NATIONAL FLOOD INSURANCE PROGRAM

CLAIMS MANUAL

MAY 2020

FEMA

NATIONAL FLOOD
INSURANCE PROGRAM

The 2020 NFIP Claims Manual is published as a service to those who work with the National Flood Insurance Program. The publisher recognizes that Adjusters, Insureds, Insurers, Policy Makers and other stakeholders may benefit from a quality printed copy. It is important that users of this book read the purpose and disclaimer located on page 1 of the content. The NFIP regularly makes changes, updates, and new policy which may supersede this manual.

If your organization would like a custom printed version of this book with or without additional content and a custom cover please contact the publisher for more information.

Should you have suggestions or feedback on ways to improve this book please send email to Books@OcotilloPress.com

Edited 2021 Ocotillo Press
ISBN 978-1-954285-30-9

Printed in the United States of America

Ocotillo Press
Houston, TX 77017
Books@OcotilloPress.com

NATIONAL FLOOD INSURANCE PROGRAM

CLAIMS MANUAL

MAY 2020

FEMA

NATIONAL FLOOD
INSURANCE PROGRAM

This page was intentionally left blank.

Table of Contents

Purpose

The purpose of the NFIP Claims Manual is to improve clarity of claims guidance to WYOs, vendors, adjusters, and examiners so that policyholders experience consistent and reliable service. The manual provides processes for handling claims from the notice of loss to final payment.

All NFIP bulletins, other than those announcing Flood Insurance Claims Office numbers, Flood Response Office locations, claims adjuster briefings, and current and future program changes, are superseded by this manual and of no further effect.

May 1, 2020

This page was intentionally left blank.

Introduction

Message to National Flood Insurance Program Claims Professionals

Over the past several years, the Federal Emergency Management Agency (FEMA) has highlighted our commitment to our policyholders. We are transforming the ways we manage the National Flood Insurance Program (NFIP). This transformation will enable our partners and stakeholders, Write Your Own (WYO) insurance companies, insurance company vendors, agents, adjusting firms, adjusters, and examiners as claims professionals, to improve our policyholders' experience when they have a flood claim.

David Maurstad, Deputy Associate Administrator for Insurance and Mitigation

We are getting policyholders on the road to recovery faster through a more robust advance payment process. We are committed to making our products and processes easier to understand from the policyholder's point of view. This includes rewriting of our claims and underwriting manuals in plain language so insurance professionals understand the NFIP and can provide policyholders with consistency and reliability of service.

One of FEMA's strategic goals is to build a culture of preparedness, which promotes the idea that everyone should be prepared when disaster strikes. One way an individual can be prepared is to purchase proper insurance coverage. As representatives of FEMA and the NFIP, we will treat each policyholder with empathy and respect, ensuring the NFIP adjusts each claim fairly, without unnecessary delay, and handles each claim as if it were our home or business. Policyholders' positive word-of-mouth to family, friends, neighbors, and the wider community regarding their claims experience can influence these individuals to purchase flood insurance.

All of you represent the NFIP and our improved customer experience. You will likely be the first and maybe the only NFIP representative the policyholder engages with after a flood event. FEMA depends on your continued expertise and compassion to help our policyholders recover from what may be a devastating experience for them.

As a claims professional, you are the one that will guide the policyholders through the entire NFIP claims process – from the notice of loss to their final payment. With your knowledge of the Standard Flood Insurance Policy (SFIP), you can make the policyholder's recovery smoother by communicating what they should do to move their claim along the adjustment journey.

I would like to take a moment to recognize the hard work you do on our behalf. I have had the pleasure of observing quality adjusting by riding along on several loss adjustments. I saw first-hand how much time, effort, and care claims adjusters put into serving our policyholders. It is a tough job entering dangerous spaces, dealing with conditions such as mold and other hazards, and meeting the needs of NFIP policyholders still processing the toll of a recent flood.

May 1, 2020

I know first-hand how tough this is because my dad was an adjuster. In addition, during my 20+ years as an agent, I experienced the challenge of settling property losses many times. I understand the dilemma claims professionals face trying to provide as much assistance to someone in need within the constraints of the flood insurance contract.

We recognize your job is not easy. However, you have the opportunity to affect the claims experience positively for NFIP policyholders. I appreciate that you go the extra mile to make sure we are treating our policyholders with integrity and respect and getting every dollar allowed to them from the policy they purchased. Together we can help close the insurance gap and create more resilient communities.

1   National Flood Insurance Program

The National Flood Insurance Act of 1968 (Title XII of the Housing and Urban Development Act of 1968, Public Law 90-448, codified as amended at 42 U.S.C § 4001 *et seq.*) created the National Flood Insurance Program (NFIP). The NFIP is a cooperative venture involving the Federal Government, state and local governments, and the private insurance industry. The Federal Government develops and sets insurance rates, provides the necessary risk studies to communities, and establishes floodplain management criteria guiding construction in the floodplain.

Communities must adopt and enforce minimum floodplain management standards for new, substantially improved, and substantially damaged structures for the NFIP to provide insurance within their boundaries. Private insurance companies, under an arrangement known as the Write Your Own (WYO) program, sell and service federal flood insurance policies and retain part of the premium for their efforts. FEMA also sells and services federal flood insurance policies through the NFIP Direct Servicing Agent (NFIP Direct).

The Federal Insurance Directorate (FID) under the Federal Insurance and Mitigation Administration (FIMA) is the component of FEMA charged with administering the NFIP.

2   Standard Flood Insurance Policy

The NFIP offers three Standard Flood Insurance Policy (SFIP) forms – Dwelling Form[1], General Property Form[2], and the Residential Condominium Building Association Policy (RCBAP) Form.[3] Each SFIP form has an insuring agreement between the policyholder and the insurer, which details the terms and conditions explaining coverage and non-coverage provisions.[4]

---

[1] 44 C.F.R. pt. 61, App. A(1) (2018)
[2] 44 C.F.R. pt. 61, App. A(2) (2018)
[3] 44 C.F.R. pt. 61, App. A(3) (2018)
[4] See 44 C.F.R. § 61.13 (2018); see also id. pt. 61, App. A(1), A(2), A(3)

2.1 Dwelling Form

Insures a single-family dwelling, a two- to four-family dwelling, a residential renter, or a residential condominium unit owner. See Section 1 for more information.

2.2 General Property Form

Insures a non-residential building or unit, a residential-detached garage or outbuilding, a non-residential leaseholder's contents, a multi-family dwelling (other residential) such as an apartment building, or a condominium association's building, that has less than 75 percent of its square footage for residential use, and any other building that does not meet the definition of a Dwelling or RCBAP. See Section 1 for more information.

2.3 Residential Condominium Building Association Policy Form

Insures a residential condominium building owned by a condominium association that has 75 percent or more of its square footage for residential use. See Section 1 for more information.

3 Emergency and Regular Programs

NFIP only sells flood insurance in communities that participate in the NFIP. See the Community Status Book for more information.

3.1 Emergency Program

A community may initially participate in the NFIP in the Emergency Program. The Emergency Program is in place when FEMA has not made a Flood Insurance Rate Map (FIRM). The NFIP makes a limited amount of flood insurance coverage available for all residents of the community. The community must adopt minimum floodplain management standards to control future use of its floodplains.[5]

3.2 Regular Program

The community joins the Regular Program of the NFIP after FEMA completes a detailed engineering study for the community. The study allows FEMA to release the engineering-driven FIRM that provides flood data. The community must adopt or amend its floodplain management regulations to incorporate the new flood data contained in the FIRM. FEMA provides higher amounts of flood insurance coverage under the Regular Program than under the Emergency Program and charges new construction actuarial rates to reflect the risk of flooding.[6]

---

[5] See P.L. 90-448 § 1336, as added P.L. 91-152 § 91-152 § 408, 83 Stat. 396 (1969), 42 U.S.C. § 4056; 44 C.F.R. § 59.3 (2018)
[6] See 44 C.F.R. § 59.2 (2018)

4   Amounts of Insurance Available

Table 1 shows the maximum amounts of insurance currently available under the SFIP for building coverage and contents coverage, in both Emergency Program and Regular Program communities. The aggregate limits for building coverage are the maximum coverage amounts allowed by statute for each building included in the relevant occupancy category. These limits apply to all single condominium units and all other buildings, not in a condominium form of ownership, including cooperatives and timeshares.[7]

Table 1. Amounts of Insurance Available: Dwelling, General Property, and RCBAP Forms

Coverage Type	Property Type	Emergency Program	Regular Program
Building	Single – Family Dwelling	$35,000[1]	$250,000
	2 – 4 Family Building	$35,000[1]	$250,000
	Other Residential Building	$100,000[2]	$500,000
	Non-Residential Building (including Business Buildings and Other Non-Residential Buildings)	$100,000[2]	$500,000
	Residential Condominium Building Association	N/A	$250,000 x number of units or replacement cost of the building, whichever is less.
Contents	Residential Property (Dwelling)	$10,000	$100,000
	Non-Residential Business, Other Non-Residential Property	$100,000	$500,000
	Residential Property (RCBAP)	N/A	$100,000

1 In Alaska, Guam, Hawaii, and U.S. Virgin Islands, the amount of building coverage available in the Emergency Program for a single-family dwelling and 2-4 family dwelling available is $50,000.

2 In Alaska, Guam, Hawaii, and U.S. Virgin Islands, the amount of building coverage available in the Emergency Program for Other Residential and Non-Residential buildings is $150,000.

---

[7] See P.L 90-448 § 1306, 82 Stat. 575 (1968) (42 U.S.C. § 4013); 44 C.F.R. § 61.6 (2018)

5   Deductibles

Table 2 shows the minimum deductibles available under the SFIP for building coverage and contents coverage, in both Emergency Program and Regular Program communities.

Table 2. Minimum Deductibles[1]

Program Type	Rating	Minimum Deductible for Coverage of $100,000 or Less[2]	Minimum Deductible for Coverage Over $100,000
Emergency	All	$1,500	$2,000
Regular	All pre-FIRM subsidized zones[3]: A, AE, A1-A30, AH, AO, V, VE, and V1-V30, AR/AR Dual Zones without Elevation Data	$1,500	$2,000
	All Full-Risk[4] zones: A, AE, A1-A30, AH, AO, V, VE, and V1-V30, AR/AR Dual Zones without Elevation Data and B, C, X, A99, and D	$1,000	$1,250
	Tentative and Provisional	$1,000	$1,250

1 The deductible for the Preferred Risk Policy, Mortgage Portfolio Protection Program, and Newly Mapped policies will be $1,000 for both building and contents if the building coverage is less than or equal to $100,000 and $1,250 if building coverage is over $100,000. A contents-only policy will have a $1,000 deductible.

2 Use this column if building coverage is $100,000 or less, regardless of the contents coverage amount. This includes policies issued with contents coverage only.

3 Pre-FIRM subsidized policies are those policies covering a pre-FIRM building that are rated in zones unnumbered A, AE, A1–A30, AH, AO, VE, and V1–V30 without elevation data from an Elevation Certificate. Also included among pre-FIRM subsidized policies are policies covering certain pre-FIRM buildings rated in zones D and unnumbered V, for which the pre-FIRM subsidized rate remains more favorable than full-risk rating in zone D or unnumbered V.

4 Full-risk rates apply to all policies rated with elevation data from an Elevation Certificate in zones unnumbered A, AE, A1–A30, AH, AO, VE, and V1–V30, regardless of whether the building is pre-FIRM or post-FIRM. Post-FIRM buildings rated in zones D or unnumbered V and pre-FIRM buildings in zones D or unnumbered V using post-FIRM rate tables are considered full-risk. Full-risk rates are also applied to all policies rated in zones B, C, or X, regardless of product type or the building classification as pre-FIRM or post-FIRM. Grandfathered standard-X zone policies and grandfathered policies using elevation data from an Elevation Certificate are considered full-risk.

Refer to the Flood Insurance Manual for more information on deductibles, including maximum and optional deductibles.

6   Group Flood Insurance Policy

A Group Flood Insurance Policy (GFIP) is an insurance certificate covering all individuals named by a state as recipients under Section 408 of the Robert T. Stafford Disaster Relief and Emergency Assistance Act (P.L. 93-288 § 408, 42 U.S.C. § 5174) of an Individuals and Households Program (IHP) award for flood damage because of a Presidential disaster declaration.[8] The NFIP Direct handles all GFIPs. The term of the GFIP is for 36 months and begins 60 days after the date of the disaster declaration. IHP funds the GFIP certificate, which is good for three years, from the date of award to the recipient. Table 3 outlines the coverage details of the GFIP.

Table 3. GFIP Policy Details

Section	Details
Coverage Amount	The amount of coverage is equivalent to the maximum grant amount established under section 408 of the Stafford Act (42 U.S.C. § 5174), which FEMA determines annually.[1] See the Federal Register for the current grant amount.
Covered Property	The GFIP covers the building and personal property of an owner. As of the publication of this manual, the policyholder has the choice of whether to use the funds solely for building damages, solely for personal property damages, or for a combination of building and personal property. For renter policyholders, the GFIP is for damaged personal property owned by the policyholder. A renter cannot have building coverage under the GFIP. There is no Increased Cost of Compliance (ICC) coverage under the GFIP.
Term	The term of the GFIP is for 36 months and begins 60 days after the date of the disaster declaration. Coverage for individual grantees begins on the 30th day after NFIP Direct receives the required data for the grantees and their premium payments. The NFIP Direct will send a Certificate of Flood Insurance to each individual under the GFIP.[2]
Deductible	The GFIP uses the SFIP Dwelling Form, except that Section VI. Deductibles do not apply. FEMA applies separate deductibles of $200 each to any building loss and any personal property loss. This deductible applies to flood-damaged losses sustained to the insured property during the term of the GFIP. The deductible does not apply to the SFIP Section III.C.2. Loss Avoidance Measures, or Section III. C.3. Condominium Loss Assessments Coverage.
	The following sections of the SFIP do not apply to the GFIP: • Section VII. General Conditions, E. Cancellation of Policy by You • Section VII. General Conditions, H. Policy Renewal.[3]

---

[8] See 44 C.F.R. § 61.17(a) (2018); see also id. 206.119(d) (explaining purchase of GFIP)

Section	Details
Cancellation	The policyholder cannot cancel a GFIP. However, the policyholder may purchase a regular SFIP through the NFIP. Upon the purchase of an SFIP, the group flood certificate becomes void and the NFIP does not refund the GFIP premium.
Renewal	NFIP Direct will send a notice to the GFIP certificate holders approximately 60 days before the end of the 36-month term of the GFIP. The notice encourages the certificate holder to contact an insurance agent or private insurance company selling NFIP policies under the WYO program to purchase the amount of flood insurance coverage they must have to maintain their eligibility for future disaster assistance.[4]

1 See 44 C.F.R. § 61.17(c) (2018); 42 U.S.C. § 5174(h) (setting the limit at $25,000 with an annual adjustment)
2 See 44 C.F.R. § 61.17 (d)-(f)
4 See 44 C.F.R. § 61.17(g)
4 See 44 C.F.R. § 61.17(h)

7   Disaster Response

Every year disasters put millions of Americans in danger and cause billions of dollars of property damage. FEMA is always ready, helping communities reduce their risk, helping emergency officials prepare for all hazards, and assisting our insured survivors on their road to recovery. Following are disaster response efforts and offices established in support of disasters.

7.1   FEMA Joint Field Office

The FEMA Joint Field Office (JFO) is a temporary federal facility established close to a disaster or a multi-state event. FEMA may establish JFOs that function as central points for federal, state, local, and tribal executives with responsibility for incident oversight, direction, or assistance to coordinate protection, prevention, preparedness, response, and recovery actions.

Federal Insurance assists the JFO in several capacities pre- and post-disaster. It oversees and coordinates response efforts between other divisions of FEMA and the NFIP to ensure the execution of flood response activities.

7.2   Disaster Response NFIP Field Offices

A.   Adjuster Control Office

NFIP Direct establishes the Adjuster Control Office (ACO) to control the assignment and coordination of NFIP Direct claims, including the GFIP, Repetitive Loss (RL), and Severe Repetitive Loss (SRL) policies.

B.   Integrated Flood Insurance Claims Office

NFIP Direct establishes an on-site Integrated Flood Insurance Claims Office (IFICO) following a major flooding event to process NFIP Direct flood claim payments. Examiner staff and general adjuster staff assist flood adjusters, agents, and policyholders in the handling of NFIP Direct flood claims.

C.   Flood Response Office

The NFIP authorizes the Bureau and Statistical Agent (NFIP BSA) to establish a Flood Response Office (FRO) to provide a local NFIP presence and base of operations during a flood event. The NFIP BSA General Adjusters (GAs), NFIP BSA Regional Support staff, and others may be deployed to a FRO to conduct a variety of activities to support the NFIP stakeholders, including policyholders, adjusters, local officials, agents, WYO Companies, the NFIP Direct, and FEMA. FRO activities are conducted in cooperation with other Government operations, including FEMA Disaster Field Offices (DFOs), FEMA Joint Field Offices (JFOs), and others.

At the FRO, the NFIP BSA:

- Coordinates with the insurers to guide the scope of coverage.

- Facilitates the adjustment of losses sustained by NFIP policyholders.

- Educates and informs the insured public, agents, adjusters, and federal and state officials in matters related to the NFIP's total catastrophic response procedures through the distribution of posters, notices, and NFIP material, and attendance and support of FEMA at community meetings.

- Conducts special adjuster briefings, surveys flood disaster areas, assesses the extent of damage, and advises FEMA of findings.

- Implements the re-inspection program and performs claims troubleshooting activities.

7.3 Adjuster Briefings

The NFIP BSA General Adjusters and FEMA conduct adjuster briefings immediately after major storms. These briefings address regional problems, construction issues, adjuster authorization, community and state ordinances, etc. FEMA posts the date, time, and location of the briefings at www.nfipservices.floodsmart.gov. Independent adjusters, adjusting firms, and WYO Company claims examiners and representatives should attend these briefings.

8   Claims Professionals Expectations

FEMA expects that all claims professionals be committed to the following NFIP core values of compassion, fairness, integrity, respect, and diversity. See Appendix L, NFIP Customer Service Standards.

8.1 NFIP Core Values

A. Compassion

Be empathetic to the stressful circumstances the policyholder may be experiencing and your crucial role in helping their recovery. Every interaction with the policyholder is an opportunity to cultivate a relationship.

B. Fairness

Strive to achieve principled, well-reasoned, and just outcomes in the execution of all claims and adjust each claim fairly and without unnecessary delay, bias, or preference.

C. Integrity

Integrity is the foundation of all our actions and is central to our conduct. Maintain the highest standards of integrity by creating a culture of honesty, consistency, and predictability. Trust is the earned result of conducting our actions with integrity. Failure to adhere to the highest standards reflects poorly on the NFIP.

D. Respect

Treat all policyholders with dignity and respect. This is not only important, but it is also their right.

E. Diversity

Diversity is one of the defining strengths of our Nation. Our policyholders reflect the full spectrum of cultures, beliefs, backgrounds, and commitments. The NFIP is committed to serving the needs of every policyholder and recognizing that diversity is central in our work every day.

8.2 Customer Service Standards

A. Be Professional

FEMA expects:

- Claims professionals to respond promptly to telephone inquiries, be available to answer questions, update the policyholder about the status of their claim, and present clear and correct information about their claim.

- Claims professionals to include all allowances payable in the policy in the estimate. NFIP coverage differs from other insurance policies therefore claims professionals may need to spend additional time addressing differences with the policyholder.

- Claims professionals to explain coverage early in the claim process in a clear manner. For example, post-FIRM elevated building and basement coverage can confuse the policyholder and require additional explanation.

- Claims professionals to inform the policyholder of the exclusions in the SFIP and the steps necessary to pay their claim promptly.

- Claims professionals to be considerate of the policyholder's time, keep appointments, and honor their commitments.

- NFIP adjusters to review and explain the building estimate and proactively assist policyholders with the contents claim and proof of loss.

- NFIP examiners to confirm that all payment recommendations made by the adjuster are in line with the SFIP.

B.   Be Prepared

FEMA expects:

- Claims professionals to have their resources on hand and to understand all three SFIP forms Dwelling, General Property, and RCBAP and the GFIP. All claims professionals must have a good command of the SFIP and its application of coverages so they can successfully support the policyholder.

- Claims professionals to ensure adjusting software is calibrated correctly for the geographic area where the loss occurred and accounts for post-disaster and property-specific issues.

- Claims professionals to offer an advance payment to the policyholder with an eligible claim and always check for new guidance on advance payments.

- Claims professionals to know when to engage outside professional services on adjustments and, when necessary, seek the appropriate authorization in a timely manner.

C.   Be Compassionate

FEMA expects:

- Claims professionals to remember the flood loss may create a traumatic experience and response by the policyholder. Claims professionals often work with people under stress and should recognize this and create a positive policyholder claims experience.

- Claims professionals to be flexible based on the circumstances affecting the policyholder. This may mean making reasonable changes to accommodate the needs of the policyholder when it comes to inspecting the loss, discussing the claim, and returning phone calls.

9   NFIP Adjuster Participation

FEMA's goal is to ensure that claims professionals adjust each claim fairly and without unnecessary delay. Adjusters should treat each policyholder with respect, fairness, and equity during this stressful time in their lives.

Adjusters represent the NFIP and demonstrate its commitment to improved customer experience. Adjusters will likely be the first and perhaps the only NFIP representative a policyholder meets after a flood. The NFIP depends on the adjusters' expertise and compassion to help our policyholders recover from what may be a devastating experience for them.

The adjuster works in concert with the claims examiner to guide a policyholder through the NFIP claims process.

9.1   Adjuster Authority

FEMA expects every adjuster handling NFIP flood losses:

- To understand and communicate to the policyholders that the adjuster does not have the authority to approve or deny a claim but should explain the policy to the policyholder and make recommendations to the insurer.

- To understand that all adjustments are only recommendations and subject to review by the NFIP insurer.

Important: Adjusters should follow the insurer's guidelines, however, any questions requiring clarification should be forwarded through their internal chain of command.

9.2   NFIP Knowledge

FEMA expects every adjuster handling NFIP flood losses:

- To know the provisions of the applicable SFIP forms and the GFIP.

- To know the coverage interpretations issued by FEMA and explained at the NFIP Claims Presentations.

- To communicate the coverage and limitations to policyholders during the inspection.

- To adjust all claims in compliance with these provisions.

- To help the policyholder to document their loss as completely and accurately as reasonably possible.

9.3   Required NFIP Adjuster Authorization

Independent adjusters must register with the NFIP BSA to adjust flood losses for NFIP insurers and possess an active Flood Control Number (FCN). Adjusters must have the qualifications noted below and attend an annual NFIP claims presentation to become a registered adjuster or to maintain active status. The NFIP BSA verifies credentials before an adjuster receives an FCN.

FEMA holds annual NFIP claims presentations to keep the adjusting community current on claims procedures and guidance required to adjust losses under the three forms of the SFIP.

9.4   Adjuster Qualifications

The NFIP requires adjusters to have different levels of qualifications to adjust different property types. Table 4 details what types of properties an adjuster can adjust for a given level of training.

Table 4. Adjuster Qualifications

Property Type	Authorization Requirements
Residential, Manufactured Home, Travel Trailer, and Commercial Losses	<ul><li>Have at least four consecutive years of full-time property loss adjusting experience.</li><li>Be capable of preparing an accurate scope of damage and dollar estimate to</li><li>$50,000 for manufactured homes and travel trailers, $250,000 for residential losses, and up to $500,000 for commercial losses.</li><li>Attend the annual NFIP claims presentation.</li><li>Demonstrate knowledge of the SFIP and NFIP adjustment criteria for all policy forms.</li><li>Have expert knowledge of manufactured home and travel trailer construction and valuation.</li><li>Be familiar with Increased Cost of Compliance coverages and criteria.</li><li>The NFIP encourages adjusters to have Errors and Omissions (E & O) insurance coverage. Some WYO Companies require adjusters assigned to their claims to have E & O coverage.</li></ul>
Large Commercial and RCBAP Losses	<ul><li>Have at least five consecutive years of full-time large-loss property adjusting experience.</li><li>For large commercial losses, be capable of preparing an accurate scope of damage and dollar estimate of $500,000 or more.</li><li>For RCBAP, be capable of preparing an accurate scope of damage and dollar estimate of $1,000,000 or more.</li><li>Attend the annual NFIP claims presentation.</li><li>Provide written recommendations from three insurance company supervisors or claims management personnel. The recommendations must reflect adjusting experience only.</li><li>The NFIP encourages adjusters to have Errors and Omissions (E & O) insurance coverage. Some WYO Companies require adjusters assigned to their claims to have E & O coverage.</li></ul>

9.5   Adjuster Authorization Process

NFIP recognizes that specialized knowledge is required for an adjuster to adjust NFIP losses. Adjusters must know the differences between the SFIP forms and differences with private industry property insurance forms. They must know the interpretations of coverage made by FEMA and the unique reporting requirements of the NFIP.

A.   NFIP BSA

The NFIP, through its NFIP BSA, issues FCNs and maintains a database of active authorized independent flood adjusters and inactive flood adjusters. The NFIP BSA also maintains records of the date and location of adjusters' attendance at an annual NFIP Claims Presentation, or attendance at a FEMA-approved claims presentation conducted by independent adjusting firms or WYO Companies.

B.   WYO Staff Adjusters

WYO Companies can use staff adjusters to adjust their flood losses. Though not required, FEMA encourages WYO staff adjusters handling flood claims to have an FCN and to attend an annual NFIP claims presentation.

C.   Adjuster Registration

The Adjuster Registration Application contains five registration categories. Adjusters can register for any or all categories if they meet adjuster qualification requirements. The categories are:

- Residential

- Manufactured (Mobile) Home/Travel Trailer

- Small Commercial (<$100,000)

- Large Commercial ($100,001 - $500,000)

- Condominium (RCBAP)

New applicants and adjusters seeking upgrades to their existing registration must submit a completed Adjuster Registration Application to the NFIP BSA via any of the following methods:

E-mail: NFIPAdjusterMailbox@fema.dhs.gov

Mail: NFIP BSA, PO Box 310, Lanham, MD 20703-0310

Adjusters seeking to maintain their active registered status do not need to submit an application. The NFIP BSA will automatically renew previously registered adjusters when they attend an annual NFIP Claims Presentation for the current calendar year.

The NFIP BSA will email new adjusters and adjusters who request an upgrade to their classification of the approval or denial of their application. All approved adjusters who attend the annual NFIP claims presentation receive an emailed FCN card confirming their registration to handle NFIP flood claims.

Important: Adjusters who do not attend an annual NFIP Claims Presentation become inactive and cannot adjust flood claims until they attend an approved NFIP claims presentation and are reactivated.

9.6   Independent Adjuster Registration and Code of Conduct

A. Adjuster Registration to Adjust Claims on Behalf of the NFIP

Adjuster trainees and experienced adjusters must hold an active registration and FCN to work flood claims for the NFIP. Only properly registered adjusters can perform flood claim inspections in their approved category displayed on the FCN card.

B. Code of Conduct

FEMA is committed to the core values of compassion, fairness, integrity, and respect. By handling NFIP claims, claims professionals agree to adhere to these principles of conduct:

All individuals handling NFIP claims will maintain the highest standards of honesty, impartiality, character, and conduct to ensure the proper performance of NFIP business and the continued trust and confidence of the NFIP policyholders. Claims professionals must conduct themselves with courtesy and integrity, a deep sense of responsibility for policyholder trust, and promptness in dealing with and serving the policyholder. Claims professionals will display a standard of professional behavior that reflects positively upon and will be a credit to both themselves and the NFIP.

FEMA does not accept any professional conflict of interest. Any independent adjuster or adjusting firm who performs work on behalf of the NFIP or registered in the Flood Adjuster Capacity Program (FACP), may not work in any capacity that provides support, inspections, consulting, or estimating, for or as a public adjuster (licensed or not), or to provide representation adverse to the NFIP. Adjusters also may not adjust claims for a property in which the adjuster (or immediate family member) owns an interest, nor can an adjuster accept any money from a third party to steer business to a specific firm or individual. Adjusters and adjusting firms may not accept monetary or non- monetary incentives from policyholders. If a conflict is identified, an adjuster's registration will be deferred for one year to ensure interests have ended and will not reoccur. In addition, the use of the FCN for any purpose other than adjusting a flood insurance claim on behalf of an NFIP insurer (WYO companies and NFIP Direct) is improper and, furthermore, may result in immediate suspension or revocation of the FCN. FEMA may refer improper usage of the FCN to investigators as necessary to protect the integrity of the NFIP.

C. Complaint Handling

When FEMA receives a complaint asserting a violation of the Code of Conduct, an investigation is required to confirm the validity of the complaint. WYO companies, NFIP Direct, and adjusting firms also have an obligation to protect the integrity of the NFIP. When a WYO company, NFIP Direct, or adjusting firm becomes aware of a violation, they are required to conduct an internal investigation. If a violation is confirmed, they will immediately notify FEMA and provide all supporting documentation that includes their findings and recommendations. If FEMA determines that there was a violation of the NFIP's Code of Conduct, FEMA will act to revoke the FCN for a period of one year or longer and provide notification to the adjuster.

Documentation should be mailed to: NFIP BSA, Attn: Adjuster Authorization, Post Office Box 310, Lanham, MD 20706; or sent via email to: NFIPAdjusterMailbox@fema.dhs.gov.

Once FEMA revokes the FCN, the adjuster can no longer adjust claims on behalf of the NFIP or hold an FCN. If code of conduct violations are evident within the firm, the firm may lose the authority to adjust claims on behalf of the NFIP.

An adjusting firm or adjuster may appeal a temporary suspension or indefinite revocation by submitting a request with supporting documentation to the Assistant Administrator for Federal Insurance for review and consideration. The Assistant Administrator for Federal Insurance is responsible for reviewing and making final determinations concerning all revocation appeals. The Assistant Administrator for Federal Insurance holds the ultimate authority to revoke or reinstate an FCN.

D. Applicability

This applies to all past, present, and future authorized adjusters and adjusting firms.

9.7   NFIP Fee Schedule

Adjusters may bill based on the current NFIP Adjuster Fee Schedule:

- Current Adjuster Fee Schedule effective August 24, 2017 (See Appendix A)

- For ICC claims, use the ICC fee schedule effective September 1, 2004 (See Appendix B)

A.   Gross Loss

The Adjuster Fee Schedule sets compensation amounts based on the claim's gross loss. Gross loss is the agreed cost to repair or replace before application of depreciation, applicable deductible(s), and salvage buy-back. Gross loss must not exceed any or all of the following policy limitations: Building and personal property policy limits stated in the Declarations Page; Program Limits building or personal property; damage values no greater than 10% for a detached garage (Dwelling Form); Special Limits ($2,500); Loss Avoidance Measures for Sandbags, Supplies, and Labor ($1,000); Property Removed to Safety ($1,000); Pollution Damage - General Property form ($10,000); Policy Exclusions.

B.   Increased Cost of Compliance (ICC) Claims

For Increased Cost of Compliance claims, use the ICC Fee Schedule whether the claim is paid or closed without payment.

10 Examiner Participation in the NFIP

FEMA's goal is to ensure that claims professionals handle each claim quickly and fairly and to see that everyone involved in the flood claim process treats each policyholder with respect and empathy.

NFIP insurers have the authority to act on behalf of the NFIP to examine claims, make coverage decisions, and communicate the NFIP's position to policyholders. How the examiner handles their oversight of flood claims can positively influence the customer experience. The examiner must be knowledgeable of the NFIP, stay up to date on program guidance, and be compassionate about the situations that policyholders are facing. The examiner can help NFIP policyholders recover from what may be a devastating experience for them by being responsive to policyholder inquiries, proactively examining reports, timely issuing payments, and providing appropriate and professional communications.

Examiners work in concert with the adjuster to guide policyholders through the entire NFIP claims process – from the Notice of Loss to their final payment. Their knowledge of the SFIP can make the policyholder's recovery smoother by communicating what they should do to move their claim along the claims journey.

10.1 Authority

Examiners are the claims administrators of the NFIP insurers and have the authority through their management, to pay claims, make and confirm coverage determinations, and to deny coverage when appropriate. Examiners should provide guidance to adjusters as needed.

FEMA expects every examiner handling NFIP flood losses to:

- Understand their first obligation to a policyholder is to identify coverage under the SFIP.

- Understand they should not take their authority lightly to determine coverage under the SFIP and be aware that their decisions have a direct impact on policyholders.

- Understand their payment decisions must be in accordance with the SFIP.

- Though not required, FEMA encourages WYO examiners handling flood claims to attend an Annual NFIP Claims Presentations.

Important: Examiners should follow their insurers' internal settlement authority guidelines. Examiners should also refer coverage questions that require clarification through their internal chain of command.

May 1, 2020

10.2   Responsibilities

Claims examiner responsibilities include:

- Assigning an adjuster within 24 hours of receipt of claim or document why they did not make the assignment in the time required.

- Managing the claim file including:

  - Issuing advances.

  - Resolving rating issues and coverage issues.

  - Overseeing adjusters to ensure timely reporting of settlement recommendations.

  - Recommending and hiring experts.

  - Issuing proper payment.

- Claims reporting and forms management including:

  - PIVOT (NFIP system of record) reporting.

  - Proper expense payments.

- Communicating with policyholders, including information on reservation of rights, non-waiver agreements, partial and full denial letters, and other communications as necessary.

- Handling of Increased Cost of Compliance (ICC) claims.

10.3   Knowledge of the NFIP

FEMA expects every examiner handling NFIP flood losses:

- To know the provisions of the three forms of the SFIP and the GFIP.

- To know the guidance issued by FEMA and as explained at the NFIP claims presentations.

- To communicate coverage and limitations to policyholders.

- To oversee all flood claims in compliance with these provisions.

11   Training for Claims Professionals

11.1   NFIP Sponsored Training

A.   Emergency Management Institute

FEMA's Emergency Management Institute (EMI) offers independent study courses for claims professionals that reinforce information offered at the NFIP Adjuster Claims Presentations. EMI

Independent Study courses are free and available to anyone. All students must have a FEMA Student Identification (SID) number to take a course and can register for a SID at https://cdp.dhs.gov/FEMASID.

Find out more about EMI Independent Study Courses at https://training.fema.gov/is/searchis.aspx?search=claims, and NFIP Perspectives informational videos along with other training information at https://nfipservices.floodsmart.gov/home/training. The Independent Study catalog is available at https://training.fema.gov/is/crslist.aspx. Below is a list of relevant courses.

B.   Adjuster Courses

- IS-1104   NFIP Claims Review for Adjusters

- IS-1107   Adjuster Customer Service

- IS-1109.a   Understanding Basement Coverage

- IS-1111   Introduction to Commercial Claims

- IS-1112   Introduction to Flood Claims

C.   Agent Courses

- IS-1100.a   Increased Cost of Compliance

- IS-1101.b   Basic Agent Tutorial

- IS-1102   Theory of Elevation Rating

- IS-1108   Insuring Condominiums

- IS-1110.a   Writing Commercial Exposures

- IS-1113   Coastal Barrier Resources

- IS-1115   Claims Process for Agents

- IS-1116   Sales for Agents

- IS-1117   Severe Repetitive Loss for Agents

D.   All Audiences

- IS-1100.a   Increased Cost of Compliance

- IS-1105a   EC Made Easy: Elevation Certificate Overview

- IS-1106a   FEMA Mapping Changes

11.2   Annual NFIP Claims Presentations

NFIP claims presentations keep the insurer examiners and the adjusting community current on claims procedures and guidance required to adjust or oversee losses under the three forms of the SFIP. FEMA does not charge a fee to attend the presentations, but you must register. Click here to sign up for NFIP adjuster training emails.

11.3   Other Training

A.   Associate in National Flood Insurance (ANFI)

Claims professionals may obtain the designation through the American Institute for Chartered Property Casualty Underwriters, The Institutes, Risk & Insurance Knowledge Group. There may be a cost associated with the ANFI designation that is not borne by the NFIP. An ANFI designation is not required by FEMA to handle NFIP claims, and we do not endorse or control the course content.

May 1, 2020

This page was intentionally left blank.

Section 1: SFIP Forms

1 Overview

The SFIP specifies the terms and conditions of the insuring agreement between either FEMA, as the insurer for policies issued by the NFIP Direct, or the WYO Company as the insurer for policies issued through the WYO Program.

There are three policy forms:

1. Dwelling Form

2. General Property (GP) Form

3. Residential Condominium Building Association Policy (RCBAP) Form

Each form insures a different type of property; however, many coverage terms and conditions are the same. This manual will detail coverages for each of the three forms. The following tables include the actual policy language in the left columns, with commentary in the right columns.

2   Dwelling Form

Please read the policy carefully. The flood insurance provided is subject to limitations, restrictions, and exclusions. This policy covers only:

1. A non-condominium residential building designed for principal use as a dwelling place of one to four families; or

2. 2. A single-family dwelling unit in a condominium building.

I. Agreement

Policy Language	Additional Explanation
The Federal Emergency Management Agency (FEMA) provides flood insurance under the terms of the National Flood Insurance Act of 1968 and its Amendments, and Title 44 of the Code of Federal Regulations. We will pay you for direct physical loss by or from flood to your insured property if you: 1. Have paid the correct premium; 2. Comply with all terms and conditions of this policy; and 3. Have furnished accurate information and statements. We have the right to review the information you give us at any time and to revise your policy based on our review.	This policy is under Federal law, unlike other property lines. Relevant definition at II.B.12 (direct physical loss). Policyholder responsibilities appear at Section VII.J, K. post-loss underwriting at Section VII.G.

II. Definitions

Policy Language	Additional Explanation
A. In this policy, "you" and "your" refer to the insured(s) shown on the Declarations Page of this policy and your spouse, if a resident of the same household. Insured(s) includes: Any mortgagee and loss payee named in the Application and Declarations Page, as well as any other mortgagee or loss payee determined to exist at the time of loss in the order of precedence. "We," "us," and "our" refer to the insurer. Some definitions are complex because they are provided as they appear in the law or regulations or result from court cases. The precise definitions are intended to protect you.	

Flood, as used in this flood insurance policy, means:
1. A general and temporary condition of partial or complete inundation of two or more acres of normally dry land area or of two or more properties (one of which is your property) from:
  a. Overflow of inland or tidal waters,
  b. Unusual and rapid accumulation or runoff of surface waters from any source,
  c. Mudflow.
	For a general condition of flood to exist, the inundation must cover two or more acres of normally dry land or two or more parcels of land, one of which can be public property (such as a roadway).
	
	The reference to "partial or complete inundation of two or more acres of normally dry land area or of two or more properties" requires that the two or more acres must be continuous acres, and that the two or more inundated parcels of land must touch.
	
	For mudflow definition, see SFIP Section II.B.19.

2. Collapse or subsidence of land along the shore of a lake or similar body of water as a result of erosion or undermining caused by waves or currents of water exceeding anticipated cyclical levels that result in a flood as defined in A.1.a. above.	The SFIP also defines a flood as the collapse or subsidence of land along the shore of a lake or similar body of water from erosion or undermining caused by waves or currents of water (velocity flow) exceeding anticipated cyclical levels during a flood from the overflow of inland or tidal waters. The SFIP does not cover damage from any other cause, form, or type of earth movement or gradual erosion. See Exclusions at SFIP Section V.C.
B. The following are the other key definitions we use in this policy:	
1. Act The National Flood Insurance Act of 1968 and any amendments to it.	N/A
2. Actual Cash Value The cost to replace an insured item of property at the time of loss, less the value of its physical depreciation.	The cost to replace a building, a building item or a personal property item that includes all charges related to material, labor, and equipment. This price may include charges such as delivery, assembly, sales tax, and any applicable overhead and profit, and the like. Actual cash value is this cost to replace less applicable depreciation on all components of the cost.

II. Definitions

Policy Language	Additional Explanation
3. Application The statement made and signed by you or your agent in applying for this policy. The application gives information we use to determine the eligibility of the risk, the kind of policy to be issued, and the correct premium payment. The application is part of this flood insurance policy. For us to issue you a policy, the correct premium payment must accompany the application.	The statement made and signed by the prospective policyholder or the agent when applying for a policy. The application contains information including the property description, information to determine eligibility, the policy form selected, the selected coverage and limits, deductible, and the premium amount.
4. Base Flood A flood having a one percent chance of being equaled or exceeded in any given year.	N/A
5. Basement Any area of the building, including any sunken room or sunken portion of a room, having its floor below ground level (subgrade) on all sides.	The SFIP definition for a basement means the floor level of a room or any area of a floor level in a building that is below the ground level on all sides. This definition may differ from what policyholders consider as their "basement." The SFIP considers a sunken room or sunken portion of a room to be a basement if the floor level is below the ground level on all sides. The entire below-ground-floor-level area, including walls and the ceiling that may extend above grade, is subject to basement coverage limitations.

II. Definitions

Policy Language	Additional Explanation
5. Basement continued	 Figure 2. Sunken Room Photograph credit Amber Flooring Ground-level is the surface of the ground immediately along the perimeter of the building. If an exterior area of egress out of the building is below the ground level on all sides, installed over a subgrade, the area of egress is below ground level. A subgrade is a surface of ground leveled off to receive a foundation such as a concrete slab of a building.  Figure 3. Ground Level vs. Below Ground Level

II. Definitions

Policy Language	Additional Explanation
5. Basement continued	Figure 4. Egress The insurer may need to engage a qualified, licensed professional (for example: a surveyor) to measure the floor level in question. See Section 2 of this manual. Sump wells are not basements because they are not a floor level.
6. Building a. A structure with two or more outside rigid walls and a fully secured roof, that is affixed to a permanent site; b. A manufactured home (a "manufactured home," also known as a mobile home, is a structure: built on a permanent chassis, transported to its site in one or more sections, and affixed to a permanent foundation); or c. A travel trailer without wheels, built on a chassis and affixed to a permanent foundation, that is regulated under the community's floodplain management and building ordinances or laws. Building does not mean a gas or liquid storage tank or a recreational vehicle, park trailer or other similar vehicle, except as described in B.6.c. above.	• The SFIP covers a building, manufactured home (mobile home), or travel trailer located at the described location as shown on the Declaration Page and only insures one building. • The SFIP requires a building to be affixed to a permanent site, whereas it requires a manufactured home and a travel trailer to be affixed to a permanent foundation. • A travel trailer (recreational vehicle) with attached wheels is not a building. • A storage or shipping container, if it is used as a shed, storage building or residence, must meet the definition of an eligible building. • "Affixed by weight" does not constitute affixed to a permanent site as used in the SFIP.
7. Cancellation	• The NFIP Flood Insurance Manual provides a list of all valid policy cancellation reasons.

II. Definitions

Policy Language	Additional Explanation
The ending of the insurance coverage provided by this policy before the expiration date.	• The expiration date is the ending of the policy term, the period of coverage provided by the insurance policy. • The policy term for the SFIP is one year, after any applicable waiting period.
8. Condominium That form of ownership of real property in which each unit owner has an undivided interest in common elements.	N/A
9. Condominium Association The entity made up of the unit owners responsible for the maintenance and operation of: a. Common elements owned in undivided shares by unit owners; and b. Other real property in which the unit owners have use rights; where membership in the entity is a required condition of unit ownership.	A condominium association is an entity recognized by a state. Homeowners' associations, townhome associations, and cooperatives, and the like are not condominium associations.
10. Declarations Page A computer-generated summary of information you provided in the application for insurance. The Declarations Page also describes the term of the policy, limits of coverage, and displays the premium and our name. The Declarations Page is a part of this flood insurance policy.	N/A
11. Described Location The location where the insured building(s) or personal property are found. The described location is shown on the Declarations Page.	Each SFIP insures only one building. Under the Dwelling Form, an eligible detached garage can be covered along with the dwelling at the option of the policyholder. Part of this eligibility requires the detached garage to be located at the described location stated on the Declarations Page. Personal property is covered within any building, but only at the described location.
12. Direct Physical Loss By or From Flood Loss or damage to insured property, directly caused by a flood. There must be evidence of physical changes to the property.	The SFIP only pays for damage caused by a direct physical loss by or from flood, as defined by the SFIP. A direct physical loss means flood must physically contact the insured property and there must be evidence of physical change by or from flood to the insured building or to insured personal property. Several SFIP provisions, each with its own criteria, address specific situations where the condition of direct physical loss by or from flood occurs despite an exclusion. In these particular situations, listed below, the insurer must thoroughly document the

II. Definitions

Policy Language	Additional Explanation
	presence of the relevant criteria in the claim file for coverage and payment:
	• Losses from mudflow and collapse or subsidence of land as a result of erosion specifically covered under the SFIP definition of flood (see SFIP Section V.C., as well as II.A.1.c and II.A.2)
	• Back up of water and water-borne material through sewers or drains, where a flood is the proximate cause of the sewer or drain backup (see SFIP Section V.D.5.a.)
	• Discharge or overflow from a sump, sump pump, or related equipment, where a flood is the proximate cause of the sump pump discharge or overflow (see SFIP Section V.D.5.b.)
	• Seepage or leakage on or through the insured building, where a flood is the proximate cause of the seepage of water (see SFIP Section V.D.5.c.)
	• Pressure or weight of water, where a flood is the proximate cause of the damage from the pressure or weight of water (see SFIP Section V.D.6.)
13. Dwelling A building designed for use as a residence for no more than four families or a single-family unit in a building under a condominium form of ownership.	N/A
14. Elevated Building A building that has no basement and that has its lowest elevated floor raised above ground level by foundation walls, shear walls, posts, piers, pilings, or columns.	For more information about elevated buildings, see Section 2 of this manual, Lowest Floor Elevation. If an elevated floor in the building is in part supported by a structural slab-on-grade foundation, additional documentation may be necessary to verify the elevated rating for the building.
15. Emergency Program The initial phase of a community's participation in the National Flood Insurance Program. During this phase, only limited amounts of insurance are available under the Act.	N/A
16. Expense Constant A flat charge you must pay on each new or renewal policy to defray the expenses of the Federal Government related to flood insurance.	There is no longer an Expense Constant charge.

II. Definitions

Policy Language	Additional Explanation
17. Federal Policy Fee A flat charge you must pay on each new or renewal policy to defray certain administrative expenses incurred in carrying out the National Flood Insurance Program. This fee covers expenses not covered by the Expense Constant.	N/A
18. Improvements Fixtures, alterations, installations, or additions comprising a part of the insured dwelling or the apartment in which you reside.	N/A
19. Mudflow A river of liquid and flowing mud on the surface of normally dry land areas, as when earth is carried by a current of water. Other earth movements, such as landslide, slope failure, or a saturated soil mass moving by liquidity down a slope, are not mudflows.	A mudflow is liquified soil flowing in a manner akin to water flowing, which causes damage in a manner similar to moving water.
20. National Flood Insurance Program (NFIP) The program of flood insurance coverage and floodplain management administered under the Act and applicable Federal regulations in Title 44 of the Code of Federal Regulations, Subchapter B.	N/A
21. Policy The entire written contract between you and us. It includes: a. This printed form; b. The application and Declarations Page; c. Any endorsement(s) that may be issued; and d. Any renewal certificate indicating that coverage has been instituted for a new policy and new policy term. b. Only one dwelling, which you specifically described in the application, may be insured under this policy.	N/A
22. Pollutants Substances that include, but are not limited to, any solid, liquid, gaseous, or thermal irritant or contaminant, including smoke, vapor, soot, fumes, acids, alkalis, chemicals, and waste. "Waste" includes, but is not limited to, materials to	Testing for or monitoring of pollutants is not covered unless required by law. See Section V.F. of the SFIP.

II. Definitions

Policy Language	Additional Explanation
be recycled, reconditioned, or reclaimed.	
23. Post-FIRM Building A building for which construction or substantial improvement occurred after December 31, 1974, or on or after the effective date of an initial Flood Insurance Rate Map (FIRM), whichever is later.	Community Status Book
24. Probation Premium A flat charge you must pay on each new or renewal policy issued covering property in a community the NFIP has placed on probation under the provisions of 44 CFR 59.24.	N/A
25. Regular Program The final phase of a community's participation in the National Flood Insurance Program. In this phase, a Flood Insurance Rate Map is in effect and full limits of coverage are available under the Act.	N/A
26. Special Flood Hazard Area An area having special flood or mudflow, and/or flood-related erosion hazards, and shown on a Flood Hazard Boundary Map or Flood Insurance Rate Map as Zone A, AO, A1–A30, AE, A99, AH, AR, AR/A, AR/AE, AR/AH, AR/AO, AR/A1–A30, V1–V30, VE, or V.	All zones listed are SFHAs. However, the post-FIRM elevated building coverage limitations apply only to Zones A1–A30, AE, AH, AR, AR/A, AR/AE, AR/AH, AR/A1–A30, V1–V30, and VE, at SFIP Section III.A.8.
27. Unit A single-family unit you own in a condominium building.	N/A
28. Valued Policy A policy in which the insured and the insurer agree on the value of the property insured, that value being payable in the event of a total loss. The Standard Flood Insurance Policy is not a valued policy.	The SFIP is not a valued policy; it is a direct physical loss policy. The insurer agrees to pay a policyholder for insured property damaged by direct physical by or from flood, subject to the terms, conditions, and exclusion of the SFIP.

III. Property Covered

Policy Language	Additional Explanation
A. Coverage A—Building Property We insure against direct physical loss by or from flood to:	
1. The dwelling at the described location, or for a period of 45 days at another location as set forth in III.C.2.b., Property Removed to Safety.	N/A
2. Additions and extensions attached to and in contact with the dwelling by means of a rigid exterior wall, a solid load-bearing interior wall, a stairway, an elevated walkway, or a roof. At your option, additions and extensions connected by any of these methods may be separately insured. Additions and extensions attached to and in contact with the building by means of a common interior wall that is not a solid load-bearing wall are always considered part of the dwelling and cannot be separately insured.	A property owner has the option to separately insure an addition under its own SFIP if the addition, considered by itself, meets the definition of a building at SFIP II.B.6. Otherwise, the Dwelling Form covers an addition or extension as part of the building. Roof Elevated walkways Exterior rigid walls Load-bearing (solid) interior walls Stairs Figure 5. Examples of additions and extensions and the five means of connection

III. Property Covered

	Policy Language	Additional Explanation
3.	A detached garage at the described location. Coverage is limited to no more than 10% of the limit of liability on the dwelling. Use of this insurance is at your option but reduces the building limit of liability. We do not cover any detached garage used or held for use for residential (i.e., dwelling), business, or farming purposes.	The SFIP covers one detached garage. The garage must meet the definition of a building (SFIP Section II.B.6) and have a garage door or opening large enough to physically accommodate an automobile. A policyholder must purchase a separate policy to cover a detached garage used for residential, business, or farming purposes. The term "residential" means used as a residence, dwelling place, domicile, or providing living accommodations. There must be evidence of the capability for an individual to live in the building overnight or longer. The presence of household property, installed kitchen appliances, HVAC equipment, sink, bathroom, exercise room, hobby room, or workshop, does not necessarily disqualify a detached garage from coverage under this provision. This provision disqualifies a detached garage used entirely or partly as or held for sleeping space. If the claim recommendation denies coverage to a detached garage used for residential, business, or farming purposes, the claim file must include documentation or detailed explanation that supports the decision.
4.	Materials and supplies to be used for construction, alteration, or repair of the dwelling or a detached garage while the materials and supplies are stored in a fully enclosed building or on an adjacent property.	N/A
5.	A building under construction, alteration, or repair at the described location. a. If the structure is not yet walled or roofed as described in the definition for building (see II.B. 6.a.) then coverage applies: (1) Only while such work is in progress; or (2) If such work is halted, only for a period of up to 90 continuous days thereafter. b. However, coverage does not apply until the building is walled and roofed if the lowest floor, including the basement floor, of a non-elevated building or the lowest elevated floor of an elevated building is: (1) Below the base flood elevation in Zones AH, AE, A1–A30, AR, AR/AE, AR/AH, AR/A1–A30, AR/A, AR/ AO; or	The SFIP only covers buildings under construction affixed to a permanent site. For example, NFIP does not cover a building on temporary cribbing and not affixed to a permanent site. The SFIP covers building materials and supplies for the insured building under construction stored in an eligible detached garage under Coverage A, up to building policy limits per Section III.A.4. When a building under construction, alteration, or repair does not have at least two rigid exterior walls and a fully secured roof at the time of loss, your deductible amount will be two times the deductible that would otherwise apply to a completed building. See Dwelling Form – Section VI. Deductibles. The SFIP does not cover a building under construction if work stops for more than 90 continuous days. Coverage resumes when work resumes. The SFIP does not cover tools for construction, such as forms, cribbing, power tools,

III. Property Covered

Policy Language	Additional Explanation
(2) Below the base flood elevation adjusted to include the effect of wave action in Zones VE or V1–V30. The lowest floor levels are based on the bottom of the lowest horizontal structural member of the floor in Zones VE or V1–V30 and the top of the floor in Zones AH, AE, A1–A30, AR, AR/AE, AR/AH, AR/A1–A30, AR/A, AR/AO.	etc. Figure 6 and Figure 7 show a dwelling elevated but temporarily supported on cribbing. The structure becomes eligible for SFIP coverage once it is affixed to a permanent site, as shown in Figure 8. Figure 6. Building in the process of Elevating Photograph credit Leesa Tomsett, FEMA Figure 7. Temporary Cribbing Photograph credit Leesa Tomsett, FEMA

III. Property Covered

Policy Language	Additional Explanation
	Figure 8. Building Affixed to a Permanent Site Photograph credit Leesa Tomsett, FEMA
6. A manufactured home or a travel trailer as described in the Definitions section (see II.B.6.b. and II.B.6.c.). If the manufactured home or travel trailer is in a special flood hazard area, it must be anchored in the following manner at the time of the loss: a. By over-the-top or frame ties to ground anchors; or b. In accordance with the manufacturer's specifications; or c. In compliance with the community's floodplain management requirements unless it has been continuously insured by the NFIP at the same described location since September 30, 1982.	A manufactured (mobile) home is a structure built on a permanent chassis, transported to its site in one or more sections, and affixed to a permanent foundation. A travel trailer is not self-propelled and must be affixed to a permanent foundation in a manner that the community regulates under its floodplain management and building ordinances. The travel trailer must have its wheels removed in order to be eligible for coverage. A recreational vehicle is self-propelled and is not insurable. See SFIP Section IV. Property Not Covered, 4. For the SFIP to insure a manufactured home, the owner must affix it to a permanent foundation. A permanent foundation for a manufactured home may be a poured masonry slab, foundation walls, piers, or block supports. The foundation, not the wheels and or the axles, must support all the weight of the manufactured (mobile) home. If the mobile home is in an SFHA, the owner must anchor it to a permanent foundation to resist flotation, collapse, or lateral movement by: • Providing over-the-top or frame ties to ground anchors. • Following the manufacturer's specification for anchoring. • Complying with the community's floodplain management requirements.
7. The following items of property, which are covered under Coverage A only: a. Awnings and canopies;	• Blinds include vertical and horizontal types. • Central air conditioners include related built-in equipment for dehumidification, air filtering, and ventilation.

III. Property Covered

Policy Language	Additional Explanation
b. Blinds; c. Built-in dishwashers; d. Built-in microwave ovens; e. Carpet permanently installed over unfinished flooring; f. Central air conditioners; g. Elevator equipment; h. Fire sprinkler systems; i. Walk-in freezers; j. Furnaces and radiators; k. Garbage disposal units; l. Hot water heaters, including solar water heaters; m. Light fixtures; n. Outdoor antennas and aerials fastened to buildings; o. Permanently installed cupboards, bookcases, cabinets, paneling, and wallpaper; p. Plumbing fixtures; q. Pumps and machinery for operating pumps; r. Ranges, cooking stoves, and ovens; s. Refrigerators; and, t. Walls and mirrors, permanently installed.	• Walk-in freezers and coolers must be permanently installed or built in. • Furnaces and radiators include heat pumps, boilers, and related installed equipment for humidification, air filtering, and ventilation. • Ranges, cooking stoves, ovens include cooktops, range hoods, and built-in cooking exhaust apparatuses. • Refrigerators include beverage coolers and other major appliances that refrigerate. • Refurbished collectible or antique major appliances, such as a refrigerator, stove, and the like, are paid at functional value less depreciation.
8. Items of property in a building enclosure below the lowest elevated floor of an elevated post-FIRM building located in Zones A1-A30, AE, AH, AR, AR/A, AR/AE, AR/AH, AR/A1-A30, V1-V30, or VE, or in a basement, regardless of the zone. Coverage is limited to the following: a. Any of the following items, if installed in their functioning locations and, if necessary for operation, connected to a power source:	When the Declarations Page reflects two zones, the current zone and the zone used for rating, the rating zone is used for coverage. This rating zone may be a grandfathered zone that remains in effect for coverage unless or until the home is substantially damaged, substantially improved, or there is a lapse in coverage. The current zone may be a different zone that reflects the zone designation in the current flood map. This zone is intended only for non-claim related purposes such as underwriting premiums and ICC applicability.

III. Property Covered

Policy Language	Additional Explanation
	Post-FIRM elevated building limitations do not apply to SFHA Zones A, AO, A99, AR/AO, V, and VO. Basement limitations apply regardless of zones.
	The SFIP only covers items specifically listed under this provision.
	Basement limitations apply to the complete area defined as a basement-- floors, walls, and ceilings.
	For aa Post-FIRM elevated building located in Zones A1-A30, AE, AH, AR, AR/A, AR/AH, AR/A1-A30, V1-V30, VE, full coverage begins at the lowest elevated floor. This is the lowest floor raised above ground, even if the pilings extend beyond it (see Lowest Elevated Floor Determination, in Section 2 this manual).
	For items of property below, at, or level with the lowest elevated floor, the item(s) is subject to the coverage limitation. For example, a cabinet, door, window, or refrigerator that originates below, at, or level with the lowest elevated floor is not covered, even that portion or value at or above the lowest elevated floor.
	However, coverage can be provided for building materials and finishes installed above the lowest elevated floor level, even if the item originates or overlaps the lowest elevated floor level, when the function of the building material or finish is not reduced by cutting or removing the damaged and otherwise excluded building material physically located at or below the line-level equal with the lowest elevated floor. Examples include exterior siding, wood trim, drywall, paint, or insulation, even if the same item extends below the level of the lowest elevated floor. The building materials and finishes below the line level with the lowest elevated floor are still excluded. This coverage interpretation is in sync with new FEMA-approved building codes for new construction and substantially improved buildings.
	The SFIP does not cover items, interior or exterior, located below the lowest elevated floor of a post-FIRM elevated building in the stated zones.
(1) Central air conditioners;	Central air conditioners include related built-in equipment for dehumidification, air filtering, and ventilation.
(2) Cisterns and the water in them;	See Section 2 Claims Processes and Guidance in this manual.

III. Property Covered

Policy Language	Additional Explanation
(3) Drywall for walls and ceilings in a basement and the cost of labor to nail it, unfinished and unfloated and not taped, to the framing;	The SFIP covers unfinished, unfloated, and not taped drywall installed anywhere in a basement. The SFIP will also pay for unfinished, unfloated, and not taped drywall in lieu of paneling or any finished wall or ceiling treatment. The SFIP does not cover non-structural building elements, including non-load bearing floor, wall, or ceiling framing components, such as when installed for the purpose to improve a basement or enclosure area with finished floors, walls, and ceilings.
(4) Electrical junction and circuit breaker boxes; (5) Electrical outlets and switches;	Electrical junction and circuit breaker boxes include a junction box, which serves as an unfinished basic light fixture. See Figure 9 below. The SFIP does not cover finished lighting, which is an improvement as defined in Section II.B.18, of the SFIP. Figure 9. Unfinished basic light fixture and Outlet
(6) Elevators, dumbwaiters, and related equipment, except for related equipment installed below the base flood elevation after September 30, 1987;	An elevator or dumbwaiter is covered if within the covered building enclosure or attached to and in contact with the insured building or directly attached to the 16 square foot landing area used for egress if unattached. For elevators and dumbwaiters installed below the BFE after September 30, 1987, coverage is limited to the cab and the included controls installed on or in the cab. Related equipment is everything except the cab and the included controls and is not covered unless the damaged equipment is installed above the level at or above the BFE.

III. Property Covered

Policy Language	Additional Explanation
	A chair lift is covered if within the covered building enclosure or attached to and in contact with the insured building or attached directly to the 16 square foot landing area attached to the building and used for egress (See Figures 10 and 11).
	  Figure 10. Example of a covered chair lift attached directly to a building or covered 4x4 16 SF landing
	Photograph credit BFA, LLC
	  Figure 11. Example of a non-covered chair lift.
(7) Fuel tanks and the fuel in them;	Fuel tanks and the fuel in them include a connected fuel gauge or fuel filter.
(8) Furnaces and hot water heaters;	Furnaces and hot water heaters include boilers and permanently installed equipment for humidification, air filtering, and ventilation. This includes those portions of the central HVAC in a building enclosure below the Lowest Floor

III. Property Covered

Policy Language	Additional Explanation
	Elevation (LFE) or basement, including boilers and connected radiators and hot water baseboards. This does not include electric baseboard heaters whether hardwired to the electrical system or not.
(9) Heat pumps	Heat pumps and other central HVAC units permanently installed equipment related to humidification, dehumidification, air filtering, and ventilation.
(10) Nonflammable insulation in a basement;	Nonflammable insulation in a basement includes: • Nonflammable insulation in walls and ceilings. For post-FIRM elevated buildings in SFHAs, coverage applies to: • Insulation installed between joists within the lowest elevated floor including plywood and any other material used to hold in the insulation. • Unfinished protective weather barriers affixed to the floor framing. The SFIP covers unattached protective barriers located in a crawlspace as personal property provided the area is not subject to basement or post-FIRM coverage limitations and the policyholder purchased contents coverage. When installed underneath a building in a crawlspace the barrier must be physically attached to the building's foundation or floor framing for Coverage A — Building.
(11) Pumps and tanks used in solar energy systems;	N/A
(12) Stairways and staircases attached to the building, not separated from it by elevated walkways;	The SFIP covers unfinished base support material for staircases and stairways (underneath the finished treads and risers) attached to the building, not separated from it by elevated walkways, including an exterior staircase into a basement that is part of the building and enclosed by an addition defined under SFIP Section III.A.2. This also includes an interior basement or post-FIRM elevated building staircases. The SFIP does not pay to treat, paint, or stain the base support material in a basement, or below the lowest elevated floor of a post-FIRM elevated building in an SFHA. The SFIP does not cover damage to finish materials used for a tread, riser, or stringer if such material is installed onto unfinished base support material

III. Property Covered

Policy Language	Additional Explanation
	for stairways and staircases. If the finish material is the base support material, such as with a floating staircase or step, the finish material is covered but not the cost to apply a finish coating, or paint.
	Figure 12. Unfinished base stairs (left) are covered in a basement or below a post-FIRM elevated building; however, improvements to paint or add finish treads, risers, and stringers (right) are not:
	Figure 13. Covered stairs where the finish material is the base material; however, no coverage to paint, stain, or coat:
	The SFIP does not cover the basement exterior egress staircase located outside of the perimeter building walls, even if covered by a roof or door. See SFIP Section IV.9.

III. Property Covered

Policy Language	Additional Explanation
(13) Sump pumps	N/A
(14) Water softeners and the chemicals in them, water filters, and faucets installed as an integral part of the plumbing system;	The SFIP allows for a faucet that is affixed directly to the plumbing line, as opposed to a faucet that is connected to plumbing lines but mounted onto a sink as a finished fixture. See Section 2: Water Softeners in this manual.
(15) Well water tanks and pumps;	Well water tanks and pumps include the pressure switch, pressure valve, and gauge.
(16) Required utility connections for any item in this list; and	N/A
(17) Footings, foundations, posts, pilings, piers, or other foundation walls and anchorage systems required to support a building.	Footings, foundations, posts, pilings, piers, or other foundation walls and anchorage systems required to support a building: • Includes windows and doors installed in the perimeter foundation walls of an SFIP-defined basement area such as a perimeter wall basement garage door or sliding glass door. • Includes vents installed in and considered part of the covered foundation walls of a post-FIRM elevated building. However, there is no coverage for breakaway walls or vents in breakaway walls. • Does not include screen or storm doors, or a door covering or enclosing an exterior egress in a basement, such as a Bilco™ door. • Does not include doors and windows of any type in an enclosure subject to post-FIRM limitations when located below the lowest elevated floor.
b. Clean-up.	Clean-up includes: • Pumping out trapped floodwater • Labor to remove or extract spent cleaning solutions • Treatment for mold and mildew • Structural drying of salvageable interior foundation elements The SFIP does not cover clean-up of an item or property located in areas subject to basement and post-FIRM coverage limitations — that is, the property must itself be covered under SFIP Section III(A)(8) –or for items or loss otherwise excluded under this policy.

III. Property Covered

Policy Language	Additional Explanation
	Clean-up is not the removal of flood-damaged items or debris removal. See SFIP Section III.C.1 for Debris Removal.
B Coverage B—Personal Property	
1. If you have purchased personal property coverage, we insure against direct physical loss by or from flood to personal property inside a building at the described location, if: a. The property is owned by you or your household family members; and b. At your option, the property is owned by guests or servants. Personal property is also covered for a period of 45 days at another location as set forth in III.C.2.b., Property Removed to Safety. Personal property in a building that is not fully enclosed must be secured to prevent flotation out of the building. If the personal property does float out during a flood, it will be conclusively presumed that it was not reasonably secured. In that case there is no coverage for such property.	• The personal property may be inside any SFIP-defined building at the described location. • The SFIP does not cover personal property that floats out of a partially enclosed building. • See SFIP Section III.C.2.b. for Property Removed to Safety. • Property leased under a "capital lease," a contract that entitles a renter the temporary use of an item and to account for the financial effect of ownership on their balance sheet, qualifies as an insurable interest and can be claimed even if the property is not solely owned by the policyholder. • In contrast, an "operating lease" is a contract that entitles a renter the temporary use of an item but does not convey ownership rights. According to Generally Accepted Accounting Principles (GAAP), property in possession of a policyholder obtained through an operating lease, cannot be represented in balancing sheet financials. Therefore, it is not covered under the SFIP Coverage B–Personal Property.
2. Coverage for personal property includes the following property, subject to B.1. above, which is covered under Coverage B only: a. Air conditioning units, portable or window type; b. Carpets, not permanently installed, over unfinished flooring; c. Carpets over finished flooring; d. Clothes washers and dryers; e. "Cook-out" grills; f. Food freezers, other than walk-in, and food in any freezer; and g. Portable microwave ovens and portable dishwashers.	• Coverage A – Building Property covers through-the-wall air conditioning units that are permanently installed. • Clothes washers and dryers, including the dryer exhaust vent kit. The connectors and plumbing lines for a gas dryer are covered under building coverage only. • Coverage B applies to food freezers only. NFIP considers an appliance that both refrigerates and freezes as a refrigerator and covers it under Coverage A – Building Property. • Drapes and hardware are contents, whether physically attached to the building or not.

III. Property Covered

	Policy Language	Additional Explanation
3.	Coverage for items of property in a building enclosure below the lowest elevated floor of an elevated post-FIRM building located in Zones A1–A30, AE, AH, AR, AR/A, AR/AE, AR/AH, AR/A1–A30, V1–V30, or VE, or in a basement, regardless of the zone, is limited to the following items, if installed in their functioning locations and, if necessary for operation, connected to a power source: a. Air conditioning units, portable or window type; b. Clothes washers and dryers; and c. Food freezers, other than walk-in, and food in any freezer.	• Coverage A – Building Property covers through-the-wall air conditioning units that are permanently installed. • Clothes washers and dryers include a dryer exhaust vent kit. • Coverage B applies to food freezers only. NFIP considers an appliance that both refrigerates and freezes as a refrigerator and covers it under Coverage A – Building Property. This provision does not apply to Zones A, AO, A99, AR/AO, V, and VO.
4.	If you are a tenant and have insured personal property under Coverage B in this policy, we will cover such property, including your cooking stove or range and refrigerator. The policy will also cover improvements made or acquired solely at your expense in the dwelling or apartment in which you reside, but for not more than 10% of the limit of liability shown for personal property on the Declarations Page. Use of this insurance is at your option but reduces the personal property limit of liability.	The SFIP considers tenant-owned appliances such as refrigerators, stoves, and ovens as personal property, not as building improvements, therefore they are not subject to the 10 percent building improvement limitation.
5.	If you are the owner of a unit and have insured personal property under Coverage B in this policy, we will also cover your interior walls, floor, and ceiling (not otherwise covered under a flood insurance policy purchased by your condominium association) for not more than 10% of the limit of liability shown for personal property on the Declarations Page. Use of this insurance is at your option but reduces the personal property limit of liability.	This provision applies only to a condominium unit owner, who purchased Coverage B – Personal Property under the Dwelling Form. This provision does not provide coverage for loss assessments charged to the unit owner by a condominium association and does not require an assessment to trigger coverage (see SFIP Section III.C.3. Condominium Loss Assessments). This provision is comparable to the provision that provides coverage to a tenant's betterments and improvements to the building. The RCBAP is the primary insurance coverage. The RCBAP pays for flood damage to interior walls, floors, and ceilings within the unit when the unit owner is responsible for those items of property. The Condominium Association's bylaws or articles of incorporation detail the unit owner's responsibility if there is no RCBAP or if there is no remaining RCBAP building coverage because of coinsurance provisions. For example, when an association purchases RCBAP coverage to 80 percent of the full replacement cost of the condominium building, no coinsurance applies. If the damages exceed the coverage purchased, this provision provides coverage to the unit owner of up to 10 percent of

III. Property Covered

Policy Language	Additional Explanation
	the amount of coverage purchased under Coverage B – Personal Property. This provision allows coverage for damages to building property (interior walls, floors, and ceilings) within the unit not to exceed 10 percent of the Coverage B limits of liability even when the unit owner has not purchased coverage under Coverage A – Building Property.
	A payment made under this provision is not an additional amount of insurance and reduces the Coverage B limit available to pay for personal property (contents) damages.
	Claims professionals must coordinate the RCBAP claim and the unit-owner claim under the Dwelling Form to prevent payment that exceeds:
	• The maximum insurance available that can be paid for the condominium building, which is $250,000 times the number of units.
	• The maximum insurance available for a single-family residence, including a unit in a condominium, which is $250,000.
	See Section 2 for detailed information on condominium claims handling.
6. **Special Limits.** We will pay no more than $2,500 for any one loss to one or more of the following kinds of personal property:	Payments for these items may not exceed $2,500.00 in aggregate.
a. Artwork, photographs, collectibles, or memorabilia, including but not limited to, porcelain or other figures, and sports cards;	Personal clothing used for work. For example: uniforms are the same as a business suit, or any other clothing used for work, and not subject to special limits.
b. Rare books or autographed items;	
c. Jewelry, watches, precious and semi-precious stones, or articles of gold, silver, or platinum;	
d. Furs or any article containing fur which represents its principal value; or	
e. Personal property used in any business.	
7. We will pay only for the functional value of antiques.	The SFIP does not value an antique based on the rarity of the item, nor does it apply depreciation based solely on age or its physical condition.
	Example: A 400-year-old fully restored chair formerly owned by a historical figure is appraised by a certified industry professional at $25,000. The chair has seen general usage for 3-years after its restoration date. Applying judgment, a new chair with the same or similar functional design, material quality, and craftsmanship is

III. Property Covered

Policy Language	Additional Explanation
	comparably worth $3,500. Less 10 percent depreciation, the SFIP would pay the functional value of $3,150.
C. Coverage C—Other Coverages	
1. Debris Removal	Insured property means the insured dwelling, the SFIP-eligible detached garage, and covered personal property.
a. We will pay the expense to remove non-owned debris that is on or in insured property and debris of insured property anywhere.	The SFIP does not pay for removal of:
b. If you or a member of your household perform the removal work, the value of your work will be based on the Federal minimum wage.	• Non-covered debris anywhere, such as a non-covered damaged property or debris located in the yard, driveway, or on another parcel of land.
c. This coverage does not increase the Coverage A or Coverage B limit of liability.	• Non-covered items of property, even if the removal of the item facilitates cleanup of covered building repairs, such as the removal of carpet installed inside a basement, or the removal of plants, shrubs, or trees along the perimeter of the building to access foundation or siding repairs.
2. Loss Avoidance Measures	The SFIP only covers those items specifically noted. The policyholder must provide receipts for covered materials they purchased. Additionally, the NFIP reimburses the policyholder and members of the policyholder's household labor at the Federal minimum wage at the time of the loss.
a. Sandbags, Supplies, and Labor	
(1) We will pay up to $1,000 for costs you incur to protect the insured building from a flood or imminent danger of flood, for the following:	Water-filled bladders, as shown in Figure 14, are considered a temporary levee for the purposes of loss avoidance coverage. However, because these are reusable, the SFIP will pay the cost to purchase the bladder once, but only when the initial purchase is in connection to the claimed flood event. After that event, any future claim for loss avoidance here is limited to the labor and fill material.
(a) Your reasonable expenses to buy:	
(i) Sandbags, including sand to fill them;	
(ii) Fill for temporary levees;	
(iii) Pumps; and	
(iv) Plastic sheeting and lumber used in connection with these items.	
(b) The value of work, at the Federal minimum wage, that you or a member of your household perform.	
(2) This coverage for Sandbags, Supplies, and Labor only applies if damage to insured property by or from flood is imminent and the threat of flood damage is apparent enough to lead a person of common prudence to anticipate flood damage. One of the following must also occur:	**Figure 14. Water-filled Bladder** Photograph credit Randy Wagner

III. Property Covered

Policy Language	Additional Explanation
(a) A general and temporary condition of flooding in the area near the described location must occur, even if the flood does not reach the insured building; or (b) A legally authorized official must issue an evacuation order or other civil order for the community in which the insured building is located calling for measures to preserve life and property from the peril of flood. This coverage does not increase the Coverage A or Coverage B limit of liability. b. Property Removed to Safety (1) We will pay up to $1,000 for the reasonable expenses you incur to move insured property to a place other than the described location that contains the property in order to protect it from flood or the imminent danger of flood. Reasonable expenses include the value of work, at the Federal minimum wage, you or a member of your household perform. If you move insured property to a location other than the described location that contains the property, in order to protect it from flood or the imminent danger of flood, we will cover such property while at that location for a period of 45 consecutive days from the date you begin to move it there. The personal property that is moved must be placed in a fully enclosed building or otherwise reasonably protected from the elements. Any property removed, including a moveable home described in II.B.6.b. and c., must be placed above ground level or outside of the special flood hazard area. (2) This coverage does not increase the Coverage A or Coverage B limit of liability.	• The SFIP coverage of "reasonable expenses" under this provision is limited to the policyholder's removal, storage, and return of covered building and personal property to the location described on the declarations page. The insurer may reimburse the policyholder for related expenses for the labor of the policyholder and family members at the Federal minimum wage and incurred transportation and storage costs. The policyholder must itemize and support these expenses with valid proof of payment. Coverage here is limited only to the length of time that a flood or the imminent danger of flood exists. Payment under this provision does not increase Coverage A – Building Property or Coverage B – Personal Property limits of liability. • The SFIP will cover from the peril of flood, the property relocated to another location for a period of 45 consecutive days from the date the policyholder began to move the property. If the policyholder does not place the property in a fully enclosed building, the property must be secured to prevent flotation out of the building. If the property floats out or away from the structure used to reasonably protect the property from the elements, it will be conclusively presumed that the policyholder did not reasonably secure the property. In that case, there is no coverage for the property. • Regarding the provision "must be placed above ground level or outside of the SFHA", the relocated site of the property must be a reasonable location to prevent loss compared to the described location. For example, where the surrounding terrain is sloped, the site of the relocated property must be on a higher elevation than the floor level of the building at the described location where the property was originally located; the policyholder may not relocate the property to a basement. Where the surrounding terrain is level and the site of the relocated property is considered within the same flood hazard area, the

III. Property Covered

Policy Language	Additional Explanation
	property must be placed on a floor level in the relocated building that is a higher elevation compared to the floor level in the building at the described location where the property was originally located. The property may not be relocated into a lower enclosure below an elevated floor within a post-FIRM building located in an SFHA.
Condominium Loss Assessments a. If this policy insures a unit, we will pay, up to the Coverage A limit of liability, your share of loss assessments charged against you by the condominium association in accordance with the condominium association's articles of association, declarations and your deed. The assessment must be made as a result of direct physical loss by or from flood during the policy term, to the building's common elements.	The Dwelling Form covers a condominium association's loss assessments to a covered property for direct physical damage by flood. This does not include an assessment from the Condominium Association for property not covered by the SFIP, such as the cleanup of debris, sand, landscape lighting, repairs to parking lots, decks, sidewalks, pools, etc.
b. We will not pay any loss assessment charged against you: (1) And the condominium association by any governmental body; (2) That results from a deductible under the insurance purchased by the condominium association insuring common elements; (3) That results from a loss to personal property, including contents of a condominium building; (4) That results from a loss sustained by the condominium association that was not reimbursed under a flood insurance policy written in the name of the association under the Act because the building was not, at the time of loss, insured for an amount equal to the lesser of: (a) 80% or more of its full replacement cost; or (b) The maximum amount of insurance permitted under the Act; (5) To the extent that payment under this policy for a condominium building loss, in combination with payments under any other NFIP policies for the same building loss, exceeds the maximum amount of insurance permitted under the Act for that kind of building; or	The Dwelling Form covers assessments if the Association does not have insurance for 80 percent of the RCV or the maximum insurance available for the condominium building. The Dwelling Form does not cover assessments for non-covered items. This provision does not increase building limits. The SFIP will not pay more than once for any building item regardless of the number of policies. The total payments for an individual unit from all NFIP policies may not exceed $250,000, the maximum insurance available for a single-family residence.

III. Property Covered

Policy Language	Additional Explanation
(6) To the extent that payment under this policy for a condominium building loss, in combination with any recovery available to you as a tenant in common under any NFIP condominium association policies for the same building loss, exceeds the amount of insurance permitted under the Act for a single-family dwelling. Loss assessment coverage does not increase the Coverage A limit of liability.	
D. Coverage D—Increased Cost of Compliance	
1. General	N/A
This policy pays you to comply with a State or local floodplain management law or ordinance affecting repair or reconstruction of a structure suffering flood damage. Compliance activities eligible for payment are: elevation, floodproofing, relocation, or demolition (or any combination of these activities) of your structure. Eligible floodproofing activities are limited to:	
a. Non-residential structures.	
b. Residential structures with basements that satisfy FEMA's standards published in the Code of Federal Regulations [44 CFR 60.6 (b) or (c)].	
2. Limit of Liability	All three SFIP forms provide Increased Cost of Compliance (ICC) benefits as Coverage D. ICC provides up to $30,000 toward the cost of bringing a flood-damaged structure into compliance with state or community floodplain management laws or ordinances governing repair or reconstruction following a flood.
We will pay you up to $30,000 under this Coverage D—Increased Cost of Compliance, which only applies to policies with building coverage (Coverage A). Our payment of claims under Coverage D is in addition to the amount of coverage which you selected on the application and which appears on the Declarations Page. But the maximum you can collect under this policy for both Coverage A— Building Property and Coverage D—Increased Cost of Compliance cannot exceed the maximum permitted under the Act. We do not charge a separate deductible for a claim under Coverage D.	
3. Eligibility	To be eligible for ICC, the community must declare the building substantially damaged. The amount paid for Coverage D – ICC and Coverage A – Building Property combined cannot exceed the maximum program limits of $250,000 for the Dwelling Form.
a. A structure covered under Coverage A—Building Property sustaining a loss caused by a flood as defined by this policy must:	ICC is not available in Emergency Program communities. ICC is not available for:
(1) Be a "repetitive loss structure." A repetitive loss structure is one that meets the following conditions:	• Contents-only policies.

III. Property Covered

Policy Language	Additional Explanation
(a) The structure is covered by a contract of flood insurance issued under the NFIP.	• Group Flood Insurance policies.
(b) The structure has suffered flood damage on two occasions during a 10-year period which ends on the date of the second loss.	• Dwelling Form policies on individual condominium units in a multi-unit building.
(c) The cost to repair the flood damage, on average, equaled or exceeded 25% of the market value of the structure at the time of each flood loss.	In a multi-unit condominium building, ICC coverage is available through the condominium association's flood policy. No separate deductible applies.
(d) In addition to the current claim, the NFIP must have paid the previous qualifying claim, and the State or community must have a cumulative, substantial damage provision or repetitive loss provision in its floodplain management law or ordinance being enforced against the structure; or	For 3.b.(2) and (3) to apply, the community must first adopt and enforce new preliminary or advisory base flood elevations, or best available data provided by FEMA, and an ICC claim cannot proceed until on or after the effective date of the new base flood elevations AND the policyholder receives notice from the community requiring the home to be brought into compliance with the new flood elevations.
(2) Be a structure that has had flood damage in which the cost to repair equals or exceeds 50% of the market value of the structure at the time of the flood. The State or community must have a substantial damage provision in its floodplain management law or ordinance being enforced against the structure.	There are situations where the community may have its own elevation or floodproofing requirements, which it enforces within a non-SFHA. This would be specified in the community's floodplain ordinance. However, the community must be able to demonstrate this requirement and enforcement is at least based in part on guidance from FEMA, and not entirely on its own.
b. This Coverage D pays you to comply with State or local floodplain management laws or ordinances that meet the minimum standards of the National Flood Insurance Program found in the Code of Federal Regulations at 44 CFR 60.3. We pay for compliance activities that exceed those standards under these conditions:	**ICC Claims** The date of loss of the ICC claim is the date of loss of the underlying flood claim that triggers the requirement to comply with a community law or ordinance.
(1) 3.a.(1) above.	Policyholders have up to six years from the date of the underlying flood loss to complete the eligible mitigation activity. Policyholders should know that initiating a mitigation project before receiving a substantial damage declaration from the community may jeopardize their eligibility to receive an ICC payment.
(2) Elevation or floodproofing in any risk zone to preliminary or advisory base flood elevations provided by FEMA which the State or local government has adopted and is enforcing for flood-damaged structures in such areas. (This includes compliance activities in B, C, X, or D zones which are being changed to zones with base flood elevations. This also includes compliance activities in zones where base flood elevations are being increased, and a flood-damaged structure must comply with the higher advisory base flood elevation.) Increased Cost of Compliance coverage does not apply to situations in B, C, X, or D zones where the	For buildings in Zones B, C, X, D, unnumbered A and V, and A99, the adjuster must document why a building must undergo mitigation and obtain a written statement from the community to substantiate the ICC claim. ICC does not pay for testing, monitoring, clean up, removal, containment, treatment, detoxification, or neutralization of pollutants even if required by community ordinance. **Repetitive Loss Properties** If a state or community adopts and enforces a cumulative substantial damage provision or repetitive loss provision requiring action by property owners to comply with floodplain management laws or ordinances, this may also qualify a structure for an ICC claim after a flood loss. The community must declare the structure to be substantially damaged and the structure must meet the NFIP's repetitive loss

III. Property Covered

Policy Language	Additional Explanation
community has derived its own elevations and is enforcing elevation or floodproofing requirements for flood-damaged structures to elevations derived solely by the community. (3) Elevation or floodproofing above the base flood elevation to meet State or local "freeboard" requirements, i.e., that a structure must be elevated above the base flood elevation. c. Under the minimum NFIP criteria at 44 CFR 60.3 (b)(4), States and communities must require the elevation or floodproofing of structures in unnumbered A zones to the base flood elevation where elevation data is obtained from a Federal, State, or other source. Such compliance activities are also eligible for Coverage D. d. This coverage will also pay for the incremental cost, after demolition or relocation, of elevating or floodproofing a structure during its rebuilding at the same or another site to meet State or local floodplain management laws or ordinances, subject to Exclusion D.5.g. below. e. This coverage will also pay to bring a flood-damaged structure into compliance with state or local floodplain management laws or ordinances even if the structure had received a variance before the present loss from the applicable floodplain management requirements.	structure definition. The NFIP defines a repetitive loss structure as an NFIP-insured building that has incurred flood-related damages on two occasions during a 10-year period ending on the date of the event for which the insured makes a second claim. The cost of repairing the flood damage, on the average, must equal or exceed 25 percent of the market value of the building at the time of each flood. The adjuster or insurer must verify that the NFIP paid a claim for both qualifying losses and that the state or community is enforcing a cumulative substantial damage or repetitive loss provision in its law or ordinance and declared the building substantially damaged on that basis. **Substantial Damage** Insurers may only open an ICC claim when the community declares a building substantially damaged in writing. Neither FEMA nor the insurer can determine substantial damage or issue a substantial damage declaration. The community has the sole authority to determine substantial damage. Note that in some cases a community may declare a building substantially damaged, based in whole or in part on non-flood-related damage. While having more than 50 percent damage may trigger a requirement to comply with the local floodplain management ordinances, the SFIP requires the percentage of damage to be by or from flood, whether covered by the SFIP or not. See <u>Section 3</u> Increased Cost of Compliance in this manual for more detail.
4. Conditions a. When a structure covered under Coverage A—Building Property sustains a loss caused by a flood, our payment for the loss under this Coverage D will be for the increased cost to elevate, floodproof, relocate, or demolish (or any combination of these activities) caused by the enforcement of current State or local floodplain management ordinances or laws. Our payment for eligible demolition activities will be for the cost to demolish and clear the site of the building debris or a portion thereof caused by the enforcement of current State or local floodplain management ordinances or laws. Eligible activities for the cost of clearing the site will include those necessary to discontinue	ICC pays for the following mitigation activities or a combination of the following: Floodproofing to reduce the potential for flood damage by keeping floodwater out of a building, for nonresidential structures and for certain residential structures that satisfy FEMA's standards under 44 C.F.R. 60.6(b) or (c). <ul><li>Elevation to raise a building to or above the BFE plus freeboard adopted by a community, adopted Advisory Base Flood Elevations (ABFE), or the best available data provided by FEMA.</li><li>Demolition when a building is in such poor condition that elevation and relocation are not technically feasible or cost-effective.</li><li>Relocation to move a building outside of the floodplain.</li></ul>See <u>Section 3</u> Increased Cost of Compliance in this manual for more detail.

III. Property Covered

Policy Language	Additional Explanation
utility service to the site and ensure proper abandonment of on-site utilities.	
b. When the building is repaired or rebuilt, it must be intended for the same occupancy as the present building unless otherwise required by current floodplain management ordinances or laws.	

5. Exclusions
 	
Under this Coverage D - Increased Cost of Compliance, we will not pay for:
 	
a. The cost to comply with any floodplain management law or ordinance in communities participating in the Emergency Program.
 	
b. The cost associated with enforcement of any ordinance or law that requires any insured or others to test for, monitor, clean up, remove, contain, treat, detoxify or neutralize, or in any way respond to, or assess the effects of pollutants.
 	
c. The loss in value to any insured building or other structure due to the requirements of any ordinance or law.
 	
d. The loss in residual value of the undamaged portion of a building demolished as a consequence of enforcement of any State or local floodplain management law or ordinance.
 	
e. Any Increased Cost of Compliance under this Coverage D:
 	
  (1) Until the building is elevated, floodproofed, demolished, or relocated on the same or to another premises; and
 	
  (2) Unless the building is elevated, floodproofed, demolished, or relocated as soon as reasonably possible after the loss, not to exceed two years.
 	
f. Any code upgrade requirements, e.g., plumbing or electrical wiring, not specifically related to the State or local floodplain management law or ordinance.
	N/A

III. Property Covered

Policy Language	Additional Explanation
g. Any compliance activities needed to bring additions or improvements made after the loss occurred into compliance with State or local floodplain management laws or ordinances.	
h. Loss due to any ordinance or law that you were required to comply with before the current loss.	
i. Any rebuilding activity to standards that do not meet the NFIP's minimum requirements. This includes any situation where the insured has received from the State or community a variance in connection with the current flood loss to rebuild the property to an elevation below the base flood elevation.	
j. Increased Cost of Compliance for a garage or carport.	
k. Any structure insured under an NFIP Group Flood Insurance Policy.	
l. Assessments made by a condominium association on individual condominium unit owners to pay increased costs of repairing commonly owned buildings after a flood in compliance with State or local floodplain management ordinances or laws.	
6. Other Provisions	N/A
a. Increased Cost of Compliance coverage will not be included in the calculation to determine whether coverage meets the 80% insurance-to-value requirement for replacement cost coverage as set forth in VII. General Conditions, V. Loss Settlement.	
b. All other conditions and provisions of the policy apply.	

IV. Property Not Covered

We do not cover any of the following

	Policy Language	Additional Explanation
1.	Personal property not inside a building;	N/A
2.	A building, and personal property in it, located entirely in, on, or over water or seaward of mean high tide if it was constructed or substantially improved after September 30, 1982;	• The SFIP allows coverage for a building not entirely over water, for example: when part of the exterior perimeter wall and foundation of the building is on land or the landward side of mean high tide (mean high water). • When the exterior perimeter walls of the building are completely over water and the support system or foundation underneath the insured building extends onto land, or the extension of any mechanism for access into a building (including, but not limited to, stairs, decks, walkways, piers, posts, pilings, docks, or driveways), even if the mechanism is on or partially on land, the building or the access will not be eligible for coverage. • If the exterior perimeter walls of a building are completely over water, but connected to another eligible building by means of an elevated walkway, stairway, roof, or rigid exterior wall, or there is an appurtenant structure on the same slab, foundation, or other continuous support system that is on land (such as a shed or garage), the presence of the connected building or appurtenant structure on land does not allow coverage to be afforded to the building that has its exterior perimeter walls entirely over water.
3.	Open structures, including a building used as a boathouse or any structure or building into which boats are floated, and personal property located in, on, or over water;	The SFIP does not cover boathouses or buildings into which boats can float and personal property located within buildings used solely as boathouses. When a boathouse is also used as a dwelling, the SFIP covers the dwelling portion and its foundation, even when the foundation includes the foundation and other building elements shared with the boathouse subject to the provisions of the SFIP including IV. Property Not Covered. The SFIP does not cover a building and personal property within it, located in, on, or over water or seaward of mean high tide if the building was constructed or substantially improved after September 30, 1982.

IV. Property Not Covered	
Policy Language	**Additional Explanation**
4. Recreational vehicles other than travel trailers described in the Definitions section (see II.B.6.c.) whether affixed to a permanent foundation or on wheels;	Figure 15. A recreation vehicle is a self-propelled vehicle Photograph credit Fleetwood RV Figure 16. A travel trailer is not self-propelled and is towed behind a road vehicle
5. Self-propelled vehicles or machines, including their parts and equipment. However, we do cover self-propelled vehicles or machines not licensed for use on public roads that are: a. Used mainly to service the described location or b. Designed and used to assist handicapped persons, while the vehicles or machines are inside a building at the described location;	The SFIP does not cover self-propelled vehicles or machinery. There are two specific instances where coverage is provided, so long as: (1) the vehicle or machinery is not licensed for use on public roads. (2) specific documentation is provided to support the claim. Under (a), the described location must be the type that would reasonably require service by means of the vehicle or machinery in question. Secondly, there must be evidence the described location is routinely serviced in support of what is claimed under this provision. Vehicles and machinery that are part of or service a business operation at the described location do not qualify for coverage under this provision. Under (b) a vehicle or machinery is covered if it is designed and used as mobility vehicles for persons with disabilities. The vehicle or machinery is not covered if it is not designed to assist persons with disabilities, or not used by persons with disabilities. As an example, a typical golf cart is not covered under this provision, even if it is used by persons with disabilities unless designed or modified specifically to assist persons with disabilities.

IV. Property Not Covered

	Policy Language	Additional Explanation
		Under both (a) and (b), the vehicle or machinery must be inside a building at the location described on the declarations page for coverage, provided all other policy terms and conditions apply.
		This exclusion does not apply to motorized toys and machinery designed, marketed, or sold for the exclusive use by a youth, including children's dirt bikes solely powered by a battery. If a motorized toy or machinery can be reasonably used by an adult, it is not a youth's toy and is not covered property.
6.	Land, land values, lawns, trees, shrubs, plants, growing crops, or animals;	• The SFIP does not cover any type of live plant located inside or outside of the building. This provision does not apply to artificial plants used as indoor decor.
		• The SFIP will pay the cost to replace land removed by sudden erosion caused by waves or currents of water during a specific type of flood as defined at SFIP Section II.A. when such soil directly supports the insured building.
7.	Accounts, bills, coins, currency, deeds, evidences of debt, medals, money, scrip, stored value cards, postage stamps, securities, bullion, manuscripts, or other valuable papers;	• Scrip is a form of money issued by a local government or private organization, such as gift cards, coupons, or any substitute for legal tender.
		• The SFIP does not cover financial loss from damage or destruction of electronic data or the cost of restoring that data.
		• Other valuable papers include stocks, certificates, and bonds.
8.	Underground structures and equipment, including wells, septic tanks, and septic systems;	• Underground structures and equipment include, but are not limited to, wires, conduits, pipes, sewers, tanks, tunnels, sprinkler systems, similar property, and any apparatus connected beneath the surface of the ground. The SFIP provides coverage if other SFIP requirements are met for equipment installed and used in the operation of underground structures and equipment installed above ground and within a building, for example, a sprinkler timer.
		• When installed, a sewage grinder pump is an integral part of the building's septic system. The grinder pump pulverizes waste for discharge into the septic drainage field. This item of property is not covered. However, the SFIP covers the sewage grinder pump's alarm service panel if installed above ground level and affixed to the building or its foundation. The SFIP does not cover the pump's alarm service panel installed to an item of property that is not covered, such as a support post to a deck.

IV. Property Not Covered

Policy Language	Additional Explanation
9. Those portions of walks, walkways, decks, driveways, patios and other surfaces, all whether protected by a roof or not, located outside the perimeter, exterior walls of the insured building or the building in which the insured unit is located;	The SFIP pays to repair or replace damage to any existing egress on the sides of a building, including underneath an elevated building. For each existing egress, the SFIP covers one 16 square foot (SF) landing and a single set of stairs, and one landing per staircase. The SFIP covers materials of a like kind and quality, such as concrete, wood, or composite wood material. Covered items include any existing hand or support rail, support posts, and hardware. The SFIP does not cover improvements such as lighting or finishing (paint or preservative stains). Figure 17 shows a deck with a single set of stairs providing access to the building through two doors. The SFIP would cover one 16 SF landing and the existing single set of stairs. Figure 17. Deck with Single Set of Stairs The SFIP does not cover the second set of stairs of the double staircase, as shown in Figure 18, because a single set of stairs provides egress. Figure 18. Deck with Double Staircase The SFIP does not cover the cost to comply with Americans with Disabilities Act of 1990 (ADA) regulations; however, the SFIP will repair or replace an existing flood

IV. Property Not Covered

Policy Language	Additional Explanation
	damaged handicap ramp shown in Figure 19 for egress, in lieu of the 16 SF of landing and stairs. Figure 19. Existing Handicap Ramp
10. Containers, including related equipment, such as, but not limited to, tanks containing gases or liquids;	The SFIP does not cover fuel tanks, pressure tanks, and well water tanks located outside of the insured building or an eligible detached garage. The SFIP does not cover containers outside of the building, including shipping containers used for storage or residential purposes, unless the container meets the definition of a building. The SFIP covers fuel tanks, water tanks, and pressure tanks inside or directly underneath the building, including in a basement or crawlspace, under Coverage A – Building Property, when installed as part of a utility system that services the building. Under Coverage B – Personal Property, the SFIP will cover any container inside of a building that is used for household or personal purposes such as oxygen tanks for medical reasons, small fuel tanks for filling lawn equipment, or sealed portable fuel canisters for cooking such as for camping or outdoor grilling. Containers used for the storage of food do not apply to this provision. Containers such as paint cans can be covered but only for the value of what is stored, and not for the value of the container. Because containers and tanks are either sealed or made of material meant for contact with liquid, including corrosive liquids, the claim should take into account the proper scope of damage and first consider if the item is reusable after rinsing and cleaning.
11. Buildings or units and all their contents if more than 49% of the actual cash value of the building is below ground, unless the lowest	A building must have over 51 percent of its actual cash value above ground level. This calculation relies solely upon the ACV, not on concepts like square footage, volume,

IV. Property Not Covered

	Policy Language	Additional Explanation
	level is at or above the base flood elevation and is below ground by reason of earth having been used as insulation material in conjunction with energy efficient building techniques;	or otherwise. Items of property that are not covered under Coverage A – Building Property, should not be included in the building valuation. Claims handling should pay close attention to subterranean or earth dwellings and certain buildings located at sanitation facilities.
12.	Fences, retaining walls, seawalls, bulkheads, wharves, piers, bridges, and docks;	FEMA considers these items covered when physically connected to a building and directly supportive and integral to the building's foundation, even if it has a secondary purpose such as a retaining wall.
13.	Aircraft or watercraft, or their furnishings and equipment;	• The SFIP covers remote-controlled boats, aircraft, and drones or UAVs (Unmanned Aerial Vehicles) designed and intended for recreational use only, and not used to carry people or cargo, or for commercial use. The same policy provisions that apply to other personal property apply to these items. • The SFIP does not cover drones or UAVs registered with the Federal Aviation Administration for purposes other than recreational model aircraft. • Watercraft includes any vessel that travels on water, including surfboards. Pool toys are not watercraft. • The SFIP does not cover furnishings and equipment for non-covered watercraft and aircraft including parts and other items identified for use with watercraft and aircraft. • This exclusion does not apply to fishing equipment like fishing poles, lures, and the like.
14.	Hot tubs and spas that are not bathroom fixtures, and swimming pools, and their equipment, such as, but not limited to, heaters, filters, pumps, and pipes, wherever located;	N/A
15.	Property not eligible for flood insurance pursuant to the provisions of the Coastal Barrier Resources Act and the Coastal Barrier Improvement Act and amendments to these Acts;	The SFIP does not provide flood insurance coverage for a building constructed or substantially improved after the U.S. Department of Interior's Fish and Wildlife Service designates it as within Coastal Barrier Resources System (CBRS) boundaries or as Otherwise Protected Areas (OPAs). See FWS website for more information.
16.	Personal property you own in common with other unit owners comprising the membership of a condominium association.	N/A

V. Exclusions

Policy Language	Additional Explanation
A. We only pay for direct physical loss by or from flood, which means that we do not pay you for:	
1. Loss of revenue or profits;	• The SFIP does not cover the costs to pack, move, or store personal property from the insured building or return it to the building when an owner repairs the building or cannot occupy it.
2. Loss of access to the insured property or described location; Loss of use of the insured property or described location; Loss from interruption of business or production;	• The SFIP does not cover replacing non-flood damaged property required to comply with government codes, ordinances, or regulations. For example, the SFIP does not cover the cost of replacing an undamaged interior HVAC unit to match a replaced exterior HVAC unit because of a change in size, Seasonal energy efficiency ratio (SEER)-rating, refrigerant, or any other reason even if local, state, or federal code required the upgrade.
3. Any additional living expenses incurred while the insured building is being repaired or is unable to be occupied for any reason;	
4. The cost of complying with any ordinance or law requiring or regulating the construction, demolition, remodeling, renovation, or repair of property, including removal of any resulting debris. This exclusion does not apply to any eligible activities we describe in Coverage D—Increased Cost of Compliance; or,	
5. Any other economic loss you suffer.	
B. We do not insure a loss directly or indirectly caused by a flood that is already in progress at the time and date:	
1. The policy term begins; or	NFIP adjusts flood insurance losses individually. Flood insurance benefits are available if an insured property suffers a covered loss caused by a general condition of flooding, as defined by the SFIP.
2. Coverage is added at your request.	See Flood-in-Progress Exclusion in Section 2 of this manual.
C. We do not insure for loss to property caused directly by earth movement even if the earth movement is caused by flood. Some examples of earth movement that we do not cover are:	
1. Earthquake;	The SFIP is a single-peril policy that only pays for covered damage due to direct physical loss by or from flood, defined in the policy in Section II. The SFIP does not cover damage resulting from an intervening cause of loss, even if the resulting cause is due to flood. The SFIP does not cover damage that results when saturated soils cause the soil below ground level to sink, expand, compact, destabilize, or otherwise lose its load-bearing capacity such as from voids or rotten organic matter when the soil dries. The SFIP does not cover earth movement; each form of earth movement is an intervening cause of loss and a separate peril.
2. Landslide;	
3. Land subsidence;	
4. Sinkholes;	
5. Destabilization or movement of land that results from accumulation of water in subsurface land area; or	The SFIP's exclusion for other perils, such as fire, exemplifies the exclusion of earth movement as a cause of loss. When a flood causes a fire, which damages the building during inundation or after floodwaters recede, the SFIP does not cover the
6. Gradual erosion.	

V. Exclusions

Policy Language	Additional Explanation
We do, however, pay for losses from mudflow and land subsidence as a result of erosion that are specifically covered under our definition of flood (see II.A.1.c. and II.A.2.).	resulting fire and smoke damage to the building even if flood directly caused the fire. The SFIP covers damage to a building if the damage results from the collapse or subsidence of land that is the direct result of sudden erosion or undermining to the building's support soil underneath or directly along the perimeter foundation of the building from waves or currents of floodwater (velocity flow) during a flood from the overflow of inland or tidal waters or mudflow. This includes damage to the foundation of the building and any resulting damage to the interior and exterior finishes. The SFIP does not cover damage caused by gradual erosion.

D. We do not insure for direct physical loss caused directly or indirectly by any of the following:
 	
1. The pressure or weight of ice;
2. Freezing or thawing;
3. Rain, snow, sleet, hail, or water spray;
4. Water, moisture, mildew, or mold damage that results primarily from any condition:
  a. Substantially confined to the dwelling; or
  b. That is within your control, including but not limited to:
    (1) Design, structural, or mechanical defects;
    (2) Failure, stoppage, or breakage of water or sewer lines, drains, pumps, fixtures, or equipment; or
    (3) Failure to inspect and maintain the property after a flood recedes;
	N/A
	
	When the policyholder is prevented access to promptly remove wetted building and personal property items, and this delay directly results in water, moisture, mildew or mold damage to building and personal property items not in physical contact with surface floodwater, this damage could be covered.
	
	As examples:
	
	• Local authorities restrict access to the area, or
	• Prolonged inundation of floodwater prevents access to the area.
	
	The claim file must include proper documentation, such as but not limited to photographs, an acceptable explanation provided by the adjuster, or a signed statement from the policyholder or community official that supports the payment for property damages above the documented water height.
	
	For instances when coverage and payment are not recommended, the claim file should include information that documents the policyholder's failure to inspect and maintain their insured property or take reasonable measures to reduce damage when it is feasible to do so.
	
	The SFIP does not cover damage caused by long-term exposure to moisture, water, rot, and insect infestation. This includes damage from the lack of climate control inside the building when the approach to repair does not include the timely repair to the building HVAC system.
	
	The SFIP does not cover pre-existing damage to structural building components, such as damage caused by rot, or for any resulting damage to non-structural finish

V. Exclusions

Policy Language	Additional Explanation
	building material.
5. Water or water-borne material that: a. Backs up through sewers or drains; b. Discharges or overflows from a sump, sump pump or related equipment; or c. Seeps or leaks on or through the covered property; d. unless there is a flood in the area and the flood is the proximate cause of the sewer or drain backup, sump pump discharge or overflow, or the seepage of water;	The adjuster must document that a flood occurred in the area and that the flood was the proximate cause of the back-up of the sewer or drain, overflow of the sump pump, pump failure, seepage of water, or damage due to the pressure or weight of water (hydrostatic pressure) in the claim file. See SFIP Section II. A and related commentary under the definition of flood. When paying a loss due to a flood in the area proximately causing discharge or overflow of water or water-borne material from a sump, sump pump, or related equipment, the insurer must document the claim file to show that a homeowner's policy endorsement or policy rider did not also cover the loss. If the homeowner's policy does provide coverage, the SFIP payment must apply a proportional loss distribution, as stated under Section VII.C. Other Insurance. The adjuster must document a flood occurred in the area, and that the flood was the proximate cause of the back-up of the sewer or drain, overflow of the sump pump, pump failure, seepage of water, or damage caused by the pressure or weight of water (hydrostatic pressure). A flood is two or more parcels of partial or complete inundation of normally dry land, or of two or more continuous acres of normally dry land. For coverage under this provision, the condition of flood does not have to be on the parcel of land described at the location; it may be within the proximate area.
6. The pressure or weight of water unless there is a flood in the area and the flood is the proximate cause of the damage from the pressure or weight of water;	Refer to SFIP Section V.D.5. above.
7. Power, heating, or cooling failure unless the failure results from direct physical loss by or from flood to power, heating, or cooling equipment on the described location;	The SFIP does not cover damage to insured property when caused by a power surge or power outage that originates from the failure or shutting down of equipment that is not located at the described location, even if the reason is a direct result of a flood. For example, the local utility operator may shut down a section of the electrical grid to avoid system damage from a flood. When the power returns to the electrical grid, the initial surge of electricity can damage insured property. Under this loss description, the damage is not covered. The SFIP covers damage to any covered building or personal property item, such as the building's main service, home security system, a plugged-in television, or to the HVAC system, when a flood physically damages related system equipment installed at the described location. For example, if the flood damages power equipment at

V. Exclusions

Policy Language	Additional Explanation
	the described location creating an electrical short within the power system resulting in damage to another item of property part of or connected to the power system, the damage to the item is also covered, even though it was not physically touched by floodwater. Under this loss description, the damage is considered a direct physical loss by or from flood. To cover the loss described, the adjuster must document the cause of loss in the claim file to rule out the possibility of a non-covered cause, such as described in the previous paragraph.
8. Theft, fire, explosion, wind, or windstorm; 9. Anything you or any member of your household do or conspires to do to deliberately cause loss by flood; or 10. Alteration of the insured property that significantly increases the risk of flooding.	N/A
E. We do not insure for loss to any building or personal property located on land leased from the Federal Government, arising from or incident to the flooding of the land by the Federal Government, where the lease expressly holds the Federal Government harmless under flood insurance issued under any Federal Government program.	N/A
F. We do not pay for the testing for or monitoring of pollutants unless required by law or ordinance.	The SFIP only pays to test or monitor the removal of a pollutant when a law or ordinance requires it. Insurers must have a copy of the law or ordinance for the file to support their decision to pay for the testing for or monitoring of pollutants. The law or ordinance must be in effect at the date of loss to apply.

VI. Deductibles

Policy Language	Additional Explanation
A. When a loss is covered under this policy, we will pay only that part of the loss that exceeds your deductible amount, subject to the limit of liability that applies. The deductible amount is shown on the Declarations Page. However, when a building under construction, alteration, or repair does not have at least two rigid exterior walls and a fully secured roof at the time of loss, your deductible amount will be two times the deductible that would otherwise apply to a completed building.	
B. In each loss from flood, separate deductibles apply to the building and personal property insured by this policy.	
C. The deductible does NOT apply to:	The SFIP applies a separate deductible to both building and personal property losses. The SFIP will only pay that portion of the loss that exceeds the applicable deductibles.
1. III.C.2. Loss Avoidance Measures;	For building (residence and a detached garage) and personal property losses, the insurer should take the deductible from the gross loss before applying policy limits. For example, if the covered loss is $110,000, the policy limit is $100,000, and the deductible is $5,000, the insurer should apply the deductible to the $110,000 loss, which leaves $105,000, meaning the insurer should pay the $100,000 policy limit.
2. III.C.3. Condominium Loss Assessments; or	The SFIP does not apply coverage of excess damage from a covered detached garage to the deductible.
3. III.D. Increased Cost of Compliance.	The SFIP does not apply excess loss to items subject to Special Limits to reduce the personal property deductible.

VII. General Conditions

Policy Language	Additional Explanation
A. Pair and Set Clause	
In case of loss to an article that is part of a pair or set, we will have the option of paying you:	If the damaged property item is ruined and cannot be replaced individually as a single item, and this renders the other item in the pair or the set unusable or worthless, then the SFIP pays for the pair or set.
1. An amount equal to the cost of replacing the lost, damaged, or destroyed article, minus its depreciation, or	**Examples:** Left shoe ruined by flood, and the right shoe undamaged. The left shoe cannot be purchased without the right, rendering the undamaged right shoe unusable. The SFIP allows for a new pair of shoes. Other similar examples include a
2. The amount that represents the fair proportion of the total value of the pair or set that the lost, damaged, or destroyed article bears to	

VII. General Conditions

Policy Language	Additional Explanation
the pair or set.	ruined china base cabinet and undamaged matching china base top; half the seat ruined in a sectional sofa; a ruined left window curtain and an undamaged right window curtain.
	If the damaged property item is ruined and can be replaced individually as a single item with like kind and quality, and this renders the other item or the set usable, the SFIP will only cover the damaged/ruined item along with the reasonable cost for like kind and quality, except in the case of the Section V. Exclusion (A)(6) for ordinance or law, and the like.
	Examples: Base cabinets ruined by flood with the upper cabinets undamaged. The upper cabinets remain usable. The SFIP allows replacing the base cabinets with like kind and quality, including reasonable costs to match the new base cabinets with existing undamaged cabinets. Other similar examples include a damaged dresser and undamaged or repairable matching armoire and nightstands, a ruined dining table leaf and undamaged or repairable dining table, a ruined granite cabinet countertop, and salvageable granite island countertop.
	Example: An outdoor heating, ventilation, and air conditioning (HVAC) unit is ruined by flood, and the interior HVAC unit is undamaged. Due to Department of Energy code requirements regarding energy efficiency, or an Environmental Protection Agency (EPA)-mandate regarding refrigerant type, a replacement outdoor HVAC unit that works with the existing interior HVAC unit is unavailable, rendering the undamaged interior unit unusable. Section VII (A) Pair and Set clause is superseded by Section V Exclusions (A)(6), and the SFIP only allows to replace the outdoor HVAC unit with like kind and quality, and does not cover replacement of the undamaged interior HVAC unit.

B. Concealment or Fraud and Policy Voidance

1. With respect to all insureds under this policy, this policy:
   a. Is void;
   b. Has no legal force or effect;
   c. Cannot be renewed; and
   d. Cannot be replaced by a new NFIP policy, if, before or after a loss, you or any other insured or your agent have at any time:
      (1) Intentionally concealed or misrepresented any material fact or

	When claims professionals suspect wrongful acts or misrepresentations on a claim by a policyholder or their representatives:
	• The adjuster should promptly submit written notification with supporting documentation to the insurer. The adjuster should not draw any conclusions regarding the suspected fraud and should only present facts in written reports.
	• The examiner should engage management to determine if the insurer should refer the matter to the FEMA Fraud Unit (email:

VII. General Conditions

Policy Language	Additional Explanation
circumstance; (2) Engaged in fraudulent conduct; or (3) Made false statements; relating to this policy or any other NFIP insurance.	StopFEMAFraud@fema.dhs.gov) and the insurer's investigative unit for a Reservation of Rights.
2. This policy will be void as of the date wrongful acts described in B.1. above were committed. 3. Fines, civil penalties, and imprisonment under applicable Federal laws may also apply to the acts of fraud or concealment described above.	The SFIP will be void if the proper authorities determine any part of a claim was fraudulent.
4. This policy is also void for reasons other than fraud, misrepresentation, or wrongful act. This policy is void from its inception and has no legal force under the following conditions: a. If the property is located in a community that was not participating in the NFIP on the policy's inception date and did not join or reenter the program during the policy term and before the loss occurred; or b. If the property listed on the application is otherwise not eligible for coverage under the NFIP.	When a community no longer participates in the NFIP, an active SFIP will remain in force up to the day before the policy renewal date. Refer to the Flood Insurance Manual for other reasons why a building may be ineligible for coverage.
C. Other Insurance	
1. If a loss covered by this policy is also covered by other insurance that includes flood coverage not issued under the Act, we will not pay more than the amount of insurance you are entitled to for lost, damaged, or destroyed property insured under this policy subject to the following: a. We will pay only the proportion of the loss that the amount of insurance that applies under this policy bears to the total amount of insurance covering the loss, unless C.1.b. or c. immediately below applies. b. If the other policy has a provision stating that it is excess insurance, this policy will be primary. c. This policy will be primary (but subject to its own deductible) up to the deductible in the other flood policy (except another policy as described in C.1.b. above). When the other deductible amount is	Other insurance includes primary flood coverage provided by a private carrier or any other insurance that duplicates SFIP coverage. Personal lines and commercial policies may include endorsements for sewer and sump or drain backup. Considerations include: 1. The other insurance clause of the other policy would determine which policy is excess or primary. 2. If the other policy is silent, proportion the claim. 3. If the endorsement excludes the peril of flood, the SFIP is primary for the direct physical damage by or from flood. • Use the following formula to determine the NFIP's share of the loss: • **NFIP share** = ((SFIP policy limit ÷ total insurance) x loss) - other insurance deductible

VII. General Conditions

Policy Language	Additional Explanation
reached, this policy will participate in the same proportion that the amount of insurance under this policy bears to the total amount of both policies, for the remainder of the loss.	<ul><li>Use the following formula to determine the other insurance's share of the loss:</li><li>**Other insurance share** = ((other insurance policy limit ÷ total insurance) x loss) - other insurance deductible</li><li>Use the following formula to determine the NFIP payment:</li><li>**NFIP payment** = NFIP share + other insurance deductible – SFIP deductible</li></ul>Below is an example of how to apply the formulas to compute the insurer's shares and NFIP payment for a $480,000 loss. **Table 5: Insurance Coverage and Deductibles** <table><tr><th>Insurance</th><th>Coverage</th><th>Deductible</th></tr><tr><td>NFIP</td><td>$250,000</td><td>$5,000</td></tr><tr><td>Other</td><td>$500,000</td><td>$15,000</td></tr><tr><td>Total</td><td>$750,000</td><td></td></tr></table> <ul><li>**NFIP share:** (($250,000 ÷ $750,000) x $480,000) - $15,000 = $145,000.00</li><li>**Other insurance share:** (($500,000 ÷ $750,000) x $480,000) - $15,000 = $305,000.00</li><li>**NFIP payment:** $145,000.00 + $15,000 - $5,000 = $155,000.00</li></ul>**IMPORTANT** – Use the order of operations as shown, starting within the innermost parentheses, for accurate calculation.

VII. General Conditions

Policy Language	Additional Explanation
2. If there is other insurance in the name of your condominium association covering the same property covered by this policy, then this policy will be in excess over the other insurance.	The Biggert-Waters Flood Insurance Reform Act of 2012, Section 100214, does not allow the NFIP to deny a unit owner's claim based on flood insurance coverage purchased by a condominium association.
	The SFIP allows unit owner building payments for loss assessments when a condominium association did not purchase insurance to at least 80 percent of the full replacement cost of the condominium building or the maximum insurance available for the condominium building. The provision does not allow insurers to pay for a building item more than once.
	The SFIP cannot pay more than the maximum amount of insurance available for a single-family residence, currently $250,000 for a single condominium, even if the unit has additional insurance available under other NFIP policies.
	The legislation did not change the coverage provided under the Residential Condominium Building Association Policy (RCBAP).
	See the Biggert-Waters Flood Insurance Reform Act of 2012 for more information.

D. Amendments, Waivers, Assignment

This policy cannot be changed nor can any of its provisions be waived without the express written consent of the Federal Insurance Administrator. No action we take under the terms of this policy constitutes a waiver of any of our rights. You may assign this policy in writing when you transfer title of your property to someone else except under these conditions: 1. When this policy covers only personal property; or 2. When this policy covers a structure during the course of construction.	The SFIP allows the assignment of the policy when the title to the property transfers to a new owner. The SFIP does not allow the assignment of a claim. The only exception to this is a Coverage D – Increased Cost of Compliance (ICC) claim that can transfer in conjunction with a FEMA project, such as a Hazard Mitigation Grant Program (HMGP) grant. Typically, the policyholder assigns the claim to a community, which typically uses the payment for the community's non-Federal match for the project. The policyholder may only assign the part of the ICC benefit used to meet the project requirements.

E. Cancellation of the Policy by You

1. You may cancel this policy in accordance with the applicable rules and regulations of the NFIP. 2. If you cancel this policy, you may be entitled to a full or partial refund of premium also under the applicable rules and regulations of the NFIP.	Policyholders must have a valid reason to cancel their flood insurance coverage during a policy term. Cancellation does not automatically create a refund. See the Cancellation section of the Flood Insurance Manual.

VII. General Conditions

Policy Language	Additional Explanation
F. Non-Renewal of the Policy by Us	
Your policy will not be renewed:	When a community no longer participates in the NFIP, an active SFIP will remain in force up to the day before the policy renewal date.
1. If the community where your covered property is located stops participating in the NFIP, or	Coverage may not be available for a building constructed or altered in violation of state or local floodplain management laws, regulations, or ordinances. Section 1316 of the Act allows a state or community to declare a building in violation of its floodplain management rules. When a state or community declares that a building is in violation of Section 1316, the building and any contents in it are not eligible for SFIP coverage. Insurers have a list of buildings with Section 1316 violations that are ineligible for NFIP coverage. When the owner corrects the violation, the building becomes eligible for coverage again. The examiner should verify the building's eligibility.
2. If your building has been declared ineligible under Section 1316 of the Act.	
G. Reduction and Reformation of Coverage	
1. If the premium we received from you was not enough to buy the kind and amount of coverage you requested, we will provide only the amount of coverage that can be purchased for the premium payment we received.	If the policyholder gives the insurer a premium that will not purchase the amounts of insurance coverage requested, the insurer must issue the policy for the insurance coverage amount the premium will purchase for a one-year policy term.
2. The policy can be reformed to increase the amount of coverage resulting from the reduction described in G.1. above to the amount you requested as follows:	After a Loss:
a. Discovery of Insufficient Premium or Incomplete Rating Information Before a Loss:	• The insurer will send a bill for the required additional premium for the current policy term only. This is an exception to the SFIP Provisions requiring the current and the prior policy terms.
(1) If we discover before you have a flood loss that your premium payment was not enough to buy the requested amount of coverage, we will send you and any mortgagee or trustee known to us a bill for the required additional premium for the current policy term (or that portion of the current policy term following any endorsement changing the amount of coverage). If you or the mortgagee or trustee pay the additional premium within 30 days from the date of our bill, we will reform the policy to increase the amount of coverage to the originally requested amount effective to the beginning of the current policy term (or subsequent date of any endorsement changing the amount of	• If the insurer receives the premium within 30 days from the date of the bill, the insurer should increase the policy limits to the originally requested amount effective as of the beginning of the current policy term.
	• If the insurer does not receive the additional premium by the due date, the insurer must settle the claim based on the previously submitted premium and reduced policy limits.
	Exceptions for Incorrect Flood Zone or BFE After a Loss. When the insurer discovers that an incorrect flood zone or BFE resulted in insufficient premium, the following exceptions apply:
	• The insurer should calculate any additional premium due prospectively from the date of discovery.

VII. General Conditions

Policy Language	Additional Explanation
coverage).	• The insurer should apply the automatic reduction in policy limits effective on the date of discovery.
(2) If we determine before you have a flood loss that the rating information we have is incomplete and prevents us from calculating the additional premium, we will ask you to send the required information. You must submit the information within 60 days of our request. Once we determine the amount of additional premium for the current policy term, we will follow the procedure in G.2.a.(1) above.	Incorrect Policy Form. The insurer must use the correct policy form before making a loss payment. When the insurer issues coverage using an incorrect SFIP form, the policy is void and the insurer must rewrite the coverage under the correct form. The provisions of the correct SFIP form apply.
(3) If we do not receive the additional premium (or additional information) by the date it is due, the amount of coverage can only be increased by endorsement subject to any appropriate waiting period.	• The insurer must reform the coverage limits according to the provisions of the correct SFIP form.
b. Discovery of Insufficient Premium or Incomplete Rating Information After a Loss:	• Coverage cannot exceed the coverage issued under the incorrect policy form.
(1) If we discover after you have a flood loss that your premium payment was not enough to buy the requested amount of coverage, we will send you and any mortgagee or trustee known to us a bill for the required additional premium for the current and the prior policy terms. If you or the mortgagee or trustee pay the additional premium within 30 days of the date of our bill, we will reform the policy to increase the amount of coverage to the originally requested amount effective to the beginning of the prior policy term.	• See the Flood Insurance Manual for detailed information
(2) If we discover after you have a flood loss that the rating information we have is incomplete and prevents us from calculating the additional premium, we will ask you to send the required information. You must submit the information before your claim can be paid. Once we determine the amount of additional premium for the current and prior policy terms, we will follow the procedure in G.2.b.(1) above.	
(3) If we do not receive the additional premium by the date it is due, your flood insurance claim will be settled based on the reduced amount of coverage. The amount of coverage can only be increased by endorsement subject to any appropriate waiting	

VII. General Conditions

Policy Language	Additional Explanation
3. However, if we find that you or your agent intentionally did not tell us, or falsified, any important fact or circumstance or did anything fraudulent relating to this insurance, the provisions of Condition B. Concealment or Fraud and Policy Voidance apply.	
H. Policy Renewal	
1. This policy will expire at 12:01 a.m. on the last day of the policy term.	The SFIP is not a continuous policy. It is a contract for a one-year term. Every policy contract expires at 12:01 a.m. on the last day of the policy term. Renewal of an expiring policy establishes a new policy term and new contractual agreement. See the Flood Insurance Manual for detailed information.
2. We must receive the payment of the appropriate renewal premium within 30 days of the expiration date.	
3. If we find, however, that we did not place your renewal notice into the U.S. Postal Service, or if we did mail it, we made a mistake, e.g., we used an incorrect, incomplete, or illegible address, which delayed its delivery to you before the due date for the renewal premium, then we will follow these procedures:	The adjuster should investigate the claim under a signed non-waiver agreement or a reservation of rights by the insurer when a policyholder reports a loss and there is uncertainty as to whether a policy is active.
a. If you or your agent notified us, not later than 1 year after the date on which the payment of the renewal premium was due, of non-receipt of a renewal notice before the due date for the renewal premium, and we determine that the circumstances in the preceding paragraph apply, we will mail a second bill providing a revised due date, which will be 30 days after the date on which the bill is mailed.	
b. If we do not receive the premium requested in the second bill by the revised due date, then we will not renew the policy. In that case, the policy will remain an expired policy as of the expiration date shown on the Declarations Page.	
4. In connection with the renewal of this policy, we may ask you during the policy term to recertify, on a Recertification Questionnaire we will provide to you, the rating information used to rate your most recent application for or renewal of insurance.	
I. Conditions Suspending or Restricting Insurance	
We are not liable for loss that occurs while there is a hazard that is increased by any means within your control or knowledge.	The SFIP will not cover a flood loss or increased flood damage to insured property that the policyholder purposely or inadvertently causes. For example: a policyholder constructs a flood barrier to prevent floodwater from a river from reaching the

VII. General Conditions

Policy Language	Additional Explanation
	building; however, the improvement now causes runoff during heavy rainfall events to collect behind the barrier and flood the building and a neighboring parcel or causes a prolonged condition of inundation creating additional damage inside the building.
	When the investigation of a loss reveals this provision might apply, the adjuster should notify the insurer at once and request immediate guidance.
J. Requirements in Case of Loss	
In case of a flood loss to insured property, you must:	The policyholder's claim begins with the written notice of loss.
1. Give prompt written notice to us;	The policyholder must report the loss to the insurer immediately; failure to provide a notice of loss to the insurer could prejudice the ability of the insurer to inspect the loss, identify the cause and extent of damage, and determine applicable coverage under the SFIP. If the policyholder delays reporting a loss, adjusters cannot help policyholders protect the property and avoid further damage.
2. As soon as reasonably possible, separate the damaged and undamaged property, putting it in the best possible order so that we may examine it;	A policyholder's failure to provide timely notice of loss can be a basis for denial of a claim.
3. Prepare an inventory of damaged property showing the quantity, description, actual cash value, and amount of loss. Attach all bills, receipts, and related documents;	• The adjuster should document the reason for a delay in the policyholder reporting a loss to the insurer.
	• The adjuster should execute a non-waiver agreement when there is a delay in reporting the loss. The non-waiver agreement should include the reason for the non-waiver and the policyholder's explanation for the delay. The adjuster should have the policyholder sign the non-waiver agreement immediately. If the policyholder refuses to sign the non-waiver agreement, the insurer may decide to send a Reservation of Rights. The adjuster should continue the inspection and review.
	The SFIP requires that the policyholder separate damaged from undamaged property putting it in the best possible order, so the adjuster may examine it. It is the policyholder's duty to perform the separation described above and prepare an inventory of damaged property including quantity, description, and the total amount of loss claimed. Any bills, receipts, photographs of damages, and related documents should be attached to the inventory.
	If flood-damaged building or contents property is removed before the adjuster can examine it, the policyholder must photograph the items in their damaged location prior to moving the property and prepare the inventory.

VII. General Conditions

Policy Language	Additional Explanation
	To minimize potential documentation issues and assist the adjuster's investigation, the policyholder should, if possible, retain samples or swatches of carpeting, wallpaper, furniture upholstery, window treatments, and other items of exceptional value where the type and quality of material will influence the amount payable on the claim. Photographs should also include groups of items such as clothing, kitchen items, furniture, etc. The insurer will evaluate and consider these items and the policyholder's written inventory of damaged items.
4. Within 60 days after the loss, send us a proof of loss, which is your statement of the amount you are claiming under the policy signed and sworn to by you, and which furnishes us with the following information:	The proof of loss is the policyholder's statement of the amount of money they are requesting. The policyholder must sign and swear to the proof of loss and provide documentation to support that the loss is a direct physical loss by or from flood and the amount requested for the insurer to consider it completed. The policyholder (or Executor in the case of a deceased policyholder) is the only person who can sign the proof of loss.
a. The date and time of loss;	**SIGNED AND SWORN:**
b. A brief explanation of how the loss happened;	FEMA encourages the use of electronic signatures on proof of loss and other NFIP-related submissions. FEMA will not deny the legal effect, validity, or enforceability of a signature solely because it is in electronic form. Insurers should accept electronic signatures in accordance with their general business practices and applicable laws.
c. Your interest (for example, "owner") and the interest, if any, of others in the damaged property;	
d. Details of any other insurance that may cover the loss;	
e. Changes in title or occupancy of the covered property during the term of the policy;	**MULTIPLE PROOFS OF LOSS ALLOWED:**
f. Specifications of damaged buildings and detailed repair estimates;	Policyholders must submit a completed proof of loss and documentation to support the amount requested initially and completed proofs of loss for any additional payment requests to the insurer within 60 days after the date of loss or within any extension of that deadline granted by FEMA.
g. Names of mortgagees or anyone else having a lien, charge, or claim against the insured property;	
h. Details about who occupied any insured building at the time of loss and for what purpose; and	**ONE CLAIM PER LOSS:**
i. The inventory of damaged personal property described in J.3. above.	The proof of loss is not the claim. The claim is the policyholder's assertion that they are entitled to payment for a covered loss under the terms of the SFIP. A policyholder has only one claim from a flood event regardless of the number of proofs of loss and amount of documentation the policyholder may submit in support of that claim. The policyholder's ICC proof of loss is a request for benefits afforded under Coverage D – ICC, for that claim; it is not a separate claim.
5. In completing the proof of loss, you must use your own judgment concerning the amount of loss and justify that amount.	
6. You must cooperate with the adjuster or representative in the investigation of the claim.	
7. The insurance adjuster whom we hire to investigate your claim may furnish you with a proof of loss form, and she or he may help you complete it. However, this is a matter of courtesy only, and you must still send us a proof of loss within 60 days after the loss even if the	

VII. General Conditions

Policy Language	Additional Explanation
adjuster does not furnish the form or help you complete it.	
8. We have not authorized the adjuster to approve or disapprove claims or to tell you whether we will approve your claim.	Only the NFIP insurer has the authority to approve or deny a claim, to tell the policyholder if they will approve or deny a claim, or to provide approved payment details. The insurer must rely only upon the terms and conditions established by Federal statute, NFIP regulations, the Federal Insurance Administrator's interpretations, and the express terms of the SFIP. See 44 C.F.R. § 61.5(e) (2018).
9. At our option, we may accept the adjuster's report of the loss instead of your proof of loss. The adjuster's report will include information about your loss and the damages you sustained. You must sign the adjuster's report. At our option, we may require you to swear to the report.	The insurer, not the policyholder or their representative, determines whether to accept the adjuster's report signed and sworn to by the policyholder, instead of a proof of loss.
K. Our Options After a Loss	
Options we may, in our sole discretion, exercise after loss include the following:	This section sets forth the steps that insurers may take to require action on the part of the policyholder. If the policyholder fails to comply with the insurer's request, the policyholder is in breach of the insuring agreement, which may affect the payment of the claim.
1. At such reasonable times and places that we may designate, you must: a. Show us or our representative the damaged property;	The policyholder must make the flood-damaged property available for examination as often as needed to verify the loss and claim. Insurer representatives will give the policyholder advanced notice of the specific time and meeting place to inspect the damaged property. The policyholder should document their loss with photographs before removing or disposing of damaged items that pose a health hazard, such as perishable food.
b. Submit to examination under oath, while not in the presence of another insured, and sign the same; and	The insurer can require the policyholder to submit to an examination under oath but not in the presence of another policyholder when there are questions concerning the claim. An examination under oath is a formal proceeding, conducted prior to a lawsuit, during which the insurer's representative questions a policyholder under oath in the presence of a court reporter. The insurer should ask the policyholder to present information and documentation necessary to evaluate their claim when requiring an examination under oath. This can include books of accounts, financial records, receipts, income tax records, property settlement records, invoices, purchase orders, affidavits, and other materials to verify the loss.

VII. General Conditions

Policy Language	Additional Explanation
c. Permit us to examine and make extracts and copies of: (1) Any policies of property insurance insuring you against loss and the deed establishing your ownership of the insured real property;	The SFIP will not pay more than the amount of insurance that the policyholder is entitled to for the damaged, lost, or destroyed property insured under this policy if non-NFIP insurance covers a loss covered by the SFIP. The policyholder must confirm the availability of other insurance to determine what the NFIP will pay. Examples include a homeowner's policy water damage or sump overflow endorsement, mobile-home owner's policy, scheduled property policy, renter's policy, builder's risk policy, etc. See SFIP Section VII.C. for Other Insurance.
(2) Condominium association documents including the Declarations of the condominium, its Articles of Association or Incorporation, Bylaws, rules and regulations, and other relevant documents if you are a unit owner in a condominium building; and	A claim involving a unit in a condominium building requires the declarations of the condominium, bylaws, etc. to determine the policyholder's insurable interest in the building. Adjusters may have to determine if the RCBAP paid for any damages. NFIP will not pay for the same damage item twice nor pay a claim for a residential unit that exceeds the statutory limits. Adjusters must provide documentation that a condominium association owns the insured building, not a homeowners' association or a building cooperative.
(3) All books of accounts, bills, invoices and other vouchers, or certified copies pertaining to the damaged property if the originals are lost.	Insurers may require the policyholder to provide information that documents the extent of the loss and the amount of the claim. Examples include books of accounts, bills, invoices, vouchers, and items showing the actual amounts paid to stores, contractors, or others for repair or replacement of items. This may also include photographs of the flood-damaged property that sufficiently and reasonably document the damage, quality of the item, and describe the damaged property. The policyholder can provide certified copies when the originals are lost or destroyed.
2. We may request, in writing, that you furnish us with a complete inventory of the lost, damaged or destroyed property, including: a. Quantities and costs;	"Costs" is the amount to replace a personal property item with like kind and quality at current pricing, including the price for sales tax plus any applicable shipping and product assembly.
b. Actual cash values or replacement cost (whichever is appropriate);	• Replacement cost is the cost to replace a building, a building item, or a personal property item that includes all charges related to material, labor, equipment, any charges, if applicable, for design, delivery, assembly, sales tax, and applicable overhead and profit. • Actual cash value is replacement cost to replace, not repair, less applicable depreciation of all components of the price.
c. Amounts of loss claimed;	The amount of loss claimed is the amount of payment the policyholder asks to

VII. General Conditions

Policy Language	Additional Explanation
	receive for the damaged and covered property.
d. Any written plans and specifications for repair of the damaged property that you can reasonably make available to us; and	Written plans and specifications for repair of the damaged property include contractor estimates, subcontractor bids, invoices, architectural reports and drawings, engineering reports, etc. This also includes water restoration or structural drying invoices and supporting documentation. NFIP will not accept a non-itemized, lump sum, or single line estimate or invoice in support of a claim.
e. Evidence that prior flood damage has been repaired.	Policyholders must provide evidence that previous flood damage was repaired, whether or not they owned or insured the property at the time of the previous flood. This includes any flood damages unrepaired by a previous owner. NFIP expects policyholders to maintain proof of repairs such as receipts, canceled checks, etc. in a safe location away from the threat of flood. When policyholders do not have proof of repairs, adjusters should request other forms of documentation such as: • Pre-flood photographs (social media or other family members) to compare old and replaced items. • Credit card or bank statements showing dates and dollar amounts of payments to contractors. • Itemized statements and paid invoices from contractors.
3. If we give you written notice within 30 days after we receive your signed, sworn proof of loss, we may: a. Repair, rebuild, or replace any part of the lost, damaged, or destroyed property with material or property of like kind and quality or its functional equivalent; and b. Take all or any part of the damaged property at the value that we agree upon or its appraised value.	3.a. N/A 3.b. Refer to Section VII.O. and other guidance, including Salvage in Section 2 of this manual.

L. No Benefit to Bailee

No person or organization, other than you, having custody of covered property will benefit from this insurance.	Bailment is the delivery of personal property by one person (the bailor) to another (the bailee) who holds the property for a certain purpose, such as a service, under an expressed or implied-in-fact contract. The SFIP does not cover the bailee because bailment is a change of possession, not a

VII. General Conditions

Policy Language	Additional Explanation
	change of ownership or title. An example is when a customer (bailor) takes personal clothing to the dry cleaner (bailee). A bailment exists when the bailee has the clothing. The articles of clothing in the possession of the bailee are bailee goods and are not covered.
	Consignment is a written agreement where a consignor provides owned personal property to a consignee for sale and gives the consignee a percentage of the sale price when sold. The SFIP does not cover property on consignment.

M. Loss Payment

Policy Language	Additional Explanation
1. We will adjust all losses with you. We will pay you unless some other person or entity is named in the policy or is legally entitled to receive payment. Loss will be payable 60 days after we receive your proof of loss (or within 90 days after the insurance adjuster files the adjuster's report signed and sworn to by you in lieu of a proof of loss) and: a. We reach an agreement with you; b. There is an entry of a final judgment; or c. There is a filing of an appraisal award with us, as provided in VII.P.	Adjusters and examiners should work with a policyholder or their authorized representative to understand the loss, prepare the estimate, and reach an agreed value for the loss. The insurer's obligation to pay and the timeframe to pay begins once the policyholder meets the requirements in Paragraph J, a proof of loss that meets all NFIP requirements, or after the signed and sworn to adjuster's report is received, and, • Insurer and the policyholder agree on the payment amount, or, • There is an entry of final judgment or an appraisal award by a court of competent jurisdiction. The insurer should promptly process all claims and payment requests. The insurer should communicate to policyholders any unforeseen delays in the claim examination process and advance undisputed claimed amounts at the earliest opportunity. When the insurer cannot pay a completed proof of loss, the examiner and the adjuster should promptly communicate the necessary adjustments or documentation required to the policyholder. Insurers should work with policyholders to settle the loss without resorting to a denial of the claim by the insurer. See Section 4 Appeals of this manual for information on denial letters.
2. If we reject your proof of loss in whole or in part you may: a. Accept our denial of your claim; b. Exercise your rights under this policy; or c. File an amended proof of loss as long as it is filed within 60 days of	Courts have not accepted the language "reject your proof of loss" as sufficient to communicate to the policyholder that the insurer has denied their claim in whole or in part. Hence, insurers should not use this language to deny all or part of a claim. When the insurer issues a written denial, the policyholder has certain rights, which

VII. General Conditions

Policy Language	Additional Explanation
the date of the loss.	include filing an appeal directly to FEMA (see Section 4 Appeals), filing suit against the insurer, or submitting an amended proof of loss with the documentation to support the requested loss and payment amount.
	The one-year statute of limitations for filing suit begins when the insurer issues the first denial letter (42 U.S.C. § 4072; 44 C.F.R. § 62.22(a)). Submitting subsequent additional or amended proofs of loss does not reset the one-year statute of limitations. Adjusters and examiners must assist policyholders in identifying all opportunities for payment. This helps the policyholder recover, ensures customer satisfaction, and prevents unnecessary appeals and lawsuits.
N. Abandonment	
You may not abandon to us damaged or undamaged property insured under this policy.	N/A
O. Salvage	
We may permit you to keep damaged property insured under this policy after a loss, and we will reduce the amount of the loss proceeds payable to you under the policy by the value of the salvage.	The insurer always has the right to seek salvage or to take possession of damaged property. Insurers should pursue opportunities for financial recovery when available. See Salvage in Section 2 of this manual.
P. Appraisal	
If you and we fail to agree on the actual cash value or, if applicable, replacement cost of your damaged property to settle upon the amount of loss, then either may demand an appraisal of the loss. In this event, you and we will each choose a competent and impartial appraiser within 20 days after receiving a written request from the other. The two appraisers will choose an umpire. If they cannot agree upon an umpire within 15 days, you or we may request that the choice be made by a judge of a court of record in the State where the covered property is located. The appraisers will separately state the actual cash value, the replacement cost, and the amount of loss to each item. If the appraisers submit a written report of an agreement to us, the amount agreed upon will be the amount of loss. If they fail to agree, they will submit their differences to the umpire. A decision agreed to by any two will set the amount of actual cash value and loss, or if it applies, the replacement cost and loss.	See Appraisal in Section 2 of this manual.

VII. General Conditions

Policy Language	Additional Explanation
Each party will: 1. Pay its own appraiser; and 2. Bear the other expenses of the appraisal and umpire equally.	
Q. Mortgage Clause	
The word "mortgagee" includes trustee. Any loss payable under Coverage A—Building Property will be paid to any mortgagee of whom we have actual notice, as well as any other mortgagee or loss payee determined to exist at the time of loss, and you, as interests appear. If more than one mortgagee is named, the order of payment will be the same as the order of precedence of the mortgages. If we deny your claim, the denial will not apply to a valid claim of the mortgagee, if the mortgagee: 1. Notifies us of any change in the ownership or occupancy, or substantial change in risk of which the mortgagee is aware; 2. Pays any premium due under this policy on demand if you have neglected to pay the premium; and 3. Submits a signed, sworn proof of loss within 60 days after receiving notice from us of your failure to do so. All of the terms of this policy apply to the mortgagee. The mortgagee has the right to receive loss payment even if the mortgagee has started foreclosure or similar action on the building. If we decide to cancel or not renew this policy, it will continue in effect for the benefit of the mortgagee only for 30 days after we notify the mortgagee of the cancellation or non-renewal. If we pay the mortgagee for any loss and deny payment to you, we are subrogated to all the rights of the mortgagee granted under the mortgage on the property. Subrogation will not impair the right of the mortgagee to recover the full amount of the mortgagee's claim.	The SFIP pays claims for building property to the named policyholder, mortgage holders, lienholders, other loss payees for whom we have actual notice, and any loss payee determined to exist at the time of loss. The mortgage clause is a contract within a contract. It is a contract between the mortgagee and the insurer within the contract between the policyholder and the insurer. Including the name of the mortgagee on each building claim payment is the surest way to keep this promise to the mortgagee. For all building payments, except Coverage C – Other Coverages and Coverage D – ICC, include all known mortgagees, as they are additional insureds. The insurer may potentially include a loss payee or lienholder on Coverage B – Personal Property of whom the insurer received actual notice such as from the U.S. Small Business Administration (SBA). If the insurer receives a letter of an SBA-approved loan, the SBA must be included on the building check(s) and the contents check(s) if the loan is for both real estate and personal or business property.
R. Suit Against Us	
You may not sue us to recover money under this policy unless you have complied with all the requirements of the policy. If you do sue, you must start	The statute of limitations begins with the insurer's first written denial of the claim. Subsequent denial letters do not re-start the statute of limitations. Policyholders

VII. General Conditions

Policy Language	Additional Explanation
the suit within 1 year after the date of the written denial of all or part of the claim, and you must file the suit in the United States District Court of the district in which the covered property was located at the time of loss. This requirement applies to any claim that you may have under this policy and to any dispute that you may have arising out of the handling of any claim under the policy.	must file suit in a U.S. District Court in the district where the loss occurred within one year after the insurer's first written denial. Neither the Federal Insurance Administrator nor the insurer may extend the one-year statute of limitations to file suit.
S. Subrogation	
Whenever we make a payment for a loss under this policy, we are subrogated to your right to recover for that loss from any other person. That means that your right to recover for a loss that was partly or totally caused by someone else is automatically transferred to us, to the extent that we have paid you for the loss. We may require you to acknowledge this transfer in writing. After the loss, you may not give up our right to recover this money or do anything that would prevent us from recovering it. If you make any claim against any person who caused your loss and recover any money, you must pay us back first before you may keep any of that money.	When the adjuster believes there may be potential for subrogation, the adjuster completes FEMA Form 086-0-16 – Cause of Loss and Subrogation Report, to identify a potentially responsible third party; and characterize how their actions may have caused or worsened flood damage. When the adjuster believes the cause of loss may be completely or in part due to an intentional or human cause, the adjuster should complete the NFIP Subrogation Form. Claim handling, review, and payment should proceed as normal. The insurer should make sure the subrogation form Cause of Loss and Subrogation Report is complete and escalate the matter for a subrogation review. See Subrogation in Section 2 of this manual.
T. Continuous Lake Flooding	
1. If an insured building has been flooded by rising lake waters continuously for 90 days or more and it appears reasonably certain that a continuation of this flooding will result in a covered loss to the insured building equal to or greater than the building policy limits plus the deductible or the maximum payable under the policy for any one building loss, we will pay you the lesser of these two amounts without waiting for the further damage to occur if you sign a release agreeing: a. To make no further claim under this policy; b. Not to seek renewal of this policy; c. Not to apply for any flood insurance under the Act for property at the described location; and d. Not to seek a premium refund for current or prior terms. If the policy term ends before the insured building has been flooded	N/A

VII. General Conditions

Policy Language	Additional Explanation
continuously for 90 days, the provisions of this paragraph T.1. will apply when the insured building suffers a covered loss before the policy term ends.	The only Closed Basin Lake recognized by FEMA at this time is Devils Lake, North Dakota.
c. If your insured building is subject to continuous lake flooding from a closed basin lake, you may elect to file a claim under either paragraph T.1. above or T.2. (A "closed basin lake" is a natural lake from which water leaves primarily through evaporation and whose surface area now exceeds or has exceeded 1 square mile at any time in the recorded past. Most of the nation's closed basin lakes are in the western half of the United States where annual evaporation exceeds annual precipitation and where lake levels and surface areas are subject to considerable fluctuation due to wide variations in the climate. These lakes may overtop their basins on rare occasions.) Under this paragraph T.2. we will pay your claim as if the building is a total loss even though it has not been continuously inundated for 90 days, subject to the following conditions:	Subject to all other provisions of the SFIP, if an insured building is subject to continuous lake flooding from Devils Lake, the following requirements must be met to be eligible for coverage under the terms of all SFIP forms: • The building must be in a participating community eligible for this coverage; and, • The subject building must have had NFIP flood insurance coverage continuously beginning on November 30, 1999, and any subsequent owner on or after November 30, 1999, must have an NFIP policy in effect within 60 days of the transfer of title (see: T. 2. g.); and, • The policyholder must grant a conservation easement (see: T. 2. b. (2), and the community must have adopted a permanent land-use ordinance on or before July 15, 2001 (see: T. 2. e. (1), (2), and (3).
d. Lake flood waters must damage or imminently threaten to damage your building. e. Before approval of your claim, you must: (1) Agree to a claim payment that reflects your buying back the salvage on a negotiated basis; and Grant the conservation easement described in FEMA's "Policy Guidance for Closed Basin Lakes" to be recorded in the office of the local recorder of deeds. FEMA, in consultation with the community in which the property is located, will identify on a map an area or areas of special consideration (ASC) in which there is a potential for flood damage from continuous lake flooding. FEMA will give the community the agreed-upon map showing the ASC. This easement will only apply to that portion of the property in the ASC. It will allow certain agricultural and recreational uses of the land. The only structures it will allow on any portion of the property within the ASC are certain simple	FEMA will not recognize any increases in coverage limits with effective dates on or after November 30, 1999 (see: T. 2. g.), except when offered by the insurer as a routine inflation-guard increase and purchased by the policyholder. Insured buildings not eligible for the provisions of T. 2. described above, but damaged by continuous lake flooding, will be eligible for those provisions described at T. 1. of the SFIP, subject to the terms and conditions of the T. 1. and the SFIP. Buildings in eligible communities that are subject to damage from the effects of the Closed Basin Lake, Devils Lake, North Dakota, may file claims if any portion of the insured building, as defined in the SFIP, is at the still-water level derived by official National Weather Service (NWS) still-water levels. See Appendix C in this manual for FEMA's "Policy Guidance for Closed Basin Lakes".

VII. General Conditions

Policy Language	Additional Explanation
agricultural and recreational structures. If any of these allowable structures are insurable buildings under the NFIP and are insured under the NFIP, they will not be eligible for the benefits of this paragraph T.2. If a U.S. Army Corps of Engineers certified flood control project or otherwise certified flood control project later protects the property, FEMA will, upon request, amend the ASC to remove areas protected by those projects. The restrictions of the easement will then no longer apply to any portion of the property removed from the ASC; and (3) Comply with paragraphs T.1.a. through T.1.d. above. f. Within 90 days of approval of your claim, you must move your building to a new location outside the ASC. FEMA will give you an additional 30 days to move if you show there is sufficient reason to extend the time. g. Before the final payment of your claim, you must acquire an elevation certificate and a floodplain development permit from the local floodplain administrator for the new location of your building. h. Before the approval of your claim, the community having jurisdiction over your building must: (1) Adopt a permanent land use ordinance, or a temporary moratorium for a period not to exceed 6 months to be followed immediately by a permanent land use ordinance that is consistent with the provisions specified in the easement required in paragraph T.2.b. above. (2) Agree to declare and report any violations of this ordinance to FEMA so that under Section 1316 of the National Flood Insurance Act of 1968, as amended, flood insurance to the building can be denied; and (3) Agree to maintain as deed-restricted, for purposes compatible with open space or agricultural or recreational use only, any affected property the community acquires an interest in. These deed restrictions must be consistent with	

VII. General Conditions

Policy Language	Additional Explanation
the provisions of paragraph T.2.b. above, except that, even if a certified project protects the property, the land use restrictions continue to apply if the property was acquired under the Hazard Mitigation Grant Program or the Flood Mitigation Assistance Program. If a non-profit land trust organization receives the property as a donation, that organization must maintain the property as deed-restricted, consistent with the provisions of paragraph T.2.b. above.	
i. Before the approval of your claim, the affected State must take all action set forth in FEMA's "Policy Guidance for Closed Basin Lakes."	
j. You must have NFIP flood insurance coverage continuously in effect from a date established by FEMA until you file a claim under paragraph T.2. If a subsequent owner buys NFIP insurance that goes into effect within 60 days of the date of transfer of title, any gap in coverage during that 60-day period will not be a violation of this continuous coverage requirement. For the purpose of honoring a claim under this paragraph T.2., we will not consider to be in effect any increased coverage that became effective after the date established by FEMA. The exception to this is any increased coverage in the amount suggested by your insurer as an inflation adjustment.	
k. This paragraph T.2. will be in effect for a community when the FEMA Regional Administrator for the affected region provides to the community, in writing, the following:	
(1) Confirmation that the community and the State are in compliance with the conditions in paragraphs T.2.e. and T.2.f. above, and	
(2) The date by which you must have flood insurance in effect.	

U. Duplicate Policies Not Allowed

Policy Language	Additional Explanation
1. We will not insure your property under more than one NFIP policy. If we find that the duplication was not knowingly created, we will give you written notice. The notice will advise you that you may choose one	The policyholder cannot benefit from the duplicate flood insurance coverage if a policyholder has two NFIP policies insuring the same property. The first policy purchased is the policy in force at the time of loss.

VII. General Conditions

Policy Language	Additional Explanation
of several options under the following procedures: a. If you choose to keep in effect the policy with the earlier effective date, you may also choose to add the coverage limits of the later policy to the limits of the earlier policy. The change will become effective as of the effective date of the later policy. b. If you choose to keep in effect the policy with the later effective date, you may also choose to add the coverage limits of the earlier policy to the limits of the later policy. The change will be effective as of the effective date of the later policy. In either case, you must pay the pro rata premium for the increased coverage limits within 30 days of the written notice. In no event will the resulting coverage limits exceed the permissible limits of coverage under the Act or your insurable interest, whichever is less. We will make a refund to you, according to applicable NFIP rules, of the premium for the policy not being kept in effect. 2. Your option under Condition U. Duplicate Policies Not Allowed to elect which NFIP policy to keep in effect does not apply when duplicates have been knowingly created. Losses occurring under such circumstances will be adjusted according to the terms and conditions of the earlier policy. The policy with the later effective date must be canceled.	When there is no loss involved, the policyholder may choose to keep either policy. The effective date of the increased coverage begins on the renewal date of the second policy purchased if the policyholder chooses to combine the coverage amounts purchased, and the combined coverage does not exceed the maximum statutory limits. The policyholder may not purchase an SFIP as excess insurance above the coverage provided by the GFIP if a policyholder has a Group Flood Insurance Policy (GFIP) from a Federal Disaster Declaration. The policyholder may cancel the GFIP and have the coverage purchased under the SFIP become effective on the date no sooner than 30 days after the date the insurer receives the application and payment. GFIP does not refund the unused portion of the premium.
V. Loss Settlement 1. Introduction This policy provides three methods of settling losses: Replacement Cost, Special Loss Settlement, and Actual Cash Value. Each method is used for a different type of property, as explained in a–c. below. a. Replacement Cost loss settlement, described in V.2. below, applies to a single-family dwelling provided: (1) It is your principal residence, which means that, at the time of loss, you or your spouse lived there for 80% of: (a) The 365 days immediately preceding the loss; or (b) The period of your ownership, if you owned the dwelling for less than 365 days; and	N/A

VII. General Conditions

Policy Language	Additional Explanation
(2) At the time of loss, the amount of insurance in this policy that applies to the dwelling is 80% or more of its full replacement cost immediately before the loss or is the maximum amount of insurance available under the NFIP.	
b. Special loss settlement, described in V.3. below, applies to a single-family dwelling that is a manufactured or mobile home or a travel trailer.	
c. Actual Cash Value loss settlement applies to a single-family dwelling not subject to replacement cost or special loss settlement, and to the property listed in V.4. below.	
2. Replacement Cost Loss Settlement	The insurer does not have to withhold the recoverable depreciation until the owner makes the building repairs as required in SFIP Section VII.V.2.c above when the dwelling is eligible for replacement cost loss settlement.
The following loss settlement conditions apply to a single-family dwelling described in V.1.a. above:	
a. We will pay to repair or replace the damaged dwelling after application of the deductible and without deduction for depreciation, but not more than the least of the following amounts:	
(1) The building limit of liability shown on your Declarations Page;	
(2) The replacement cost of that part of the dwelling damaged, with materials of like kind and quality and for like use; or	
(3) The necessary amount actually spent to repair or replace the damaged part of the dwelling for like use.	
b. If the dwelling is rebuilt at a new location, the cost described above is limited to the cost that would have been incurred if the dwelling had been rebuilt at its former location.	
c. When the full cost of repair or replacement is more than $1,000 or more than 5 percent of the whole amount of insurance that applies to the dwelling, we will not be liable for any loss under V.2.a. above or V.4.a.(2) below unless and until actual repair or replacement is completed.	
d. You may disregard the replacement cost conditions above and make claim for loss to dwellings on an actual cash value basis. You may then make claim for any additional liability according	

VII. General Conditions

Policy Language	Additional Explanation
to V.2.a., b., and c. above, provided you notify us of your intent to do so within 180 days after the date of loss. e. If the community in which your dwelling is located has been converted from the Emergency Program to the Regular Program during the current policy term, then we will consider the maximum amount of available NFIP insurance to be the amount that was available at the beginning of the current policy term. 3. Special Loss Settlement a. The following loss settlement conditions apply to a single-family dwelling that: (1) Is a manufactured or mobile home or a travel trailer, as defined in II.B.6.b. and c., (2) Is at least 16 feet wide when fully assembled and has an area of at least 600 square feet within its perimeter walls when fully assembled, and (3) Is your principal residence, as specified in V.1.a.(1) above. b. If such a dwelling is totally destroyed or damaged to such an extent that, in our judgment, it is not economically feasible to repair, at least to its pre-damage condition, we will, at our discretion pay the least of the following amounts: (1) The lesser of the replacement cost of the dwelling or 1.5 times the actual cash value, or (2) The building limit of liability shown on your Declarations Page. c. If such a dwelling is partially damaged and, in our judgment, it is economically feasible to repair it to its pre-damage condition, we will settle the loss according to the Replacement Cost conditions in V.2. above.	There are two ways to settle a loss on a manufactured or mobile home or a travel trailer: ■ Total loss is a property that is either not repairable (example: destroyed) or the cost to repair exceeds the value of the property: ● If the dwelling is 16 feet wide, at least 600 total square feet, and the principal residence, the loss adjustment is the lesser of the following: – Replacement cost, i.e., the value of a new manufactured or mobile home, or travel trailer of like kind and quality, delivered to and installed at the described location. – 1.5 times the actual cash value, i.e., 1.5 times the documented book value for the year of the existing manufactured or mobile home, or travel trailer, delivered to and installed at the described location. – Amount of coverage purchased under Coverage A - Building. ■ Repairable loss or a loss not considered a total loss: ● If the dwelling is 16 feet wide, at least 600 total square feet, and the principal residence, settle the loss under Replacement Cost Loss Settlement. (See Section VII.V.2.) ● If the dwelling is not 16 feet wide, or not at least 600 total square feet, or not the principal residence, settle the loss under Actual Cash Value Loss Settlement. (See Section VII.V.4.) The requirement for a policyholder to purchase building coverage to at least 80 percent of the dwelling's replacement cost value does not apply under Special Loss Settlement.

VII. General Conditions

Policy Language	Additional Explanation
4. Actual Cash Value Loss Settlement The types of property noted below are subject to actual cash value (or in the case of V.4.a.(2), below, proportional) loss settlement. a. A dwelling, at the time of loss, when the amount of insurance on the dwelling is both less than 80% of its full replacement cost immediately before the loss and less than the maximum amount of insurance available under the NFIP. In that case, we will pay the greater of the following amounts, but not more than the amount of insurance that applies to that dwelling: (1) The actual cash value, as defined in II.B.2., of the damaged part of the dwelling; or (2) A proportion of the cost to repair or replace the damaged part of the dwelling, without deduction for physical depreciation and after application of the deductible. This proportion is determined as follows: If 80% of the full replacement cost of the dwelling is less than the maximum amount of insurance available under the NFIP, then the proportion is determined by dividing the actual amount of insurance on the dwelling by the amount of insurance that represents 80% of its full replacement cost. But if 80% of the full replacement cost of the dwelling is greater than the maximum amount of insurance available under the NFIP, then the proportion is determined by dividing the actual amount of insurance on the dwelling by the maximum amount of insurance available under the NFIP.	An actual cash value loss settlement is the cost to repair or replace insured building items at the time of the loss, less the building deductible and less its physical depreciation. When the dwelling is a single-family building and the policyholder's principal residence, but the insurance carried does not meet the criteria for the replacement cost loss settlement (80 percent of the dwelling's full replacement cost or maximum policy limits), proportional loss settlement can be more advantageous than the actual cash value settlement. If proportional settlement benefits the policyholder, use the following formulas to calculate a proportional loss settlement: • **RCV to pay** = (Insurance carried ÷ insurance required) x RCV loss • **Proportional loss payable** = RCV to pay – deductible Proportional loss payments should not be: • Less than the ACV payable loss, because you would then settle at ACV; • More than the RCV payable loss; • More than the policy building limit; or, • More than the maximum statutory amount available for the coverage.

VII. General Conditions

Policy Language	Additional Explanation
	Below is an example of how to calculate a proportional loss settlement.

Table 6: Proportional Loss Settlement Example

Item	Value
Building RCV	$135,000
Insurance Required (80%) RCV	$108,000
Insurance Carried	$92,000
Deductible	$2,000
RCV Loss	$50,500

- (($92,000 ÷ $108,000) x $50,500) = $43,018.52
- $43,018.52 - $2,000 = $41,018.52

IMPORTANT – Use the order of operations as shown, starting within the innermost parentheses, for accurate calculation.

Appliances include refrigerators, stoves, ovens, ranges, trash compactors, garbage disposals, and the like.

b. A two-, three-, or four-family dwelling.

c. A unit that is not used exclusively for single-family dwelling purposes.

d. Detached garages.

e. Personal property.

f. Appliances, carpets, and carpet pads.

g. Outdoor awnings, outdoor antennas or aerials of any type, and other outdoor equipment.

h. Any property covered under this policy that is abandoned after a loss and remains as debris anywhere on the described location.

i. A dwelling that is not your principal residence.

VII. General Conditions

Policy Language	Additional Explanation
5. Amount of Insurance Required To determine the amount of insurance required for a dwelling immediately before the loss, we do not include the value of: a. Footings, foundations, piers, or any other structures or devices that are below the undersurface of the lowest basement floor and support all or part of the dwelling; b. Those supports listed in V.5.a. above, that are below the surface of the ground inside the foundation walls if there is no basement; and c. Excavations and underground flues, pipes, wiring, and drains. The Coverage D—Increased Cost of Compliance limit of liability is not included in the determination of the amount of insurance required.	The replacement cost value (RCV) and the amount of insurance required to qualify for replacement cost loss settlement are two separate amounts. The RCV of the building is pertinent to the adjuster completing the Adjuster's Preliminary Damage Assessment form or determining a potential total loss. Adjusters use adjustment valuation software to generate RCV, which typically includes the value to excavate and install foundation components that are below the ground level of a building with no basement, underneath the floor of a building with a basement, and the cost to install underground utility connections. The adjuster should not include the value of the items listed when determining the amount of insurance required. If loss meets all the criteria for replacement cost loss settlement, except for the required amount of insurance, the adjuster and examiner must adjust the RCV to exclude the value of the items listed before adjusting the loss settlement at Actual Cash Value

VIII. Liberalization Clause

Policy Language	Additional Explanation
If we make a change that broadens your coverage under this edition of our policy, but does not require any additional premium, then that change will automatically apply to your insurance as of the date we implement the change, provided that this implementation date falls within 60 days before or during the policy term stated on the Declarations Page.	Insurers cannot apply additional coverages provided through the liberalization clause retroactively to losses that have occurred; insurers can apply it prospectively. The clause permits FEMA to give existing, active policyholders beneficial amendments without needing to endorse their policies separately but does not provide any retroactive effect.

IX. What Law Governs

Policy Language	Additional Explanation
This policy and all disputes arising from the handling of any claim under the policy are governed exclusively by the flood insurance regulations issued by FEMA, the National Flood Insurance Act of 1968, as amended (42 U.S.C. 4001, et seq.), and Federal common law.	N/A

This page was intentionally left blank.

3   General Property Form

The General Property Form provides flood insurance coverage for owners or leaseholders of non-residential buildings or units, other residential buildings, and personal property in those buildings or units. The General Property form also covers residential condominium buildings that are not insurable under the Residential Condominium Building Association Policy (RCBAP).

I.   Agreement

Policy Language	Additional Explanation
The Federal Emergency Management Agency (FEMA) provides flood insurance under the terms of the National Flood Insurance Act of 1968 and its Amendments, and Title 44 of the Code of Federal Regulations. We will pay you for direct physical loss by or from flood to your insured property if you: 1. Have paid the correct premium; 2. Comply with all terms and conditions of this policy; and 3. Have furnished accurate information and statements. We have the right to review the information you give us at any time and to revise your policy based on our review.	This policy is under Federal law, unlike other property lines. Relevant definition at II.B.12 (direct physical loss). Policyholder responsibilities appear at Section VII.J, K. post-loss underwriting at Section VII.G.

II.   Definitions

Policy Language	Additional Explanation
A. In this policy, "you" and "your" refer to the insured(s) shown on the Declarations Page of this policy. Insured(s) includes: Any mortgagee and loss payee named in the Application and Declarations Page, as well as any other mortgagee or loss payee determined to exist at the time of loss in the order of precedence. "We," "us," and "our" refer to the insurer. Some definitions are complex because they are provided as they appear in the law or regulations or result from court cases. The precise definitions are intended to protect you.	
Flood, as used in this flood insurance policy, means: 1. A general and temporary condition of partial or complete inundation of two or more acres of normally dry land area or of two or more properties (one of which is your property) from:	For a general condition of flood to exist, the inundation must cover two or more acres of normally dry land or two or more parcels of land, one of which can be public property such as a roadway. The reference to "partial or complete inundation of two or more acres of normally

II. Definitions

Policy Language	Additional Explanation
a. Overflow of inland or tidal waters; b. Unusual and rapid accumulation or runoff of surface waters from any source; c. Mudflow.	dry land area or of two or more properties" requires that the two or more acres must be continuous acres, and that the two or more inundated parcels of land must touch. For mudflow definition, see SFIP Section II.B.19.
2. Collapse or subsidence of land along the shore of a lake or similar body of water as a result of erosion or undermining caused by waves or currents of water exceeding anticipated cyclical levels which result in a flood as defined in A.1.a. above	The SFIP also defines a flood as the collapse or subsidence of land along the shore of a lake or a similar body of water from erosion or undermining caused by waves or currents of water (velocity flow) exceeding anticipated cyclical levels during a flood from the overflow of inland or tidal waters. The SFIP does not cover damage from any other cause, form, or type of earth movement or gradual erosion. See Exclusions at SFIP Section V.C.

B. The following are the other key definitions we use in this policy:

Policy Language	Additional Explanation
1. **Act** The National Flood Insurance Act of 1968 and any amendments to it.	N/A
2. **Actual Cash Value** The cost to replace an insured item of property at the time of loss, less the value of its physical depreciation.	The cost to replace a building, a building item or a personal property item that Includes all charges related to material, labor, and equipment. This price may include charges such as delivery, assembly, sales tax, and any applicable overhead and profit, and the like. Actual cash value is the cost to replace, less applicable depreciation on all components of the cost.
3. **Application** The statement made and signed by you or your agent in applying for this policy. The application gives information we use to determine the eligibility of the risk, the kind of policy to be issued, and the correct premium payment. The application is part of this flood insurance policy. For us to issue you a policy, the correct premium payment must accompany the application.	The statement made and signed by the prospective policyholder or the agent when applying for a policy. The application contains information including the property description, information to determine eligibility, the policy form selected, selected coverage and limits, deductible, and the premium amount.
4. **Base Flood** A flood having a one percent chance of being equaled or exceeded in any given year.	N/A
5. **Basement** Any area of the building, including any sunken room or sunken portion of	The SFIP definition for a basement means the floor level of a room or any area of a floor level in a building is below the ground level on all sides. This definition may differ from what policyholders consider as their "basement." The SFIP considers a

II. Definitions

Policy Language	Additional Explanation
a room, having its floor below ground level (subgrade) on all sides.	sunken room or sunken portion of a room is a basement if the floor level is below the ground level on all sides. The entire below-ground-floor-level area, including walls and the ceiling that may extend above grade, is subject to basement coverage limitations.
	Ground-level is the surface of the ground immediately along the perimeter of the building. If an exterior area of egress out of the building is below the ground level on all sides, installed over a subgrade, the area of egress is below ground level. A subgrade is a surface of earth leveled off to receive a foundation such as a concrete slab of a building.
	The insurer may need to engage a qualified, licensed professional (example: surveyor) to measure the floor level in question. See Section 2 of this manual.
	Sump wells are not basements because they are not a floor level.
6. Building a. A structure with two or more outside rigid walls and a fully secured roof, that is affixed to a permanent site; b. A manufactured home (a "manufactured home," also known as a mobile home, is a structure: built on a permanent chassis, transported to its site in one or more sections, and affixed to a permanent foundation); or c. A travel trailer without wheels built on a chassis and affixed to a permanent foundation, that is regulated under the community's floodplain management and building ordinances or laws. Building does not mean a gas or liquid storage tank or a recreational vehicle, park trailer, or other similar vehicle, except as described in B.6.c., above.	• The SFIP covers a building, manufactured home (mobile home), or travel trailer if located at the described location, as shown on the Declaration Page and only insures one building. • The SFIP requires a building to be affixed to a permanent site, whereas it requires a manufactured home and a travel trailer to be affixed to a permanent foundation. • A travel trailer (recreational vehicle) with attached wheels is not a building. • A storage or shipping container, if used as a shed, storage building or residence, must meet the definition of an eligible building. • "Affixed by weight" does not constitute affixed to a permanent site as used in the SFIP.
7. Cancellation Represents the ending of the insurance coverage provided by this policy before the expiration date.	• The NFIP Flood Insurance Manual provides an exhaustive list for all valid policy cancellation reasons. • The expiration date is the ending of the policy term, the period of coverage provided by the insurance policy. • The policy term for the SFIP is one year, after any applicable waiting period.
8. Condominium	N/A

II. Definitions

Policy Language	Additional Explanation
A form of ownership of real property in which each unit owner has an undivided interest in common elements.	A Condominium Association is an entity recognized by a state.
9. Condominium Association The entity, formed by the unit owners, responsible for the maintenance and operation of: a. Common elements owned in undivided shares by unit owners; and b. Other real property in which the unit owners have use rights where membership in the entity is a required condition of unit ownership.	Homeowners' associations, townhome associations, and cooperatives, and the like are not condominium associations.
10. Declarations Page A computer-generated summary of information you provided in the application for insurance. The Declarations Page also describes the term of the policy, limits of coverage, and displays the premium and our name. The Declarations Page is a part of this flood insurance policy.	N/A
11. Described Location The location where the insured building or personal property is found. The described location is shown on the Declarations Page.	N/A
12. Direct Physical Loss By or From Flood Loss or damage to insured property, directly caused by a flood. There must be evidence of physical changes to the property.	The SFIP only pays for damage caused by a direct physical loss by or from flood, as defined by the SFIP. A direct physical loss means flood must physically contact the insured property and there must be evidence of physical change by or from flood to the insured building or insured personal property. Several SFIP provisions, each with its own criteria, address specific situations where the condition of direct physical loss by or from flood occurs despite an exclusion. In these specific situations, listed below, the insurer must thoroughly document the presence of the relevant criteria in the claim file for coverage and payment: • Losses from mudflow and collapse or subsidence of land as a result of erosion specifically covered under the SFIP definition of flood (see SFIP Section V.C., as well as II.A.1.c and II.A.2) • Back up of water and water-borne material through sewers or drains, where a flood is the proximate cause of the sewer or drain backup (see SFIP Section V.D.5.a.) • Discharge or overflow from a sump, sump pump, or related equipment, where

II. Definitions

Policy Language	Additional Explanation
	a flood is the proximate cause of the sump pump discharge or overflow (see SFIP Section V.D.5.b.) • Seepage or leakage on or through the insured building, where a flood is the proximate cause of the seepage of water (see SFIP Section V.D.5.c.) • Pressure or weight of water, where a flood is the proximate cause of the damage from the pressure or weight of water (see SFIP Section V.D.6.)
13. Elevated Building A building that has no basement and has its lowest elevated floor raised above ground level by foundation walls, shear walls, posts, piers, pilings, or columns.	For more information about elevated buildings, see Section 2 of this manual, Lowest Floor Elevation. If an elevated floor in the building is in part supported by a structural slab-on-grade foundation, additional documentation may be necessary to verify the elevated rating for the building.
14. Emergency Program The initial phase of a community's participation in the National Flood Insurance Program; only limited amounts of insurance are available under the Act.	N/A
15. Expense Constant A flat charge you must pay on each new or renewal policy to defray the expenses of the Federal Government related to flood insurance.	There is no longer an Expense Constant charge.
16. Federal Policy Fee A flat charge you must pay on each new or renewal policy to defray certain administrative expenses incurred in carrying out the National Flood Insurance Program. This fee covers expenses not covered by the expense constant.	N/A
17. Improvements Fixtures, alterations, installations, or additions comprising a part of the insured building.	N/A
18. Mudflow A river of liquid and flowing mud on the surfaces of normally dry land areas, as when earth is carried by a current of water. Other earth movements, such as landslide, slope failure, or a saturated soil mass moving by liquidity down a slope, are not mudflows.	A mudflow is liquified soil flowing in a manner akin to water flowing, which causes damage in a manner similar to moving water.

II. Definitions

Policy Language	Additional Explanation
19. National Flood Insurance Program (NFIP) The program of flood insurance coverage and floodplain management administered under the Act and applicable Federal regulations in Title 44 of the Code of Federal Regulations, Subchapter B.	N/A
20. Policy The entire written contract between you and us. It includes: a. This printed form; b. The application and Declarations Page; c. Any endorsement(s) that may be issued; and, d. Any renewal certificate indicating that coverage has been instituted for a new policy and new policy term. Only one building, which you specifically described in the application, may be insured under this policy.	N/A
21. Pollutants Substances that include, but that are not limited to, any solid, liquid, gaseous or thermal irritant or contaminant, including smoke, vapor, soot, fumes, acids, alkalis, chemicals, and waste. "Waste" includes, but is not limited to, materials to be recycled, reconditioned, or reclaimed.	The policy covers up to $10,000 damage caused by pollutants to covered property if the discharge, seepage, migration, release, or escape of the pollutants is caused by or results from flood. Testing for or monitoring of pollutants is not covered unless required by law. See the General Property Form Section III.C.3.
22. Post-FIRM Building A building for which construction or substantial improvement occurred after December 31, 1974, or on or after the effective date of an initial Flood Insurance Rate Map (FIRM), whichever is later.	Community Status Book
23. Probation Premium A flat charge you must pay on each new or renewal policy issued covering property in a community that has been placed on probation under the provisions of 44 CFR 59.24.	N/A
24. Regular Program The final phase of a community's participation in the National Flood Insurance Program. In this phase, a Flood Insurance Rate Map is in effect and full limits	N/A

II. Definitions

Policy Language	Additional Explanation
of coverage are available under the Act.	
25. Residential Condominium Building A building owned and administered as a condominium, containing one or more family units and in which at least 75% of the floor area is residential.	N/A
26. Special Flood Hazard Area (SFHA) An area having special flood or mudflow, and/or flood-related erosion hazards, and shown on a Flood Hazard Boundary Map or Flood Insurance Rate Map as Zone A, AO, A1-A30, AE, A99, AH, AR, AR/A, AR/AE, AR/AH, AR/AO, AR/A1-A30, V1-V30, VE, V.	All zones listed are SFHAs. However, the post-FIRM elevated building coverage limitations apply only to Zones A1–A30, AE, AH, AR, AR/A, AR/AE, AR/AH, AR/A1–A30, V1–V30, and VE, at SFIP Section III.A.8.

27. Stock
 Merchandise held in storage or for sale, raw materials, and in-process or finished goods, including supplies used in their packing or shipping. Stock does not include any property not covered under Section IV. Property Not Covered, except the following:
   a. Parts and equipment for self-propelled vehicles;
   b. Furnishings and equipment for watercraft;
   c. Spas and hot-tubs, including their equipment; and
   d. Swimming pool equipment.
	N/A

28. Unit A unit in a condominium building.	N/A
29. Valued Policy A policy in which the insured and the insurer agree on the value of the property insured, that value being payable in the event of a total loss. The Standard Flood Insurance Policy is not a valued policy.	The SFIP is not a valued policy; it is a direct physical loss policy. The insurer agrees to pay a policyholder for insured property damaged by direct physical by or from flood, subject to the terms, conditions, and exclusion of the SFIP.

III. Property Covered

Policy Language	Additional Explanation
A. Coverage A—Building Property We insure against direct physical loss by or from flood to:	
1. The building described on the Declarations Page at the described location. If the building is a condominium building and the named insured is the condominium association, Coverage A includes all units within the building and the improvements within the units, provided the units are owned in common by all unit owners.	N/A
2. We also insure building property for a period of 45 days at another location, as set forth in III.C.2.b. Property Removed to Safety.	N/A
3. Additions and extensions attached to and in contact with the building by means of a rigid exterior wall, a solid loadbearing interior wall, a stairway, an elevated walkway, or a roof. At your option, additions and extensions connected by any of these methods may be separately insured. Additions and extensions attached to and in contact with the building by means of a common interior wall that is not a solid load-bearing wall are always considered part of the building and cannot be separately insured.	A property owner has the option to separately insure an SFIP-defined addition if the insured property meets the definition of a building. Otherwise, an addition or extension meeting the requirements of General Property Form III.A.3. is covered under the General Property Form as part of the building.
4. The following fixtures, machinery, and equipment, which are covered under Coverage A only: a. Awnings and canopies; b. Blinds; c. Carpet permanently installed over unfinished flooring; d. Central air conditioners; e. Elevator equipment; f. Fire extinguishing apparatus; g. Fire sprinkler systems; h. Walk-in freezers; i. Furnaces; j. Light fixtures; k. Outdoor antennas and aerials attached to buildings;	• Blinds include vertical, horizontal, and wood or wood-like blinds. • Central air conditioners include related built-in equipment for dehumidification, air filtering, and ventilation. • Walk-in freezers and coolers must be permanently installed or built in. Furnaces and radiators include heat pumps, boilers, and related installed equipment for humidification, air filtering, and ventilation. • Ranges, cooking stoves, ovens include cooktops, range hoods, and built-in cooking exhaust apparatuses. • Refrigerators include beverage coolers and other major appliances that refrigerate.

III. Property Covered

Policy Language	Additional Explanation
l. Permanently installed cupboards, bookcases, paneling, and wallpaper;	
m. Pumps and machinery for operating pumps;	
n. Ventilating equipment; and	
o. Wall mirrors, permanently installed;	
p. In the units within the building, installed:	
(1) Built-in dishwashers;	
(2) Built-in microwave ovens;	
(3) Garbage disposal units;	
(4) Hot water heaters, including solar water heaters;	
(5) Kitchen cabinets;	
(6) Plumbing fixtures;	
(7) Radiators;	
(8) Ranges;	
(9) Refrigerators; and	
(10) Stoves.	
5. Materials and supplies to be used for construction, alteration, or repair of the insured building while the materials and supplies are stored in a fully enclosed building at the described location or on an adjacent property.	N/A
6. A building under construction, alteration, or repair at the described location:	The SFIP only covers buildings under construction affixed to a permanent site. For example, NFIP does not cover a building on temporary cribbing and not affixed to a permanent site.
a. If the structure is not yet walled or roofed as described in the definition for building (see II.6.a.), then coverage applies:	The SFIP covers building materials and supplies for the insured building under construction stored in a fully enclosed building up to building policy limits per General Property Form Section III.A.5.
(1) Only while such work is in progress; or	
(2) If such work is halted, only for a period of up to 90 continuous days thereafter.	When a building under construction, alteration, or repair does not have at least two rigid exterior walls and a fully secured roof at the time of loss, your deductible amount will be two times the deductible that would otherwise apply to a completed building. See General Property Form Section VI. Deductibles.
b. However, coverage does not apply until the building is walled and roofed if the lowest floor, including the basement floor, of a non-elevated building or the lowest elevated floor of an elevated building is:	The SFIP does not cover a building under construction if work stops for
(1) Below the base flood elevation in Zones AH, AE, A1–A30, AR, AR/AE,	

III. Property Covered

Policy Language	Additional Explanation
AR/AH, AR/A1–A30, AR/A, AR/AO; or (2) Below the base flood elevation adjusted to include the effect of wave action in Zones VE or V1–V30. The lowest floor levels are based on the bottom of the lowest horizontal structural member of the floor in Zones VE or V1–V30 and the top of the floor in Zones AH, AE, A1–A30, AR, AR/AE, AR/AH, AR/A1–A30, AR/A, AR/AO.	more than 90 continuous days. Coverage will resume when work resumes. The SFIP does not cover tools for construction, such as forms, cribbing, power tools, etc.
7. A manufactured home or a travel trailer as described in the Definitions Section (see II.B.6.b. and II.B.6.c.). If the manufactured home or travel trailer is in a special flood hazard area, it must be anchored in the following manner at the time of the loss: a. By over-the-top or frame ties to ground anchors; or b. In accordance with the manufacturer's specifications; or c. In compliance with the community's floodplain management requirements unless it has been continuously insured by the NFIP at the same described location since September 30, 1982.	A manufactured (mobile) home is a structure built on a permanent chassis, transported to its site in one or more sections, and affixed to a permanent foundation. A travel trailer is not self-propelled and must be affixed to a permanent foundation in a manner that the community regulates under its floodplain management and building ordinances. The travel trailer must have its wheels removed in order to be eligible for coverage. A recreational vehicle is self-propelled and is not insurable. See SFIP Section IV. Property Not Covered. For the SFIP to insure a manufactured home, the owner must affix it to a permanent foundation. A permanent foundation for a manufactured home may be a poured masonry slab, foundation walls, piers, or block supports. The foundation, not the wheels and or the axles, must support all the weight of the manufactured (mobile) home. If the mobile home is in an SFHA, the owner must anchor it to a permanent foundation to resist flotation, collapse, or lateral movement by: • Providing over-the-top or frame ties to ground anchors. • Following the manufacturer's specification for anchoring. • Complying with the community's floodplain management requirements.
8. Items of property in a building enclosure below the lowest elevated floor of an elevated post-FIRM building located in zones A1–A30, AE, AH, AR, AR/A, AR/AE, AR/AH, AR/A1–A30, V1– V30, or VE, or in a basement, regardless of the zone. Coverage is limited to the following: a. Any of the following items, if installed in their functioning locations and, if necessary for operation, connected to a power source:	When the Declarations Page reflects two zones, the current zone and the zone used for rating, the rating zone is used for coverage. This zone may be a grandfathered zone that remains in effect for coverage unless or until the home is substantially damaged, substantially improved, or there is a lapse in coverage. The current zone may be a different zone that reflects the zone designation in the current flood map. This zone is intended only for non-claim related purposes such as underwriting premiums and ICC applicability.

III. Property Covered

Policy Language	Additional Explanation
	Post-FIRM elevated building limitations do not apply to SFHA Zones A, AO, A99, AR/AO, V, and VO. Basement limitations apply regardless of zone.
	Basement limitations apply to the complete area defined as a basement-- floors, walls, and ceilings.
	For an elevated building located in an SFHA, full coverage begins at the lowest elevated floor. This is the lowest floor raised above ground, even if the pilings extend beyond it (see Lowest Elevated Floor Determination in Section 2 of this manual).
	For items of property below, at, or level with the lowest elevated floor, the item(s) is subject to the coverage limitation. For example, a cabinet, door, window, or refrigerator that originates below, or straddles the line-level equal with the lowest elevated floor is not covered, even that portion or value at or above the lowest elevated floor.
	However, coverage can be provided for building materials and finishes installed above the lowest elevated floor, even if the items originate or overlaps the lowest elevated floor level, when the function of the building material or finish is not reduced by cutting or removing the damaged and otherwise excluded building material physically located at or below the line-level equal with the lowest elevated floor. Examples include exterior siding, wood trim, drywall, paint, or insulation, even if the same item extends below the level of the lowest elevated floor. The building materials and finishes below the line level with the lowest elevated floor are still excluded. This coverage interpretation is in sync with new FEMA-approved building codes for new construction and substantially improved buildings.
	The SFIP does not cover items, interior or exterior, located below the lowest elevated floor of a post-FIRM elevated building in the stated zones.
(1) Central air conditioners;	Central air conditioners include related built-in equipment for dehumidification, air filtering, and ventilation.
(2) Cisterns and the water in them;	See Section 2 Cisterns in this manual.
(3) Drywall for walls and ceilings in a basement and the cost of labor to nail it, unfinished and unfloated and not taped, to the framing;	The SFIP covers unfinished, unfloated, and not taped drywall installed anywhere in a basement. The SFIP will also pay for unfinished, unfloated, and not taped drywall in lieu of paneling or any finished wall or ceiling treatment.

III. Property Covered

Policy Language	Additional Explanation
	The SFIP does not cover non-structural building elements, including non-load bearing floor, wall, or ceiling framing components, such as when installed for the purpose to improve a basement or enclosed area with finish floors, walls, and ceilings.
(4) Electrical junction and circuit breaker boxes; (5) Electrical outlets and switches;	Electrical junction and circuit breaker boxes include a junction box, which serves as an unfinished basic light fixture. See Figure 20 below. The SFIP does not cover finished lighting, which is an improvement as defined in Section II.B.17 of the SFIP. Figure 20: Unfinished basic light fixture and outlet
(6) Elevators, dumbwaiters, and related equipment, except for related equipment installed below the base flood elevation after September 30, 1987;	An elevator or dumbwaiter is covered if within the covered building enclosure or attached to and in contact with the insured building or directly attached to the 16 square foot landing area used for egress if unattached. For elevators and dumbwaiters installed below the BFE after September 30, 1987, coverage is limited to the cab and the included controls installed on or in the cab. Related equipment is everything except the cab and the included controls and is not covered unless the damaged part of the equipment is installed above the level at or above the BFE. A chair lift is covered if within the covered building enclosure or attached to and in contact with the insured building or attached directly to the 16 square foot landing area attached to the building and used for egress (See **Figures 21 and 22**).

III. Property Covered

Policy Language	Additional Explanation
	Figure 21. Example of a covered chair lift attached directly to a building or covered 4x4 16SF landing Photograph credit BFA, LLC Figure 22: Example of a non-covered chair lift.
(7) Fuel tanks and the fuel in them;	Fuel tanks and the fuel in them include a connected fuel gauge or fuel filter.
(8) Furnaces and hot water heaters;	Furnaces and hot water heaters include boilers and permanently installed equipment for humidification, air filtering, and ventilation. This includes those portions of the central HVAC in a building enclosure below the LFE or basement, including boilers and connected radiators and hot water baseboards. This does not include electric baseboard heaters, whether hardwired to the electrical system or not.
(9) Heat pumps;	Heat pumps and other central HVAC units permanently installed equipment related to humidification, dehumidification, air filtering, and ventilation.
(10) Nonflammable insulation in a basement;	Nonflammable insulation in a basement includes: • Nonflammable insulation in walls and ceilings. For post-FIRM elevated buildings in SFHAs, coverage applies to: • Insulation installed between joists within the lowest elevated floor including plywood and any other material used to hold in the insulation. • Unfinished protective weather barriers affixed to the floor framing.

III. Property Covered

Policy Language	Additional Explanation
	When installed underneath a building in a crawlspace the barrier must be physically attached to the building's foundation or floor framing for Coverage A – Building.
(11) Pumps and tanks used in solar energy systems;	N/A
(12) Stairways and staircases attached to the building, not separated from it by elevated walkways;	The SFIP covers unfinished base support material for staircases and stairways (underneath the finished treads and risers) attached to the building, not separated from it by elevated walkways, includes an exterior staircase into a basement that is part of the building and enclosed by an addition defined under SFIP Section III.A.2. This also includes interior basement or post-FIRM elevated building staircases.
	The SFIP does not pay to treat, paint, or stain the base support material in a basement, or below the lowest elevated floor of a post-FIRM elevated building in an SFHA.
	The SFIP does not cover damage to finish materials used for a tread, riser, or stringer, if such material is installed onto unfinished base support material for stairways and staircases. If finish material is the base support material, such as with a floating staircase or step, the finish material is covered but not the cost to apply a finish, coating, or paint.
	Figure 23. Unfinished base stairs (left) are covered in a basement or below post-FIRM elevated building; however, improvements to paint or added finish to treads, risers, and stringers (right) are not: 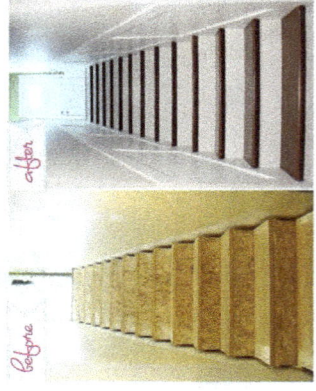

III. Property Covered

Policy Language	Additional Explanation
Figure 24: Covered stairs where the finish material is the base material; however, no coverage to paint, stain, or coat:

The SFIP does not cover the basement exterior egress staircase located outside of the perimeter building walls, even if covered by a roof or door. See SFIP Section IV.9. |
(13) Sump pumps	N/A
(14) Water softeners and the chemicals in them, water filters, and faucets installed as an integral part of the plumbing system;	The SFIP allows for a faucet that is affixed directly to the plumbing line, as opposed to a faucet that is connected to plumbing lines but mounted onto a sink as a finished fixture. See Section 2: Water Softeners in this manual.
(15) Well water tanks and pumps;	Well water tanks and pumps include the pressure switch, pressure valve, and gauge.
(16) Required utility connections for any item in this list; and	N/A
(17) Footings, foundations, posts, pilings, piers, or other foundation walls and anchorage systems required to support a building.	Footings, foundations, posts, pilings, piers, or other foundation walls and anchorage systems required to support a building:

• Includes windows and doors installed in the perimeter foundation walls of an SFIP-defined basement area such as a perimeter wall basement garage door or sliding glass door.

• Include vents installed in and considered part of the covered foundation walls of a post-FIRM elevated building. However, there is no coverage for breakaway walls or vents in breakaway walls.

• Does not include screen or storm doors, or a door covering or |

III. Property Covered

Policy Language	Additional Explanation
	enclosing an exterior egress in a basement, such as a Bilco™ door.
	• Does not include doors and windows of any type in an enclosure subject to post-FIRM limitations when located below the lowest elevated floor.
b. Clean-up.	Clean-up includes:
	• Pumping out trapped floodwater
	• Labor to remove or extract spent cleaning solutions
	• Treatment for mold and mildew
	• Structural drying of salvageable interior foundation elements
	The SFIP does not cover clean-up of an item or property located in areas subject to basement and post-FIRM coverage limitations – that is, the property must itself be covered under SFIP Section III(A)(8) –or for items or loss otherwise excluded under this policy.
	Clean-up is not the removal of flood-damaged items or debris. See SFIP Section III.C.1. for Debris Removal.
B. Coverage B—Personal Property	
1. If you have purchased personal property coverage, we insure, subject to B.2., 3. and 4. below, against direct physical loss by or from flood to personal property inside the fully enclosed insured building:	• The SFIP does not cover personal property items not within the fully enclosed insured building at the described location. This differs from the Dwelling Form in that the Dwelling Form covers personal property within any SFIP-defined building at the described location.
a. Owned solely by you, or in the case of a condominium, owned solely by the condominium association and used exclusively in the conduct of the business affairs of the condominium association; or	• See SFIP Section III.C.2.b. for Property Removed to Safety.
b. Owned in common by the unit owners of the condominium association.	• Property leased under a "capital lease," a contract that entitles a renter the temporary use of an item and to account for the financial effect of ownership on the balance sheet, qualifies as insurable interest and can be claimed even if the property is not solely owned by the policyholder.
We also insure such personal property for 45 days while stored at a temporary location, as set forth in III.C.2.b. Property Removed to Safety.	In contrast, an "operating lease" is a contract that entitles a renter the temporary use of an item but does not convey ownership rights. Property in the possession of a policyholder obtained through an operating lease cannot be represented in balancing sheet financials according to Generally Accepted Accounting Principles (GAAP) and is not covered

III. Property Covered

Policy Language	Additional Explanation
	under the SFIP Coverage B-Personal Property.

2. When this policy covers personal property, coverage will be either for household personal property or other than household personal property, while within the insured building, but not both.
 	
a. If this policy covers household personal property, it will insure household personal property usual to a living quarters, that:
  (1) Belongs to you, or a member of your household, or at your option:
    (a) Your domestic worker;
    (b) Your guest; or
  (2) You may be legally liable for.
 	
b. If this policy covers other than household personal property, it will insure your:
  (1) Furniture and fixtures;
  (2) Machinery and equipment;
  (3) Stock; and
  (4) Other personal property owned by you and used in your business, subject to IV. Property Not Covered.
	• The SFIP does not cover personal property items not within the building, as defined by the policy.
	
	• Church pews are furniture and fixtures whether attached to the building or not.
	
	• Drapes and hardware are contents whether physically attached to the building or not.

3. Coverage for personal property includes the following property, subject to B.1.a. and B.1.b. above, which is covered under Coverage B only: a. Air conditioning units installed in the building; b. Carpet, not permanently installed, over unfinished flooring; c. Carpets over finished flooring; d. Clothes washers and dryers; e. "Cook-out" grills; f. Food freezers, other than walk-in, and food in any freezer; g. Outdoor equipment and furniture stored inside the insured building; h. Ovens and the like; and i. Portable microwave ovens and portable dishwashers.	• Coverage A – Building Property covers through-the-wall air conditioning units that are permanently installed. • Clothes washers and dryers, including the dryer exhaust vent kit. • Coverage B applies to food freezers only. NFIP considers an appliance that both refrigerates and freezes as a refrigerator and covers it under Coverage A–Building Property This provision does not apply to Zones A, AO, A99, AR/AO, V, and VO.
4. Items of property in a building enclosure below the lowest elevated floor of	• Coverage A – Building Property covers through-the-wall air

III. Property Covered

Policy Language	Additional Explanation
an elevated post-FIRM building located in Zones A1-A30, AE, AH, AR, AR/A, AR/AE, AR/AH, AR/A1-A30, V1-V30, or VE, or in a basement, regardless of the zone, is limited to the following items, if installed in their functioning locations and, if necessary for operation, connected to a power source: a. Air conditioning units, portable or window type; b. Clothes washers and dryers; and c. Food freezers, other than walk-in, and food in any freezer.	conditioning units that are permanently installed. • Clothes washers and dryers include a dryer exhaust vent kit. The connectors and plumbing lines for a gas dryer are covered under building coverage only. • Coverage B applies to food freezers only. NFIP considers an appliance that both refrigerates and freezes as a refrigerator and covers it under Coverage A – Building Property. This provision does not apply to Zones A, AO, A99, AR/AO, V, and VO.
5. Special Limits: We will pay no more than $2,500 for any loss to one or more of the following kinds of personal property: a. Artwork, photographs, collectibles, or memorabilia, including but not limited to, porcelain or other figures, and sports cards; b. Rare books or autographed items; c. Jewelry, watches, precious and semi-precious stones, articles of gold, silver, or platinum; d. Furs or any article containing fur which represents its principal value.	Payments for these items may not exceed $2,500.00 in aggregate.
6. We will pay only for the functional value of antiques.	The SFIP does not value an antique based on the rarity of the item, nor does it apply depreciation based solely on age or its physical condition. Example: A 400-year-old fully restored chair formerly owned by a historical figure is appraised by a certified industry professionally at $25,000. The chair has seen general usage for 3-years after its restoration date. Applying judgment, a new chair with the same or similar functional design, material quality, and craftsmanship is comparably worth $3,500. Less 10 percent depreciation, the SFIP would pay the functional value of $3,150.
7. If you are a tenant, you may apply up to 10% of the Coverage B limit to improvements: a. Made a part of the building you occupy; and b. You acquired, or made at your expense, even though you cannot legally remove. This coverage does not increase the amount of insurance that applies to insured personal property.	The SFIP does not allow duplication of benefits with another NFIP policy. Insurers may not pay for property as tenant improvements and pay for the same scope for the same items under a building owner's policy. The insurer must obtain the lease agreement to verify the insurable interest before making a payment under this provision. For policyholders who are tenants, appliances such as refrigerators, stoves, ovens, ranges, and dishwashers are not subject to the 10 percent limitation.

III. Property Covered

Policy Language	Additional Explanation
8. If you are a condominium unit owner, you may apply up to 10% of the Coverage B limit to cover loss to interior: a. Walls, b. Floors, and c. Ceilings, that are not covered under a policy issued to the condominium association insuring the condominium building. This coverage does not increase the amount of insurance that applies to insured personal property.	N/A
9. If you are a tenant, personal property must be inside the fully enclosed building.	N/A
C. Coverage C—Other Coverages	
1. Debris Removal a. We will pay the expense to remove non-owned debris that is on or in insured property and debris of insured property anywhere. b. If you or a member of your household perform the removal work, the value of your work will be based on the Federal minimum wage. c. This coverage does not increase the Coverage A or Coverage B limit of liability	Insured property means the insured dwelling and covered personal property. The SFIP does not pay for removal of: • Non-covered debris anywhere, such as a non-covered damaged property or debris located in the yard, driveway, or on another parcel of land. • Non-covered items of property, even if the removal of the item facilitates cleanup of covered building repairs, such as the removal of carpet installed inside a basement, or the removal of plants, shrubs, or trees along the perimeter of the building to access foundation or siding repairs.
2. Loss Avoidance Measures a. Sandbags, Supplies, and Labor (1) We will pay up to $1,000 for the costs you incur to protect the insured building from a flood or imminent danger of flood, for the following: (a) Your reasonable expenses to buy: (i) Sandbags, including sand to fill them;	The SFIP only covers those items specifically noted. The policyholder must provide receipts for covered materials they purchased. Additionally, the NFIP reimburses the policyholder labor at the Federal minimum wage at the time of the loss. Water-filled bladders, as shown in Figure 25, are considered a temporary levee for the purposes of loss avoidance coverage. However, because these are reusable, the SFIP will pay the cost to purchase the bladder once, but only when the initial purchased is in connection to the claimed flood event. After that event, any future claim for loss avoidance here is limited to the labor and

III. Property Covered

Policy Language	Additional Explanation
(ii) Fill for temporary levees; (iii) Pumps; and (iv) Plastic sheeting and lumber used in connection with these items; and (b) The value of work, at the Federal minimum wage, that you perform. (2) This coverage for Sandbags, Supplies, and Labor only applies if damage to insured property by or from flood is imminent and the threat of flood damage is apparent enough to lead a person of common prudence to anticipate flood damage. One of the following must also occur: (a) General and temporary condition of flooding in the area near the described location must occur, even if the flood does not reach the insured building; or (b) A legally authorized official must issue an evacuation order or other civil order for the community in which the insured building is located calling for measures to preserve life and property from the peril of flood. This coverage does not increase the Coverage A or Coverage B limit of liability. b. Property Removed to Safety (1) We will pay up to $1,000 for the reasonable expenses you incur to move insured property to a place other than the described location that contains the property, in order to protect it from flood or the imminent danger of flood. Reasonable expenses include the value of work, at the Federal minimum wage, that you perform. (2) If you move insured property to a place other than the described location that contains the property, in order to protect it from flood or the imminent danger of flood, we will cover such property while at that location for a period of 45 consecutive days from the date you begin to move it there. The personal property that is moved must be placed in a fully enclosed building, or otherwise	fill material. Figure 25: Water-Filled Bladder Photograph credit Randy Wagner • The SFIP coverage of "reasonable expenses" under this provision is limited to the policyholder's removal, storage, and return of covered building and personal property to the location described on the declarations page. The insurer may reimburse the policyholder for related expenses for the labor of the policyholder and family members at Federal minimum wage and incurred transportation and storage costs. The policyholder must itemize and support these expenses with valid proof of payment. Coverage here is limited only to the length of time that a flood or the imminent danger of flood exists. Payment under this provision does not increase Coverage A – Building Property or Coverage B – Personal Property limits of liability. • The SFIP will cover from the peril of flood, the property relocated to another location for a period of 45 consecutive days from the date the policyholder began to move the property. If the policyholder does not

III. Property Covered

Policy Language	Additional Explanation
reasonably protected from the elements. Any property removed, including a moveable home described in II.6.b. and c., must be placed above ground level or outside of the special flood hazard area. This coverage does not increase the Coverage A or Coverage B limit of liability.	place the property in a fully enclosed building, the property must be secured to prevent flotation out of the building. If the property floats out or away from the building used to reasonably protect the property from the elements, it will be conclusively presumed that the policyholder did not reasonably secure the property. In that case, there is no coverage for the property. • Regarding the provision "must be placed above ground level or outside of the SFHA", the relocated site of the property must be a reasonable location to prevent loss compared to the described location. For example, where the surrounding terrain is sloped, the site of the relocated property must be on a higher elevation than the floor level of the building at the described location where the property was originally located; the policyholder may not relocate the property to a basement. Where the surrounding terrain is level and the site of the relocated property is considered within the same flood hazard area, the property must be placed on a floor level in the relocated building that is a higher elevation compared to the floor level in the building at the described location where the property was originally located. The property may not be relocated into a lower enclosure below an elevated floor within a post-FIRM building located in an SFHA.
3. Pollution Damage We will pay for damage caused by pollutants to covered property if the discharge, seepage, migration, release, or escape of the pollutants is caused by or results from flood. The most we will pay under this coverage is $10,000. This coverage does not increase the Coverage A or Coverage B limits of liability. Any payment under this provision when combined with all other payments for the same loss cannot exceed the replacement cost or actual cash value, as appropriate, of the covered property. This coverage does not include the testing for or monitoring of pollutants unless required by law or ordinance.	N/A
D. Coverage D— Increased Cost of Compliance	N/A
1. General This policy pays you to comply with a State or local floodplain management law or ordinance affecting repair or reconstruction of a structure suffering flood damage.	

III. Property Covered

Policy Language	Additional Explanation
Compliance activities eligible for payment are: elevation, floodproofing, relocation, or demolition (or any combination of these activities) of your structure. Eligible floodproofing activities are limited to: a. Non-residential structures. b. Residential structures with basements that satisfy FEMA's standards published in the Code of Federal Regulations [44 CFR 60.6 (b) or (c)].	
2. Limit of Liability We will pay you up to $30,000 under this Coverage D—Increased Cost of Compliance, which only applies to policies with building coverage (Coverage A). Our payment of claims under Coverage D is in addition to the amount of coverage which you selected on the application and which appears on the Declarations Page. But the maximum you can collect under this policy for both Coverage A (Building Property) and Coverage D (Increased Cost of Compliance) cannot exceed the maximum permitted under the Act. We do NOT charge a separate deductible for a claim under Coverage D.	All three SFIP forms provide Increased Cost of Compliance (ICC) benefits as Coverage D. Increased Cost of Compliance. ICC provides up to $30,000 toward the cost of bringing a flood-damaged structure into compliance with state or community floodplain management laws or ordinances governing repair or reconstruction following a flood.
3. Eligibility a. A structure covered under Coverage A—Building Property sustaining a loss caused by a flood as defined by this policy must: (1) Be a "repetitive loss structure." A "repetitive loss structure" is one that meets the following conditions: (a) The structure is covered by a contract of flood insurance issued under the NFIP. (b) The structure has suffered flood damage on 2 occasions during a 10-year period that ends on the date of the second loss. The cost to repair the flood damage, on average, equaled or exceeded 25% of the market value of the structure at the time of each flood loss. (d) In addition to the current claim, the NFIP must have paid the previous qualifying claim, and the State or community must have a cumulative, substantial damage provision or repetitive loss provision in its floodplain management law or ordinance being enforced against the structure; or	To be eligible for ICC, the community must declare the building substantially damaged. The amount paid for Coverage D – ICC and Coverage A – Building Property cannot exceed the maximum program limits of $500,000 General Property Form. ICC is not available in Emergency Program communities. ICC is not available for: • Contents-only policies. • Group Flood Insurance policies. • Dwelling Form policies on individual condominium units in a multi-unit building. ICC coverage is available through the condominium association's flood policy. No separate deductible applies. For 3.b.(2) and (3) to apply, the community must first adopt and enforce new preliminary or advisory base flood elevations and an ICC claim cannot proceed until on or after the effective date of the new base flood elevations AND the policyholder receives notice from the community requiring the home to be

III. Property Covered

Policy Language	Additional Explanation
(2) Be a structure that has had flood damage in which the cost to repair equals or exceeds 50% of the market value of the structure at the time of the flood. The State or community must have a substantial damage provision in its floodplain management law or ordinance being enforced against the structure.	brought into compliance with the new flood elevations. However, there are situations where the community may enforce elevation requirements in a non-SFHA and this would be specified in the ordinance.
b. This Coverage D pays you to comply with State or local floodplain management laws or ordinances that meet the minimum standards of the National Flood Insurance Program found in the Code of Federal Regulations at 44 CFR 60.3. We pay for compliance activities that exceed those standards under these conditions:	There are situations where the community may have its own elevation or flood-proofing requirements, which it enforces within a non-SFHA. This would be specified in the community's floodplain ordinance, but the community must be able to demonstrate this requirement and enforcement is at least based in part on guidance from FEMA, and not entirely on its own.
(1) 3.a.(1) above.	**ICC Claims**
(2) Elevation or floodproofing in any risk zone to preliminary or advisory base flood elevations provided by FEMA which the State or local government has adopted and is enforcing for flood-damaged structures in such areas. (This includes compliance activities in B, C, X, or D zones which are being changed to zones with base flood elevations. This also includes compliance activities in zones where base flood elevations are being increased, and a flood-damaged structure must comply with the higher advisory base flood elevation.) Increased Cost of Compliance coverage does not apply to situations in B, C, X, or D zones where the community has derived its own elevations and is enforcing elevation or floodproofing requirements for flood-damaged structures to elevations derived solely by the community.	The date of loss of the ICC claim is the date of loss of the underlying flood claim that triggers the requirement to comply with a community law or ordinance.

Policyholders have up to six years from the date of the underlying flood loss to complete the eligible mitigation activity. Policyholders should know that initiating a mitigation project before receiving a substantial damage declaration from the community may jeopardize their eligibility to receive an ICC payment.

For buildings in Zones B, C, X, D, unnumbered A and V, and A99, the adjuster must document why a building must undergo mitigation and obtain a written statement from the community to substantiate the ICC claim.

ICC does not pay for testing, monitoring, clean up, removal, containment, treatment, detoxification, or neutralization of pollutants even if required by community ordinance. |
Elevation or floodproofing above the base flood elevation to meet State or local "freeboard" requirements, i.e., that a structure must be elevated above the base flood elevation.	**Repetitive Loss Properties**
c. Under the minimum NFIP criteria at 44 CFR 60.3 (b)(4), States and communities must require the elevation or floodproofing of structures in unnumbered A zones to the base flood elevation where elevation data is obtained from a Federal, State, or other source. Such compliance activities are also eligible for Coverage D.	If a state or community adopts and enforces a cumulative substantial damage provision or repetitive loss provision requiring action by property owners to comply with floodplain management laws or ordinances, this may also qualify a structure for an ICC claim after a flood loss. The community must declare the structure to be substantially damaged and the structure must meet the NFIP's repetitive loss structure definition. The NFIP defines a
d. This coverage will also pay for the incremental cost, after demolition or relocation, of elevating or floodproofing a structure during its rebuilding at	repetitive loss structure as an NFIP-insured building that has incurred flood-related damages on two occasions during a 10-year period ending on the

III. Property Covered

Policy Language	Additional Explanation
the same or another site to meet State or local floodplain management laws or ordinances, subject to Exclusion D.5.g. below. (c) This coverage will also pay to bring a flood damaged structure into compliance with State or local floodplain management laws or ordinances even if the structure had received a variance before the present loss from the applicable floodplain management requirements	date of the event for which the insured makes a second claim. The cost of repairing the flood damage, on the average, must equal or exceed 25 percent of the market value of the building at the time of each flood. The adjuster or insurer must verify that the NFIP paid a claim for both qualifying losses and that the state or community is enforcing a cumulative substantial damage or repetitive loss provision in its law or ordinance and declared the building substantially damaged on that basis. **Substantial Damage** Insurers may only open an ICC claim when the community declares a building substantially damaged in writing. Neither FEMA nor the insurer can determine substantial damage or issue a substantial damage declaration. The community has the sole authority to determine substantial damage. Note that, in some cases, a community may declare a building substantially damaged, based in whole or in part on non-flood-related damage. While having more than 50 percent damage may trigger a requirement to comply with the local floodplain management ordinances, the SFIP requires the percentage of damage to be by or from flood, whether covered by the SFIP or not. See Section 3 Increased Cost of Compliance in this manual for more detail.
4. Conditions a. When a structure covered under Coverage A-Building Property sustains a loss caused by a flood, our payment for the loss under this Coverage D will be for the increased cost to elevate, floodproof, relocate, or demolish (or any combination of these activities) caused by the enforcement of current State or local floodplain management ordinances or laws. Our payment for eligible demolition activities will be for the cost to demolish and clear the site of the building debris or a portion thereof caused by the enforcement of current State or local floodplain management ordinances or laws. Eligible activities for the cost of clearing the site will include those necessary to discontinue utility service to the site and ensure proper abandonment of on-site utilities. b. When the building is repaired or rebuilt, it must be intended for the same	ICC pays for the following mitigation activities or combination thereof: • Floodproofing to reduce the potential for flood damage by keeping floodwater out of a building, for nonresidential structures and for certain residential structures that satisfy FEMA's standards under 44 C.F.R. 60.6(b) or (c). • Elevation to raise a building to or above the BFE plus freeboard adopted by a community, adopted Advisory Base Flood Elevations (ABFE), or the best available data provided by FEMA. • Demolition when a building is in such poor condition that elevation and relocation are not technically feasible or cost-effective. • Relocation to move a building outside of the floodplain. See Section 3 Increased Cost of Compliance in this manual for more detail.

III. Property Covered

Policy Language	Additional Explanation
occupancy as the present building unless otherwise required by current floodplain management ordinances or laws.	N/A
5. Exclusions	
Under this Coverage D-Increased Cost of Compliance, we will not pay for:	
a. The cost to comply with any floodplain management law or ordinance in communities participating in the Emergency Program.	
b. The cost associated with enforcement of any ordinance or law that requires any insured or others to test for, monitor, clean up, remove, contain, treat, detoxify or neutralize, or in any way respond to, or assess the effects of pollutants.	
c. The loss in value to any insured building or other structure due to the requirements of any ordinance or law.	
d. The loss in residual value of the undamaged portion of a building demolished as a consequence of enforcement of any State or local floodplain management law or ordinance.	
e. Any Increased Cost of Compliance under this Coverage D:	
(1) Until the building is elevated, floodproofed, demolished, or relocated on the same or to another premises; and	
(2) Unless the building is elevated, floodproofed, demolished, or relocated as soon as reasonably possible after the loss, not to exceed two years.	
f. Any code upgrade requirements, e.g., plumbing or electrical wiring, not specifically related to the State or local floodplain management law or ordinance.	
g. Any compliance activities needed to bring additions or improvements made after the loss occurred into compliance with State or local floodplain management laws or ordinances.	
h. Loss due to any ordinance or law that you were required to comply with before the current loss.	
i. Any rebuilding activity to standards that do not meet the NFIP's minimum requirements. This includes any situation where the insured has received from the State or community a variance in connection with the current flood	

III. Property Covered

Policy Language	Additional Explanation
loss to rebuild the property to an elevation below the base flood elevation.	
j. Increased Cost of Compliance for a garage or carport.	
k. Any structure insured under an NFIP Group Flood Insurance Policy.	
Assessments made by a condominium association on individual condominium unit owners to pay increased costs of repairing commonly owned buildings after a flood in compliance with State or local floodplain management ordinances or laws.	

6. Other Provisions

All other conditions and provisions of this policy apply.	N/A

IV. Property Not Covered

Policy Language	Additional Explanation
We do not cover any of the following property:	
1. Personal property not inside the fully enclosed building;	This provision applies to tenants and building owners for personal property inside the insured building.
2. A building, and personal property in it, located entirely in, on, or over water or seaward of mean high tide, if it was constructed or substantially improved after September 30, 1982;	• The SFIP allows coverage for a building not entirely over water, for example: when part of the exterior perimeter wall and foundation of the building is on land or the landward side of mean high tide (mean high water).
	• When the exterior perimeter walls of the building are completely over water and the support system or foundation underneath the insured building extends onto land, or the extension of any mechanism for access into a building (including, but not limited to, stairs, decks, walkways, piers, posts, pilings, docks, or driveways), even if the mechanism is on or partially on land, the building or the access will not be eligible for coverage.
	• If the exterior perimeter walls of a building are completely over water, but connected to another eligible building by means of an elevated walkway, stairway, roof, and/or rigid exterior wall, or there is an appurtenant structure on the same slab, foundation, or other continuous support system that is on land (such as a shed or garage), the presence of the connected building or appurtenant structure on land does not allow coverage to be afforded to the building that has its exterior perimeter walls entirely over water.
3. Open structures, including a building used as a boathouse or any structure or building into which boats are floated, and personal property located in, on, or over water;	The SFIP does not cover boathouses or buildings into which boats can float and personal property located within buildings used solely as boathouses.
	The SFIP does not cover a building and personal property within it, located in, on, or over water or seaward of mean high tide if the building was constructed or substantially improved after September 30, 1982.

IV. Property Not Covered

Policy Language	Additional Explanation
4. Recreational vehicles other than travel trailers described in II.B.6.c., whether affixed to a permanent foundation or on wheels;	Figure 26. A recreational vehicle is a self-propelled vehicle Photograph credit Fleetwood RV Figure 27. A travel trailer is not self-propelled and is towed behind a road vehicle

5. Self-propelled vehicles or machines, including their parts and equipment. However, we do cover self-propelled vehicles or machines, provided they are not licensed for use on public roads and are:
  a. Used mainly to service the described location; or
  b. Designed and used to assist handicapped persons, while the vehicles or machines are inside a building at the described location;
	The SFIP does not cover self-propelled vehicles or machinery. There are two specific instances where coverage is provided, so long as:
	
	  (1) the vehicle or machinery is not licensed for use on public roads.
	  (2) specific documentation is provided to support the claim.
	
	Under (a), the described location must be the type that would reasonably require service by means of the vehicle or machinery in question. Secondly, there must be evidence the described location is routinely serviced in support of what is claimed under this provision. Vehicles and machinery that are part of or service a business operation at the described location do not qualify for coverage under this provision.
	
	Under (b), a vehicle or machinery is covered if it is designed and used as mobility vehicles for persons with disabilities. The vehicle or machinery is not covered if it is not designed to assist persons with disabilities, or not used by persons with disabilities. As an example, a typical golf cart is not covered under this provision, even if it is used by persons with disabilities, unless

	IV. Property Not Covered	
	Policy Language	**Additional Explanation**
		designed or modified specifically to assist persons with disabilities.
		Under both (a) and (b), the vehicle or machinery must be inside a building at the location described on the declarations page for coverage, provided all other policy terms and conditions apply.
6.	Land, land values, lawns, trees, shrubs, plants, growing crops, or animals;	• The SFIP does not cover any type of live plant located inside or outside of the building. This provision does not apply to artificial plants used as indoor decor.
		• The SFIP will pay the cost to replace land removed by sudden erosion caused by waves or currents of water during a specific type of flood as defined at SFIP Section II.A. when such soil directly supports the insured building.
7.	Accounts, bills, coins, currency, deeds, evidences of debt, medals, money, scrip, stored value cards, postage stamps, securities, bullion, manuscripts, or other valuable papers;	• Scrip is a form of money issued by a local government or private organization, such as gift cards, coupons, or any substitute for legal tender.
		• The SFIP does not cover financial loss from damage or destruction of electronic data or the cost of restoring that data.
		• Other valuable papers include stocks certificates and bonds.
8.	Underground structures and equipment, including wells, septic tanks, and septic systems;	• Underground structures and equipment include, but are not limited to, wires, conduits, pipes, sewers, tanks, tunnels, sprinkler systems, similar property, and any apparatus connected beneath the surface of the ground. The SFIP provides coverage if other SFIP requirements are met for equipment installed used in the operation of underground structures and equipment installed above ground and within a building, for example, a sprinkler timer.
		• When installed, a sewage grinder pump is an integral part of the building's septic system. The grinder pump pulverizes waste for discharge into the septic drainage field. This item of property is not covered. However, the SFIP covers the sewage grinder pump's alarm service panel if installed above ground level and affixed to the building or its foundation. The SFIP does not cover alarm service panels installed to an item of property that is not covered, such as a support post to a deck.

IV. Property Not Covered

Policy Language	Additional Explanation
9. Those portions of walks, walkways, decks, driveways, patios, and other surfaces, all whether protected by a roof or not, located outside the perimeter, exterior walls of the insured building;	The SFIP pays to repair or replace damage to any existing egress on the sides of a building, including underneath an elevated building. For each existing egress, NFIP covers one 16 square foot landing and a single set of stairs, and one landing per staircase. The SFIP covers materials of a like kind and quality, such as concrete, wood, or composite wood material. Covered items include any existing hand or support rail, support posts, and hardware. The SFIP does not cover improvements such as lighting or finishing (paint or preservative stains).

The SFIP does not cover the cost to comply with Americans with Disabilities Act of 1990 (ADA) regulations; however, the SFIP will repair or replace an existing flood damaged handicap ramp shown in Figure 28 for egress, in lieu of the 16 SF of landing and steps.

Figure 28. Existing Handicap Ramp |
| 10. Containers including related equipment, such as, but not limited to, tanks containing gases or liquids; | The SFIP does not cover fuel tanks, pressure tanks, and well water tanks located outside of the insured building or an eligible detached garage. The SFIP does not cover containers outside of the building, including shipping containers used for storage or residential purposes, unless the container meets the definition of a building.

The SFIP covers fuel tanks, water tanks, and pressure tanks inside or directly underneath the building, including in a basement or crawlspace, under Coverage A – Building Property, when installed as part of a utility system that services the building.

Under Coverage B – Personal Property, the SFIP will cover any container |

IV. Property Not Covered

Policy Language	Additional Explanation
	inside of a building that is used for household or personal purposes such as oxygen tanks for medical reasons, small fuel tanks for filling lawn equipment, or sealed portable fuel canisters for cooking such as for camping or outdoor grilling. Containers used for the storage of food are not applicable to this provision. Containers such as paint cans can be covered but only for the value of what is stored, and not for the value of the container.
	Because containers and tanks are either sealed or made of material meant for contact with liquid, including corrosive liquids, the claim should take into account the proper scope of damage and first consider if the item is reusable after rinsing and cleaning.
11. Buildings or units and all their contents if more than 49% of the actual cash value of the building or unit is below ground, unless the lowest level is at or above the base flood elevation and is below ground by reason of earth having been used as insulation material in conjunction with energy efficient building techniques;	A building must have over 51 percent of its actual cash value above ground level. This calculation relies solely upon the ACV, not on concepts like square footage, volume, or otherwise.
	Items of property that are not covered under Coverage A – Building Property, should not be included in the building valuation. Claims handling should pay close attention to subterranean or earth dwellings and certain buildings located at sanitation facilities.
12. Fences, retaining walls, seawalls, bulkheads, wharves, piers, bridges, and docks;	FEMA considers these items covered when physically connected to a building and directly supportive and integral to the building's foundation, even if it has a secondary purpose such as a retaining wall.
13. Aircraft or watercraft, or their furnishings and equipment;	• The SFIP covers remote-controlled boats, aircraft, and drones or UAVs (Unmanned Aerial Vehicles) designed and intended for recreational use only, and not used to carry people or cargo, or for commercial use. The same policy provisions that apply to other personal property apply to these items. • The SFIP does not cover drones or UAVs registered with the Federal Aviation Administration for purposes other than recreational model aircraft. • Watercraft includes any vessel that travels on water, including surfboards. Pool toys are not watercraft. • The SFIP does not cover furnishings and equipment for non-covered

IV. Property Not Covered

Policy Language	Additional Explanation
	watercraft and aircraft, including parts and other items identified for use with watercraft or aircraft.
	• This exclusion does not apply to fishing equipment like fishing poles, lures, and the like.
14. Hot tubs and spas that are not bathroom fixtures, and swimming pools, and their equipment such as, but not limited to, heaters, filters, pumps, and pipes, wherever located;	N/A
15. Property not eligible for flood insurance pursuant to the provisions of the Coastal Barrier Resources Act and the Coastal Barrier Improvement Act of 1990 and amendments to these Acts;	The SFIP does not provide flood insurance coverage for a building constructed or substantially improved after the U.S. Department of Interior's Fish and Wildlife Service (FWS) designates it as within Coastal Barrier Resources System (CBRS) boundaries or as Otherwise Protected Areas (OPAs). See FWS website for more information.
16. Personal property owned by or in the care, custody or control of a unit owner, except for property of the type and under the circumstances set forth under III. Coverage B–Personal Property of this policy;	The SFIP covers household property usually found in living quarters (See General Property Form Section III.B.2.a.)
17. A residential condominium building located in a Regular Program community.	N/A

V. Exclusions

Policy Language	Additional Explanation
A. We only pay for direct physical loss by or from flood, which means that we do not pay you for:	
1. Loss of revenue or profits;	The SFIP does not cover the costs to pack, move, or store personal property from the insured building or return it to the building when an owner repairs the building or cannot occupy it.
2. Loss of access to the insured property or described location;	
3. Loss of use of the insured property or described location;	
4. Loss from interruption of business or production;	
5. Any additional expenses incurred while the insured building is being repaired or is unable to be occupied for any reason;	

V. Exclusions

	Policy Language	Additional Explanation
6.	The cost of complying with any ordinance or law requiring or regulating the construction, demolition, remodeling, renovation, or repair of property, including removal of any eligible debris. This exclusion does not apply to any eligible activities we describe in Coverage D—Increased Cost of Compliance; or	The SFIP does not cover replacing non-flood damaged property required to comply with government codes, ordinances, or regulations. For example, the SFIP does not cover the cost of replacing an undamaged interior HVAC unit to match a replaced exterior HVAC unit because of a change in size, SEER-rating, refrigerant, or any other reason even if local, state, or federal code required the upgrade.
7.	Any other economic loss you suffer.	
B.	We do not insure a loss directly or indirectly caused by a flood that is already in progress at the time and date:	
1.	The policy term begins; or	NFIP adjusts flood insurance losses individually. Flood insurance benefits are available if an insured property suffers a covered loss caused by a general condition of flooding, as defined by the SFIP.
2.	Coverage is added at your request.	See Flood-In-Progress Exclusion in Section 2 of this manual.
C.	We do not insure for loss to property caused directly by earth movement even if the earth movement is caused by flood. Some examples of earth movement that we do not cover are:	The SFIP is a single-peril policy that only pays for covered damage due to direct physical loss by or from flood, defined in the policy in Section II. The SFIP does not cover damage resulting from an intervening cause of loss, even if the resulting cause is due to flood. The SFIP does not cover damage that results when saturated soils cause the soil below ground level to sink, expand, compact, destabilize, or otherwise lose its load-bearing capacity such as from voids or rotten organic matter when the soil dries. The SFIP does not cover earth movement; each form of earth movement is an intervening cause of loss and a separate peril.
1.	Earthquake;	
2.	Landslide;	
3.	Land subsidence;	
4.	Sinkholes;	
5.	Destabilization or movement of land that results from accumulation of water in subsurface land areas; or	The SFIP's exclusion for other perils, such as fire, exemplifies the exclusion of earth movement as a cause of loss. When a flood causes a fire, which damages the building during inundation or after floodwaters recede, NFIP does not cover the resulting fire and smoke damage to the building even if flood directly caused the fire.
6.	Gradual erosion	
	We do, however, pay for losses from mudflow and land subsidence as a result of erosion that are specifically covered under our definition of flood (see A.1.c. and II.A.2.).	The SFIP covers damage to a building if the damage results from the collapse or subsidence of land that is the direct result of sudden erosion or undermining to the building's support soil underneath or directly along the perimeter foundation of the building from waves or currents of floodwater (velocity flow) during a flood from the overflow of inland or tidal waters or mudflow. This includes damage to the foundation of the building and any resulting damage to interior and exterior finishes.

V. Exclusions

Policy Language	Additional Explanation
D. We do not insure for direct physical loss caused directly or indirectly by:	The SFIP does not cover damage caused by gradual erosion.
1. The pressure or weight of ice;	N/A
2. Freezing or thawing;	
3. Rain, snow, sleet, hail, or water spray;	When the policyholder is prevented access to promptly remove wetted building and personal property items, and this delay directly results in water, moisture, mildew or mold damage to building and personal property items not in physical contact with surface floodwater, this damage could be covered.
4. Water, moisture, mildew, or mold damage that results primarily from any condition:	As examples:
a. Substantially confined to the insured building; or	• Local authorities restrict access to the area, or
b. That is within your control including, but not limited to:	• Prolonged inundation of floodwater prevents access to the area.
(1) Design, structural, or mechanical defects;	The claim file must include proper documentation, such as but not limited to photographs, an acceptable explanation provided by the adjuster, or a signed statement from the policyholder or community official that supports the payment for property damages above the documented water height.
(2) Failures, stoppages, or breakage of water or sewer lines, drains, pumps, fixtures, or equipment; or	For instances when coverage and payment are not recommended, the claim file should include information that documents the policyholder's failure to inspect and maintain their insured property or take reasonable measures to reduce damage when it is feasible to do so.
(3) Failure to inspect and maintain the property after a flood recedes;	The SFIP does not cover damage caused by long-term exposure to moisture, water, rot, and insect infestation. This includes damage from the lack of climate control inside the building when the approach to repair does not include the timely repair to the building HVAC system.
	The SFIP does not cover pre-existing damage to structural building components, such as damage caused by rot, or for any resulting damage to non-structural finish building material.
5. Water or water-borne material that:	The adjuster must document that a flood occurred in the area and that the flood was the proximate cause of the back-up of the sewer or drain, overflow of the sump pump, pump failure, seepage of water, or damage due to the pressure or weight of water (hydrostatic pressure), in the claim file. See SFIP Section II.A and related commentary under the definition of flood.
a. Backs up through sewers or drains;	
b. Discharges or overflows from a sump, sump pump, or related equipment; or	When paying a loss due to a flood in the area proximately causing discharge or overflow of water or water-borne material from a sump, sump pump, or related
c. Seeps or leaks on or through the covered property;	

V. Exclusions

Policy Language	Additional Explanation
unless there is a flood in the area and the flood is the proximate cause of the sewer or drain backup, sump pump discharge or overflow, or the seepage of water;	equipment, the insurer must document the claim file to show that a property policy endorsement or policy rider did not also cover the loss. If the property policy does provide coverage, the SFIP payment must apply a proportional loss distribution, as stated under Section VII.C. "Other Insurance". The adjuster must document a flood occurred in the area, and that the flood was the proximate cause of the back-up of the sewer or drain, overflow of the sump pump, pump failure, seepage of water, or damage due to the pressure or weight of water (hydrostatic pressure). A flood is two or more parcels of partial or complete inundation of normally dry land, or two or more continuous acres of normally dry land. For coverage under this provision, the condition of flood does not have to be on the parcel of land described at the location; it may be within the proximate area.
6. The pressure or weight of water unless there is a flood in the area and the flood is the proximate cause of the damage from the pressure or weight of water;	Refer to SFIP Section V.D.5. above.
7. Power, heating, or cooling failure unless the failure results from direct physical loss by or from flood to power, heating, or cooling equipment situated on the described location;	The SFIP does not cover damage to insured property when caused by a power surge or power outage that originates from the failure or shutting down of equipment that is not located at the described location, even if the reason is a direct result of a flood. For example, the local utility operator may shut down a section of the electrical grid to avoid system damage from a flood. When the power returns to the electrical grid, the initial surge of electricity can damage insured property. Under this loss description, the damage is not covered. The SFIP covers damage to any covered building or personal property item, such as the building's main service, home security system, a plugged-in television, or to the HVAC system, when a flood physically damages related system equipment installed at the described location. For example, if the flood damages power equipment at the described location creating an electrical short within the power system resulting in damage to another item of property part of or connected to the power system, the damage to the item is also covered, even though it was not physically touched by floodwater. Under this loss description, the damage is considered a direct physical loss by or from flood. To cover the loss described, the adjuster must document the cause of loss in the claim file to rule out the possibility of a non-covered cause, such as described in the previous paragraph.

V. Exclusions

Policy Language	Additional Explanation
8. Theft, fire, explosion, wind, or windstorm;	N/A
9. Anything that you or your agents do or conspire to do to cause loss by flood deliberately; or	
10. Alteration of the insured property that significantly increases the risk of flooding.	
E. We do not insure for loss to any building or personal property located on land leased from the Federal Government, arising from or incident to the flooding of the land by the Federal Government, where the lease expressly holds the Federal Government harmless under flood insurance issued under any Federal Government program.	N/A

VI. Deductibles

Policy Language	Additional Explanation
A. When a loss is covered under this policy, we will pay only that part of the loss that exceeds the applicable deductible amount, subject to the limit of liability that amount, subject to the limit of liability that applies. The deductible amount is shown on the Declarations Page. However, when a building under construction, alteration, or repair does not have at least two rigid exterior walls and a fully secured roof at the time of loss, your deductible amount will be two times the deductible that would otherwise apply to a completed building.	
B. In each loss from flood, separate deductibles apply to the building and personal property insured by this policy.	
C. No deductible applies to: 1. III.C.2. Loss Avoidance Measures; or 2. III.D. Increased Cost of Compliance.	The SFIP applies a separate deductible to both building and personal property losses. The SFIP will only pay that portion of the loss that exceeds the applicable deductibles. For building and personal property losses, the insurer should take the deductible from the gross loss before applying policy limits. For example, if the covered loss is $340,000, the policy limit is $300,000, and the deductible is $10,000. The insurer should apply the deductible to the $340,000 loss, which leaves $330,000, meaning the insurer should pay the $300,000 policy limit. The SFIP does not apply the excess loss to items subject to Special Limits to reduce the personal property deductible.

VII. General Conditions

Policy Language	Additional Explanation
A. Pair and Set Clause In case of loss to an article that is part of a pair or set, we will have the option of paying you: 1. An amount equal to the cost of replacing the lost, damaged, or destroyed article, less depreciation, or 2. An amount which represents the fair proportion of the total value of the pair or set that the lost, damaged, or destroyed article bears to the pair or set.	If the damaged property item is ruined, and cannot be replaced individually as a single item, and this renders the other item in the pair or the set unusable or worthless, then the SFIP pays for the pair or set. **Examples:** Left shoe ruined by flood, and the right shoe undamaged. The left shoe cannot be purchased without the right, rendering the undamaged right shoe unusable. The SFIP covers a new pair of shoes. Other similar examples include a ruined china base cabinet and undamaged matching china base top; half the seats

VII. General Conditions

Policy Language	Additional Explanation
	ruined in a sectional sofa; a ruined left window curtain and an undamaged right window curtain.
	If the damaged property item is ruined and can be replaced individually as a single item with like kind and quality, and this renders the other item or the set usable, the SFIP will only cover the damaged/ruined item along with the reasonable cost for like kind and quality, except in the case of the Section V. Exclusion (A)(6) for ordinance or law, and the like.
	Examples: Base cabinets ruined by flood with the upper cabinets undamaged. The upper cabinets remain usable. The SFIP allows replacing the base cabinets with like kind and quality, including reasonable costs to match the new base cabinets with existing undamaged cabinets. Other similar examples include a damaged dresser and undamaged or repairable matching armoire and nightstands; a ruined dining table leaf and undamaged or repairable dining table; a ruined granite cabinet countertop and salvageable granite island countertop.
	Example: An outdoor heating, ventilation, and air conditioning (HVAC) unit is ruined by flood, and the interior HVAC unit is undamaged. Due to Department of Energy code requirements regarding energy efficiency, or an Environmental Protection Agency (EPA)–mandate regarding refrigerant type, a replacement outdoor HVAC unit that works with the existing interior HVAC unit is unavailable, rendering the undamaged interior unit unusable. Section VII (A) Pair and Set clause is superseded by Section V Exclusions (A)(6) and the SFIP only allows to replace the outdoor HVAC unit with like kind and quality, and does not cover replacement of the undamaged interior HVAC unit.

B. Concealment of Fraud and Policy Voidance

1. With respect to all insureds under this policy, this policy: a. Is void, b. Has no legal force or effect, c. Cannot be renewed, and d. Cannot be replaced by a new NFIP policy, if, before or after a loss, you or any other insured or your agent have at any time: (1) Intentionally concealed or misrepresented any material fact or circumstance,	When claims professionals suspect wrongful acts or misrepresentations on a claim by a policyholder or their representatives: • The adjuster should promptly submit written notification with supporting documentation to the insurer. The adjuster should not draw any conclusions regarding the suspected fraud and should only present facts in written reports. • The examiner should engage management to determine if the insurer should refer the matter to the FEMA Fraud Unit (email: StopFEMAFraud@fema.dhs.gov) and the insurer's investigative unit for a Reservation of Rights.

VII. General Conditions

Policy Language	Additional Explanation
(2) Engaged in fraudulent conduct, or (3) Made false statements relating to this policy or any other NFIP insurance.	
2. This policy will be void as of the date wrongful acts described in B.1. above were committed.	The SFIP will be void if the proper authorities determine any part of a claim was fraudulent.
3. Fines, civil penalties, and imprisonment under applicable Federal laws may also apply to the acts of fraud or concealment described above.	
4. This policy is also void for reasons other than fraud, misrepresentation, or wrongful act. This policy is void from its inception and has no legal force under the following conditions: a. If the property is located in a community that was not participating in the NFIP on the policy's inception date and did not join or re-enter the program during the policy term and before the loss occurred; or b. If the property listed on the application is otherwise not eligible for coverage under the NFIP.	When a community no longer participates in the NFIP, an active SFIP will remain in force up to the day before the policy renewal date. Refer to the Flood Insurance Manual for other reasons why a building may be ineligible for coverage.
C. Other Insurance	
1. If a loss covered by this policy is also covered by other insurance that includes flood coverage not issued under the Act, we will not pay more than the amount of insurance that you are entitled to for lost, damaged, or destroyed property insured under this policy subject to the following: a. We will pay only the proportion of the loss that the amount of insurance that applies under this policy bears to the total amount of insurance covering the loss, unless C.1.b. or c. below applies. b. If the other policy has a provision stating that it is excess insurance, this policy will be primary. c. This policy will be primary (but subject to its own deductible) up to the deductible in the other flood policy (except another policy as described in C.1.b. above). When the other deductible amount is reached, this policy will participate in the same proportion that the	Other insurance includes primary flood coverage provided by a private carrier or any other insurance that duplicates SFIP coverage. Personal lines and commercial policies may have endorsements for sewer and sump or drain backup. Considerations include: 1. The other insurance clause of the other policy would determine which policy is excess or primary. 2. If the other policy is silent, proportion the claim. 3. If the endorsement excludes the peril of flood, the SFIP is primary for the direct physical damage by or from flood. • Use the following formula to determine the NFIP's share of the loss: **NFIP share** = ((SFIP policy limit ÷ total insurance) x loss) - other insurance deductible • Use the following formula to determine the other insurance's share of the loss:

VII. General Conditions

Policy Language	Additional Explanation
amount of insurance under this policy bears to the total amount of both policies, for the remainder of the loss.	• **Other insurance share** = ((other insurance policy limit ÷ total insurance) x loss) - other insurance deductible • Use the following formula to determine the NFIP payment: **NFIP payment** = NFIP share + other insurance deductible – SFIP deductible Below is an example of how to apply the formulas to compute the insurer's shares and NFIP payment for a $480,000 loss. Table 7: Insurance Coverage and Deductibles <table><tr><th>Insurance</th><th>Coverage</th><th>Deductible</th></tr><tr><td>NFIP</td><td>$250,000</td><td>$5,000</td></tr><tr><td>Other</td><td>$500,000</td><td>$15,000</td></tr><tr><td>Total</td><td>$750,000</td><td></td></tr></table> • **NFIP share:** (($250,000 ÷ $750,000) x $480,000) - $15,000 = $145,000 • **Other insurance share:** (($500,000 ÷ $750,000) x $480,000) - $15,000 = $305,000.00 • **NFIP payment:** $145,000.00 + $15,000 - $5,000 = $155,000.00 **IMPORTANT** – Use the order of operations as shown, starting with the innermost parentheses, for accurate calculation.
2. Where this policy covers a condominium association and there is a flood insurance policy in the name of a unit owner that covers the same loss as this policy, then this policy will be primary.	N/A
D. Amendments, Waivers, Assignment	
This policy cannot be changed nor can any of its provisions be waived without the express written consent of the Federal Insurance Administrator. No action that we take under the terms of this policy can constitute a waiver of any of our rights. You may assign this policy in writing when you transfer title of your property to someone else except under these conditions: 1. When this policy covers only personal property; or 2. When this policy covers a structure during the course of construction.	The SFIP allows the assignment of the policy when the title to the property transfers to a new owner. The SFIP does not allow the assignment of a claim. The only exception to this is a Coverage D – Increased Cost of Compliance (ICC) claim that can transfer in conjunction with a FEMA project, such as a Hazard Mitigation Grant Program (HMGP) grant. Typically, the policyholder assigns the claim to a community, which typically uses the payment for the community's non-Federal match for the project. The

VII. General Conditions

Policy Language	Additional Explanation
	policyholder may only assign the part of the ICC benefit used to meet the project requirements.
E. Cancellation of Policy by You	
1. You may cancel this policy in accordance with the applicable rules and regulations of the NFIP.	Policyholders must have a valid reason to cancel their flood insurance coverage during a policy term.
2. If you cancel this policy, you may be entitled to a full or partial refund of premium also under the applicable rules and regulations of the NFIP.	See the Flood Insurance Manual for detailed information.
F. Non-Renewal of Policy by Us	
Your policy will not be renewed:	When a community no longer participates in the NFIP, an active SFIP will remain in force up to the day before the policy renewal date.
1. If the community where your covered property is located stops participating in the NFIP; or	Coverage may not be available for a building constructed or altered in violation of state or local floodplain management laws, regulations, or ordinances. Section 1316 of the Act allows a state or community to declare a building in violation of its floodplain management rules. When a state or community declares that a building is in violation of Section 1316, the building and any contents in it are not eligible for SFIP coverage. Insurers have a list of buildings with Section 1316 violations that are ineligible for NFIP coverage. When the owner corrects the violation, the building becomes eligible for coverage again. The examiner should verify the building's eligibility.
2. If your building has been declared ineligible under section 1316 of the Act.	
G. Reduction and Reformation Coverage	
1. If the premium we received from you was not enough to buy the kind and amount of coverage that you requested, we will provide only the amount of coverage that can be purchased for the premium payment we received.	If the policyholder gives the insurer a premium that will not purchase the amounts of insurance requested, the insurer must issue the policy for the insurance coverage amount the premium will purchase for a one-year policy term.
2. The policy can be reformed to increase the amount of coverage resulting from the reduction described in G.1. above to the amount you requested as follows:	After a Loss:
a. Discovery of Insufficient Premium or Incomplete Rating Information Before a Loss.	• The insurer will send a bill for the required additional premium for the current policy term only. This is an exception to the SFIP Provisions requiring the current and the prior policy terms.
(1) If we discover before you have a flood loss that your premium payment was not enough to buy the requested amount of	• If the insurer receives the premium within 30 days from the date of the bill, the insurer should increase the policy limits to the originally requested amount effective as of the beginning of the current policy term.

VII. General Conditions

Policy Language	Additional Explanation
coverage, we will send you and any mortgagee or trustee known to us a bill for the required additional premium for the current policy term (or that portion of the current policy term following any endorsement changing the amount of coverage). If you or the mortgagee or trustee pay the additional premium within 30 days from the date of our bill, we will reform the policy to increase the amount of coverage to the originally requested amount effective to the beginning of the current policy term (or subsequent date of any endorsement changing the amount of coverage).	• If the insurer does not receive the additional premium by the due date, the insurer must settle the claim based on the previously submitted premium and results in reduced policy limits. Exceptions for Incorrect Flood Zone or BFE After a Loss. When the insurer discovers that an incorrect flood zone or BFE resulted in insufficient premium, the following exceptions apply:
(2) If we determine before you have a flood loss that the rating information we have is incomplete and prevents us from calculating the additional premium, we will ask you to send the required information. You must submit the information within 60 days of our request. Once we determine the amount of additional premium for the current policy term, we will follow the procedure in G.2.a.(1) above.	• The insurer should calculate any additional premium due prospectively from the date of discovery. • The insurer should apply the automatic reduction in policy limits effective on the date of discovery. Incorrect Policy Form. The insurer must use the correct policy form before making a loss payment. When the insurer issues coverage using an incorrect SFIP form, the policy is void and the insurer must rewrite the coverage under the correct form. The provisions of the correct SFIP form apply.
(3) If we do not receive the additional premium (or additional information) by the date it is due, the amount of coverage can only be increased by endorsement subject to any appropriate waiting period.	• The insurer must reform the coverage limits according to the provisions of the correct SFIP form. • Coverage cannot exceed the coverage issued under the incorrect policy form. See the Flood Insurance Manual for detailed information.
b. Discovery of Insufficient Premium or Incomplete Rating Information After a Loss. (1) If we discover after you have a flood loss that your premium payment was not enough to buy the requested amount of coverage, we will send you and any mortgagee or trustee known to us a bill for the required additional premium for the current and the prior policy terms. If you or the mortgagee or trustee pay the additional premium within 30 days of the date of our bill, we will reform the policy to increase the amount of coverage to the originally requested amount effective to the beginning of the prior policy term. (2) If we discover after you have a flood loss that the rating information we have is incomplete and prevents us from	

VII. General Conditions

Policy Language	Additional Explanation
calculating the additional premium, we will ask you to send the required information. You must submit the information before your claim can be paid. Once we determine the amount of additional premium for the current and prior policy terms, we will follow the procedure in G.2.b.(1) above.	
(3) If we do not receive the additional premium by the date it is due, your flood insurance claim will be settled based on the reduced amount of coverage. The amount of coverage can only be increased by endorsement subject to any appropriate waiting period.	
3. However, if we find that you or your agent intentionally did not tell us, or falsified any important fact or circumstance or did anything fraudulent relating to this insurance, the provisions of Condition B. above apply.	
H. Policy Renewal	
1. This policy will expire at 12:01 a.m. on the last day of the policy term.	The SFIP is not a continuous policy. It is a contract for a one-year term. Every policy contract expires at 12:01 a.m. on the last day of the policy term. Renewal of an expiring policy establishes a new policy term and new contractual agreement. See the Flood Insurance Manual for detailed information.
2. We must receive the payment of the appropriate renewal premium within 30 days of the expiration date.	
3. If we find, however, that we did not place your renewal notice into the U.S. Postal Service, or if we did mail it, we made a mistake, e.g., we used an incorrect, incomplete, or illegible address, which delayed its delivery to you before the due date for the renewal premium, then we will follow these procedures:	The adjuster should investigate the claim under a signed non-waiver agreement or a reservation of rights by the insurer when a policyholder reports a loss and there is uncertainty as to whether a policy is active.
a. If you or your agent notified us, not later than one year after the date on which the payment of the renewal premium was due, of nonreceipt of a renewal notice before the due date for the renewal premium, and we determine that the circumstances in the preceding paragraph apply, we will mail a second bill providing a revised due date, which will be 30 days after the date on which the bill is mailed.	
b. If we do not receive the premium requested in the second bill by the revised due date, then we will not renew the policy. In that case, the policy will remain as an expired policy as of the expiration date shown on the Declarations Page.	

VII. General Conditions

Policy Language	Additional Explanation
4. In connection with the renewal of this policy, we may ask you during the policy term to re-certify, on a Recertification Questionnaire that we will provide to you, the rating information used to rate your most recent application for or renewal of insurance.	
I. Conditions Suspending or Restricting Insurance	
We are not liable for loss that occurs while there is a hazard that is increased by any means within your control or knowledge.	The SFIP will not cover a flood loss or increased flood damage to insured property that the policyholder purposely or inadvertently causes. For example: a policyholder constructs a flood barrier to prevent floodwater from a river form reaching the building; however, the improvement now causes runoff during heavy rainfall events to collect behind the barrier and flood the building and a neighboring parcel or causes a prolonged condition of inundation creating additional damage inside the building.
	When the investigation of a loss reveals this provision might apply, the adjuster should notify the insurer at once and request immediate guidance.
J. Requirements in Case of Loss	
In case of a flood loss to insured property, you must:	The policyholder's claim begins with the written notice of loss.
1. Give prompt written notice to us;	The policyholder must report the loss to the insurer immediately; failure to provide a notice of loss to the insurer could prejudice the ability of the insurer to inspect the loss, identify the cause and extent of damage, and determine applicable coverage under the SFIP. If the policyholder delays reporting a loss, adjusters cannot help policyholders protect the property and avoid further damage.
	A policyholder's failure to provide timely notice of loss can be a basis for denial of a claim.
	• The adjuster should document the reason for a delay in the policyholder reporting a loss to the insurer.
	• The adjuster should execute a non-waiver agreement when there is a delay in reporting the loss. The non-waiver agreement should include the reason for the non-waiver and the policyholder's explanation for the delay. The adjuster should have the policyholder sign the non-waiver agreement immediately. If the policyholder refuses to sign the non-waiver agreement,

VII. General Conditions

Policy Language	Additional Explanation
	the insurer may decide to send a Reservation of Rights. The adjuster should continue the inspection and review.
2. As soon as reasonably possible, separate the damaged and undamaged property, putting it in the best possible order so that we may examine it;	The SFIP requires that the policyholder separate damaged from undamaged property, putting it in the best possible order so that the adjuster may examine it. It is the policyholder's duty to perform the separation described above and prepare an inventory of damaged property, including quantity, description, and the total amount of loss claimed. Any bills, receipts, photographs of damages, and related documents should be attached to the inventory.
3. Prepare an inventory of damaged property showing the quantity, description, actual cash value, and amount of loss. Attach all bills, receipts, and related documents;	If flood-damaged building or contents property is removed before the adjuster can examine it, the policyholder must photograph the items in their damaged location prior to moving the property and prepare the inventory.
	To minimize potential documentation issues, if possible, the policyholder should retain for the adjuster, samples or swatches of carpeting, wallpaper, furniture upholstery, window treatments, and other items of exceptional value where the type and quality of the material will influence the amount payable on the claim. Photographs should also include groups of items such as clothing, kitchen items, furniture, etc. The insurer will evaluate and consider these items and the policyholder's written inventory of damaged items.
4. Within 60 days after the loss, send us a proof of loss, which is your statement of the amount you are claiming under the policy signed and sworn to by you, and which furnishes us with the following information:	The proof of loss is the policyholder's statement of the amount of money they are requesting. The policyholder must sign and swear to the proof of loss and provide documentation to support that the loss is a direct physical loss by or from flood and the amount requested for the insurer to consider it completed. The policyholder (or Executor in the case of a deceased policyholder) is the only person who can sign the proof of loss.
a. The date and time of loss;	**SIGNED AND SWORN:**
b. A brief explanation of how the loss happened;	FEMA encourages the use of electronic signatures on proofs of loss and other NFIP-related submissions. FEMA will not deny the legal effect, validity, or enforceability of a signature solely because it is in electronic form. Insurers should accept electronic signatures in accordance with their general business practices and applicable laws.
c. Your interest (for example, "owner") and the interest, if any, of others in the damaged property;	**MULTIPLE PROOFS OF LOSS ALLOWED:**
d. Details of any other insurance that may cover the loss;	Policyholders must submit a completed proof of loss and documentation to support the amount requested initially and completed proofs of loss for any additional
e. Changes in title or occupancy of the insured property during the term of the policy;	
f. Specifications of damaged buildings and detailed repair estimates;	
g. Names of mortgagees or anyone else having a lien, charge, or claim against the insured property;	

VII. General Conditions

Policy Language	Additional Explanation
h. Details about who occupied any insured building at the time of loss and for what purpose; and	payment requests to the insurer within 60 days after the date of loss or within any extension of that deadline granted by FEMA.
i. The inventory of damaged property described in J.3. above.	**ONE CLAIM PER LOSS:**
5. In completing the proof of loss, you must use your own judgment concerning the amount of loss and justify that amount.	The proof of loss is not the claim. The claim is the policyholder's assertion that they are entitled to payment for a covered loss under the terms of the SFIP. A policyholder has only one claim from a flood event regardless of the number of proofs of loss and amount of documentation the policyholder may submit in support of that claim. The policyholder's ICC proof of loss is a request for benefits afforded under Coverage D – ICC, for that claim; it is not a separate claim.
6. You must cooperate with the adjuster or representative in the investigation of the claim.	N/A
7. The insurance adjuster whom we hire to investigate your claim may furnish you with a proof of loss form, and she or he may help you complete it. However, this is a matter of courtesy only, and you must still send us a proof of loss within sixty days after the loss even if the adjuster does not furnish the form or help you complete it.	
8. We have not authorized the adjuster to approve or disapprove claims or to tell you whether we will approve your claim.	Only the NFIP insurer has the authority to approve or deny a claim, to tell the policyholder if they will approve or deny a claim, or to provide approved payment details. The insurer must rely only upon the terms and conditions established by Federal statute, NFIP regulations, the Federal Insurance Administrator's interpretations, and the express terms of the SFIP. See 44 C.F.R. § 61.5(e) (2018).
9. At our option, we may accept the adjuster's report of the loss instead of your proof of loss. The adjuster's report will include information about your loss and the damages you sustained. You must sign the adjuster's report. At our option, we may require you to swear to the report.	The insurer, not the policyholder or their representative, determines whether to accept the adjuster's report signed and sworn to by the policyholder, instead of a proof of loss.
K. Our Options After Loss	
Options we may, in our sole discretion, exercise after loss includes the following:	This section sets forth the steps that insurers may take to require action on the part of the policyholder. If the policyholder fails to comply with the insurer's request, the policyholder is in breach of the insuring agreement, which may affect the payment of the claim.

VII. General Conditions

Policy Language	Additional Explanation
1. At such reasonable times and places that we may designate, you must:	
a. Show us or our representative the damaged property;	The policyholder must make the flood-damaged property available for examination as often as needed to verify the loss and claim. Insurer representatives will give the policyholder advanced notice of the specific time and meeting place to inspect the damaged property.
	The policyholder should document their loss with photographs before removing or disposing of damaged items that pose a health hazard, such as perishable food.
b. Submit to examination under oath, while not in the presence of another insured, and sign the same; and	The insurer can require the policyholder to submit to an examination under oath but not in the presence of another policyholder when there are questions concerning the claim. An examination under oath is a formal proceeding, typically conducted prior to a lawsuit, during which the insurer's representative questions a policyholder under oath in the presence of a court reporter. When requiring an examination under oath, the insurer should ask the policyholder to present information and documentation necessary to evaluate their claim. This can include books of accounts, financial records, receipts, income tax records, property settlement records, invoices, purchase orders, affidavits, and other materials to verify the loss.
c. Permit us to examine and make extracts and copies of:	The SFIP will not pay more than the amount of insurance that the policyholder is entitled to for the damaged, lost, or destroyed property insured under this policy if non-NFIP insurance covers a loss covered by the SFIP.
(1) Any policies of property insurance insuring you against loss and the deed establishing your ownership of the insured real property;	The policyholder must confirm the availability of other insurance to determine what the NFIP will pay. Examples include a homeowner's policy water damage or sump overflow endorsement, mobile homeowner's policy, scheduled property policy, renter's policy, builder's risk policy, etc.
	See SFIP Section VII.C. for Other Insurance.
(2) Condominium association documents including the Declarations of the condominium, its Articles of Association or Incorporation, Bylaws, and rules and regulations; and	A claim involving a unit in a condominium building requires the declarations of the condominium, bylaws, etc. to determine the policyholder's insurable interest in the building. Adjusters may have to determine if the RCBAP paid for any damages. NFIP will not pay for the same damage item twice or pay a claim for a residential unit that exceeds the statutory limits. Adjusters must provide documentation that a condominium association owns the insured building, not a homeowners' association or a building cooperative.

VII. General Conditions

Policy Language	Additional Explanation
(3) All books of accounts, bills, invoices, and other vouchers, or certified copies pertaining to the damaged property if the originals are lost.	Insurers may require the policyholder to provide information that documents the extent of the loss and the amount of the claim. Examples include books of accounts, bills, invoices, vouchers, and items showing the actual amounts paid to stores, contractors, or others for repair or replacement of items. This may also include photographs of the flood-damaged property that sufficiently and reasonably document the damage, quality of the item, and describe the damaged property. The policyholder can provide certified copies when the originals are lost or destroyed.
2. We may request, in writing, that you furnish us with a complete inventory of the lost, damaged, or destroyed property, including:	
a. Quantities and costs;	"Costs" is the amount to replace a personal property item with like kind and quality at current pricing, including the price for sales tax plus any applicable shipping and product assembly.
b. Actual cash values;	The actual cash value represents the replacement cost to replace, not repair, less applicable depreciation of all components of the price.
c. Amounts of loss claimed;	The amount of loss claimed is the amount of payment the policyholder asks to receive for the damaged and covered property.
d. Any written plans and specifications for repair of the damaged property that you can reasonably make available to us; and	Written plans and specifications for repair of the damaged property include contractor estimates, subcontractor bids, invoices, architectural reports and drawings, engineering reports, etc. This also includes water restoration or structural drying invoices and supporting documentation. NFIP will not accept a non-itemized, lump sum, or single line estimate or invoice in support of a claim.
e. Evidence that prior flood damage has been repaired.	Policyholders must provide evidence of repair from the previous flood damage whether or not they owned or insured the property. This includes any damage unrepaired by a previous owner. NFIP expects policyholders to maintain proof of repairs such as receipts, canceled checks, etc. in a safe location away from the threat of flood. When policyholders do not have proof of repairs, adjusters should request other forms of documentation such as: • Pre-flood photographs (social media or other family members) to compare old and replaced items. • Credit card or bank statements showing dates and dollar amounts of payments to contractors.

VII. General Conditions

Policy Language	Additional Explanation
	• Itemized statements and paid invoices from contractors.
3. If we give you written notice within 30 days after we receive your signed, sworn proof of loss, we may:	3.a. N/A
	3.b. Refer to Section VII.O. and other guidance including Salvage in Section 2 of this manual.
a. Repair, rebuild, or replace any part of the lost, damaged, or destroyed property with material or property of like kind and quality or its functional equivalent; and	
b. Take all or any part of the damaged property at the value we agree upon or its appraised value.	

L. No Benefit to Bailee

Policy Language	Additional Explanation
No person or organization, other than you, having custody of covered property will benefit from this insurance.	Bailment is the delivery of personal property by one person (the bailor) to another (the bailee) who holds the property for a certain purpose, such as service, under an expressed or implied-in-fact contract.
	The SFIP does not cover the bailee because bailment is a change of possession, not a change of ownership or title. When a customer (bailor) takes personal clothing to the dry cleaner (bailee) illustrates a good example. A bailment exists when the bailee has the clothing. The articles of clothing in the possession of the bailee are bailee goods and are not covered.
	Consignment is a written agreement where a consignor provides owned personal property to a consignee for sale and gives the consignee a percentage of the sale price when sold. The SFIP does not cover property on consignment.

M. Loss Payment

Policy Language	Additional Explanation
1. We will adjust all losses with you. We will pay you unless some other person or entity is named in the policy or is legally entitled to receive payment. Loss will be payable 60 days after we receive your proof of loss (or within 90 days after the insurance adjuster files an adjuster's report signed and sworn to by you in lieu of a proof of loss) and:	Adjusters and examiners should work with a policyholder or their authorized representative to understand the loss, prepare the estimate, and reach an agreed value for the loss.
	The insurer's obligation to pay and the 60-day timeframe to pay begin once the policyholder meets the requirements in Paragraph J, a proof of loss that meets all NFIP requirements, or after the signed and sworn to adjuster's report is received, and,
a. We reach an agreement with you;	
b. There is an entry of a final judgment; or	
c. There is a filing of an appraisal award with us, as provided in VII.P.	• Insurer and the policyholder agree on the payment amount, or

VII. General Conditions

Policy Language	Additional Explanation
	• There is an entry of final judgment or an appraisal award by a court of competent jurisdiction.

The insurer should promptly process all claims and payment requests. The insurer should communicate to policyholders any unforeseen delays in the claim examination process and advance undisputed claimed amounts at the earliest opportunity.

When the insurer cannot pay a completed proof of loss, the examiner and the adjuster should promptly communicate the necessary adjustments or documentation required to the policyholder. Insurers should work with policyholders to settle the loss without resorting to a denial of the claim by the insurer.

See Section 4 Appeals of this manual for information on denial letters |
| 2. If we reject your proof of loss in whole or in part you may:

a. Accept such denial of your claim;

b. Exercise your rights under this policy; or

c. File an amended proof of loss, as long as it is filed within 60 days of the date of the loss. | Courts have not accepted "reject your proof of loss" as sufficient language to communicate to the policyholder that the insurer has denied their claim in whole or in part. Hence, insurers should not use this language to deny all or part of a claim.

When the insurer issues a written denial, the policyholder has certain rights, which include filing an appeal directly to FEMA, filing suit against the insurer, or submitting an amended proof of loss with the documentation to support the requested loss and payment amount.

The one-year statute of limitations for filing suit begins when the insurer issues the first denial letter (42 U.S.C. § 4072; 44 C.F.R. § 62.22(a)). Submitting subsequent additional or amended proofs of loss does not reset the one-year statute of limitations. Adjusters and examiners must assist policyholders in identifying all opportunities for payment. This helps the policyholder recover, ensures customer satisfaction, and prevents unnecessary appeals and lawsuits. |

N. Abandonment

You may not abandon damaged or undamaged insured property to us.	N/A

O. Salvage

We may permit you to keep damaged insured property after a loss, and we will reduce the amount of the loss proceeds payable to you under the policy by the value of the salvage.	The insurer always has the right to seek salvage or to take possession of damaged property. Insurers should pursue opportunities for financial recovery when available.

See Salvage in Section 2 of this manual. |

VII. General Conditions

Policy Language	Additional Explanation

P. Appraisal

If you and we fail to agree on the actual cash value of the damaged property so as to determine the amount of loss, either may demand an appraisal of the loss. In this event, you and we will each choose a competent and impartial appraiser within 20 days after receiving a written request from the other. The two appraisers will choose an umpire. If they cannot agree upon an umpire within 15 days, you or we may request that the choice be made by a judge of a court of record in the state where the insured property is located. The appraisers will separately state the actual cash value and the amount of loss to each item. If the appraisers submit a written report of an agreement to us, the amount agreed upon will be the amount of loss. If they fail to agree, they will submit their differences to the umpire. A decision agreed to by any two will set the amount of actual cash value and loss.

Each party will:

1. Pay its own appraiser; and
2. Bear the other expenses of the appraisal and umpire equally. | See Appraisal in Section 2 of this manual. |

Q. Mortgage Clause

The word "mortgagee" includes trustee.

Any loss payable under Coverage A—Building Property will be paid to any mortgagee of whom we have actual notice, as well as any other mortgagee or loss payee determined to exist at the time of loss, and you, as interests appear. If more than one mortgagee is named, the order of payment will be the same as the order of precedence of the mortgages. If we deny your claim, that denial will not apply to a valid claim of the mortgagee, if the mortgagee:

1. Notifies us of any change in the ownership or occupancy, or substantial change in risk of which the mortgagee is aware;
2. Pays any premium due under this policy on demand if you have neglected to pay the premium; and
3. Submits a signed, sworn proof of loss within 60 days after receiving notice from us of your failure to do so.

All terms of this policy apply to the mortgagee. | The SFIP pays claims for building property to the named policyholder, mortgage holders, lienholders, other loss payees for whom we have actual notice, and any loss payee determined to exist at the time of loss. The mortgage clause is a contract within a contract. It is a contract between the mortgagee and the insurer within the contract between the policyholder and the insurer. Including the name of the mortgagee on each building claim payment is the surest way to keep this promise to the mortgagee. For all building payments, except Coverage C – Other Coverages and Coverage D – ICC, include all known mortgagees, as they are additional insureds.

The insurer may potentially include a loss payee or lienholder on Coverage B – Personal Property of whom the insurer received actual notice, such as from the U.S. Small Business Administration (SBA). If the insurer receives a letter of an SBA-approved loan, the SBA must be included on the building check(s) and the contents check(s) if the loan is for both real estate and personal or business property. |

VII. General Conditions	
Policy Language	Additional Explanation
The mortgagee has the right to receive loss payment even if the mortgagee has started foreclosure or similar action on the building. If we decide to cancel or not renew this policy, it will continue in effect for the benefit of the mortgagee only for 30 days after we notify the mortgagee of the cancellation or non-renewal. If we pay the mortgagee for any loss and deny payment to you, we are subrogated to all the rights of the mortgagee granted under the mortgage on the property. Subrogation will not impair the right of the mortgagee to recover the full amount of the mortgagee's claim.	
R. Suit Against Us	
You may not sue us to recover money under this policy unless you have complied with all the requirements of the policy. If you do sue, you must start the suit within one year of the date of the written denial of all or part of the claim, and you must file the suit in the United States District Court of the district in which the insured property was located at the time of loss. This requirement applies to any claim that you may have under this policy and to any dispute that you may have arising out of the handling of any claim under the policy.	The statute of limitations begins with the insurer's first written denial of the claim. Subsequent denial letters do not re-start the statute of limitations. Policyholders must file suit in a U.S. District Court in the district where the loss occurred within one year after the insurer's first written denial. Neither the Federal Insurance Administrator nor the insurer may extend the one-year statute of limitations to file suit.
S. Subrogation	
Whenever we make a payment for a loss under this policy, we are subrogated to your right to recover for that loss from any other person. That means that your right to recover for a loss that was partly or totally caused by someone else is automatically transferred to us, to the extent that we have paid you for the loss. We may require you to acknowledge this transfer in writing. After the loss, you may not give up our right to recover this money or do anything that would prevent us from recovering it. If you make any claim against any person who caused your loss and recover any money, you must pay us back first before you may keep any of that money.	When the adjuster believes there may be potential for subrogation, the adjuster completes FEMA Form 086-0-16 – Cause of Loss and Subrogation Report, to identify a potentially responsible third party; and characterize how their actions may have caused or worsened flood damage. Claim handling, review, and payment should proceed as normal. The insurer should make sure the Cause of Loss and Subrogation Report is complete and escalates the matter for a subrogation review. See Subrogation in Section 2 of this manual.
T. Continuous Lake Flooding	
1. If an insured building has been flooded by rising lake waters continuously for 90 days or more and it appears reasonably certain that a continuation	N/A

VII. General Conditions

Policy Language	Additional Explanation
of this flooding will result in a covered loss to the insured building equal to or greater than the building policy limits plus the deductible or the maximum payable under the policy for any one building loss, we will pay you the lesser of these two amounts without waiting for the further damage to occur if you sign a release agreeing: a. To make no further claim under this policy; b. Not to seek renewal of this policy; c. Not to apply for any flood insurance under the Act for property at the described location; and d. Not to seek a premium refund for current or prior terms. If the policy term ends before the insured building has been flooded continuously for 90 days, the provisions of this paragraph T.1. will apply when as the insured building suffers a covered loss before the policy term ends.	
2. If your insured building is subject to continuous lake flooding from a closed basin lake, you may elect to file a claim under either paragraph T.1. above or this paragraph T.2. (A "closed basin lake" is a natural lake from which water leaves primarily through evaporation and whose surface area now exceeds or has exceeded one square mile at any time in the recorded past. Most of the nation's closed basin lakes are in the western half of the United States, where annual evaporation exceeds annual precipitation and where lake levels and surface areas are subject to considerable fluctuation due to wide variations in the climate. These lakes may overtop their basins on rare occasions.) Under this paragraph T.2 we will pay your claim as if the building is a total loss even though it has not been continuously inundated for 90 days, subject to the following conditions: a. Lake flood waters must damage or imminently threaten to damage your building. b. Before approval of your claim, you must: (1) Agree to a claim payment that reflects your buying back the salvage on a negotiated basis; and (2) Grant the conservation easement described in FEMA's "Policy Guidance for Closed Basin Lakes," to be recorded in the office of the local recorder of deeds. FEMA, in consultation with the	The only Closed Basin Lake recognized by FEMA at this time is Devils Lake, North Dakota. Subject to all other provisions of the SFIP, if an insured building is subject to continuous lake flooding from Devils Lake, the following requirements must be met to be eligible for coverage under the terms of all SFIP forms: • The building must be in a participating community eligible for this coverage; and, • The subject building must have had NFIP flood insurance coverage continuously beginning on November 30, 1999, and any subsequent owner on or after November 30, 1999, must have an NFIP policy in effect within 60 days of the transfer of title (see: T. 2. g.) and, • The policyholder must grant a conservation easement (see: T. 2. b. (2), and the community must have adopted a permanent land-use ordinance on or before July 15, 2001 (see: T. 2. e. (1), (2), and (3). FEMA will not recognize any increases in coverage limits with effective dates on or after November 30, 1999 (see: T. 2. g.), except when offered by the insurer as a routine inflation-guard increase and purchased by the policyholder. Insured buildings not eligible for the provisions of T. 2. described above, but damaged by continuous

VII. General Conditions

Policy Language	Additional Explanation
community in which the property is located, will identify on a map an area or areas of special consideration (ASC) in which there is a potential for flood damage from continuous lake flooding. FEMA will give the community the agreed-upon map showing the ASC. This easement will only apply to that portion of the property in the ASC. It will allow certain agricultural and recreational uses of the land. The only structures that it will allow on any portion of the property within the ASC are certain, simple agricultural and recreational structures. If any of these allowable structures are insurable buildings under the NFIP and are insured under the NFIP, they will not be eligible for the benefits of this paragraph T.2. If a U.S. Army Corps of Engineers certified flood control project or otherwise certified flood control project later protects the property, FEMA will, upon request, amend the ASC to remove areas protected by those projects. The restrictions of the easement will then no longer apply to any portion of the property removed from the ASC; and (3) Comply with paragraphs T.1.a. through T.1.d. above. c. Within 90 days of approval of your claim, you must move your building to a new location outside the ASC. FEMA will give you an additional 30 days to move if you show that there is sufficient reason to extend the time. d. Before the final payment of your claim, you must acquire an elevation certificate and a floodplain development permit from the local floodplain administrator for the new location of your building. e. Before the approval of your claim, the community having jurisdiction over your building must: (1) Adopt a permanent land use ordinance, or a temporary moratorium for a period not to exceed 6 months to be followed immediately by a permanent land use ordinance, that is consistent with the provisions specified in the easement required in paragraph T.2.b. above; (2) Agree to declare and report any violations of this ordinance to FEMA so that under Sec. 1316 of the National Flood Insurance	lake flooding, will be eligible for those provisions described at T. 1. of the SFIP, subject to the terms and conditions of the T. 1. and the SFIP. Buildings in eligible communities that are subject to damage from the effects of the Closed Basin Lake, Devils Lake, North Dakota, may file claims if any portion of the insured building, as defined in the SFIP, is at the still-water level derived by official National Weather Service (NWS) still-water levels. See Appendix C in this manual for FEMA's "Policy Guidance for Closed Basin Lakes".

VII. General Conditions

Policy Language	Additional Explanation
Act of 1968, as amended, flood insurance to the building can be denied; and	
(3) Agree to maintain as deed-restricted, for purposes compatible with open space or agricultural or recreational use only, any affected property the community acquires an interest in. These deed restrictions must be consistent with the provisions of paragraph T.2.b. above except that even if a certified project protects the property, the land use restrictions continue to apply if the property was acquired under the Hazard Mitigation Grant Program or the Flood Mitigation Assistance Program. If a non-profit land trust organization receives the property as a donation, that organization must maintain the property as deed-restricted, consistent with the provisions of paragraph T.2.b. above.	
f. Before the approval of your claim, the affected State must take all action set forth in FEMA's "Policy Guidance for Closed Basin Lakes."	
g. You must have NFIP flood insurance coverage continuously in effect from a date established by FEMA until you file a claim under this paragraph T.2. If a subsequent owner buys NFIP insurance that goes into effect within 60 days of the date of transfer of title, any gap in coverage during that 60-day period will not be a violation of this continuous coverage requirement. For the purpose of honoring a claim under this paragraph T.2, we will not consider to be in effect any increased coverage that became effective after the date established by FEMA. The exception to this is any increased coverage in the amount suggested by your insurer as an inflation adjustment.	
h. This paragraph T.2. will be in effect for a community when the FEMA Regional Administrator for the affected region provides to the community, in writing, the following:	
(1) Confirmation that the community and the State are in compliance with the conditions in paragraphs T.2.e. and T.2.f. above, and	
(2) The date by which you must have flood insurance in effect.	

VII. General Conditions

Policy Language	Additional Explanation
U. Duplicate Policies Not Allowed	

1. Property may not be insured under more than one NFIP policy.
 	
If we find that the duplication was not knowingly created, we will give you written notice. The notice will advise you that you may choose one of several options under the following procedures:
 	
  a. If you choose to keep in effect the policy with the earlier effective date, you may also choose to add the coverage limits of the later policy to the limits of the earlier policy. The change will become effective as of the effective date of the later policy.
 	
  b. If you choose to keep in effect the policy with the later effective date, you may also choose to add the coverage limits of the earlier policy to the limits of the later policy. The change will be effective as of the effective date of the later policy.
 	
In either case, you must pay the pro rata premium for the increased coverage limits within 30 days of the written notice. In no event will the resulting coverage limits exceed the permissible limits of coverage under the Act or your insurable interest, whichever is less.
 	
We will make a refund to you, according to applicable NFIP rules, of the premium for the policy not being kept in effect.
 	
2. Your option under this Condition U. Duplicate Policies Not Allowed to elect which NFIP policy to keep in effect does not apply when duplicates have been knowingly created. Losses occurring under such circumstances will be adjusted according to the terms and conditions of the earlier policy. The policy with the later effective date must be canceled.
	The policyholder cannot benefit from the duplicate flood insurance coverage if a policyholder has two NFIP policies insuring the same property. The first policy purchased is the policy in force at the time of loss.
	
	When there is no loss involved, the policyholder may choose to keep either policy. If the policyholder chooses to combine the coverage amounts purchased, and the combined coverage does not exceed the maximum statutory limits, the effective date of the increased coverage begins on the renewal date of the second policy purchased.

V. Loss Settlement	
We will pay the least of the following amounts after application of the deductible: 1. The applicable amount of insurance under this policy; 2. The actual cash value; or 3. The amount it would cost to repair or replace the property with material of like kind and quality within a reasonable time after the loss.	An actual cash value loss settlement is the cost to repair or replace insured building items at the time of the loss, less the building deductible and less its physical depreciation.

VIII. Liberalization Clause

Policy Language	Additional Explanation
If we make a change that broadens your coverage under insurance as of the date we implement the change, provided this edition of our policy, but does not require any additional that this implementation date falls within 60 days before, or premium, then that change will automatically apply to your during, the policy term stated on the Declarations Page.	Insurers cannot apply additional coverages provided through the liberalization clause retroactively to losses that have occurred; insurers can apply it prospectively. The clause permits FEMA to give existing, active policyholders beneficial amendments without needing to separately endorse their policies but does not provide any retroactive effect.

IX. What Law Governs

Policy Language	Additional Explanation
This policy and all disputes arising from the handling of any Insurance Act of 1968, as amended (42 U.S.C. 4001, et seq.), claim under the policy are governed exclusively by the flood and Federal common law insurance regulations issued by FEMA, the National Flood Insurance Act of 1968, as amended (42 U.S.C. 4001, et seq.), and Federal common law.	N/A

This page was intentionally left blank.

4. Residential Condominium Building Association Policy

I. Agreement

Policy Language	Additional Explanation
Please read the policy carefully. The flood insurance provided is subject to limitations, restrictions, and exclusions. This policy covers only a residential condominium building in a regular program community. If the community reverts to emergency program status during the policy term and remains as an emergency program community at time of renewal, this policy cannot be renewed. The Federal Emergency Management Agency (FEMA) provides flood insurance under the terms of the National Flood Insurance Act of 1968 and its Amendments, and Title 44 of the Code of Federal Regulations. We will pay you for direct physical loss by or from flood to your insured property if you: 1. Have paid the correct premium; 2. Comply with all terms and conditions of this policy; and 3. Have furnished accurate information and statements. We have the right to review the information you give us at any time and to revise your policy based on our review.	This policy is under Federal law, unlike other property lines. Relevant definition at II.B.12 (direct physical loss). Policyholder responsibilities appear at Section VIII.J, K. post-loss underwriting at Section VIII.G.

II. Definitions

Policy Language	Additional Explanation
A. In this policy, "you" and "your" refer to the insured(s) shown on the Declarations Page of this policy. Insured(s) includes: Any mortgagee and loss payee named in the Application and Declarations Page, as well as any other mortgagee or loss payee, determined to exist at the time of loss in the order of precedence. "We," "us," and "our" refer to the insurer. Some definitions are complex because they are provided as they appear in the law or regulations or result from court cases. The precise definitions are intended to protect you.	
Flood	
1. A general and temporary condition of partial or complete inundation of two or more acres of normally dry land area or of two or more properties (one of which is your property) from:	For a general condition of flood to exist, the inundation must cover two or more acres of normally dry land or two or more parcels of land, one of which can be public property such as a roadway).
a. Overflow of inland or tidal waters,	The reference to "partial or complete inundation of two or more acres of normally dry land area or two or more properties" requires that the two or more acres must be continuous acres, and that the two or more inundated parcels of land must touch.
b. Unusual and rapid accumulation or runoff of surface waters from any source,	For mudflow definition, see SFIP Section II.B.19.
c. Mudflow.	
2. Collapse or subsidence of land along the shore of a lake or similar body of water as a result of erosion undermining caused by waves or currents of water exceeding anticipated cyclical levels which result in a flood as defined in A.1.a. above.	The SFIP also defines a flood as the collapse or subsidence of land along the shore of a lake or similar body of water from erosion or undermining caused by waves or currents of water (velocity flow) exceeding anticipated cyclical levels during a flood from the overflow of inland or tidal waters.
	The SFIP does not cover damage from any other cause, form, or type of earth movement. It also does not cover gradual erosion. See Exclusions at SFIP Section V.C.
B. The following are the other key definitions we use in this policy:	
1. Act	N/A
The National Flood Insurance Act of 1968 and any amendments to it.	
2. Actual Cash Value	The cost to replace a building, a building item, or a personal property item that includes all charges related to material, labor, and equipment. This price may include charges such as delivery, assembly, sales tax, and any applicable overhead and profit, and the like. Actual cash value is this cost to replace less applicable depreciation on all components of the cost.
The cost to replace an insured item of property at the time of loss, less the value of its physical depreciation.	
3. Application	The statement made and signed by the prospective policyholder or the agent when applying for a policy. The application contains information including the property description, information to determine eligibility, the policy form chosen, selected
The statement made and signed by you or your agent in applying for this policy. The application gives information we use to determine the eligibility of	

	II. Definitions	
Policy Language		**Additional Explanation**
the risk, the kind of policy to be issued, and the correct premium payment. The application is part of this flood insurance policy. For us to issue you a policy, the correct premium payment must accompany the application.		coverage and limits, deductible, and the premium amount.
4. Base Flood A flood having a one percent chance of being equaled or exceeded in any given year.		N/A
5. Basement Any area of the building, including any sunken room or sunken portion of a room, having its floor below ground level (subgrade) on all sides.		The SFIP definition for a basement means the floor level of a room or any area of a floor level in a building is below the ground level on all sides. This definition may differ from what policyholders may consider as their "basement." The SFIP considers a sunken room or sunken portion of a room to be a basement if the floor level is below the ground level on all sides. The entire below-ground-floor-level area, including walls and ceiling that may extend above grade, is subject to basement coverage limitations. Figure 29. Sunken Room Photograph credit Amber Flooring Ground-level is the surface of the ground immediately along the perimeter of the building. If an exterior area of egress out of the building is below the ground level on all sides, installed over a subgrade, the area of egress is below ground level. A subgrade is a surface of earth leveled off to receive a foundation such as a concrete slab of a building.

Policy Language	II. Definitions	Additional Explanation
		Figure 30. Ground Level vs. Below Ground Level

Below ground level   Ground level

Figure 31. Egress

Basement with below ground level egress

The insurer may need to engage a qualified, licensed professional (example: surveyor) to measure the floor level in question. See Section 2 of this manual. Sump wells are not basements because they are not a floor level.

6. Building

a. A structure with two or more outside rigid walls and a fully secured roof, that is affixed to a permanent site;

b. A manufactured home ("a manufactured home," also known as a mobile home, is a structure: built on a permanent chassis,

- The SFIP covers a building, manufactured home (mobile home), or travel trailer if it is located at the described location, as shown on the Declaration Page and only insures one building.

Policy Language	II. Definitions	Additional Explanation
transported to its site in one or more sections, and affixed to a permanent foundation); or A travel trailer without wheels, built on a chassis and affixed to a permanent foundation, that is regulated under the community's floodplain management and building ordinances or laws. c. Building does not mean a gas or liquid storage tank or a recreational vehicle, park trailer or other similar vehicle, except as described in B.6.c., above.		• The SFIP requires a building to be affixed to a permanent site, whereas it requires a manufactured home and a travel trailer to be affixed to a permanent foundation. • A travel trailer (recreational vehicle) with attached wheels is not a building. • A storage or shipping container, if it is used as a shed, storage building, or residence, must meet the definition of an eligible building. • "Affixed by weight" does not constitute affixed to a permanent site as used in the SFIP.
7. Cancellation The ending of the insurance coverage provided by this policy before the expiration date.		• The NFIP Flood Insurance Manual provides an exhaustive list for all valid policy cancellation reasons. • The expiration date is the ending of the policy term, the period of coverage provided by the insurance policy. • The policy term for the SFIP is one year, after any applicable waiting period.
8. Condominium That form of ownership of real property in which each unit owner has an undivided interest in common elements.	N/A	
9. Condominium Association The entity made up of the unit owners responsible for the maintenance and operation of: a. Common elements owned in undivided shares by unit owners; and b. Other real property in which the unit owners have use rights; where membership in the entity is a required condition of unit ownership.		A condominium association is an entity recognized by a state. Homeowners' associations, townhome associations, and cooperatives, and the like, are not condominium associations.
10. Declarations Page A computer-generated summary of information you provided in the application for insurance. The Declarations Page also describes the term of the policy, limits of coverage, and displays the premium and our name. The Declarations Page is a part of this flood insurance policy.	N/A	
11. Described Location The location where the insured building(s) or personal property are found. The described location is shown on the Declarations Page.	N/A	

Policy Language	II. Definitions	Additional Explanation
12. Direct Physical Loss By or From Flood Loss or damage to insured property, directly caused by a flood. There must be evidence of physical changes to the property.		The SFIP only pays for damage caused by a direct physical loss by or from flood, as defined by the SFIP. A direct physical loss means flood must physically contact the insured property and there must be evidence of physical change by or from flood to the insured building or insured personal property. Several SFIP provisions, each with its own criteria, address specific situations where the condition of direct physical loss by or from flood occurs despite an exclusion. In these specific situations, listed below, the insurer must thoroughly document the presence of the relevant criteria in the claim file for coverage and payment: • Losses from mudflow and collapse or subsidence of land as a result of erosion specifically covered under the SFIP definition of flood (see SFIP Section V.C., as well as II.A.1.c and II.A.2) • Back up of water and water-borne material through sewers or drains, where a flood is the proximate cause of the sewer or drain backup (see SFIP Section V.D.5.a.) • Discharge or overflow from a sump, sump pump, or related equipment, where a flood is the proximate cause of the sump pump discharge or overflow (see SFIP Section V.D.5.b.) • Seepage or leakage on or through the insured building, where a flood is the proximate cause of the seepage of water (see SFIP Section V.D.5.c.) • Pressure or weight of water, where a flood is the proximate cause of the damage from the pressure or weight of water (see SFIP Section V.D.6.)
13. Elevated Building A building that has no basement and that has its lowest elevated floor raised above ground level by foundation walls, shear walls, posts, piers, pilings, or columns.		For more information about elevated buildings, see Section 2 of this manual, Floor Elevation Lowest Floor Elevation. If the elevated floor in the building is in part supported by a structural slab-on-grade foundation, additional documentation may be necessary to verify the elevated rating for the building.
14. Emergency Program The initial phase of a community's participation in the National Flood Insurance Program. During this phase, only limited amounts of insurance are available under the Act.		N/A
15. Expense Constant A flat charge you must pay on each new or renewal policy to defray the expenses of the Federal Government related to flood insurance.		There is no longer an Expense Constant charge.

II. Definitions

Policy Language	Additional Explanation
16. Federal Policy Fee A flat charge you must pay on each new or renewal policy to defray certain administrative expenses incurred in carrying out the National Flood Insurance Program. This fee covers expenses not covered by the Expense Constant.	N/A
17. Improvements Fixtures, alterations, installations, or additions comprising a part of the insured dwelling or the apartment in which you reside.	N/A
18. Mudflow A river of liquid and flowing mud on the surface of normally dry land areas, as when earth is carried by a current of water. Other earth movements, such as landslide, slope failure, or a saturated soil mass moving by liquidity down a slope, are not mudflows.	A mudflow is liquified soil flowing in a manner akin to water flowing, which causes damage in a manner similar to moving water.
19. National Flood Insurance Program (NFIP) The program of flood insurance coverage and floodplain management administered under the Act and applicable Federal regulations in Title 44 of the Code of Federal Regulations, Subchapter B.	N/A
20. Policy The entire written contract between you and us. It includes: a. This printed form; b. The application and Declarations Page; c. Any endorsement(s) that may be issued; and d. Any renewal certificate indicating that coverage has been instituted for a new policy and new policy term. b. Only one dwelling, which you specifically described in the application, may be insured under this policy.	N/A
21. Pollutants Substances that include, but are not limited to, any solid, liquid, gaseous, or thermal irritant or contaminant, including smoke, vapor, soot, fumes, acids,	Testing for or monitoring of pollutants is not covered unless required by law. See Section V.F. of the SFIP.

II. Definitions

Policy Language	Additional Explanation
alkalis, chemicals, and waste. "Waste" includes, but is not limited to, materials to be recycled, reconditioned, or reclaimed.	
22. Post-FIRM Building A building for which construction or substantial improvement occurred after December 31, 1974, or on or after the effective date of an initial Flood Insurance Rate Map (FIRM), whichever is later.	Community Status Book
23. Probation Premium A flat charge you must pay on each new or renewal policy issued covering property in a community the NFIP has placed on probation under the provisions of 44 CFR 59.24.	N/A
24. Regular Program The final phase of a community's participation in the National Flood Insurance Program. In this phase, a Flood Insurance Rate Map is in effect and full limits of coverage are available under the Act.	N/A
25. Residential Condominium Building A building, owned and administered as a condominium, containing one or more family units and in which at least 75% of the floor area is residential.	N/A
26. Special Flood Hazard Area An area having special flood or mudflow, and/or flood-related erosion hazards, and shown on a Flood Hazard Boundary Map or Flood Insurance Rate Map as Zone A, AO, A1–A30, AE, A99, AH, AR, AR/A, AR/AE, AR/AH, AR/AO, AR/A1– A30, V1–V30, VE, or V.	All zones listed are SFHAs. However, the post-FIRM elevated building coverage limitations apply only to Zones A1–A30, AE, AH, AR, AR/A, AR/AE, AR/AH, AR/A1–A30, V1–V30, and VE, at SFIP Section III.A.8.
27. Unit A single-family unit you own in a condominium building.	N/A
28. Valued Policy A policy in which the insured and the insurer agree on the value of the property insured, that value being payable in the event of a total loss. The Standard Flood Insurance Policy is not a valued policy.	The SFIP is not a valued policy; it is a direct physical loss policy. The insurer agrees to pay a policyholder for insured property damaged by direct physical by or from flood, subject to the terms, conditions, and exclusion of the SFIP.

III. Property Covered

Policy Language	Additional Explanation
A. Coverage A—Building Property We insure against direct physical loss by or from flood to:	
1. The residential condominium building described on the Declarations Page at the described location, including all units within the building and the improvements within the units.	N/A
2. We also insure such building property for a period of 45 days at another location, as set forth in III.C.2.b., Property Removed to Safety.	N/A

III. Property Covered

Policy Language	Additional Explanation
3. Additions and extensions attached to and in contact with the dwelling by means of a rigid exterior wall, a solid load-bearing interior wall, a stairway, an elevated walkway, or a roof. At your option, additions and extensions connected by any of these methods may be separately insured. Additions and extensions attached to and in contact with the building by means of a common interior wall that is not a solid load-bearing wall are always considered part of the dwelling and cannot be separately insured.	A property owner has the option to separately insure an addition under its own SFIP if the addition, considered by itself, meets the definition of a building. Otherwise, an addition or extension is covered under the RCBAP as part of the building. **Figure 32. Examples of Additions and Extensions and the Five Means of Connection** Roof Elevated walkways Exterior rigid walls Load-bearing (solid) interior walls Stairs
4. The following fixtures, machinery and equipment, including its units, which are covered under Coverage A only: a. Awnings and canopies; b. Blinds; c. Carpet permanently installed over unfinished flooring;	• Blinds include vertical and horizontal types. • Central air conditioners include related built-in equipment for dehumidification, air filtering, and ventilation. • Walk-in freezers and coolers must be permanently installed or built in. Furnaces and radiators include heat pumps, boilers, and related installed equipment for humidification, air filtering, and ventilation.

III. Property Covered

Policy Language	Additional Explanation

d. Central air conditioners;
e. Elevator equipment;
f. Fire extinguishing apparatus;
g. Fire sprinkler systems;
h. Walk-in freezers;
i. Furnaces;
j. Light fixtures;
k. Outdoor antennas and aerials fastened to buildings;
l. Permanently installed cupboards, bookcases, paneling, and wallpaper;
m. Pumps and machinery for operating pumps;
n. Ventilating equipment;
o. Wall mirrors, permanently installed; and
p. In the units within the building, installed:
  (1) Built-in dishwashers;
  (2) Built-in microwave ovens;
  (3) Garbage disposal units;
  (4) Hot water heaters, including solar water heaters;
  (5) Kitchen cabinets;
  (6) Plumbing fixtures;
  (7) Radiators;
  (8) Ranges;
  (9) Refrigerators; and
  (10) Stoves.
	• Ranges, cooking stoves, ovens include cooktops, range hoods, and built-in cooking exhaust apparatuses.
	• Refrigerators include beverage coolers and other major appliances that refrigerate.
	• Refurbished collectible or antique major appliances, such as a refrigerator, stove, and the like, are paid at functional value less depreciation.

5. Materials and supplies to be used for construction, alteration or repair of the insured building while the materials and supplies are stored in a fully enclosed building at the described location or on an adjacent property.	N/A
6. A building under construction, alteration or repair at the described location.	The SFIP only covers buildings under construction affixed to a permanent site. For example, NFIP does not cover a building on temporary cribbing and not affixed to a permanent site.

III. Property Covered

Policy Language	Additional Explanation
a. If the structure is not yet walled or roofed as described in the definition for building (see II.B.6.a.), then coverage applies: (1) Only while such work is in progress; or (2) If such work is halted, only for a period of up to 90 continuous days thereafter. b. However, coverage does not apply until the building is walled and roofed if the lowest floor, including the basement floor, of a non-elevated building or the lowest elevated floor of an elevated building is: (1) Below the base flood elevation in Zones AH, AE, A1–30, AR, AR/AE, AR/AH, AR/A1–30, AR/A, AR/AO; or Below the base flood elevation adjusted to include the effect of wave action in Zones VE or V1–30. (2) The lowest floor levels are based on the bottom of the lowest horizontal structural member of the floor in Zones VE or V1–V30 and the top of the floor in Zones AH, AE, A1–A30, AR, AR/AE, AR/AH, AR/ A1–A30, AR/A, AR/AO.	The SFIP covers building materials and supplies for the insured building under construction stored in a fully enclosed building up to building policy limits per RCBAP Section III.A.5. When a building under construction, alteration, or repair does not have at least two rigid exterior walls and a fully secured roof at the time of loss, your deductible amount will be two times the deductible that would otherwise apply to a completed building. See RCBAP – Section VI.A. The SFIP does not cover a building under construction if work stops for more than 90 continuous days. Coverage will resume when work resumes. The SFIP does not cover tools for construction, such as forms, cribbing, power tools, etc.
7. A manufactured home or a travel trailer as described in the Definitions Section (See II.B.b. and c.). If the manufactured home is in a special flood hazard area, it must be anchored in the following manner at the time of the loss: a. By over-the-top or frame ties to ground anchors; or b. In accordance with the manufacturer's specifications; or c. In compliance with the community's floodplain management requirements unless it has been continuously insured by the NFIP at the same described location since September 30, 1982.	A manufactured (mobile) home is a structure built on a permanent chassis, transported to its site in one or more sections, and affixed to a permanent foundation. A travel trailer is not self-propelled and must be affixed to a permanent foundation in a manner that the community regulates under its floodplain management and building ordinances. The travel trailer must have its wheels removed in order to be eligible for coverage. A recreational vehicle is self-propelled and is not insurable. See SFIP Section IV. Property Not Covered, 4. For the SFIP to insure a manufactured home, the owner must affix it to a permanent foundation. A permanent foundation for a manufactured home may be a poured masonry slab, foundation walls, piers, or block supports. The foundation, not the wheels and or the axles, must support all of the weight of the manufactured (mobile) home. If the mobile home is in an SFHA, the owner must anchor it to a permanent foundation to resist flotation, collapse, or lateral movement by: • Providing over-the-top or frame ties to ground anchors.

III. Property Covered

Policy Language	Additional Explanation
	• Following the manufacturer's specification for anchoring.
	• Complying with the community's floodplain management requirements.
8. Items of property in a building enclosure below the lowest elevated floor of an elevated post-FIRM building located in zones A1-A30, AE, AH, AR, AR/A, AR/AE, AR/AH, AR/ A1-A30, V1-V30, or VE, or in a basement, regardless of the zone. Coverage is limited to the following:	When the Declarations Page reflects two zones, the current zone and the zone used for rating, the rating zone is used for coverage. This zone may be a grandfathered zone that remains in effect for coverage unless or until the home is substantially damaged, substantially improved, or there is a lapse in coverage.
a. Any of the following items, if installed in their functioning locations and, if necessary for operation, connected to a power source:	The current zone may be a different zone that reflects the zone designation in the current flood map. This zone is intended only for non-claim related purposes such as underwriting premiums and ICC applicability.
	Post-FIRM elevated building limitations do not apply to SFHA Zones A, AO, A99, AR/AO, V, and VO. Basement limitations apply regardless of zones.
	Basement limitations apply to the complete area defined as a basement--floors, walls, and ceilings.
	For an elevated building located in an SFHA, full coverage begins at the lowest elevated floor. This is the lowest floor raised above ground, even if the pilings extend beyond it (see Lowest Elevated Floor Determination in Section 2 of this manual.
	For items of property below, at, or level with the lowest elevated floor, the item(s) is subject to the coverage limitation. For example, a cabinet, door, window, or refrigerator that originates below, or straddles the line-level with the lowest elevated floor is not covered, even that portion or value at or above the lowest elevated floor.
	However, coverage can be provided for building materials and finishes installed above the lowest elevated floor, even if the items originate or overlaps the lowest elevated floor level when the function of the building material or finish is not reduced by cutting or removing the damaged and otherwise excluded building material physically located at or below the line-level equal with the lowest elevated floor. Examples include exterior siding, wood trim, drywall, paint, or insulation, even if the same item extends below the level of the lowest elevated floor. The building materials and finishes below the line level with the lowest elevated floor are still excluded. This coverage interpretation is in sync with new FEMA-approved building codes for new construction and substantially improved buildings.
	The SFIP does not cover items, interior or exterior, located below the lowest

III. Property Covered

Policy Language	Additional Explanation
	elevated floor of a post-FIRM elevated building in the stated zones.
(1) Central air conditioners;	Central air conditioners include related built-in equipment for dehumidification, air filtering, and ventilation.
(2) Cisterns and the water in them;	See Section 2 Claims Processes and Guidance in this manual.
(3) Drywall for walls and ceilings in a basement and the cost of labor to nail it, unfinished and unfloated and not taped, to the framing;	Unfinished, unfloated, and not taped drywall installed anywhere in a basement. The SFIP will also pay for unfinished, unfloated, and not taped drywall in lieu of paneling or any finished wall treatment.
	The SFIP does not cover interior framed walls or interior partition walls.
	For an elevated building located in an SFHA, full coverage begins at the lowest elevated floor. This is the lowest floor raised above ground, even if the pilings extend beyond it (see Lowest Elevated Floor Determination in Section 2, this manual). Items of property that include but not limited to, garage doors, exterior doors, windows, and drywall that originate below the lowest elevated floor are subject to the post-FIRM limitations and excluded.
	The SFIP does not cover items, interior or exterior, located below the lowest elevated floor of a post-FIRM elevated building.
(4) Electrical junction and circuit breaker boxes; (5) Electrical outlets and switches;	Electrical junction and circuit breaker boxes include a junction box, which serves as an unfinished basic light fixture. See Figure 33 below. NFIP does not cover finished lighting, which is an improvement as defined in Section II.B.17, of the SFIP. Figure 33 Unfinished light fixture and outlet
(6) Elevators, dumbwaiters, and related equipment, except for related equipment installed below the base flood elevation after September 30, 1987;	An elevator or dumbwaiter is covered if within the covered building enclosure or attached to and in contact with the insured building or directly attached to the 16 square foot landing area used for egress if unattached.

III. Property Covered

Policy Language	Additional Explanation
	For elevators and dumbwaiters installed below the BFE after September 30, 1987, coverage is limited to the cab and the included controls installed on or in the cab. Related equipment is everything except the cab and the included controls and is not covered unless the damaged part of the equipment is installed above the level at or above the BFE.
	A chair lift is covered if within the covered building enclosure or attached to an in contact with the insured building or attached directly to the 16 square foot landing area used for egress (See Figures 34 and 35).

Figure 34. Example of a covered chair lift attached to the building

Photograph credit BFA, LLC

Figure 35. Example of a non-covered chair lift.

III. Property Covered

Policy Language	Additional Explanation
(7) Fuel tanks and the fuel in them;	Fuel tanks and the fuel in them include a connected fuel gauge or fuel filter.
(8) Furnaces and hot water heaters;	Furnaces and hot water heaters include boilers and permanently installed equipment for humidification, air filtering, and ventilation. This includes those portions of the central HVAC in a building enclosure below the LFE or basement, including boilers and connected radiators and hot water baseboards. This does not include electric baseboard heaters, whether hardwired to the electrical system or not.
(9) Heat pumps	Heat pumps and other central HVAC units permanently installed equipment related to humidification, dehumidification, air filtering, and ventilation.
(10) Nonflammable insulation in a basement;	Nonflammable insulation in a basement includes: • Nonflammable insulation in walls and ceilings. For post-FIRM elevated buildings in SFHAs, coverage applies to: • Insulation installed between joists within the lowest elevated floor, including plywood and any other material used to hold in the insulation. • Unfinished protective weather barriers affixed to the floor framing. The SFIP covers unattached protective barriers located in a crawlspace as personal property provided the area is not subject to basement or post-FIRM coverage limitations and the policyholder purchased contents coverage. When installed underneath a building in a crawlspace, the barrier must be physically attached to the building's foundation or floor framing for Coverage A - Building.
(11) Pumps and tanks used in solar energy systems;	N/A
(12) Stairways and staircases attached to the building, not separated from it by elevated walkways;	The SFIP covers unfinished base support material for staircases and stairways (underneath the finished treads and risers) attached to the building, not separated from it by elevated walkways, includes an exterior staircase into a basement that is part of the building and enclosed by an addition defined under SFIP Section III.A.2. This also includes an interior basement or post-FIRM elevated building staircases. The SFIP does not pay to treat, paint, or stain the base support material in a basement, or below the lowest elevated floor of a post-FIRM elevated building in an SFHA. The SFIP does not cover damage to finish materials used for a tread, riser, or stringer if such material is installed onto unfinished base support material for stairways and staircases. If the finish material is the base support material, such as with a floating

III. Property Covered

Policy Language	Additional Explanation
	staircase or step, the finish material is covered but not the cost to apply a finish coating, or paint.
	Figure 36. Unfinished base stairs (left) are covered in a basement or below post-FIRM elevated building; however, improvements to paint or add finish to treads, risers, and stringers (right) are not:
	Figure 37. Covered stairs where the finished material is the base material; however, no coverage to paint, stain, or coat
	The SFIP does not cover the basement exterior egress staircase located outside of the perimeter building walls, even if covered by a roof or door. See SFIP Section IV.9.
(13) Sump pumps	N/A
(14) Water softeners and the chemicals in them, water filters, and faucets installed as an integral part of the plumbing system;	The SFIP allows for a faucet that is affixed directly to the plumbing line, as opposed to a faucet that is connected to plumbing lines but mounted onto a sink as a finished fixture. See Section 2: Water Softeners in this manual.

III. Property Covered

Policy Language	Additional Explanation
(15) Well water tanks and pumps;	Well water tanks and pumps include the pressure switch, pressure valve, and gauge.
(16) Required utility connections for any item in this list; and	N/A
(17) Footings, foundations, posts, pilings, piers, or other foundation walls and anchorage systems required to support a building.	• Footings, foundations, posts, pilings, piers, or other foundation walls and anchorage systems required to support a building: • Include windows and doors installed in the perimeter foundation walls of an SFIP-defined basement area such as a perimeter wall basement garage door or sliding glass door. • Include vents installed in and considered part of the covered foundation walls of a post-FIRM elevated building. However, there is no coverage for breakaway walls or vents in breakaway walls. • Does not include screen or storm doors, or a door covering or enclosing an exterior egress in a basement, such as a Bilco™ door. • Does not include doors and windows of any type in an enclosure subject to post-FIRM limitations when located below the lowest elevated floor.
b. Clean-up.	Clean-up includes: • Pumping out trapped floodwater • Labor to remove or extract spent cleaning solutions Treatment for mold and mildew • Structural drying of salvageable interior foundation elements The SFIP does not cover clean-up of an item or property located in areas subject to basement and post-FIRM coverage limitations – that is, the property must itself be covered under SFIP Section III(A)(8) – or for items or loss otherwise excluded under this policy. Clean-up is not the removal of flood-damaged items or debris removal. See SFIP Section III.C.1 for Debris Removal.
B. Coverage B—Personal Property	
1. If you have purchased personal property coverage, we insure, subject to B.2. and B.3. below, against direct physical loss by or from flood to personal property that is inside the fully enclosed insured building and is:	• The SFIP does not cover personal property items not within the fully enclosed insured building at the described location. This differs from the Dwelling Form in that the Dwelling Form covers personal property within any SFIP-defined building at the described location.

May 1, 2020

III. Property Covered

Policy Language	Additional Explanation
a. Owned by the unit owners of the condominium association in common, meaning property in which each unit owner has an undivided ownership interest; or b. Owned solely by the condominium association and used exclusively in the conduct of the business affairs of the condominium association. We also insure such personal property for 45 days while stored at a temporary location, as set forth in III.C.2.b., Property Removed to Safety.	• Property leased under a "capital lease", a contract that entitles a renter the temporary use of an item and to account for the financial effect of ownership on their balance sheet qualifies as an insurable interest and can be claimed even if the property is not solely owned by the policyholder. • In contrast, an "operating lease" is a contract that entitles a renter the temporary use of an item but does not convey ownership rights. According to Generally Accepted Accounting Principles (GAAP), property in possession of a policyholder obtained through an operating lease, cannot be represented in balancing sheet financials. Therefore, it is not covered under the SFIP Coverage B-Personal Property.
2. Coverage for personal property includes the following property, subject to B.1. above, which is covered under Coverage B only: a. Air conditioning units-portable or window type; b. Carpet, not permanently installed, over unfinished flooring; c. Carpets over finished flooring; d. Clothes washers and dryers; e. "Cook-out" grills; f. Food freezers, other than walk-in, and the food in any freezer; g. Outdoor equipment and furniture stored inside the insured building; h. Ovens and the like; and i. Portable microwave ovens and portable dishwashers	• Coverage A – Building Property covers through-the-wall air conditioning units that are permanently installed. • Clothes washers and dryers, including the dryer exhaust vent kit. The connectors and plumbing lines for a gas dryer are covered under building coverage only. • Coverage B applies to food freezers only. NFIP considers an appliance that both refrigerates and freezes as a refrigerator and covers it under Coverage A – Building Property. • Drapes and hardware are contents, whether physically attached to the building or not.
3. Coverage for items of property in a building enclosure below the lowest elevated floor of an elevated post-FIRM building located in Zones A1–A30, AE, AH, AR, AR/A, AR/AE, AR/AH, AR/A1–A30, V1–V30, or VE, or in a basement, regardless of the zone, is limited to the following items, if installed in their functioning locations and, if necessary for operation, connected to a power source: a. Air conditioning units-portable or window type; b. Clothes washers and dryers; and c. Food freezers, other than walk-in, and food in any freezer.	• Coverage A – Building Property covers through-the-wall air conditioning units that are permanently installed. • Clothes washers and dryers including the dryer exhaust vent kit. • Coverage B applies to food freezers only. NFIP considers an appliance that both refrigerates and freezes, a refrigerator, and covers it under Coverage A – Building Property. This provision does not apply to Zones A, AO, A99, AR/AO, V, and VO.

III. Property Covered

Policy Language	Additional Explanation
4. Special Limits. We will pay no more than $2,500 for any one loss to one or more of the following kinds of personal property:	Payments for these items may not exceed $2,500.00 in aggregate.
a. Artwork, photographs, collectibles, or memorabilia, including but not limited to, porcelain or other figures, and sports cards;	
b. Rare books or autographed items;	
c. Jewelry, watches, precious and semi-precious stones, or articles of gold, silver, or platinum;	
d. Furs or any article containing fur which represents its principal value.	
5. We will pay only for the functional value of antiques.	The SFIP does not value an antique based on the rarity of the item, nor does it apply depreciation based solely on age or its physical condition. The SFIP bases the value of an antique item on its functional value considering its quality. The adjuster should apply depreciation based on its restored condition at the time of the loss.
	SFIP-covered Functional value for an antique = Agreed appraised value – Intangible value – Depreciation
	As an example, a 400-year-old fully restored chair formerly owned by a historical figure is appraised by a certified industry professionally at $25,000. The chair has seen general usage for 3-years after its restoration date.
	Applying judgment, a new chair with the same or similar functional design, material quality, and craftsmanship is comparably worth $3,500. Less 3 percent depreciation, the SFIP would pay the functional value of $3,395, as the functional value must also consider depreciation.

C. Coverage C—Other Coverages

Policy Language	Additional Explanation
1. Debris Removal	Insured property means the insured dwelling and covered personal property. The SFIP does not pay for removal of:
a. We will pay the expense to remove non-owned debris that is on or in insured property and debris of insured property anywhere.	• Non-covered debris anywhere, such as a non-covered damaged property or debris located in the yard, driveway, or on another parcel of land.
b. If you or a member of your household perform the removal work, the value of your work will be based on the Federal minimum wage.	• Non-covered items of property, even if the removal of the item facilitates cleanup of covered building repairs, such as the removal of carpet installed inside a basement, or the removal plants, shrubs, or trees along the perimeter of the building to access foundation or siding repairs.
c. This coverage does not increase the Coverage A or Coverage B limit of liability.	

III. Property Covered

Policy Language	Additional Explanation
2. Loss Avoidance Measures a. Sandbags, Supplies, and Labor (1) We will pay up to $1,000 for costs you incur to protect the insured building from a flood or imminent danger of flood, for the following: (a) Your reasonable expenses to buy: (i) Sandbags, including sand to fill them; (ii) Fill for temporary levees; (iii) Pumps; and (iv) Plastic sheeting and lumber used in connection with these items; and (b) The value of work, at the Federal minimum wage, that you perform. (2) This coverage for Sandbags, Supplies, and Labor applies only if damage to insured property by or from flood is imminent and the threat of flood damage is apparent enough to lead a person of common prudence to anticipate flood damage. One of the following must also occur: (a) A general and temporary condition of flooding in the area near the described location must occur, even if the flood does not reach the insured building; or (b) A legally authorized official must issue an evacuation order or other civil order for the community in which the insured building is located calling for measures to preserve life and property from the peril of flood. This coverage does not increase the Coverage A or Coverage B limit of liability. b. Property Removed to Safety (1) We will pay up to $1,000 for the reasonable expenses you incur to move insured property to a place other than the described location that contains the property in order to protect it from flood or the imminent danger of flood.	The SFIP only covers those items specifically noted. The policyholder must provide receipts for covered materials they purchased. Additionally, the NFIP reimburses the policyholder and members of the policyholder's household labor at the Federal minimum wage at the time of the loss. Water-filled bladders, as shown in Figure 38, are considered a temporary levee for the purposes of loss avoidance coverage. However, because these are reusable, the SFIP will pay the cost to purchase the bladder once, but only when the initial purchase is in connection to the claimed flood event. After that event, any future claim for loss avoidance here is limited to the labor and fill material. **Figure 38. Water-filled Bladder** Photograph credit Randy Wagner • The SFIP coverage of "reasonable expenses" under this provision is limited to the policyholder's removal, storage, and return of covered building and personal property to the location described on the declarations page. The insurer may reimburse the policyholder for related expenses for the labor of the policyholder and family members at the Federal minimum wage, and incurred transportation and storage costs. The policyholder must itemize and support

III. Property Covered

Policy Language	Additional Explanation
Reasonable expenses include the value of work, at the Federal minimum wage, that you perform. (2) If you move insured property to a location other than the described location that contains the property, in order to protect it from flood or the imminent danger of flood, we will cover such property while at that location for a period of 45 consecutive days from the date you begin to move it there. The personal property that is moved must be placed in a fully enclosed building, or otherwise reasonably protected from the elements. Any property removed, including a moveable home described in II.6.b. and c., must be placed above ground level or outside of the special flood hazard area. This coverage does not increase the Coverage A or Coverage B limit of liability.	these expenses with valid proof of payment. Coverage here is limited only to the length of time that a flood or the imminent danger of flood exists. Payment under this provision does not increase Coverage A – Building Property or Coverage B – Personal Property limits of liability. • The SFIP will cover from the peril of flood, the property relocated to another location for a period of 45 consecutive days from the date the policyholder began to move the property. If the policyholder does not place the property in a fully enclosed building, the property must be secured to prevent flotation out of the building. If the property floats out or away from the structure used to reasonably protect the property from the elements, it will be conclusively presumed that the policyholder did not reasonably secure the property. In that case, there is no coverage for the property. • Regarding the provision "must be placed above ground level or outside of the SFHA", the relocated site of the property must be a reasonable location to prevent loss compared to the described location. For example, where the surrounding terrain is sloped, the site of the relocated property must be on a higher elevation than the floor level of the building at the described location where the property was originally located; the policyholder may not relocate the property to a basement. Where the surrounding terrain is level and the site of the relocated property is considered within the same flood hazard area, the property must be placed on a floor level in the relocated building that is a higher elevation compared to the floor level in the building at the described location where the property was originally located. The property may not be relocated into a lower enclosure below an elevated floor within a post-FIRM building located in an SFHA.

D. Coverage D—Increased Cost of Compliance

1. General	N/A
This policy pays you to comply with a State or local floodplain management law or ordinance affecting repair or reconstruction of a structure suffering flood damage. Compliance activities eligible for payment are: elevation, floodproofing, relocation, or demolition (or any combination of these activities) of your structure. Eligible floodproofing activities are limited to: a. Non-residential structures.	

III. Property Covered

Policy Language	Additional Explanation
b. Residential structures with basements that satisfy FEMA's standards published in the Code of Federal Regulations [44 CFR 60.6 (b) or (c)].	
2. Limit of Liability We will pay you up to $30,000 under this Coverage D—Increased Cost of Compliance, which only applies to policies with building coverage (Coverage A). Our payment of claims under Coverage D is in addition to the amount of coverage which you selected on the application and which appears on the Declarations Page. But the maximum you can collect under this policy for both Coverage A— Building Property and Coverage D—Increased Cost of Compliance cannot exceed the maximum permitted under the Act. We do not charge a separate deductible for a claim under Coverage D.	All three SFIP forms provide Increased Cost of Compliance (ICC) benefits as Coverage D. Increased Cost of Compliance. ICC provides up to $30,000 toward the cost of bringing a flood-damaged structure into compliance with state or community floodplain management laws or ordinances governing repair or reconstruction following a flood.
3. Eligibility a. A structure covered under Coverage A— Building Property sustaining a loss caused by a flood as defined by this policy must: (1) Be a "repetitive loss structure." A repetitive loss structure is one that meets the following conditions: (a) The structure is covered by a contract of flood insurance issued under the NFIP. (b) The structure has suffered flood damage on two occasions during a 10-year period which ends on the date of the second loss. (c) The cost to repair the flood damage, on average, equaled or exceeded 25% of the market value of the structure at the time of each flood loss. (d) In addition to the current claim, the NFIP must have paid the previous qualifying claim, and the State or community must have a cumulative, substantial damage provision or repetitive loss provision in its floodplain management law or ordinance being enforced against the structure; or (2) Be a structure that has had flood damage in which the cost to repair equals or exceeds 50% of the market value of the structure at the time of the flood. The State or community	To be eligible for ICC, the community must declare the building substantially damaged. The amount paid for Coverage D – ICC and Coverage A – Building Property combined cannot exceed the maximum program limits $250,000 x the number of units under the RCBAP Form. ICC is not available in Emergency Program communities. ICC is not available for: • Contents-only policies. • Group Flood Insurance policies. • Dwelling Form policies on individual condominium units in a multi-unit building. In a multi-unit condominium building, ICC coverage is available through the condominium association's flood policy. No separate deductible applies. For 3.b.(2) and (3) to apply, the community must first adopt and enforce new preliminary or advisory base flood elevations and an ICC claim cannot proceed until on or after the effective date of the new base flood elevations AND the policyholder receives notice from the community requiring the home to be brought into compliance with the new flood elevations. However, there are situations where the community may enforce elevation requirements in a non-SFHA and this would be specified in the ordinance. There are situations where the community may have its own elevation or floodproofing requirements, which it enforces within a non-SFHA. This would be

III. Property Covered

Policy Language	Additional Explanation
must have a substantial damage provision in its floodplain management law or ordinance being enforced against the structure.	specified in the community's floodplain ordinance, but the community must be able to demonstrate this requirement and enforcement is at least based in part on guidance from FEMA, and not entirely on its own.
b. This Coverage D pays you to comply with State or local floodplain management laws or ordinances that meet the minimum standards of the National Flood Insurance Program found in the Code of Federal Regulations at 44 CFR 60.3. We pay for compliance activities that exceed those standards under these conditions:	**ICC Claims** The date of loss of the ICC claim is the date of loss of the underlying flood claim that triggers the requirement to comply with a community law or ordinance.
(1) 3.a.(1) above.	Policyholders have up to six years from the date of the underlying flood loss to complete the eligible mitigation activity. Policyholders should know that initiating a mitigation project before receiving a substantial damage declaration from the community may jeopardize their eligibility to receive an ICC payment.
(2) Elevation or floodproofing in any risk zone to preliminary or advisory base flood elevations provided by FEMA which the State or local government has adopted and is enforcing for flood-damaged structures in such areas. (This includes compliance activities in B, C, X, or D zones which are being changed to zones with base flood elevations. This also includes compliance activities in zones where base flood elevations are being increased, and a flood-damaged structure must comply with the higher advisory base flood elevation.) Increased Cost of Compliance coverage does not apply to situations in B, C, X, or D zones where the community has derived its own elevations and is enforcing elevation or floodproofing requirements for flood-damaged structures to elevations derived solely by the community.	For buildings in Zones B, C, X, D, unnumbered A and V, and A99, the adjuster must document why a building must undergo mitigation and obtain a written statement from the community to substantiate the ICC claim. ICC does not pay for testing, monitoring, clean up, removal, containment, treatment, detoxification, or neutralization of pollutants even if required by community ordinance. **Repetitive Loss Properties** If a state or community adopts and enforces a cumulative substantial damage provision or repetitive loss provision requiring action by property owners to comply with floodplain management laws or ordinances, this may also qualify a structure for an ICC claim after a flood loss. The community must declare the structure to be substantially damaged and the structure must meet the NFIP's repetitive loss structure definition. The NFIP defines a repetitive loss structure as an NFIP-insured building that has incurred flood-related damages on two occasions during a 10-year period ending on the date of the event for which the insured makes a second claim. The cost of repairing the flood damage, on the average, must equal or exceed 25 percent of the market value of the building at the time of each flood. The adjuster or insurer must verify that the NFIP paid a claim for both qualifying losses and that the state or community is enforcing a cumulative substantial damage or repetitive loss provision in its law or ordinance and declared the building substantially damaged on that basis.
(3) Elevation or floodproofing above the base flood elevation to meet State or local "freeboard" requirements, i.e., that a structure must be elevated above the base flood elevation.	
c. Under the minimum NFIP criteria at 44 CFR 60.3 (b)(4), States and communities must require the elevation or floodproofing of structures in unnumbered A zones to the base flood elevation where elevation data is obtained from a Federal, State, or other source. Such compliance activities are also eligible for Coverage D.	**Substantial Damage** Insurers may only open an ICC claim when the community declares a building
d. This coverage will also pay for the incremental cost, after demolition or relocation, of elevating or floodproofing a structure during its	

III. Property Covered

Policy Language	Additional Explanation
rebuilding at the same or another site to meet State or local floodplain management laws or ordinances, subject to Exclusion D.5.g. below relating to improvements.	substantially damaged in writing. Neither FEMA nor the insurer can determine substantial damage or issue a substantial damage declaration. The community has the sole authority to determine substantial damage.
e. This coverage will also pay to bring a flood-damaged structure into compliance with State or local floodplain management laws or ordinances even if the structure had received a variance before the present loss from the applicable floodplain management requirements	Note that in some cases a community may declare a building substantially damaged, based in whole or in part on non-flood-related damage. While having more than 50 percent damage may trigger a requirement to comply with the local floodplain management ordinances, the SFIP requires the percentage of damage to be by or from flood, whether covered by the SFIP or not.
	See Section 3 Increased Cost of Compliance, of this manual for more detail.
4. Conditions	ICC pays for the following mitigation activities or combination thereof:
a. When a structure covered under Coverage A-Building Property sustains a loss caused by a flood, our payment for the loss under this Coverage D will be for the increased cost to elevate, floodproof, relocate, or demolish (or any combination of these activities) caused by the enforcement of current State or local floodplain management ordinances or laws. Our payment for eligible demolition activities will be for the cost to demolish and clear the site of the building debris or a portion thereof caused by the enforcement of current State or local floodplain management ordinances or laws. Eligible activities for the cost of clearing the site will include those necessary to discontinue utility service to the site and ensure proper abandonment of on-site utilities.	• Floodproofing to reduce the potential for flood damage by keeping floodwater out of a building. • Elevation to raise a building to or above the BFE plus freeboard adopted by a community, adopted Advisory Base Flood Elevations (ABFE), or the best available data provided by FEMA. • Demolition when a building is in such poor condition that elevation and relocation are not technically feasible or cost-effective. • Relocation to move a building outside of the floodplain. See Section 3 Increased Cost of Compliance, of this manual for more detail.
b. When the building is repaired or rebuilt, it must be intended for the same occupancy as the present building unless otherwise required by current floodplain management ordinances or laws.	
5. Exclusions Under this Coverage D—Increased Cost of Compliance, we will not pay for: a. The cost to comply with any floodplain management law or ordinance in communities participating in the Emergency Program. b. The cost associated with enforcement of any ordinance or law that requires any insured or others to test for, monitor, clean up,	N/A

III. Property Covered

Policy Language	Additional Explanation
remove, contain, treat, detoxify or neutralize, or in any way respond to, or assess the effects of pollutants.	
c. The loss in value to any insured building or other structure due to the requirements of any ordinance or law.	
d. The loss in residual value of the undamaged portion of a building demolished as a consequence of enforcement of any State or local floodplain management law or ordinance.	
e. Any Increased Cost of Compliance under this Coverage D:	
(1) Until the building is elevated, floodproofed, demolished, or relocated on the same or to another premises; and	
(2) Unless the building is elevated, floodproofed, demolished, or relocated as soon as reasonably possible after the loss, not to exceed two years.	
f. Any code upgrade requirements, e.g., plumbing or electrical wiring, not specifically related to the State or local floodplain management law or ordinance.	
g. Any compliance activities needed to bring additions or improvements made after the loss occurred into compliance with State or local floodplain management laws or ordinances.	
h. Loss due to any ordinance or law that you were required to comply with before the current loss.	
i. Any rebuilding activity to standards that do not meet the NFIP's minimum requirements. This includes any situation where the insured has received from the State or community a variance in connection with the current flood loss to rebuild the property to an elevation below the base flood elevation.	
j. Increased Cost of Compliance for a garage or carport.	
k. Any structure insured under an NFIP Group Flood Insurance Policy.	
Assessments made by a condominium association on individual condominium unit owners to pay increased costs of repairing	

III. Property Covered

Policy Language	Additional Explanation
commonly owned buildings after a flood in compliance with State or local floodplain management ordinances or laws.	N/A
6. Other Provisions a. Increased Cost of Compliance coverage will not be included in the calculation to determine whether coverage meets the coinsurance requirement for replacement cost coverage under VIII. General Conditions, V. Loss Settlement. b. All other conditions and provisions of the policy apply.	

IV. Property Not Covered

Policy Language	Additional Explanation
We do not cover any of the following property:	
1. Personal property not inside the fully enclosed building;	N/A
2. A building, and personal property in it, located entirely in, on, or over water or seaward of mean high tide, if constructed or substantially improved after September 30, 1982;	• The SFIP allows coverage for a building not entirely over water, for example: when part of the exterior perimeter wall and foundation of the building is on land or on the landward side of mean high tide (mean high water). • When the exterior perimeter walls of the building are completely over water and the support system or foundation underneath the insured building extends onto land, or the extension of any mechanism for access into a building (including, but not limited to, stairs, decks, walkways, piers, posts, pilings, docks, or driveways), even if the mechanism is on or partially on land, the building or the access will not be eligible for coverage. • If the exterior perimeter walls of a building are completely over water, but connected to another eligible building by means of an elevated walkway, stairway, roof, and/or rigid exterior wall, or there is an appurtenant structure on the same slab, foundation, or other continuous support system that is on land (such as a shed or garage), the presence of the connected building or appurtenant structure on land does not allow coverage to be afforded to the building that has its exterior perimeter walls entirely over water.

IV. Property Not Covered

Policy Language	Additional Explanation
3. Open structures, including a building used as a boathouse or any structure or building into which boats are floated, and personal property located in, on, or over water;	The SFIP does not cover boathouses or buildings into which boats can float and personal property located within buildings used solely as boathouses. The SFIP does not cover a building and personal property within it, located in, on, or over water or seaward of mean high tide if the building was constructed or substantially improved after September 30, 1982. Figure 39. A recreational vehicle is a self-propelled vehicle Photograph credit Fleetwood RV
4. Recreational vehicles other than travel trailers described in the Definitions Section (see II.B.6.c.) whether affixed to a permanent foundation or on wheels;	 Figure 40. A travel trailer is not self-propelled and is towed behind a road vehicle
5. Self-propelled vehicles or machines, including their parts and equipment. However, we do cover self-propelled vehicles or machines, provided they are not licensed for use on public roads and are: a. Used mainly to service the described location; or b. Designed and used to assist handicapped persons, while the vehicles or machines are inside a building at the described location;	The SFIP does not cover self-propelled vehicles or machinery. There are two specific instances where coverage is provided, so long as: (1) the vehicle or machinery is not licensed for use on public roads. (2) specific documentation is provided to support the claim. Under (a) the described location must be the type that would reasonably require service by means of the vehicle or machinery in question. Secondly, there must be evidence the described location is routinely serviced in support of what is claimed under this provision. Vehicles and machinery that are part of or service a business operation at the described location do not qualify for coverage under this provision. Under (b) a vehicle or machinery is covered if it is designed and used as mobility vehicles for persons with disabilities. The vehicle or machinery is not covered if it is

IV. Property Not Covered

Policy Language	Additional Explanation
	not designed to assist persons with disabilities, or not used by persons with disabilities. As an example, a typical golf cart is not covered under this provision, even if it is used by persons with disabilities unless designed or modified specifically to assist persons with disabilities.
	Under both (a) and (b), the vehicle or machinery must be inside a building at the location described on the declarations page for coverage, provided all other policy terms and conditions apply.
	This exclusion does not apply to motorized toys and machinery designed, marketed, or sold for the exclusive use by a youth, including children's dirt bikes solely powered by a battery. If a motorized toy or machinery can be reasonably used by an adult, it is not a youth's toy and is not covered property.
6. Land, land values, lawns, trees, shrubs, plants, growing crops, or animals;	<ul><li>The SFIP does not cover any type of live plant located inside or outside of the building. This provision does not apply to artificial plants used as indoor decor.</li><li>The SFIP will pay the cost to replace land removed by sudden erosion caused by waves or currents of water during a specific type of flood as defined at SFIP Section II.A. when such soil directly supports the insured building.</li></ul>
7. Accounts, bills, coins, currency, deeds, evidences of debt, medals, money, scrip, stored value cards, postage stamps, securities, bullion, manuscripts, or other valuable papers;	<ul><li>Scrip is a form of money issued by a local government or private organization, such as gift cards, coupons, or any substitute for legal tender.</li><li>The SFIP does not cover financial loss from damage or destruction of electronic data or the cost of restoring that data.</li><li>Other valuable papers include stocks, certificates, and bonds.</li></ul>
8. Underground structures and equipment, including wells, septic tanks, and septic systems;	<ul><li>Underground structures and equipment include, but are not limited to, wires, conduits, pipes, sewers, tanks, tunnels, sprinkler systems, similar property, and any apparatus connected beneath the surface of the ground. The SFIP provides coverage if other SFIP requirements are met for equipment installed used in the operation of underground structures and equipment installed above ground and within a building, for example, sprinkler timer.</li><li>When installed, a sewage grinder pump is an integral part of the building's septic system. The grinder pump pulverizes waste for discharge into the septic drainage field. This item of property is not covered. However, the SFIP covers the sewage grinder pump's alarm service panel if installed above ground level and affixed to the building or its foundation. The SFIP does not cover the</li></ul>

IV. Property Not Covered

Policy Language	Additional Explanation
	pump's alarm service panels installed to an item of property that is not covered, such as a support post to a deck.
9. Those portions of walks, walkways, decks, driveways, patios, and other surfaces, all whether protected by a roof or not, located outside the perimeter, exterior walls of the insured building;	The SFIP pays to repair or replace damage to any existing egress on the sides of a building, including underneath an elevated building. For each existing egress, the SFIP covers one 16 square foot (SF) landing and a single set of stairs, one landing per staircase. The SFIP covers materials of a like kind and quality, such as concrete, wood or composite wood material. Covered items include any existing hand or support rail, support posts, and hardware. The SFIP does not cover improvements such as lighting or finishing (paint or preservative stains).
	The SFIP does not cover the cost to comply with Americans with Disabilities Act of 1990 (ADA) regulations; however, the SFIP will repair and/or replace an existing flood damaged handicap ramp for egress, in lieu of the 16 SF of landing and steps.
10. Containers including related equipment, such as, but not limited to, tanks containing gases or liquids;	The SFIP does not cover fuel tanks, pressure tanks, and well water tanks located outside of the insured building. The SFIP does not cover containers outside of the building, including shipping containers used for storage or residential purposes, unless the container meets the definition of a building.
	The SFIP covers fuel tanks, water tanks, and pressure tanks inside or directly underneath the building, including in a basement or crawlspace, under Coverage A – Building Property, when installed as part of a utility system that services the building.
	Under Coverage B – Personal Property, the SFIP will cover any container inside of a building that is used for household or personal purposes such as oxygen tanks for medical reasons, small fuel tanks for filling lawn equipment, or sealed portable fuel canisters for cooking such as for camping or outdoor grilling. Containers used for the storage of food do not apply to this provision. Containers such as paint cans can be covered but only for the value of what is stored, and not for the value of the container.
	Because containers and tanks are either sealed or made of material meant for contact with liquid, including corrosive liquids, the claim should take into account the proper scope of damage and first consider if the item is reusable after rinsing and cleaning.
11. Buildings or units and all their contents if more than 49% of the actual cash value of the building or unit is below ground, unless the lowest level is at or above the base flood elevation and is below ground by reason of	A building must have over 51 percent of its actual cash value above ground level. This calculation relies solely upon the ACV, not on concepts like square footage, volume, or otherwise.

IV. Property Not Covered

Policy Language	Additional Explanation
earth having been used as insulation material in conjunction with energy efficient building techniques;	Items of property that are not covered under Coverage A – Building Property, should not be included in the building valuation. Claims handling should pay close attention to subterranean or earth dwellings and certain buildings located at sanitation facilities.
12. Fences, retaining walls, seawalls, bulkheads, wharves, piers, bridges, and docks;	FEMA considers these items covered when physically connected to a building and directly supportive and integral to the building's foundation, even if it has a secondary purpose such as a retaining wall.
13. Aircraft or watercraft, or their furnishings and equipment;	• The SFIP covers remote-controlled boats, aircraft, and drones or UAVs (Unmanned Aerial Vehicles) designed and intended for recreational use only and not used to carry people or cargo, or commercial use. The same policy provisions that apply to other personal property apply to these items. • The SFIP does not cover drones or UAVs registered with the Federal Aviation Administration for purposes other than recreational model aircraft. • Watercraft includes any vessel that travels on water, including surfboards. Pool toys are not watercraft. • The SFIP does not cover furnishings and equipment for non-covered watercraft and aircraft, including parts and other items identified for use with watercraft and aircraft.
14. Hot tubs and spas that are not bathroom fixtures, and swimming pools, and their equipment such as, but not limited to, heaters, filters, pumps, and pipes, wherever located;	N/A
15. Property not eligible for flood insurance pursuant to the provisions of the Coastal Barrier Resources Act and the Coastal Barrier Improvement Act of 1990 and amendments to these Acts;	The SFIP cannot provide flood insurance coverage for a building constructed or substantially improved after the U.S. Department of Interior's Fish and Wildlife Service designates it as within Coastal Barrier Resources System (CBRS) boundaries or as Otherwise Protected Areas (OPAs). See USFWS website for more details.
16. Personal property owned by or in the care, custody or control of a unit owner, except for property of the type and under the circumstances set forth under III. Coverage B-Personal Property of this policy;	N/A

V. Exclusions

Policy Language	Additional Explanation
A. We only pay for direct physical loss by or from flood, which means that we do not pay you for:	
1. Loss of revenue or profits;	The SFIP does not cover the costs to pack, move, or store personal property from the insured building or return it to the building when an owner repairs the building or cannot occupy it.
2. Loss of access to the insured property or described location;	
3. Loss of use of the insured property or described location;	
4. Loss from interruption of business or production;	
5. Any additional living expenses incurred while the insured building is being repaired or is unable to be occupied for any reason;	
6. The cost of complying with any ordinance or law requiring or regulating the construction, demolition, remodeling, renovation, or repair of property, including removal of any resulting debris. This exclusion does not apply to any eligible activities we describe in Coverage D—Increased Cost of Compliance; or	The SFIP does not cover replacing non-flood damaged property required to comply with government codes, ordinances, or regulations. For example, the SFIP does not cover the cost of replacing an undamaged interior HVAC unit to match a replaced exterior HVAC unit because of a change in size, SEER-rating, refrigerant, or any other reason even if local, state, or federal code required the upgrade.
7. Any other economic loss you suffer.	
B. We do not insure a loss directly or indirectly caused by a flood that is already in progress at the time and date:	
1. The policy term begins; or	NFIP adjusts flood insurance losses individually. Flood insurance benefits are available if an insured property suffers a covered loss caused by a general condition of flooding, as defined by the SFIP.
2. Coverage is added at your request.	See Flood-In-Progress Exclusion in Section 2 of this manual.
C. We do not insure for loss to property caused directly by earth movement even if the earth movement is caused by flood. Some examples of earth movement that we do not cover are:	
1. Earthquake;	The SFIP is a single-peril policy that only pays for covered damage due to direct physical loss by or from flood, defined in the policy in Section II. The SFIP does not cover damage resulting from an intervening cause of loss, even if the resulting cause is due to flood. The SFIP does not cover damage that results when saturated soils cause the soil below ground level to sink, expand, compact, destabilize, or otherwise lose its load-bearing capacity such as from voids or rotten organic matter when the soil dries. The SFIP does not cover earth movement; each form of earth movement is an intervening cause of loss and a separate peril.
2. Landslide;	
3. Land subsidence;	
4. Sinkholes;	
5. Destabilization or movement of land that results from accumulation of water in subsurface land areas; or	
6. Gradual erosion	The SFIP's exclusion for other perils, such as fire, exemplifies the exclusion of earth movement as a cause of loss. When a flood causes a fire, which damages the

May 1, 2020

V. Exclusions

Policy Language	Additional Explanation
We do, however, pay for losses from mudflow and land subsidence as a result of erosion that are specifically covered under our definition of flood (see A.1.c. and II.A.2.).	building during inundation or after floodwaters recede, the SFIP does not cover the resulting fire and smoke damage to the building even if flood directly caused the fire.

The SFIP covers damage to a building if the damage results from the collapse or subsidence of land that is the direct result of sudden erosion or undermining to the building's support soil underneath or directly along the perimeter foundation of the building from waves or currents of floodwater (velocity flow) during a flood from the overflow of inland or tidal waters or mudflow. This includes damage to the foundation of the building and any resulting damage to the interior and exterior finishes. The SFIP does not cover damage caused by gradual erosion. |
| **D.**   We do not insure for direct physical loss caused directly or indirectly by: | |
| 1. The pressure or weight of ice;
2. Freezing or thawing;
3. Rain, snow, sleet, hail, or water spray;
4. Water, moisture, mildew, or mold damage that results primarily from any condition:
   a. Substantially confined to the insured building; or
   b. That is within your control including, but not limited to:
     (1) Design, structural, or mechanical defects;
     (2) Failures, stoppages, or breakage of water or sewer lines, drains, pumps, fixtures, or equipment; or
     (3) Failure to inspect and maintain the property after a flood recedes; | When the policyholder is prevented access to promptly remove wetted building and personal property items, and this delay directly results in water, moisture, mildew or mold damage to building and personal property items not in physical contact with surface floodwater, this damage could be covered.

As examples:

- local authorities restrict access to the area or
- prolonged inundation of floodwater prevents access to the area.

The claim file must include proper documentation, such as but not limited to photographs, an acceptable explanation provided by the adjuster, or a signed statement from the policyholder or community official that supports the payment for property damages above the documented water height.

For instances when coverage and payment are not recommended, the claim file should include information that documents the policyholder's failure to inspect and maintain their insured property or take reasonable measures to reduce damage when it is feasible to do so.

The SFIP does not cover damage caused by long-term exposure to moisture, water, rot, and insect infestation. This includes damage from the lack of climate control inside the building when the approach to repair does not include the timely repair to the building HVAC system.

The SFIP does not cover pre-existing damage to structural building components, such as damage caused by rot, or for any resulting damage to non-structural finish |

V. Exclusions

Policy Language	Additional Explanation
	building material.
5. Water or water-borne material that: a. Backs up through sewers or drains; b. Discharges or overflows from a sump, sump pump, or related equipment; or c. Seeps or leaks on or through insured property; unless there is a flood in the area and the flood is the proximate cause of the sewer, drain, or sump pump discharge or overflow, or the seepage of water;	The adjuster must document that a flood occurred in the area and that the flood was the proximate cause of the back-up of the sewer or drain, overflow of the sump pump, pump failure, seepage of water, or damage due to the pressure or weight of water (hydrostatic pressure), in the claim file. See SFIP Section II.A and related commentary under the definition of flood. When paying a loss due to a flood in the area proximately causing discharge or overflow of water or water-borne material from a sump, sump pump, or related equipment, the insurer must document the claim file to show that a homeowner's policy endorsement or policy rider did not also cover the loss. If the homeowner's policy does provide coverage, the SFIP payment must apply a proportional loss distribution, as stated under Section VIII.C. Other Insurance. The adjuster must document a flood occurred in the area, and that the flood was the proximate cause of the back-up of the sewer or drain, overflow of the sump pump, pump failure, seepage of water, or damage due to the pressure or weight of water (hydrostatic pressure). A flood is two or more parcels of partial or complete inundation of normally dry land, or of two or more continuous acres of normally dry land. For coverage under this provision, the condition of flood does not have to be on the parcel of land described at the location; it may be within the proximate area.
6. The pressure or weight of water unless there is a flood in the area and the flood is the proximate cause of the damage from the pressure or weight of water;	Refer to SFIP Section V.D.5. above.
7. Power, heating, or cooling failure unless the failure results from direct physical loss by or from flood to power, heating, or cooling equipment situated on the described location;	The SFIP does not cover damage to insured property when caused by a power surge or power outage that originates from the failure or shutting down of equipment that is not located at the described location, even if the reason is a direct result of a flood. For example, the local utility operator may shut down a section of the electrical grid to avoid system damage from a flood. When the power returns to the electrical grid, the initial surge of electricity can damage insured property. Under this loss description, the damage is not covered. The SFIP covers damage to any covered building or personal property item, such as the building's main service, home security system, a plugged-in television, or to the HVAC system, when a flood physically damages related system equipment installed at the described location. For example, if the flood damages power equipment at

V. Exclusions

Policy Language	Additional Explanation
	the described location creating an electrical short within the power system resulting in damage to another item of property part of or connected to the power system, the damage to the item is also covered, even though it was not physically touched by floodwater. Under this loss description, the damage is considered a direct physical loss by or from flood. To cover the loss described, the adjuster must document the cause of loss in the claim file to rule out the possibility of a non-covered cause, such as described in the previous paragraph.
8. Theft, fire, explosion, wind, or windstorm;	N/A
9. Anything that you or your agents do or conspire to do to cause loss by flood deliberately; or	
10. Alteration of the insured property that significantly increases the risk of flooding.	
E. We do not insure for loss to any building or personal property located on land leased from the Federal Government, arising from or incident to the flooding of the land by the Federal Government, where the lease expressly holds the Federal Government harmless under flood insurance issued under any Federal Government program.	N/A
F. We do not pay for the testing for or monitoring of pollutants unless required by law or ordinance.	The SFIP only pays to test or monitor the removal of a pollutant when a law or ordinance requires it. Insurers must have a copy of the law or ordinance for the file to support their decision to pay for the testing for or monitoring of pollutants. The law or ordinance must be in effect at the date of loss to apply.

VI. Deductibles

Policy Language	Additional Explanation
A. When a loss is covered under this policy, we will pay only that part of the loss that exceeds the applicable deductible amount, subject to the limit of insurance that applies. The deductible amount is shown on the Declarations Page. However, when a building under construction, alteration, or repair does not have at least two rigid exterior walls and a fully secured roof at the time of loss, your deductible amount will be two times the deductible that would otherwise apply to a completed building.	
B. In each loss from flood, separate deductibles apply to the building and personal property insured by this policy.	The SFIP applies a separate deductible to both building and personal property losses.
C. No deductible applies to:	The SFIP will only pay that portion of the loss that exceeds the applicable deductibles.
1. III.C.2. Loss Avoidance Measures;	For building and personal property losses, the insurer should take the deductible from the gross loss before applying policy limits. For example, if the covered loss is $110,000, the policy limit is $100,000, and the deductible is $5,000, the insurer should apply the deductible to the $110,000 loss, which leaves $105,000, meaning the insurer should pay the $100,000 policy limit unless coinsurance applies (see SFIP Section VII Coinsurance).
2. III.D. Increased Cost of Compliance.	The SFIP does not apply excess loss to items subject to Special Limits to reduce the personal property deductible.

VII. Coinsurance

Policy Language	Additional Explanation
A. This Coinsurance Section applies only to coverage on the building.	
B. We will impose a penalty on loss payment unless the amount of insurance applicable to the damaged building is:	Refer to policy definition.
1. At least 80% of its replacement cost; or	
2. The maximum amount of insurance available for that building under the NFIP, whichever is less.	

VII. Coinsurance

Policy Language	Additional Explanation
C. If the actual amount of insurance on the building is less than the required amount in accordance with the terms of VII.B. above, then loss payment is determined as follows (subject to all other relevant conditions in this policy, including those pertaining to valuation, adjustment, settlement, and payment of loss):	
1. Divide the actual amount of insurance carried on the building by the required amount of insurance.	Do not use the formula on the RCBAP form to determine the proportional loss amount. Use the formula below.
2. Multiply the amount of loss, before application of the deductible, by the figure determined in C.1. above.	**Proportional loss amount** = ((insurance purchased ÷ required insurance) x (ACV plus recoverable depreciation)) – deductible
3. Subtract the deductible from the figure determined in C.2. above.	**IMPORTANT** – Use the order of operations as shown, starting within the innermost parentheses, for accurate calculation.

We will pay the amount determined in C.3. above, or the amount of insurance carried, whichever is less. The amount of insurance carried, whichever is less. The amount of insurance carried, if in excess of the applicable maximum amount of insurance available under the NFIP, is reduced accordingly.

Example #1 (Inadequate Insurance)

Replacement value of the building	$250,000
Required amount of insurance (80% of replacement value of $250,000)	$200,000
Actual amount of insurance carried	$180,000
Amount of the loss	$150,000
Deductible	$500

Step 1: 180,000 ÷ 200,000 = .90 (90% of what should be carried.)

Step 2: 150,000 X .90 = 135,000

Step 3: 135,000 - 500 = 134,500

We will pay no more than $134,500. The remaining $15,500 is not covered due to the coinsurance penalty ($15,000) and application of the deductible ($500).

Table 8: Example of Inadequate Insurance

Item	Value
RC Value	$2,499,872.60
Required Insurance	$1,999,898.08
Insurance Purchased	$1,800,000.00
ACV plus Recoverable Depreciation	$46,132.16

- (($1,800,000.00 ÷ $1,999,898.08) x 46,132.16) = $41,521.06 - $5,000 deductible = $36,521.06 Amount Owed.

VII. Coinsurance

Policy Language	Additional Explanation
Example #2 (Adequate Insurance)	Table 9: Example of Adequate Insurance

Item	Value
RC Value	$2,500,000
Required Insurance	$2,000,000
Insurance Purchased	$2,000,000
ACV plus Recoverable Depreciation	$46,132.16
Deductible	$5,000
Amount Owed	$41,132.16

Example #2 (Adequate Insurance)

Replacement value of the building $500,000

Required amount of insurance $400,000
(80% of replacement value of $500,000)

Actual amount of insurance carried $400,000

Amount of the loss $200,000

Deductible $500

In this example, there is no coinsurance penalty, because the actual amount of insurance carried meets the required amount. We will pay no more than

$199,500 ($200,000 amount of loss minus the $500 deductible).

D. In calculating the full replacement cost of a building:

1. The replacement cost value of any covered building property will be included;

2. The replacement cost value of any building property not covered under this policy will not be included; and

3. Only the replacement cost value of improvements installed by the condominium association will be included.

Refer to policy definition.

VIII. General Conditions

Policy Language	Additional Explanation
A. Pair and Set Clause	
In case of loss to an article that is part of a pair or set, we will have the option of paying you: 1. An amount equal to the cost of replacing the lost, damaged, or destroyed article, less depreciation; or 2. An amount which represents the fair proportion of the total value of the pair or set that the lost, damaged, or destroyed article bears to the pair or set.	If the damaged property item is ruined, and cannot be replaced individually as a single item, and this renders the other item in the pair or the set unusable or worthless, then the SFIP pays for the pair or set. **Examples:** Left shoe ruined by flood, and the right shoe undamaged. The left shoe cannot be purchased without the right, rendering the undamaged right shoe unusable. The SFIP covers a new pair of shoes. Other similar examples include a ruined china base cabinet and undamaged matching china base top; half the seats ruined in a sectional sofa; a ruined left window curtain and an undamaged right window curtain. If the damaged property item is ruined and can be replaced individually as a single item with like kind and quality, and this renders the other item or the set usable, the SFIP will only cover the damaged or ruined items along with the reasonable cost for like kind and quality, except in the case of the Section V. Exclusion (A)(6) for ordinance or law, and the like. **Examples:** Base cabinets ruined by flood with the upper cabinets undamaged. The upper cabinets remain usable. The SFIP allows replacing the base cabinets with like kind and quality, including reasonable costs to match the new base cabinets with existing undamaged cabinets. Other similar examples include a damaged dresser and undamaged or repairable matching armoire and nightstands, a ruined dining table leaf and undamaged or repairable dining table, a ruined granite cabinet countertop, and salvageable granite island countertop. **Example:** An outdoor heating, ventilation, and air conditioning (HVAC) unit is ruined by flood, and the interior HVAC unit is undamaged. Due to Department of Energy code requirements regarding energy efficiency, or an Environmental Protection Agency (EPA)-mandate regarding the refrigerant type, a replacement outdoor HVAC unit that works with the existing interior HVAC unit is unavailable, rendering the undamaged interior unit unusable. Section VII (A) Pair and Set clause is superseded by Section V Exclusions (A)(6) and the SFIP only allows to replace the outdoor HVAC unit with like kind and quality, and does not cover replacement of the undamaged interior HVAC unit.

VIII. General Conditions

Policy Language	Additional Explanation
B. Concealment or Fraud and Policy Voidance	
1. With respect to all insureds under this policy, this policy: a. Is void; b. Has no legal force or effect; c. Cannot be renewed; and d. Cannot be replaced by a new NFIP policy, if, before or after a loss, you or any other insured or your agent have at any time: (1) Intentionally concealed or misrepresented any material fact or circumstance; (2) Engaged in fraudulent conduct; or (3) Made false statements; relating to this policy or any other NFIP insurance.	When claims professionals suspect wrongful acts or misrepresentations on a claim by a policyholder or their representatives: • The adjuster should promptly submit written notification with supporting documentation to the insurer. The adjuster should not draw any conclusions regarding the suspected fraud and should only present facts in written reports. • The examiner should engage management to determine if the insurer should refer the matter to the FEMA Fraud Unit (email: StopFEMAFraud@fema.dhs.gov) and the insurer's investigative unit for a Reservation of Rights.
2. This policy will be void as of the date wrongful acts described in B.1. above were committed.	The SFIP will be void if the proper authorities determine any part of a claim was fraudulent.
3. Fines, civil penalties, and imprisonment under applicable Federal laws may also apply to the acts of fraud or concealment described above.	
4. This policy is also void for reasons other than fraud, misrepresentation, or wrongful act. This policy is void from its inception and has no legal force under the following conditions: a. If the property is located in a community that was not participating in the NFIP on the policy's inception date and did not join or reenter the program during the policy term and before the loss occurred; or b. If the property listed on the application is otherwise not eligible for coverage under the NFIP.	When a community no longer participates in the NFIP, an active SFIP will remain in force up to the day before the policy renewal date. Refer to the Flood Insurance Manual for other reasons why a building may be ineligible for coverage.
C. Other Insurance	
1. If a loss covered by this policy is also covered by other insurance that includes flood coverage not issued under the Act, we will not pay more than the amount of insurance that you are entitled to for lost, damaged or destroyed property insured under this policy subject to the following: a. We will pay only the proportion of the loss that the amount of	The RCBAP is primary, and the SFIP Dwelling Form provides excess coverage for the same loss. The total amount of insurance available for the Dwelling Form and the RCBAP is $250,000 combined; the total claim payment may not exceed this amount. Other insurance includes primary flood coverage provided by a private carrier or any other insurance that duplicates SFIP coverage.

VIII. General Conditions

Policy Language	Additional Explanation

insurance that applies under this policy bears to the total amount of insurance covering the loss, unless C.1.b. or c. immediately below applies.
 	
b. If the other policy has a provision stating that it is excess insurance, this policy will be primary.
 	
2. This policy will be primary (but subject to its own deductible) up to the deductible in the other flood policy (except another policy as described in C.1.b. above). When the other deductible amount is reached, this policy will participate in the same proportion that the amount of insurance under this policy bears to the total amount of both policies, for the remainder of the loss.
	Personal lines and commercial policies may have endorsements for sewer, sump or drain backup. Considerations include:
	
	1. The other insurance clause of the other policy would determine which policy is excess or primary.
	
	2. If the other policy is silent, proportion the claim.
	
	3. If the endorsement excludes the peril of flood, the SFIP is primary for the direct physical damage by or from flood.
	• Use the following formula to determine the NFIP's share of the loss:
	  NFIP share = ((SFIP policy limit ÷ total insurance) x loss) - other insurance deductible
	• Use the following formula to determine the other insurance's share of the loss:
	  Other insurance share = ((other insurance policy limit ÷ total insurance) x loss) - other insurance deductible
	• Use the following formula to determine the NFIP payment:
	  NFIP payment = NFIP share + other insurance deductible – SFIP deductible
	
	Below is an example of how to apply the formulas to compute the insurer's shares and NFIP payment for a $480,000 loss.

Table 10: Insurance Coverage and Deductibles

Insurance	Coverage	Deductible
NFIP	$250,000	$5,000
Other	$500,000	$15,000
Total	$750,000	

- **NFIP share:** (($250,000 ÷ $750,000) x $480,000) - $15,000 = $145,000
- **Other insurance share:** (($500,000 ÷ $750,000) x $480,000) - $15,000 = $305,000.00
- **NFIP payment:** $145,000.00 + $15,000 - $5,000 = $155,000.00

IMPORTANT – Use the order of operations as shown, starting within the innermost parentheses, for accurate calculation.

3. If there is other insurance in the name of your condominium association	The Biggert-Waters Flood Insurance Reform Act of 2012, Section 100214, does not

VIII. General Conditions

Policy Language	Additional Explanation
covering the same property covered by this policy, then this policy will be in excess over the other insurance.	allow the NFIP to deny a unit owner's claim based on flood insurance coverage purchased by a condominium association.

The SFIP allows unit owner building payments for loss assessments when a condominium association did not purchase insurance to at least 80 percent of the full replacement cost of the condominium building. The provision does not allow insurers to pay for a building item more than once.

The SFIP cannot pay more than the maximum amount of insurance available for a single-family residence, currently $250,000 for a single condominium, even if the unit has additional insurance available under other NFIP policies.

The legislation did not change the coverage provided under the Residential Condominium Building Association Policy (RCBAP).

See the Biggert-Waters Flood Insurance Reform Act of 2012 for more information. |

D. Amendments, Waivers, Assignment

This policy cannot be changed nor can any of its provisions be waived without the express written consent of the Federal Insurance Administrator. No action we take under the terms of this policy constitutes a waiver of any of our rights. You may assign this policy in writing when you transfer title of your property to someone else except under these conditions:

1. When this policy covers only personal property; or
2. When this policy covers a structure during the course of construction. | The SFIP allows the assignment of the policy when the title to the property transfers to a new owner.

The SFIP does not allow the assignment of a claim. The only exception to this is a Coverage D – Increased Cost of Compliance (ICC) claim that can transfer in conjunction with a FEMA project, such as a Hazard Mitigation Grant Program (HMGP) grant. Typically, the policyholder assigns the claim to a community, which typically uses the payment for the community's non-Federal match for the project. The policyholder may only assign the part of the ICC benefit used to meet the project requirements. |

E. Cancellation of the Policy by You

1. You may cancel this policy in accordance with the applicable rules and regulations of the NFIP.
2. If you cancel this policy, you may be entitled to a full or partial refund of premium also under the applicable rules and regulations of the NFIP. | Policyholders must have a valid reason to cancel their flood insurance coverage during a policy term.

See the Flood Insurance Manual for detailed information. |

F. Non-Renewal of the Policy by Us

Your policy will not be renewed:

1. If the community where your covered property is located stops | When a community no longer participates in the NFIP, an active SFIP will remain in force up to the day before the policy renewal date.

Coverage may not be available for a building constructed or altered in violation of |

VIII. General Conditions

Policy Language	Additional Explanation
1. participating in the NFIP, or 2. If your building has been declared ineligible under Section 1316 of the Act.	state or local floodplain management laws, regulations, or ordinances. Section 1316 of the Act allows a state or community to declare a building in violation of its floodplain management rules. When a state or community declares that a building is in violation of Section 1316, the building and any contents in it are not eligible for SFIP coverage. Insurers have a list of buildings with Section 1316 violations that are ineligible for NFIP coverage. When the owner corrects the violation, the building becomes eligible for coverage again. The examiner should verify the building's eligibility.
G. Reduction and Reformation of Coverage	
1. If the premium we received from you was not enough to buy the kind and amount of coverage you requested, we will provide only the amount of coverage that can be purchased for the premium payment we received. 2. The policy can be reformed to increase the amount of coverage resulting from the reduction described in G.1. above to the amount you requested as follows: a. Discovery of Insufficient Premium or Incomplete Rating Information Before a Loss: (1) If we discover before you have a flood loss that your premium payment was not enough to buy the requested amount of coverage, we will send you and any mortgagee or trustee known to us a bill for the required additional premium for the current policy term (or that portion of the current policy term following any endorsement changing the amount of coverage). If you or the mortgagee or trustee pay the additional premium within 30 days from the date of our bill, we will reform the policy to increase the amount of coverage to the originally requested amount effective to the beginning of the current policy term (or subsequent date of any endorsement changing the amount of coverage). (2) If we determine before you have a flood loss that the rating information we have is incomplete and prevents us from calculating the additional premium, we will ask you to send the required information. You must submit the information within 60 days of our request. Once we determine the amount of	If the policyholder gives the insurer a premium that will not purchase the amounts of insurance requested, the insurer must issue the policy for the insurance coverage amount the premium will purchase for a one-year policy term. After a Loss: • The insurer will send a bill for the required additional premium for the current policy term only. This is an exception to the SFIP Provisions requiring the current and the prior policy terms. • If the insurer receives the premium within 30 days from the date of the bill, the insurer should increase the policy limits to the originally requested amount effective as of the beginning of the current policy term. • If the insurer does not receive the additional premium by the due date, the insurer must settle the claim based on the previously submitted premium and results in reduced policy limits. Exceptions for Incorrect Flood Zone or BFE After a Loss. When the insurer discovers that an incorrect flood zone or BFE resulted in insufficient premium, the following exceptions apply: • The insurer should calculate any additional premium due prospectively from the date of discovery. • The insurer should apply the automatic reduction in policy limits effective on the date of discovery. **Incorrect Policy Form.** The insurer must use the correct policy form before making a loss payment. When the insurer issues coverage using an incorrect SFIP form, the policy is void and the insurer must rewrite the coverage under the correct form. The

VIII. General Conditions

Policy Language	Additional Explanation
additional premium for the current policy term, we will follow the procedure in G.2.a.(1) above. (3) If we do not receive the additional premium (or additional information) by the date it is due, the amount of coverage can only be increased by endorsement subject to any appropriate waiting period. b. Discovery of insufficient premium or incomplete rating information after a loss. (1) If we discover after you have a flood loss that your premium payment was not enough to buy the requested amount of coverage, we will send you and any mortgagee or trustee known to us a bill for the required additional premium for the current and the prior policy terms. If you or the mortgagee or trustee pay the additional premium within 30 days of the date of our bill, we will reform the policy to increase the amount of coverage to the originally requested amount effective to the beginning of the prior policy term. (2) If we discover after you have a flood loss that the rating information we have is incomplete and prevents us from calculating the additional premium, we will ask you to send the required information. You must submit the information before your claim can be paid. Once we determine the amount of additional premium for the current and prior policy terms, we will follow the procedure in G.2.b.(1) above. (3) If we do not receive the additional premium by the date it is due, your flood insurance claim will be settled based on the reduced amount of coverage. The amount of coverage can only be increased by endorsement subject to any appropriate waiting period. 3. However, if we find that you or your agent intentionally did not tell us, or falsified, any important fact or circumstance or did anything fraudulent relating to this insurance, the provisions of Condition B. Concealment or Fraud and Policy Voidance apply.	provisions of the correct SFIP form apply. • The insurer must reform the coverage limits according to the provisions of the correct SFIP form. • Coverage cannot exceed the coverage issued under the incorrect policy form. See the Flood Insurance Manual for detailed information.

VIII. General Conditions

Policy Language	Additional Explanation
H. Policy Renewal	
1. This policy will expire at 12:01 a.m. on the last day of the policy term.	The SFIP is not a continuous policy. It is a contract for a one-year term. Every policy contract expires at 12:01 a.m. on the last day of the policy term. Renewal of an
2. We must receive the payment of the appropriate renewal premium within 30 days of the expiration date.	expiring policy establishes a new policy term and new contractual agreement. See the Flood Insurance Manual for detailed information.
3. If we find, however, that we did not place your renewal notice into the U.S. Postal Service, or if we did mail it, we made a mistake, e.g., we used an incorrect, incomplete, or illegible address, which delayed its delivery to you before the due date for the renewal premium, then we will follow these procedures:	The adjuster should investigate the claim under a signed non-waiver agreement or a reservation of rights by the insurer when a policyholder reports a loss, and there is uncertainty as to whether a policy is active.
a. If you or your agent notified us, not later than 1 year after the date on which the payment of the renewal premium was due, of non-receipt of a renewal notice before the due date for the renewal premium, and we determine that the circumstances in the preceding paragraph apply, we will mail a second bill providing a revised due date, which will be 30 days after the date on which the bill is mailed.	
b. If we do not receive the premium requested in the second bill by the revised due date, then we will not renew the policy. In that case, the policy will remain an expired policy as of the expiration date shown on the Declarations Page.	
4. In connection with the renewal of this policy, we may ask you during the policy term to recertify, on a Recertification Questionnaire we will provide to you, the rating information used to rate your most recent application for or renewal of insurance.	
I. Conditions Suspending or Restricting Insurance	
We are not liable for loss that occurs while there is a hazard that is increased by any means within your control or knowledge.	The SFIP will not cover a flood loss or increased flood damage to insured property that the policyholder purposely or inadvertently causes. For example: a policyholder constructs a flood barrier to prevent floodwater from a river form reaching the building; however, the improvement now causes runoff during heavy rainfall events to collect behind the barrier and flood the building and a neighboring parcel or causes a prolonged condition of inundation creating additional damage inside the building.

VIII. General Conditions

Policy Language	Additional Explanation
	When the investigation of a loss reveals this provision might apply, the adjuster should notify the insurer at once and request immediate guidance.
J. Requirements in Case of Loss	
In case of a flood loss to insured property, you must:	
1. Give prompt written notice to us;	The policyholder's claim begins with the written notice of loss.
	The policyholder must report the loss to the insurer immediately; failure to provide a notice of loss to the insurer could prejudice the ability of the insurer to inspect the loss, identify the cause and extent of damage, and determine applicable coverage under the SFIP. If the policyholder delays reporting a loss, the adjuster cannot help the policyholder protect the property and avoid further damage.
	A policyholder's failure to provide timely notice of loss can be a basis for denial of a claim.
	• The adjuster should document the reason for a delay in the policyholder reporting a loss to the insurer.
	• If the WYO elects, the adjuster should execute a non-waiver agreement when there is a delay in reporting the loss. The non-waiver agreement should include the reason for the non-waiver and the policyholder's explanation for the delay. The adjuster should have the policyholder sign the non-waiver agreement immediately. If the policyholder refuses to sign the non-waiver agreement, the insurer may decide to send a Reservation of Rights. The adjuster should continue the inspection and review. The insurer cannot waive FEMA's rights.
2. As soon as reasonably possible, separate the damaged and undamaged property, putting it in the best possible order so that we may examine it;	The SFIP requires that the policyholder separate damaged from undamaged property, putting it in the best possible order, so the adjuster may examine it. It is the policyholder's duty to perform the separation described above and prepare an inventory of damaged property, including quantity, description, and the total amount of loss claimed. Any bills, receipts, photographs of damages, and related documents should be attached to the inventory.
3. Prepare an inventory of damaged property showing the quantity, description, actual cash value, and amount of loss. Attach all bills, receipts, and related documents;	If flood-damaged building or contents property is removed before the adjuster can examine it, the policyholder must photograph the items in their damaged location prior to moving the property and prepare the inventory.
	To minimize potential documentation issues, if possible, the policyholder should retain for the adjuster, samples or swatches of carpeting, wallpaper, furniture upholstery, window treatments, and other items of exceptional value where the type and quality of material will influence the amount payable on the claim.

VIII. General Conditions

Policy Language	Additional Explanation
	Photographs should also include groups of items such as clothing, kitchen items, furniture, etc. The insurer will evaluate and consider these items and the policyholder's written inventory of damaged items.
4. Within 60 days after the loss, send us a proof of loss, which is your statement of the amount you are claiming under the policy signed and sworn to by you, and which furnishes us with the following information:	The proof of loss is the policyholder's statement of the amount of money they are requesting. The policyholder must sign and swear to the proof of loss and provide documentation to support that direct physical loss by or from flood occurred to covered property and the amount requested for the insurer to consider it completed. The policyholder (or Executor in the case of a deceased policyholder) is the only person who can sign the proof of losses or legally appointed representative.
a. The date and time of loss;	
b. A brief explanation of how the loss happened;	**SIGNED AND SWORN:**
c. Your interest (for example, "owner") and the interest, if any, of others in the damaged property;	FEMA encourages the use of electronic signatures on proof of loss and other NFIP-related submissions. FEMA will not deny the legal effect, validity, or enforceability of a signature solely because it is in electronic form. Insurers should accept electronic signatures in accordance with their general business practices and applicable laws.
d. Details of any other insurance that may cover the loss;	
e. Changes in title or occupancy of the covered property during the term of the policy;	
f. Specifications of damaged buildings and detailed repair estimates;	**MULTIPLE PROOFS OF LOSS ALLOWED:**
g. Names of mortgagees or anyone else having a lien, charge, or claim against the insured property;	Policyholders must submit a completed proof of loss and documentation to support the amount requested initially and completed proofs of loss for any additional payment requests to the insurer within 60 days after the date of loss or within any extension of that deadline granted by FEMA.
h. Details about who occupied any insured building at the time of loss and for what purpose; and	**ONE CLAIM PER LOSS:**
i. The inventory of damaged personal property described in J.3. above.	The proof of loss is not the claim. The claim is the policyholder's assertion that they are entitled to payment for a covered loss under the terms of the SFIP. A
5. In completing the proof of loss, you must use your own judgment concerning the amount of loss and justify that amount.	policyholder has only one claim from a flood event regardless of the number of proofs of loss and amount of documentation the policyholder may submit in support of that claim. The policyholder's ICC proof of loss is a request for benefits afforded under Coverage D – ICC, for that claim; it is not a separate claim.
6. You must cooperate with the adjuster or representative in the investigation of the claim.	N/A
7. The insurance adjuster whom we hire to investigate your claim may furnish you with a proof of loss form, and she or he may help you complete it. However, this is a matter of courtesy only, and you must still send us a proof of loss within 60 days after the loss even if the adjuster does not furnish the form or help you complete it.	

VIII. General Conditions

Policy Language	Additional Explanation
8. We have not authorized the adjuster to approve or disapprove claims or to tell you whether we will approve your claim.	Only the NFIP insurer has the authority to approve or deny a claim, to tell the policyholder if they will approve or deny a claim, or to provide approved payment details.
	The insurer must rely only upon the terms and conditions established by Federal statute, NFIP regulations, the Federal Insurance Administrator's interpretations, and the express terms of the SFIP. See 44 C.F.R. § 61.5(e) (2018).
9. At our option, we may accept the adjuster's report of the loss instead of your proof of loss. The adjuster's report will include information about your loss and the damages you sustained. You must sign the adjuster's report. At our option, we may require you to swear to the report.	The insurer, not the policyholder or their representative, determines whether to accept the adjuster's report signed and sworn to by the policyholder instead of a proof of loss.

K. Our Options After a Loss

Policy Language	Additional Explanation
Options we may, in our sole discretion, exercise after loss include the following:	This section sets forth the steps that insurers may take to require action on the part of the policyholder. If the policyholder fails to comply with the insurer's request, the policyholder is in breach of the insuring agreement, which may affect the payment of the claim.
1. At such reasonable times and places that we may designate, you must:	
a. Show us or our representative the damaged property;	The policyholder must make the flood-damaged property available for examination as often as needed to verify the loss and claim. Insurer representatives will give the policyholder advance notice of the specific time and meeting place to inspect the damaged property.
	The policyholder should document their loss with photographs before removing or disposing of damaged items that pose a health hazard, such as perishable food.
b. Submit to examination under oath, while not in the presence of another insured, and sign the same; and	The insurer can require the policyholder to submit to an examination under oath but not in the presence of another insured when there are questions concerning the claim. An examination under oath is a formal proceeding, typically conducted prior to a lawsuit, during which the insurer's representative questions an insured under oath in the presence of a court reporter. The insurer should ask the policyholder to present information and documentation necessary to evaluate their claim when requiring an examination under oath. This can include books of accounts, financial records, receipts, income tax records, property settlement records, invoices, purchase orders, affidavits, and other materials to verify the loss.
c. Permit us to examine and make extracts and copies of:	The SFIP will not pay more than the amount of insurance that the policyholder is entitled to for the damaged, lost, or destroyed property insured under this policy if

VIII. General Conditions

Policy Language	Additional Explanation
(1) Any policies of property insurance insuring you against loss and the deed establishing your ownership of the insured real property;	non-NFIP insurance covers a loss covered by the SFIP. The policyholder must confirm the availability of other insurance to determine what the NFIP will pay. Examples include a homeowner's policy water damage or sump overflow endorsement, mobile homeowner's policy, scheduled property policy, renter's policy, builder's risk policy, etc. See SFIP Section VIII.C. for Other Insurance.
(2) Condominium association documents including the Declarations of the condominium, its Articles of Association or Incorporation, Bylaws, rules and regulations, and other relevant documents if you are a unit owner in a condominium building; and	A claim involving a unit in a condominium building requires the declarations of the condominium, bylaws, etc. to determine the policyholder's insurable interest in the building. Adjusters may have to determine if the RCBAP paid for any damages. NFIP will not pay for the same damaged item twice nor pay a claim for a residential unit that exceeds the statutory limits. Adjusters must provide documentation that a condominium association owns the insured building, not a homeowners' association or a building cooperative.
(3) All books of accounts, bills, invoices and other vouchers, or certified copies pertaining to the damaged property if the originals are lost.	Insurers may require the policyholder to provide information that documents the extent of the loss and the amount of the claim. Examples include books of accounts, bills, invoices, vouchers, and items showing the actual amounts paid to stores, contractors, or others for repair or replacement of items. This may also include photographs of the flood-damaged property that sufficiently and reasonably document the damage, quality of the item, and describe the damaged property. The policyholder can provide certified copies when the originals are lost or destroyed.
2. We may request, in writing, that you furnish us with a complete inventory of the lost, damaged or destroyed property, including: a. Quantities and costs;	"Costs" is the amount to replace a personal property item with like kind and quality at current pricing, including the price for sales tax any applicable shipping and product assembly.
b. Actual cash values or replacement cost (whichever is appropriate);	• Replacement cost is the cost to replace a building, a building item, or a personal property item that includes all charges related to material, labor, equipment, any charges, if applicable, for design, delivery, assembly, sales tax, and applicable overhead and profit. • Actual cash value is replacement cost, less applicable depreciation of all components of the price.
c. Amounts of loss claimed;	The amount of loss claimed is the amount of payment the policyholder asks to receive for the damaged and covered property.
d. Any written plans and specifications for repair of the damaged	Written plans and specifications for repair of the damaged property include

VIII. General Conditions

Policy Language	Additional Explanation
property that you can reasonably make available to us; and	contractor estimates, subcontractor bids, invoices, architectural reports and drawings, engineering reports, etc. This also includes water restoration or structural drying invoices and supporting documentation. NFIP will not accept a non-itemized, lump sum, or single line estimate or invoice in support of a claim.
e. Evidence that prior flood damage has been repaired.	Policyholders must provide evidence that previous flood damage was repaired whether or not they owned or insured the property. This includes any flood damages unrepaired by a previous owner. NFIP expects policyholders to maintain proof of repairs such as receipts, canceled checks, etc. in a safe location away from the threat of flood. When policyholders do not have proof of repairs, adjusters should request other forms of documentation such as: • Pre-flood photographs (social media or other family members) to compare old and replaced items. • Credit card or bank statements showing dates and dollar amounts of payments to contractors. • Itemized statements and paid invoices from contractors.
3. If we give you written notice within 30 days after we receive your signed, sworn proof of loss, we may: a. Repair, rebuild, or replace any part of the lost, damaged, or destroyed property with material or property of like kind and quality or its functional equivalent; and b. Take all or any part of the damaged property at the value that we agree upon or its appraised value.	3.a. N/A 3.b. Refer to Section VII.O. and other guidance, including Salvage in Section 2 of this manual.
L. No Benefit to Bailee	
No person or organization, other than you, having custody of covered property will benefit from this insurance.	Bailment is the delivery of personal property by one person (the bailor) to another (the bailee) who holds the property for a certain purpose, such as a service, under an expressed or implied-in-fact contract. The SFIP does not cover the bailee because bailment is a change of possession, not a change of ownership or title. An example is when a customer (bailor) takes personal clothing to the dry cleaner (bailee). A bailment exists when the bailee has the clothing. The articles of clothing in the possession of the bailee are bailee goods and

VIII. General Conditions

Policy Language	Additional Explanation
	are not covered.
	Consignment is a written agreement where a consignor provides owned personal property to a consignee for sale and gives the consignee a percentage of the sale price when sold. The SFIP does not cover property on consignment.

M. Loss Payment

Policy Language	Additional Explanation
1. We will adjust all losses with you. We will pay you unless some other person or entity is named in the policy or is legally entitled to receive payment. Loss will be payable 60 days after we receive your proof of loss (or within 90 days after the insurance adjuster files the adjuster's report signed and sworn to by you in lieu of a proof of loss) and: a. We reach an agreement with you; b. There is an entry of a final judgment; or c. There is a filing of an appraisal award with us, as provided in VIII.P.	Adjusters and examiners should work with a policyholder or their authorized representative to understand the loss, prepare the estimate, and reach an agreed value for the loss. The insurer's obligation to pay and the 60-day timeframe to pay begin once the policyholder meets the requirements in Paragraph J, a proof of loss that meets all NFIP requirements, or after the signed and sworn to adjuster's report is received, and, • Insurer and the policyholder agree on the payment amount, or • There is an entry of final judgment or an appraisal award by a court of competent jurisdiction. The insurer should promptly process all claims and payment requests. The insurer should communicate to policyholders any unforeseen delays in the claim examination process and advance undisputed claimed amounts at the earliest opportunity. When the insurer cannot pay a completed proof of Loss, the examiner and the adjuster should promptly communicate the necessary adjustments or documentation required to the policyholder. Insurers should work with policyholders to settle the loss without resorting to a denial of the claim by the insurer. See Section 4 Appeals of this manual for information on denial letters.
2. If we reject your proof of loss in whole or in part you may: a. Accept our denial of your claim; b. Exercise your rights under this policy; or c. File an amended proof of loss as long as it is filed within 60 days of the date of the loss.	Courts have not accepted the language "reject your proof of loss" as sufficient to communicate to the policyholder that the insurer has denied their claim in whole or in part. Hence, insurers should not use this language to deny all or part of a claim. When the insurer issues a written denial, the policyholder has certain rights, which include filing an appeal directly to FEMA (see Section 4 Appeals), filing suit against the insurer, or submitting an amended proof of loss with the documentation to support the requested loss and payment amount.

VIII. General Conditions

Policy Language	Additional Explanation
	The one-year statute of limitations for filing suit begins when the insurer issues the first denial letter (42 U.S.C. § 4072; 44 C.F.R. § 62.22(a)). Submitting subsequent additional or amended proofs of loss does not reset the one-year statute of limitations. Adjusters and examiners must assist policyholders in identifying all opportunities for payment. This helps the policyholder recover, ensures customer satisfaction, and prevents unnecessary appeals and lawsuits.
N. Abandonment	
You may not abandon to us damaged or undamaged property insured under this policy.	N/A
O. Salvage	
We may permit you to keep damaged property insured under this policy after a loss, and we will reduce the amount of the loss proceeds payable to you under the policy by the value of the salvage.	The insurer always has the right to seek salvage or to take possession of damaged property. Insurers should pursue opportunities for financial recovery when available. See Salvage in Section 2 of this manual.
P. Appraisal	
If you and we fail to agree on the actual cash value or, if applicable, replacement cost of your damaged property to settle upon the amount of loss, then either may demand an appraisal of the loss. In this event, you and we will each choose a competent and impartial appraiser within 20 days after receiving a written request from the other. The two appraisers will choose an umpire. If they cannot agree upon an umpire within 15 days, you or we may request that the choice be made by a judge of a court of record in the State where the covered property is located. The appraisers will separately state the actual cash value, the replacement cost, and the amount of loss to each item. If the appraisers submit a written report of an agreement to us, the amount agreed upon will be the amount of loss. If they fail to agree, they will submit their differences to the umpire. A decision agreed to by any two will set the amount of actual cash value and loss, or if it applies, the replacement cost and loss. Each party will: 1. Pay its own appraiser; and	See Appraisal in Section 2 of this manual.

VIII. General Conditions

Policy Language	Additional Explanation
Bear the other expenses of the appraisal and umpire equally.	
Q. Mortgage Clause	
The word "mortgagee" includes trustee. Any loss payable under Coverage A—Building Property will be paid to any mortgagee of whom we have actual notice, as well as any other mortgagee or loss payee determined to exist at the time of loss, and you, as interests appear. If more than one mortgagee is named, the order of payment will be the same as the order of precedence of the mortgages. If we deny your claim, the denial will not apply to a valid claim of the mortgagee, if the mortgagee: 1. Notifies us of any change in the ownership or occupancy, or substantial change in risk of which the mortgagee is aware; 2. Pays any premium due under this policy on demand if you have neglected to pay the premium; and 3. Submits a signed, sworn proof of loss within 60 days after receiving notice from us of your failure to do so. All of the terms of this policy apply to the mortgagee. The mortgagee has the right to receive loss payment even if the mortgagee has started foreclosure or similar action on the building. If we decide to cancel or not renew this policy, it will continue in effect for the benefit of the mortgagee only for 30 days after we notify the mortgagee of the cancellation or non-renewal. If we pay the mortgagee for any loss and deny payment to you, we are subrogated to all the rights of the mortgagee granted under the mortgage on the property. Subrogation will not impair the right of the mortgagee to recover the full amount of the mortgagee's claim.	The SFIP pays claims for building property to the named policyholder, mortgage holders, lienholders, other loss payees for whom we have actual notice, and any loss payee determined to exist at the time of loss. The mortgage clause is a contract within a contract. It is a contract between the mortgagee and the insurer within the contract between the policyholder and the insurer. Including the name of the mortgagee on each building claim payment is the surest way to keep this promise to the mortgagee. For all building payments, except Coverage C – Other Coverages and Coverage D – ICC, include all known mortgagees, as they are additional insureds. The insurer may potentially include a loss payee or lienholder on Coverage B – Personal Property of whom the insurer received actual notice, such as from the U.S. Small Business Administration (SBA). If the insurer receives a letter of an SBA-approved loan, the SBA must be included on the building check(s) and the contents check(s) if the loan is for both real estate and personal or business property.

VIII. General Conditions

Policy Language	Additional Explanation
R. Suit Against Us	
You may not sue us to recover money under this policy unless you have complied with all the requirements of the policy. If you do sue, you must start the suit within 1 year after the date of the written denial of all or part of the claim, and you must file the suit in the United States District Court of the district in which the covered property was located at the time of loss. This requirement applies to any claim that you may have under this policy and to any dispute that you may have arising out of the handling of any claim under the policy.	The statute of limitations begins with the insurer's first written denial of the claim. Subsequent denial letters do not re-start the statute of limitations. Policyholders must file suit in a U.S. District Court in the district where the loss occurred within one year after the insurer's first written denial. Neither the Federal Insurance Administrator nor the insurer may extend the one-year statute of limitations to file suit.
S. Subrogation	
Whenever we make a payment for a loss under this policy, we are subrogated to your right to recover for that loss from any other person. That means that your right to recover for a loss that was partly or totally caused by someone else is automatically transferred to us, to the extent that we have paid you for the loss. We may require you to acknowledge this transfer in writing. After the loss, you may not give up our right to recover this money or do anything that would prevent us from recovering it. If you make any claim against any person who caused your loss and recover any money, you must pay us back first before you may keep any of that money.	When the adjuster believes there may be potential for subrogation, the adjuster completes FEMA Form 086-0-16 – Cause of Loss and Subrogation Report, to identify a potentially responsible third party; and characterize how their actions may have caused or worsened flood damage. When the adjuster believes the cause of loss may be completely or in part due to an intentional or human cause, the adjuster should complete the NFIP Subrogation Form. Claim handling, review, and payment should proceed as normal. The insurer should make sure the subrogation form Cause of Loss and Subrogation Report is complete and escalate the matter for a subrogation review. See Subrogation in Section 2 of this manual.
T. Continuous Lake Flooding	

1. If an insured building has been flooded by rising lake waters continuously for 90 days or more and it appears reasonably certain that a continuation of this flooding will result in a covered loss to the insured building equal to or greater than the building policy limits plus the deductible or the maximum payable under the policy for any one building loss, we will pay you the lesser of these two amounts without waiting for the further damage to occur if you sign a release agreeing:
   a. To make no further claim under this policy;
   b. Not to seek renewal of this policy;
	N/A

VIII. General Conditions

Policy Language	Additional Explanation
c. Not to apply for any flood insurance under the Act for property at the described location; and	
d. Not to seek a premium refund for current or prior terms.	
If the policy term ends before the insured building has been flooded continuously for 90 days, the provisions of this paragraph T.1. will apply when the insured building suffers a covered loss before the policy term ends.	
2. If your insured building is subject to continuous lake flooding from a closed basin lake, you may elect to file a claim under either paragraph T.1. above or T.2. (A "closed basin lake" is a natural lake from which water leaves primarily through evaporation and whose surface area now exceeds or has exceeded 1 square mile at any time in the recorded past. Most of the nation's closed basin lakes are in the western half of the United States where annual evaporation exceeds annual precipitation and where lake levels and surface areas are subject to considerable fluctuation due to wide variations in the climate. These lakes may overtop their basins on rare occasions.) Under this paragraph T.2. we will pay your claim as if the building is a total loss even though it has not been continuously inundated for 90 days, subject to the following conditions:	The only Closed Basin Lake recognized by FEMA at this time is Devils Lake, North Dakota. Subject to all other provisions of the SFIP, if an insured building is subject to continuous lake flooding from Devils Lake, the following requirements must be met to be eligible for coverage under the terms of all SFIP forms: ● The building must be in a participating community eligible for this coverage; and, ● The subject building must have had NFIP flood insurance coverage continuously beginning on November 30, 1999, and any subsequent owner on or after November 30, 1999, must have an NFIP policy in effect within 60 days of the transfer of title (see: T. 2. g.); and,
a. Lake flood waters must damage or imminently threaten to damage your building.	● The policyholder must grant a conservation easement (see: T. 2. b. (2), and the community must have adopted a permanent land-use ordinance on or before July 15, 2001 (see: T. 2. e. (1), (2), and (3).
b. Before approval of your claim, you must: (1) Agree to a claim payment that reflects your buying back the salvage on a negotiated basis; and (2) Grant the conservation easement described in FEMA's "Policy Guidance for Closed Basin Lakes" to be recorded in the office of the local recorder of deeds. FEMA, in consultation with the community in which the property is located, will identify on a map an area or areas of special consideration (ASC) in which there is a potential for flood damage from continuous lake flooding. FEMA will give the community the agreed-upon map showing the ASC. This easement will only apply to that portion of the property in the ASC. It will allow certain agricultural and recreational uses of the land. The only structures it will allow on any portion of the property within the ASC are certain simple	FEMA will not recognize any increases in coverage limits with effective dates on or after November 30, 1999 (see: T. 2. g.), except when offered by the insurer as a routine inflation-guard increase and purchased by the policyholder. Insured buildings not eligible for the provisions of T. 2. described above, but damaged by continuous lake flooding, will be eligible for those provisions described at T. 1. of the SFIP, subject to the terms and conditions of the T. 1. and the SFIP. Buildings in eligible communities that are subject to damage from the effects of the Closed Basin Lake, Devils Lake, North Dakota, may file claims if any portion of the insured building, as defined in the SFIP, is at the still-water level derived by official National Weather Service (NWS) still-water levels. See Appendix C in this manual for FEMA's "Policy Guidance for Closed Basin Lakes".

VIII. General Conditions

Policy Language	Additional Explanation
agricultural and recreational structures. If any of these allowable structures are insurable buildings under the NFIP and are insured under the NFIP, they will not be eligible for the benefits of this paragraph T.2. If a U.S. Army Corps of Engineers certified flood control project or otherwise certified flood control project later protects the property, FEMA will, upon request, amend the ASC to remove areas protected by those projects. The restrictions of the easement will then no longer apply to any portion of the property removed from the ASC; and	
(3) Comply with paragraphs T.1.a. through T.1.d. above.	
c. Within 90 days of approval of your claim, you must move your building to a new location outside the ASC. FEMA will give you an additional 30 days to move if you show there is sufficient reason to extend the time.	
d. Before the final payment of your claim, you must acquire an elevation certificate and a floodplain development permit from the local floodplain administrator for the new location of your building.	
e. Before the approval of your claim, the community having jurisdiction over your building must:	
(1) Adopt a permanent land use ordinance, or a temporary moratorium for a period not to exceed 6 months to be followed immediately by a permanent land use ordinance that is consistent with the provisions specified in the easement required in paragraph T.2.b. above.	
(2) Agree to declare and report any violations of this ordinance to FEMA so that under Section 1316 of the National Flood Insurance Act of 1968, as amended, flood insurance to the building can be denied; and	
(3) Agree to maintain as deed-restricted, for purposes compatible with open space or agricultural or recreational use only, any affected property the community acquires an interest in. These deed restrictions must be consistent with the provisions of paragraph T.2.b. above, except that, even if a certified project protects the property, the land use restrictions	

VIII. General Conditions

Policy Language	Additional Explanation
continue to apply if the property was acquired under the Hazard Mitigation Grant Program or the Flood Mitigation Assistance Program. If a non-profit land trust organization receives the property as a donation, that organization must maintain the property as deed-restricted, consistent with the provisions of paragraph T.2.b. above.	
f. Before the approval of your claim, the affected State must take all action set forth in FEMA's "Policy Guidance for Closed Basin Lakes."	
You must have NFIP flood insurance coverage continuously in effect from a date established by FEMA until you file a claim under paragraph T.2. If a subsequent owner buys NFIP insurance that goes into effect within 60 days of the date of transfer of title, any gap in coverage during that 60-day period will not be a violation of this continuous coverage requirement. For the purpose of honoring a claim under this paragraph T.2., we will not consider to be in effect any increased coverage that became effective after the date established by FEMA. The exception to this is any increased coverage in the amount suggested by your insurer as an inflation adjustment.	
h. This paragraph T.2. will be in effect for a community when the FEMA Regional Administrator for the affected region provides to the community, in writing, the following:	
(1) Confirmation that the community and the State are in compliance with the conditions in paragraphs T.2.e. and T.2.f. above, and	
g. The date by which you must have flood insurance in effect	
U. Duplicate Policies Not Allowed	
1. We will not insure your property under more than one NFIP policy.	The policyholder cannot benefit from the duplicate flood insurance coverage if a policyholder has two NFIP policies insuring the same property. The first policy purchased is the policy in force at the time of loss.
If we find that the duplication was not knowingly created, we will give you written notice. The notice will advise you that you may choose one of several options under the following procedures:	When there is no loss involved, the policyholder may choose to keep either policy. The effective date of the increased coverage begins on the renewal date of the
a. If you choose to keep in effect the policy with the earlier effective date, you may also choose to add the coverage limits of the later	second policy purchased if the policyholder chooses to combine the coverage

VIII. General Conditions

Policy Language	Additional Explanation
policy to the limits of the earlier policy. The change will become effective as of the effective date of the later policy.	amounts purchased, and the combined coverage does not exceed the statutory limits.
b. If you choose to keep in effect the policy with the later effective date, you may also choose to add the coverage limits of the earlier policy to the limits of the later policy. The change will be effective as of the effective date of the later policy.	
In either case, you must pay the pro rata premium for the increased coverage limits within 30 days of the written notice. In no event will the resulting coverage limits exceed the permissible limits of coverage under the Act or your insurable interest, whichever is less.	
We will make a refund to you, according to applicable NFIP rules, of the premium for the policy not being kept in effect.	
2. Your option under Condition U. Duplicate Policies Not Allowed to elect which NFIP policy to keep in effect does not apply when duplicates have been knowingly created. Losses occurring under such circumstances will be adjusted according to the terms and conditions of the earlier policy. The policy with the later effective date must be canceled.	

V. Loss Settlement	
1. Introduction	N/A
This policy provides three methods of settling losses: Replacement Cost, Special Loss Settlement, and Actual Cash Value. Each method is used for a different type of property, as explained in a–c. below.	
a. Replacement Cost Loss settlement described in V.2. below applies to buildings other than manufactured homes or travel trailers.	
b. Special Loss Settlement described in V.3. below applies to a residential condominium building that is a travel trailer or a manufactured home.	
c. Actual Cash Value loss settlement applies to all other property covered under this policy, as outlined in V.4. below.	
2. Replacement Cost Loss Settlement	The insurer does not have to withhold the recoverable depreciation until the owner makes the building repairs as required in SFIP Section VIII.V.2.b. and c. when the structure is eligible for replacement cost loss settlement.
a. We will pay to repair or replace a damaged or destroyed building, after application of the deductible and without deduction for	

VIII. General Conditions

Policy Language	Additional Explanation
depreciation, but not more than the least of the following amounts: (1) The amount of insurance in this policy that applies to the building; (2) The replacement cost of that part of the building damaged, with materials of like kind and quality, and for like occupancy and use; or (3) The necessary amount actually spent to repair or replace the damaged part of the building for like occupancy and use. b. We will not be liable for any loss on a Replacement Cost Coverage basis unless and until actual repair or replacement of the damaged building or parts thereof, is completed. c. If a building is rebuilt at a location other than the described location, we will pay no more than it would have cost to repair or rebuild at the described location, subject to all other terms of Replacement Cost Loss Settlement. **3. Special Loss Settlement** a. The following loss settlement conditions apply to a residential condominium building that is: (1) a manufactured home or a travel trailer, as defined in II.B.6.b. And c., and (2) at least 16 feet wide when fully assembled and has at least 600 square feet within its perimeter walls when fully assembled. b. If such a building is totally destroyed or damaged to such an extent that, in our judgment, it is not economically feasible to repair, at least to its pre-damaged condition, we will, at our discretion, pay the least of the following amounts: (1) The lesser of the replacement cost of the manufactured home or travel trailer or 1.5 times the actual cash value; or (2) The Building Limit of liability shown on your Declarations Page. c. If such a manufactured home or travel trailer is partially damaged and, in our judgment, it is economically feasible to repair it to its pre-damaged condition, we will settle the loss according to the	There are two ways to settle a loss on a manufactured or mobile home or a travel trailer. ■ Total loss is a property that is either not repairable (i.e., destroyed) or the cost to repair exceeds the value of the property: ● If the dwelling is 16 feet wide, at least 600 total square feet, and the principal residence, the loss adjustment is the lesser of the following: — Replacement cost, i.e., the value of a new manufactured or mobile home, or travel trailer of like kind and quality, delivered to and installed at the described location. — 1.5 times the actual cash value, i.e., 1.5 times the documented book value for the year of the existing manufactured or mobile home, or travel trailer, delivered to and installed at the described location. — Amount of coverage purchased under Coverage A - Building. ■ Repairable loss or a loss not considered a total loss: ● If the manufactured or mobile home or a travel trailer is 16 feet wide, at least 600 total square feet, and the principal residence, settle the loss under Replacement Cost Loss Settlement. (See Section VII.V.2.)

VIII. General Conditions

Policy Language	Additional Explanation
Replacement Cost Loss Settlement conditions in V.2. above.	• If the manufactured or mobile home or a travel trailer is not 16 feet wide, or not at least 600 total square feet, or not the principal residence, settle the loss under Actual Cash Value Loss Settlement. (See Section VII.V.4.) The requirement for a policyholder to purchase building coverage to at least 80 percent of the manufactured or mobile home or a travel trailer's replacement cost value does not apply under Special Loss Settlement.
4. Actual Cash Value Loss Settlement a. The types of property noted below are subject to actual cash value loss settlement: (1) Personal property; (2) Insured property abandoned after a loss and that remains as debris at the described location; (3) Outside antennas and aerials, awnings, and other outdoor equipment; (4) Carpeting and pads; (5) Appliances; and (6) A manufactured home or mobile home or a travel trailer as defined in II.B.6.b. or c. that does not meet the conditions for Special Loss Settlement in V.3. above. b. We will pay the least of the following amounts: (1) The applicable amount of insurance under this policy; (2) The actual cash value (as defined in II.B.2.); or (3) The amount it would cost to repair or replace the property with material of like kind and quality within a reasonable time after the loss.	An actual cash value loss settlement is the cost to repair or replace insured building items at the time of the loss, less the building deductible and less its physical depreciation. Appliances include refrigerators, stoves, ovens, ranges, trash compactors, garbage disposals, and the like.

IX. Liberalization Clause

Policy Language	Additional Explanation
If we make a change that broadens your coverage under this edition of our policy, but does not require any additional premium, then that change will automatically apply to your insurance as of the date we implement the change, provided that this implementation date falls within 60 days before or during the policy term stated on the Declarations Page.	Insurers cannot apply additional coverages provided through the liberalization clause retroactively to losses that have occurred; insurers can apply it prospectively. The clause permits FEMA to give existing, active policyholders beneficial amendments without needing to separately endorse their policies but does not provide any retroactive effect.

X. What Law Governs

Policy Language	Additional Explanation
This policy and all disputes arising from the handling of any Insurance Act of 1968, as amended (42 U.S.C. 4001, et seq.), claim under the policy are governed exclusively by the flood and Federal common law insurance regulations issued by FEMA, the National Flood Insurance Act of 1968, as amended (42 U.S.C. 4001, et seq.), and Federal common law.	N/A

This page was intentionally left blank.

Section 2: Claims Processes and Guidance

This section provides FEMA guidance and claims processes. The primary audience is claims adjusters with call-out boxes denoting the claims examiners' roles/responsibilities.

1   Adjuster Preliminary Damage Assessment

The adjuster completes the Adjuster Preliminary Damage Assessment (APDA) form when there is possible "substantial damage" to the insured building directly from flood, non-covered flood damage, and damage from other perils.

Only communities can determine substantial damage. Substantial damage is defined as damage from any origin where the cost to repair the structure to its before damaged condition equals or exceeds 50 percent of the market value of the building before the damage occurred. The adjuster should know that some communities have adopted a percentage threshold of less than 50 percent. Community officials can efficiently direct resources for substantial damage inspection when APDAs are received early in the flood disaster recovery process.

All adjusters should adhere to the following:

- For the purpose of claim handling, the adjuster should complete and submit an APDA when the estimated cost to repair flood damage approaches or exceeds 50 percent of the RCV of the building.

- While the APDA form contains space for two separate claims, ONLY submit one claim per form. Submitting one claim per form helps to avoid confusion during the review process at the community level.

- The timely submission of the APDA is important. FEMA requests that adjusters submit the APDA as soon as possible following the initial inspection. Email the APDA forms to the NFIP at NFIPClaimsMailbox@fema.dhs.gov. The subject line should read "APDA Enclosed." Submit a copy of the APDA to the company along with the Preliminary Report.

Claims Examiners

The examiner should confirm the adjuster timely submits an APDA on applicable claims by checking for a copy of the APDA with the Preliminary Report. When an APDA is not included with the Preliminary Report the examiner should assume the adjuster did not submit an APDA. The examiner should contact the adjusting firm to ensure the APDA is submitted to the NFIP BSA and to request a copy for the claim file. Note, the local building official is the authority who determines a building is substantially damaged and the requirement for compliance with the local floodplain management ordinance.

2   Advance Payments

FEMA encourages advance payments to policyholders whenever it is warranted. The adjuster should notify the policyholder that they may request an advance payment on their behalf, and to expect the payment through their local U.S. mail carrier or express mail service. Therefore, the adjuster must verify the mailing address. FEMA recommends two advance payment opportunity types for insurers to use as they find suitable:

2.1   Advance Payment Opportunity One: Pre-Inspection

$5,000 pre-inspection advance. To accommodate the needs of its policyholders during major flood events, NFIP insurers may offer policyholders an advance payment before an adjuster inspects the loss.

FEMA allows a payment of this type up to $5,000 on building and contents losses combined less deductibles. The insurer must obtain and verify the following information before the payment is issued:

1. The policyholder provides the insurer with a notice of loss in accordance with the SFIP.

2. The insurer verifies that the subject property is covered by an active flood insurance policy and confirms current coverage terms, amounts, and deductibles.

3. The policyholder gives verbal or written statements to the adjuster or examiner. The adjuster or examiner documents these statements and provides additional information to the insurer confirming the following:

   a. Relating to the flood:

      i. A flood, as defined by SFIP, directly damaged the insured property.

      ii. Names the source of the flood.

      iii. Briefly describes how the flood occurred; when in doubt, obtain supporting documentation available from an official weather bureau or reputable news media.

    iv. Explains other effects from the flood event to support that the loss is in excess of the advanced amount: Was the street flooded? Are neighboring properties and buildings also flooded?

  b. Relating to flood depth and damage:

    i. Provides the approximate depth of floodwater on the exterior of the building and the approximate depth inside the interior floor level.

    ii. Details whether the extent of damage is limited to an area subject to coverage limitations such as a basement or lower enclosure, or the extent of damage is in a ground-level floor or elevated floor level.

    iii. Briefly describes damage to the building and personal property items.

    iv. Addresses any prior loss to avoid a duplication of payment of non-repaired property items.

$20,000 pre-inspection advance (The enhanced process is only available when activated by FEMA). An NFIP insurer may issue a larger advance payment amount before the loss is inspected by an adjuster when it obtains more substantive documentation.

The NFIP allows a payment of this type up to $20,000 on building and contents losses combined less deductibles. For this type of pre-inspection advance payment, in addition to obtaining and verifying the above items 1 to 3, the insurer should also obtain the following:

1. **Photographs.** Obtain the proper number of photographs depicting floodwater depths and damage to the building and personal property items.

2. **Documentation of cost.** Verify out-of-pocket expenses related to the repair or replacement of covered property, such as with paid receipts, invoices, or estimates with canceled checks; or an estimate signed by the contractor on letterhead that itemizes the repair or the facilitation of repairs, to covered property.

2.2 Advance Payment Opportunity Two: Post-Inspection

25 percent advance. NFIP insurers may issue an advance payment amount once the adjuster inspects the property and after providing the insurer with the Preliminary Report and any other applicable documentation that is normally submitted or required with the Preliminary Report, including but not limited to the proper number of photographs, policyholder-signed Advance Payment Request form, and any underwriting memorandum, APDA, adjuster narrative addressing a prior NFIP paid loss. The NFIP allows a payment of this type up to 25 percent of the reserve amount indicated on the Preliminary Report for each coverage type, building, or contents less deductible(s).

50 percent advance. The insurer may issue a larger advance payment amount when it obtains more substantive documentation. The NFIP allows a payment of this type up to 50 percent of the reserve amount indicated on the Preliminary Report for building coverage less deductible. For this type of post-inspection advance payment, in addition to obtaining and verifying the above in the preceding paragraph, the insurer should also obtain a signed contract between the policyholder and the contractor along with the estimate of repair. The estimate should itemize the repair and cost to covered property.

Building Valuation Loss Assessment (This enhanced process is only available when activated by FEMA). The insurer may issue a post-inspection advance payment based on the FEMA-authorized Building Valuation Loss Assessment (BVLA) advance payment method. In addition to the Preliminary Report and any other applicable documentation that is normally submitted or required with the Preliminary Report, including but not limited to the proper photographs, policyholder-signed Advance Payment Request form, any underwriting memorandum, APDA or adjuster narrative addressing a prior NFIP paid loss, the adjuster must also submit a properly completed BVLA worksheet to the insurer. See Appendix J in this manual for the BVLA method and frequently asked questions.

WYO's proprietary approach. The insurer may issue a post-inspection advance payment based on the WYO Company's own proprietary estimation approach. This approach and payment method may not broaden or change any coverage term in the SFIP. The insurer must document any deviations from normal FEMA processes and include a reference to the proprietary process in the claim file. As with the BVLA advance payment method, a claim payment under the insurer's own proprietary estimation approach is subject to all standard FEMA claim documentation and payment standards.

2.3 Procedures for Issuing Advance Payment

Claims Examiners

An NFIP insurer may offer an advance payment upon written, verbal, or electronic request by the policyholder. With any advance payment, the insurer must include a written notice conditioning the advance payment on the policyholder's acknowledgment that:

1. The NFIP advance payment is not intended to provide reimbursement to the policyholder for non-SFIP insured expenses, such as costs related to evacuation, temporary housing while the home is non-inhabitable, a rental car to cover the loss of a personal vehicle, or any other expense not covered by the SFIP.
2. The issuance and acceptance of an advance payment does not prejudice or waive any claim or defense available to either the policyholder or insurer.
3. The issuance and acceptance of an advance payment does not constitute an admission of coverage under the policy.
4. The policyholder must assert the insured property has suffered a covered loss.
5. If the insurer determines the claim is not a covered loss, or if the advance payment exceeds the amount of the covered loss, the policyholder is ineligible for the payment and agrees to repay the advanced payment in excess of the covered loss.
6. Acceptance of an advance payment will not affect the policyholder's right to seek additional payment under the terms and conditions of the SFIP.
7. After the claim is settled, the insurer will reduce the final payment by the amount of any advance(s) payment made to the policyholder.

Claims Examiners

8. Building only: The insurer must include as co-payee any mortgagee shown on the Declaration Page of the policy or any known mortgagee on any advance payment for building coverage.
9. To finalize the claim, the policyholder must execute a proof of loss meeting the requirements of the SFIP for all amounts received, including the amount of the advance payment, except as may otherwise be authorized by the Administrator under any applicable waiver.

2.4 Advance Payments Exceeding the Covered Loss

Adjusters and examiners must make sure they avoid recommending and issuing advance payments that exceed the final total claim payment. Adjusters and examiners should account for the following factors when determining the amount of an advance payment in order to avoid issuing an advance payment in excess of the covered loss:

1. Amount of deductible;

2. Interior water depth;

3. Other non-flood related damage such as wind, water, etc.;

4. Pre-loss condition and ACV of damaged property, especially if a previous flood payment was issued;

5. Scope of damage such as when limited to a basement or lower enclosure with a post-FIRM elevated building subject to coverage limitations; and

6. Use of flood avoidance measures, such as sandbags or property removed to safety.

Claims Examiners

If an NFIP insurer issues an advance payment to the policyholder in excess of the covered loss, the NFIP insurer must attempt to recoup the funds. The following are the minimum steps the NFIP insurer must perform under such circumstances:

1. The insurer must send a letter via certified mail or equivalent trackable delivery service to the policyholder containing the following information:

    a. The amount due.
    b. A description of the charges.
    c. A description of the remedies available to the NFIP upon failure to repay the amount due by the deadline, including but not limited to Federal Debt Collection pursuant to 44 CFR Part 11, Subpart A.
    d. The deadline for either submitting payment or disputing the validity of the overpayment, which must be at least 30 days from the date of the letter.
    e. Contact information for an individual representing the insurer that the policyholder can contact directly to dispute the validity of the overpayment or seek more information.

2. If the policyholder does not pay the amount due by the stated deadline, the insurer must attempt to contact the policyholder via phone and then send a follow-up letter via certified mail or equivalent trackable delivery service to the policyholder's last known address.

If an NFIP insurer is not able to recoup the overpayment after making its best efforts, the NFIP insurer must provide FEMA with the following documentation:

![Claims Examiners icon] **Claims Examiners**

1. A narrative explaining the basis of the overpayment determination and identifying the insurer's efforts to recoup the funds.
2. Copies of all written correspondence with the policyholder regarding the overpayment.
3. A copy of the claim file.

See Claim Overpayment Recovery in this section of the manual.

3 Appraisal

Claims professionals should only use appraisal to resolve disputes involving the amount to pay for flood damages. The policyholder may not use appraisal to determine the scope, coverage, or causation of damage.

Appraisal is an option of last resort and does not replace the claims adjustment process. Filing a lawsuit is the last resort for settling a disputed claim.

FEMA encourages the policyholder and the insurer to exhaust all other avenues available to determine the fair price for an agreed-to loss. This includes the policyholder providing contractors' estimates, receipts, invoices, photographs, and any other relevant documentation or a written explanation to support their claim of a fair price for the agreed-to loss.

The SFIP allows appraisal under the following conditions:

- The policyholder and the insurer must agree on the scope of loss (damage). There must be an agreed list of covered items damaged by flood. Appraisal is not available if the policyholder and insurer cannot agree on the scope of loss. Insurers cannot use appraisal if the policyholder submits an appeal to FEMA or initiates litigation. Appraisal must result in a complete resolution of the entire claim.

- The policyholder must submit a timely and completed proof of loss with supporting documentation for the items the policyholder seeks appraisal. If the policyholder submitted a signed and sworn proof of loss and the insurer paid the amount in full, there is no dispute regarding pricing and no need for appraisal.

- The policyholder must provide documentation with the proof of loss that explains, supports, or otherwise justifies the increased cost. The insurer should not accept the request for appraisal simply from an estimate with increased unit pricing and no justification included. This is not a complete proof of loss.

- Appraisal is available only when the insurer and the policyholder agree on eligibility, causation, coverage, and scope of loss, except they do not agree on the value of the covered loss. Appraisal is only available under the SFIP for differences with unit pricing, which also includes differences with the scope to repair the agreed covered scope of loss.

- If the policyholder invokes the Appraisal Clause and attempts to resolve a coverage or scoping issue outside the previously agreed upon scope of the appraisal, then the policyholder did not properly invoke the Appraisal Clause. As the Appraisal Clause was not properly invoked, the appraisal process, including any award, is not valid. If the WYO inappropriately issues payment to the policyholder or if the WYO inappropriately used the Appraisal Clause, the WYO is responsible to FEMA for any erroneous payments, including fees.

Appraisers and umpires must be competent and impartial. Appraisers and umpires cannot profit from a higher claim payment made to a policyholder. If the policyholder hires a public adjuster or attorney, and the basis of their fee is securing a higher claims payment for the policyholder, no one employed, affiliated with, or related to the public adjuster or attorney can serve as the appraiser or the umpire. The same rule applies to the insurer. No one employed, affiliated with, or related to the adjuster or owner of the adjusting company who receives a fee based upon the policyholder receiving a higher payment can serve as an appraiser or umpire.

If the insurer agrees and invokes the policyholder's request for appraisal, the policyholder may not subsequently file an appeal to FEMA on the same items or the same dispute reason. Similarly, if the policyholder submits an appeal to FEMA, the insurer may not invoke the appraisal provision at their policyholder's request.

4 Cisterns, Water Softeners, and Well Water Pumps

Cisterns, their components, and the water in them are covered when installed or located within the building, an eligible detached garage, or an enclosed porch, including within an enclosure or basement.

The SFIP does not cover cisterns, components, or water, that are installed or located outside of the areas defined above, including cisterns installed underground.

Figure 41. Example of a Covered Cistern in a Basement

Photograph credit Port City Daily

Figure 42. Example of a Non-covered Cistern Outside

Figure 43. Example of a Non-covered Cistern Below Ground

Photograph credit well-water-report.com

4.1 Water Softeners

A water softener and the chemicals in it, installed in a building as defined by the SFIP, at the described location, connected to and servicing the insured building, is covered.

4.2 Well Water Pumps

A well water pump that supplies water to the insured building and is installed above ground is covered when installed in a building as defined by the SFIP, at the described location connected to and servicing the insured building.

5   Claims Adjustment

The adjuster must understand what factors may be involved with the claim that may or may not affect the covered scope of loss and the dollar amount to repair or replace an item and explain these factors in detail in the narrative to support the adjuster's recommendation.

5.1 Determine Cause of Loss

On every flood claim, the adjuster must confirm a general and temporary condition of flooding occurred, as defined by the policy. This can require canvassing the neighborhood to identify if other properties flooded, interviewing neighbors, or reviewing news articles or videos documenting the flood. For some events, contacting the nearest police department, fire department, etc., may be beneficial in confirming a questionable general and temporary condition of flood. The adjuster must document:

- When the flooding began and the source of the water
- Whether the flood caused direct physical loss to covered property.

During the claim process, the adjuster should consider utilizing information provided by FEMA (example: GIS products), from state or county government websites (example: online community building property assessor pages), from publicly available information (example: online real estate listings), or from open-source map products that show the property in its pre-disaster condition.

5.2 Building Scope and Estimate

Before adjusting losses, the adjuster must ensure the software is properly calibrated for the geographic area where the loss occurred and accounts for post-disaster pricing factors and property-specific issues. The adjuster must consistently document all state and local sales tax on applicable goods or services, subject to applicable depreciation. In the claim file, the adjuster must document the most accurate scope of loss, provide notations for exceptional scope, quantity and quality, and the adjuster must take or obtain meaningful photographs of the loss that clearly document damage and non-damaged items and support the recommendation for payment or non-payment of the claim or any portion thereof.

The adjuster must identify covered flood-damaged building components and estimate the reasonable and necessary cost of repair or replacement of the damaged property. The scope of damage includes room measurements, preliminary damage findings, and photographs that document and describe the quantity, quality, and extent of damage to covered property. The adjuster may translate the adjustment of the scope of loss into an adjusted estimate of repair. The adjuster should determine if damaged items are salvageable, requiring cleaning, refinishing, repair, or if the damages are non-salvageable requiring replacement. In the estimate of loss, the adjuster should include the itemized listing of all damaged property items, organized room by room, in the unit-cost style of estimating. The unit pricing should include all costs related to labor, material, and equipment usage, and only include the expense, which restores the property with like kind and quality material and labor. The pricing should be reasonable and customary to the loss and location.

Once the policyholder obtains a signed agreement with the contractor and, if differences exist with the insurance estimate, it may be necessary for the adjuster, supervising adjuster, or the claim examiner to communicate with the policyholder and the contractor to understand the pricing differences or explain coverage issues to reach a claim settlement.

👥 Claims Examiners

The examiner should conduct a timely review of the estimate to confirm:

- The photographs reasonably document the estimate scope. Timely request additional photographs or a re-inspection when there is a question and provide status to the policyholder.
- Ensure no manual entry errors, example: ensure the quantity matches what is in the dwelling.
- Contents manipulation estimated under building coverage is limited to covered undamaged personal items and the policyholder must have purchased personal property coverage. See Contents Manipulation in Section 2 of this manual, for more information.
- The estimate appropriately addresses necessary structural drying and makes allowances for it.
- The estimate written for covered items, example: bids used to substantiate value/repair cost, does not include undamaged items or matching equipment, examples: replacing undamaged air handlers to match external HVAC units due to change in SEER ratings or refrigerant.
- The estimate is written on a room-by-room, line item, unit cost basis with reasonable recoverable and non-recoverable depreciation applied based on age and condition.
- The adjuster has identified the proper quantity, measurements, and unit costs for items.
- Building or applicable line items, qualify for replacement cost or actual cash value settlement.
- Proper deductible applied.
- No non-covered structures, for example: sheds, garages with living quarters, carports, decks (over 16 square feet), etc., are considered in the estimate.
- Applicable coverage limitations applied for basements and elevated buildings in SFHA.
- The adjuster's quantity and unit cost calculations are accurate based on item, area, and room.

- All exceptions are fully explained by the adjuster in the narrative report.

5.3 Contents (Personal Property)

The adjuster is expected to list, document, and value the entire contents loss and provide the list to the policyholder for review. If a policyholder elects to complete the inventory, the adjuster is expected to start the inventory and ensure the policyholder understands how to document the remaining contents.

The adjuster must include documentation to support the claimed loss in terms of photographing the extent of damages, quantities, qualities, and value. The adjuster must ensure coverage and depreciation are appropriately applied to their recommendation. Adjusters must also explain their judgment regarding recommending repair vs. replacement, when it may not be apparent to the policyholder or the examiner. The contents inventory should include notations specific to the applicable line item regarding descriptions of quality, make, model and serial number when applicable, quantity, age, special limit item, and cost to replace with like-kind and quality at current pricing.

The adjuster should list damages room-by-room, priced individually with like kind and quality, and include all costs related to applicable tax, removal, shipping, assembly, etc. Each replaced item must individually include a fair and reasonable rate of depreciation representing the age and/or physical condition of the item at the time of loss.

The adjuster should address any salvage or buy-back opportunity with the policyholder or with a third-party, promptly, and provide an explanation in the interim or narrative report. When the policyholder agrees to buy-back items, this should be fully disclosed in the content loss as a credit under the applicable property line item.

5.4 Special Limits

The adjuster must apply the $2,500 special limit to the aggregate ACV of all applicable contents described in the SFIP at Section III.B.6., such as jewelry, furs, contents used in business, etc., in their recommendation. The adjuster should add documentation to the claim file to support the payment recommended under this provision. The aggregate ACV is subject to the policy deductible and any excess loss to items subject to the $2,500 special limits cannot be applied to the contents deductible.

5.5 Depreciation

The adjuster should apply depreciation based on the age and physical condition of each line item in the building estimate and the personal property inventory. The adjuster should apply depreciation to the material, labor, and equipment usage, including overhead and profit and sales tax. All estimates must reflect depreciation regardless of whether the loss qualifies for replacement cost or ACV loss settlement. The adjuster should document the claim file to support the rate of depreciation or the lack of depreciation. Lump-sum depreciation or application of the same rate of depreciation to all building and personal property items throughout the adjustment or estimate, despite the many differences in material type, age, and usage, is not acceptable.

Building materials and personal property have a certain useful life or life expectancy. Replacement of an item clearly results in betterment; however, certain repairs can also result in betterment, and the adjuster should use sound judgment in determining if depreciation is appropriate. Some examples to consider:

- A repair of a small area of drywall, called a patch, would not result in betterment, even if the repair requires multiple patches. The same could be said if replacing a section of drywall in one room; however, the replacement of drywall at a 2', 4', or 8' height in an entire room(s) or throughout the entire building is betterment and should be depreciated based on the age and condition at the time of loss.

- Replacing the feet on a sofa or hutch or repairing a split leg on a table would be a repair; however, refinishing the entire item or reupholstering the sofa would be betterment and subject to depreciation.

It is important to document any exceptions.

5.6 Progress Notes in File

The adjuster must note information in the file that:

- Adequately reflects the progress of the claim and communications with the policyholder;

- The scope of damage, calculations of replacement cost and actual cash value, and a diagram of the insured building with measurements; and

- Confirms receipt of documents or information provided by the policyholder.

Claims Examiners

The examiner should conduct a timely review of the estimate to confirm:

- The contents inventory includes description, age, and cost to replace with like kind, and quality at current year pricing.
- The photographs reasonably document the damage to support repairing or replacing an item. Timely request additional photographs or a re-inspection when there is a question and provide a status to the policyholder. Photographs should document contents items of exceptional value and quality.
- The adjuster considered a reasonable repair allowance, or the policyholder provided a repair estimate to supplement the settlement amount.
- The adjuster determined or verified local replacement costs of the damaged property based on like kind and quality.
- $2,500.00 special limits applied to the aggregate of applicable contents (jewelry, furs, contents used in business, etc.).
- The adjuster applied reasonable non-recoverable physical depreciation based on the age and condition of the item at the time of loss.
- The adjuster added appropriate sales tax and proper deductible.

6   Claim Closed Without Payment Reasons

Claims Examiners

The examiner should carefully review the adjuster's report for claims that are to be closed without payment, and use the correct Closed Without Payment (CWOP) reason code in accordance with PIVOT (NFIP system of Record). the. Proper coding is necessary to ensure the appropriate expense payment is issued. Use the erroneous assignment code when the adjuster receives an assignment in error prior to inspection.

Table 11. CWOP Reasons

Code	Reason
01	Claim denied that was less than deductible
02	Seepage
03	Backup drains
04	Shrubs not covered
05	Sea wall
06	Not actual flood
07	Loss in progress
08	Failure to pursue claim

09	Debris removal only
10	Fire
11	Fence damage
12	Hydrostatic pressure
13	Drainage clogged
14	Boat piers
15	Not insured, damage before inception of policy
16	Not insured, wind damage
17	Type of erosion not included in definition of flood or flooding
18	Landslide
19	Type of mudflow not included in definition of flood or flooding
20	No demonstrable damage
97	Other
98	Error delete claim (no assignment)
99	Erroneous assignment

7   Communications from Attorneys, Public Adjusters, and Other Policyholder Representatives

Adjusters should notify the insurer promptly when they become aware a policyholder is represented. This notification should be forwarded with the Preliminary Report or as an interim status report and include any documents received related to this representation. Adjusters and examiners should always put forth a courteous effort with policyholder representatives during the entire flood claim process. As a Federal program, all stakeholders, including FEMA, must adhere to the Privacy Act. The relevant DHS regulation (applicable to FEMA) regarding Privacy appears at 6 C.F.R. § 5.21.

Letter of Representation. Whenever the policyholder authorizes a party to speak with an NFIP stakeholder, including FEMA, about their claim, the policyholder will need to do so in writing. By law, the NFIP stakeholder must obtain this authorization to protect the policyholder's privacy.

Privacy Release. To authorize another individual to represent the policyholder, the policyholder must also submit documentation that includes all named policyholders' full name(s), address(es), date(s) and place(s) of birth, the name(s) of the representative(s), and the policyholder(s) signature(s). The policyholder must have this document notarized or include the following statement: "I declare under penalty of perjury that the foregoing is true and correct. Executed on <DATE>. <SIGNATURE>."

Attorney representation. When the policyholder becomes represented by an attorney, and the proper letter of representation and privacy release signed by the policyholder is obtained, adjusters and examiners must ensure all verbal and written communications are held directly with the attorney, unless approved by the attorney to communicate directly with the policyholder.

Public adjusters. A public adjuster is an individual who negotiates coverage, scope, and price on behalf of the policyholder. When the policyholder is represented by a public adjuster, and the proper letter of representation and privacy release signed by the policyholder is obtained, FEMA recommends that the adjuster and examiner send all written communications, including the insurer-adjuster-prepared proof of loss, to both the public adjuster and the policyholder. A best practice after verbally communicating with the public adjuster during an inspection or over the telephone is to follow up with a written correspondence or email to the public adjuster copying the policyholder. Keep in mind that a public adjuster must be licensed and in good standing in the state and have a signed contract with the policyholder before they may communicate with NFIP representatives regarding the claim.

Other types of representatives. Whether given the permission to speak with the NFIP stakeholder or not, only attorneys and public adjusters are legally permitted to negotiate coverage, scope, and price on behalf of the policyholder but are required to complete a signed privacy release or letter of representation. Neighbors, other adjusters, estimators, or contractors are not allowed to practice "public adjusting" on the claim; that is negotiating coverage, scope, and price with the insurer or one of its representatives. With the proper documentation provided, a policyholder's representative may be the spouse or an immediate family member acting on the policyholder's behalf. This is often the case when the policyholder is ill, in the hospital, out-of-the-country, or otherwise incapacitated.

Claims Examiners

When an insurer receives a communication that contains a time demand (a specific action by a specific date), a request to reopen the claim, a request for additional payment, or a proof of loss submission, the examiner should promptly review the request and determine the appropriate action.

When a policyholder or representative submits a proof of loss, the examiner should review to determine if the proof of loss supports payment of the claim in part or in whole and issue the appropriate payment. If the proof of loss is received after the 60 days (or after any extension granted by the Administrator), a proof of loss Waiver is required before payment can be made. See Proof of Loss Waiver in Section 2 of this manual.

When the information provided does not support the request for payment outlined in the proof of loss, the examiner should reject the proof of loss, in whole or in part, and communicate the decision to the policyholder or representative along with a partial denial letter when appropriate. The claims examiner should include in the communication what the policyholder or their representative needs to provide to consider an additional payment under the existing claim.

8   Condominium Claims Handling

Section 1312 of the National Flood Insurance Act (42 U.S.C. § 4019), as amended by section 100214 of the Biggert-Waters Flood Insurance Reform Act of 2012 (BW12), prohibits the NFIP insurer from denying a payment requested by the condominium unit owner, who has building coverage under the Dwelling Form, when covered damages under the Dwelling Form are not payable under the association's RCBAP due to policy limits or the application of coinsurance. In general, BW12 here allows for the unit owner's building coverage under the Dwelling Form, to act as a type of excess flood insurance coverage after the RCBAP addresses the building loss and the condominium association's claim is settled.

The RCBAP Coinsurance provision at Section VII applies a penalty when the building insurance coverage purchased by the condominium association is less than 80 percent of the full replacement cost of the RCBAP-insured condominium building or is less than the maximum amount of insurance available. When determining the coinsurance penalty, the adjuster should follow the recommended formula provided in Section 1 of this manual in SFIP RCBAP, Section VII. Coinsurance.

Section III.C.3.b(4) of the Dwelling Form precludes payment for a loss assessment if the reason for the deficiency is the application of the RCBAP's coinsurance penalty provision. Section VII.C.2 states that the RCBAP provides primary flood insurance coverage and the Dwelling Form provides excess coverage if the Dwelling Form covers a unit in a condominium building where the condominium association has purchased an RCBAP or other coverage for the condominium structure. Section 100214 of BW12 prohibits the NFIP from enforcing Section III.C.3.b(4), and that provision is waived. Under certain circumstances, application of Section VII.C.2 also prevents implementation of section 100214, and that provision is waived in part where application of the provision would deny payment due to the coinsurance penalty in the RCBAP. This will allow the Dwelling Form to respond as if the RCBAP coverage is exhausted. In all other cases, the RCBAP will continue to be primary, and the Dwelling Form will act as an excess flood insurance policy.

Section 100214 of BW12 does not alter, amend, or supersede the limits of coverage established under 42 U.S.C. § 4013 or allow more than one payment for the same damaged item. Accordingly, the combined building coverage of the RCBAP and the Dwelling Forms for units within the building covered by the RCBAP cannot exceed $250,000 times the number of units, nor can the payment for any one unit exceed $250,000 respectively.

9   Contents Manipulation

When a building or room in a building suffers damage, and the contents items stored within the building or area require movement to facilitate building repairs, the task is known as "contents manipulation." To be eligible for coverage for contents manipulation, the policyholder must have purchased both Coverage A – Building Property (building) coverage and Coverage B – Personal Property (contents) coverage.

FEMA recognizes that the policyholder may need to manipulate undamaged insured contents to repair covered building damage. These charges are often included in the contractor's unit cost(s) for items repaired or replaced and are not a separate charge to the policyholder. When contractors present an itemized breakdown of their charges and contents manipulation is a separate line item, the adjuster may separately allow for contents manipulation. Adjusters may not make lump sum allowances or room-by-room contents manipulation allowances in the estimate without providing supporting documentation of those costs. Coverage for contents manipulation is subject to the following:

- Only reasonable and necessary charges for contents manipulation.

- Contents manipulation does not extend to items already included in the contents claim as a repair or as a replacement.

- If a contents item is non-covered property, is in an area of the building that is subject to coverage limitations such as in a basement or certain lower enclosures, or exceeds special limit coverage, the cost to manipulate the item(s) is not covered.

- Manipulation of the tenant's personal property is not covered under the owner's building policy, even when the tenant has purchased contents coverage. In such cases when a tenant has contents coverage and incurs reasonable costs to move contents to facilitate flood damage repairs, the charge is covered only under the tenant's contents policy.

- Coverage for contents manipulation does not include the additional labor or cost to remove or store contents outside of the insured building, or another appurtenant building at the described location (Dwelling Form only), such as a portable storage container placed at the described location, or personal property moved to storage at a building at another location. The SFIP will only consider reasonable costs to move personal property items within the insured building or within an appurtenant structure (Dwelling Form only), to facilitate flood repairs to the building.

- Contents manipulation is not "property removed to safety," as described in Section III.C.2.b.

- Documented contents manipulation expenses may be charged against the building coverage when they are a function of the covered building repair.

10 Cooperative Buildings

Buildings in a cooperative form of ownership (referred to by FEMA as "cooperative buildings") are typically owned and managed by a corporation, and their ownership is different from the condominium form of ownership. Residents within cooperative buildings typically buy shares of the corporation, rather than the real estate (building, land, or both building and land) itself. Shareholders of the cooperative corporation are provided a preferential lease agreement from the corporation, which affords them the right to occupy a specific space or "unit" within the cooperative building. Under the rules of the NFIP, cooperative-owned buildings where at least 75 percent of the area is used for residential purposes are considered residential occupancies. These buildings in a Regular Program community can be insured for the maximum building coverage of $500,000 under the General Property Form in the cooperative corporation's name. Because they are not in the condominium form of ownership, these cooperative buildings are not eligible for insurance under the RCBAP Form.

A shareholder in a cooperative building typically does not receive a real estate interest in the building or unit, but rather shares of stock in the cooperative corporation with the right to occupy a particular "unit" under a lease or rental agreement. Similar to tenants of non-condominium apartment buildings, the shareholders of a cooperative building cannot purchase building coverage under an SFIP Dwelling Form to cover their individual units. Shareholders of a residential cooperative building can only access the maximum $100,000 contents coverage in Regular Program communities under the Dwelling Form. Under certain circumstances, at the policyholder's option, 10 percent of the content's coverage may be applied to betterments or improvements to the unit made at the insured shareholder's expense.

FEMA is aware that there may be unusual forms of cooperative ownership. In some cooperatives, a large number of the structures are owned by the individual shareholders through an arrangement whereby the shareholders lease the buildings to the cooperative, and the cooperative leases the buildings back to the shareholders, and the land on which the buildings are located is owned by the cooperative corporation. At the termination of a lease, the owner of the building may remove the structure from the land owned by the cooperative. Under this arrangement, the shareholders have an ownership interest in the buildings. Based on this information, such owner-shareholders are eligible to purchase building coverage under the appropriate SFIP.

In this situation, the cooperative corporation should be named as an additional loss payee, as its interest may appear, and any mortgagee should also be named as an additional payee. Claims on SFIPs issued to individuals or businesses owning buildings in such cooperatives are payable, subject to all other requirements and limitations.

Claims Examiners

FEMA encourages insurers to review underlying cooperative documents to determine how cooperative buildings are owned, as other cooperative arrangements may exist that allow an individual to actually own the building, and therefore be able to purchase building coverage.

---

11 Countertops

11.1 Common Countertop Types and their Repair or Replacement

When questions arise regarding the removal and resetting of countertop materials or replacing the material following a flood, the adjuster's judgment and obtained documentation are important. FEMA developed the following guidelines to enhance the adjuster's knowledge of the various types of materials and precautions regarding removal and resetting countertops:

- Post-form, roll-top laminated countertops are manufactured prior to installation. The plastic resin laminated surface is sometimes referred to as Formica®. The common identifier for this type is that the laminated surface is molded over and around the front edge and backsplash. The front edge of this type may have a more ornate style other than the common bullnose or rounded edge. Removal of single straight length roll-top countertops can be performed without damage. However, if a single section of the countertop has a mitered corner joint creating an "L-shape," the removal process may cause delamination of the top finish surface or separation of the mitered corner joint, exposing the seam, requiring replacement.

- Job-built, laid flat, or self-edge laminated countertops are similar in material to the above described "roll-top," but are built at the job site to exact specifications. Its common identifier is that the front edge and sides are always squared. When removal is necessary to facilitate repairs, replacement is often required as the finished surface may partially delaminate, resulting in damage to the substrate base material or the backsplash. When a job-built laminate countertop layout design is curved or L-shaped, damage during removal is likely, requiring replacement.

- Formed concrete and ceramic tile countertops are built on the job site to exact specifications. They are constructed over a wood or rock-board type substrate material that may be screwed or glued to the cabinet framing, or both. When removal is possible, handling may cause twisting or bending of the countertop, which will crack mortar or separate the finish material from the substrate. Replacing the top may be necessary.

- Natural or man-made stone materials such as granite and Silestone® can typically be removed and reinstalled without damage. If the top is joined by two or more individual pieces, a chemical is applied to the seam to dissolve the polymer, which bonds the material together prior to removal. If two or more slabs of stone countertop are installed over a wooden substrate, typically 2 centimeters thick type, then successful removal may not be likely. If a backsplash is made of the same material and set over top of the countertop's rear edge, it is also possible to remove it without damage. However, if the backsplash is a material such as ceramic tile, its removal is necessary to prevent damage to the countertop and replacement of the backsplash may be required. Only supervised

May 1, 2020

labor experienced in handling this material should attempt to remove this type of countertop, as the SFIP does not cover avoidable damage resulting from poor handling.

- Corian® and other solid-surface (acrylic polymer) countertops can typically be removed and reinstalled without damage. If the material cracks or breaks off during removal or handling, the countertop material can be successfully repaired with the application of an epoxy applied to the surface of each crack, creating an invisible or near-invisible bond.

FEMA is aware of unique instances when a countertop can be damaged beyond repair directly by or from flood. In cases in which an adjuster recommends replacement of the countertop, the claim file must include documentation that explains and supports the judgment to replace, rather than remove and reset.

11.2 Countertop Adjustment Concerns

A.   Adjuster Documentation

At the initial loss inspection, the adjuster should examine, photograph, and document the condition of the surface, edge, and underside of the countertop in a narrative report. The adjuster should note the number of adjoining seams of the countertop, as well as the material thickness. Typically, the thickness of the granite is in centimeters. The adjuster should note substrate material covering any cabinet framing located underneath the countertop. This documentation process applies to any countertop, sink, toilet, vanity top, bathtub, shower stall, or other such fixture.

B.   Discussion with Policyholder

The adjuster should discuss removal and re-installation with the policyholder and contractor (if present) at the initial loss inspection. The adjuster should set the expectation that the policyholder and contractor salvage any countertop, sink, toilet, vanity top, bathtub, shower stall, or other similar items for re-use. The adjuster should inform the policyholder that the policyholder should notify the adjuster immediately if damage occurs during removal and providing photographs when necessary. The policyholder must retain and not discard items damaged during removal.

C.   Determining Unavoidable Damage

Policyholders and contractors repairing or replacing damaged items must use reasonable care when removing undamaged items. When the removal process irreparably damages a previously undamaged item, the removal effort must support a finding that the damage was unavoidable. The SFIP covers direct physical loss by or from a flood. The SFIP will not cover avoidable damage.

D.   Policyholder Documentation

The policyholder can best support a request for payment when unavoidable damage occurs during the removal and replacement process with the following:

1. Clear photographs of the damage at the time of occurrence.

2. A signed detailed statement from the removal or repair contractor.

3. The signed detailed statement must:

    a. Explain the action taken to remove the item.

    b. State how the damage occurred.

    c. Address salvage.

E.   Completing the Adjustment

Once the policyholder provides the documentation noted above, the adjuster should adjust the claim accordingly. Adjusters should factor in the additional time and labor to safely remove and reset salvageable items. The adjustment should also apply the appropriate credit reflecting any previously estimated allowance to reinstall. If the adjuster recommends no payment, the adjuster should include an explanation in the estimate and narrative report.

12   Electronic Signatures

FEMA expects insurers to handle NFIP claims in a customer-centric manner as part of their normal business practices. To improve the policyholder's experience and to reduce administrative burden, FEMA is approving and encouraging the use of electronic signatures on proofs of loss and other NFIP-related submissions. FEMA will not deny the legal effect, validity, or enforceability of a signature solely because it is in electronic form.[9] Insurers should accept electronic signatures in accordance with their general business practices and applicable laws.

The General Services Administration (GSA) and the Federal Chief Information Officers Council have provided joint comprehensive guidance on the best practices for accepting electronic signatures.[10] Insurers may find this guidance helpful.

13   Expense Payments

13.1 Adjuster Fees

FEMA uses the current NFIP Adjuster Fee Schedule to make payment to insurers; the insurers, in turn, make payment to the adjusters.

Current Adjuster Fee Schedule effective August 24, 2017 (See Appendix A)

---

[9] *See* Gov't Paperwork Elimination Act (GPEA), Pub. L. 105-277 § 1707 (44 U.S.C. § 3504 note); Electronic Signatures in Glob. & Nat'l Commerce Act (E-SIGN), Pub. L. 106-229 § 101(a) (15 U.S.C. § 7001(a)).
[10] Use of Electronic Signatures in Federal Organization Transaction, Version 2 (January 25, 2013), at https://bsa.nfipstat.fema.gov/wyobull/2017/w-17008.pdf

For ICC claims, use the ICC fee schedule effective September 1, 2004 (See Appendix B)

👥 Claims Examiners

Important: FEMA expects examiners to take appropriate action when the adjuster's work performance is deficient:

1. Does not comply with NFIP standards,
2. Is improperly prepared, thereby requiring the claim to be substantially readjusted, or
3. When the claim handling is not timely or responsive to expectation with customer service and requires reassignment.

---

14. Flood-In-Progress Exclusion

When adjusting a claim for which the flood-in-progress exclusion may apply, the adjuster must investigate if a flood is already in progress at the time and date the policy's term begins. We are providing this guidance to help ensure consistency in adjusting and evaluating claims involving the flood-in-progress exclusion.

14.1 When the Flood-in-Progress Exclusions May Apply

SFIP Section V.B. excludes from coverage a loss directly or indirectly caused by a flood that is already in progress at the time and date the policy's first term begins. In other words, damage from a flood that begins before the date the policy's first term begins is not covered even if the flood event does not damage the insured property until after the policy's first term begins.

When coverage is added to an existing policy at the request of the policyholder and a flood is already in progress, damage that occurs to insured property from that same flood event after the effective date of the increased coverage will only be covered at the prior policy limits.

Whether a flood is in progress for a claim is evaluated on an individual basis. Evidence that a flood may be in progress on the date the policy's first term begins or on the date increased policy coverage is effective may include a recent:

1. Flood in the community where the insured building is located caused by the same source of flooding as the flood on the insured property, or

2. Event initiating a flood that causes damage, such as:

   a. A spillway opening,

   b. A levee breaching,

   c. A dam releasing water, or

   d. Water escaping from the banks of a waterway (stream, river, creek, etc.).

FEMA will apply the Section V.B. exclusion regardless of individual property, city, county, or parish boundaries.

FEMA does not interpret the Section V.B. exclusion as triggered only when floodwaters physically touch the insured building.

The applicability of the Section V.B. exclusion applies regardless of any waiting period provisions found at 44 C.F.R. § 61.11. An insurance policy may be purchased without the 30-day waiting period, but that does not mean that section V.B. of the SFIP does not apply.

14.2   Flood-in-Progress Exclusion Adjustment Concerns

In addition to adhering to the claims adjustment guidance in section 2.5, when a loss occurs within 30 days of the policy or the additional coverage effective date or when there is evidence that a flood may have been in progress when the policy or additional coverage became effective, the adjuster should identify and investigate the following:

1. The date the policy was purchased;

2. The date the policy or additional coverage went into effect;

3. The date the flooding as defined by the policy at Section II.A began;

4. Evidence of flood prevention prior to the effective date of the policy, e.g., temporary levees, sandbagging, constructed berms, pumps, etc.; and

5. Data sources, including:

    a. National Oceanic and Atmospheric Administration (NOAA) for data on river and lake levels;

    b. News reports and social media or other sources that may help the adjuster to determine when flooding was first reported; and

    c. The community or other official for assistance in determining lake or river levels.

The adjuster should interview the policyholder and conduct a neighborhood canvass to determine the location of the floodwaters in relation to the insured property location at the time the policy became effective. The adjuster must detail in the narrative their process and evidence used for recommending coverage or denial under the SFIP.

If the adjuster needs assistance in confirming when a flood began, the adjuster should notify the insurer. The insurer may contact the NFIP BSA for assistance at NFIPFloodDisasterResponseMailbox@fema.dhs.gov.

Claims Examiners

Carriers must determine when exclusions apply to claims on a case-by-case basis, based on the available information and adjuster's investigation. When determining whether the flood-in-progress exclusion applies to a claim as part of a coverage determination, examiners should consider:

a. Did the adjuster determine if the flood was in progress prior to the effective date and time of the flood policy or the effective date and time of when coverage is added or changed at the request of the policyholder?

b. If a different flood caused by another source damages the insured property -
   i. Determine if a separate flood-in-progress applies to this loss, requiring the exclusion. The insurer will consider the date the policy term began or additional SFIP coverage became effective and compare it to the start date of this flood.
   ii. The SFIP may cover this flood damage subject to the terms of the SFIP. *Do not forget to exclude any prior unrepaired damage.*

c. The flood-in-progress exclusion will not affect most claims. The flood-in-progress exclusion will primarily affect applicants or policyholders who wait to purchase flood insurance or increase their coverage until flooding is imminent.

14.3   Requesting Assistance and Tracking Flood-In-Progress

NFIP insurers may request assistance from FEMA in determining whether a flood began before the policy term or additional coverage became effective. In addition, the NFIP insurer must report to FEMA each claim to which an NFIP insurer applies the flood-in-progress exclusion.

The NFIP insurer will send the information to the NFIP BSA at NFIPFloodDisasterResponseMailbox@fema.dhs.gov. **Subject Line must state:** "Flood-in-Progress" and body of email must include: the reason for the submission (e.g. Requesting Assistance or Tracking Flood-in-Progress); the policyholder name; policy number; date of loss; loss address including city, state, and county or parish; new business date; the date the adjuster determined the flood began; and current term on all claims where FIP exclusion is known or may apply.

15   GFIP Claims Handling

Group Flood Insurance Policies (GFIP) are handled solely by the NFIP Direct. They are assigned to adjusters and are handled the same as the SFIP with the following exceptions:

- Maximum GFIP coverage limit is equivalent to the maximum grant amount established under section 408 of the Robert T. Stafford Disaster Relief and Emergency Assistance Act (42 U.S.C. § 5174) which FEMA updates at the start of each fiscal year through publication in the Federal Register, 83 Fed. Reg. 53,281.

- The homeowner policyholder has the choice of whether to use the funds solely for owned building damages, solely for owned contents damages, or for a combination of owned building and contents damages; but the total cannot exceed the maximum GFIP limits. A separate $200.00 deductible is applied to each coverage.

- Adjuster must verify the policyholder is the owner of the home to qualify for building coverage. The adjuster may request a copy of the deed or obtain information from the local property assessor's office or assessor's website.

- For renter policyholders, the GFIP is only for damaged contents owned by the policyholder.

- There is no underwriting review performed on a new GFIP, as it is awarded directly from FEMA's Individuals and Households Program. A GFIP policy does not include building rating information, and among other items, the ownership, property address, and loss payee may be inaccurate. The adjuster should obtain a fully completed questionnaire from the policyholder, which helps to verify this required policy information, before executing a proof of loss for the policyholder's signature.

- GFIP coverage is only available at actual cash value and does not provide Coverage D – Increased Cost of Compliance Coverage.

16 Guidance on the Use of Outside Professional Services

16.1 When to request a Building Structural Evaluation

- Cause of damage is uncertain

- Extent of the damage is unknown

- Discern the cost-effective method of repair

- Policyholder contests the recommended loss settlement due to structural issues or due to issues of causation with certain building items.

Adjusters should submit a request to the insurer to have the building's structure evaluated as soon as the need is identified. Adjusters do not have the authority to assign an expert. Table 12 details the issues that may require assistance from a qualified outside professional service.

Table 12. Issues pointing towards a Building Structural Evaluation

Type	Qualifications
Exterior	<ul><li>Any signs of foundation cracking or foundation movement.</li><li>Any piers/pilings that are out of plumb or showing displaced connections.</li><li>Any areas showing scour (washout) or erosion under or alongside the foundation.</li><li>Any evidence of vertical or lateral displacement of the brick veneer or siding.</li><li>Any displacement of an exterior wall.</li></ul>

Interior	• Any floors that are cracked, separated, uneven, or out of level. • Any structural elements that show movement including bowed or bulged walls. • Any evidence of significant cracks in the interior finishes, such as cracks above doors and windows or at the corners in wall covering material. • Any evidence of moisture, leaks, or hydrostatic pressure present in floors or walls. • Any lower-level configuration where precise elevations cannot be determined. • Allegations that the flood-damaged non-porous ceramic or porcelain tile, or the like, installed to the concrete substrate.
General	• To resolve questions concerning causation or repair methodology. • Other types of experts can also be helpful when handling large commercial losses involving damage to inventory, including salvors, accountants, etc. **Note:** Each building loss is different, so there will be instances where certain elements or circumstances fall outside of the ordinary; therefore, adjuster discretion is needed. The above items are a non-exhaustive list to look for to aid the decision to involve a qualified outside professional service.

16.2 Outside Financial Accounting Professionals

A commercial loss involving damage to a significant quantity, value, or specialized type of business contents loss may require the involvement of the services of a CPA to provide a detailed report of findings. Here the role of the expert is to help promptly document and certify the quantity and value of damaged inventory, goods in process, or raw materials. The question of financial recovery through a buy-back by the policyholder, or salvage through the involvement of a third party, can also be addressed. The CPA's involvement can also help inform the policyholder what documentation is needed and how it can be presented to best support the loss of their commercial contents quickly. A detailed report of findings is required when a financial accounting professional is engaged.

16.3 Insurers must comply with the following requirements regarding the use of outside professional services

Claims Examiners

The licensure and rules regarding professional services vary by state. The NFIP insurer is responsible for making sure the professional services it hires are familiar and compliant with state licensing requirements and the rules that regulate the profession. When a report from a professional service is used to support the decision of the NFIP insurer, the report must disclose that it complies with state rules regulating licensure and professional conduct. If a report does not meet the state's requirement, the claim decision may become invalid, and FEMA will not approve the insurer's Special Allocated Loss Adjustment Expense (SALAE) Type 1 -Expert Expense, request for reimbursement.

A. Ensuring Compliance with Applicable Laws and Use of Reports

Insurers may only rely upon the use of an outside professional service who perform work in accordance with all applicable laws regarding professional licensure and conduct. For the purposes of this requirement, insurers and their retained service providers may not assert that they are exempt from state licensing laws because they are Federal employees, Federal contractors, or performing work for the Federal Government unless FEMA expressly authorizes an exemption in writing.

FEMA will not pre-authorize an assignment to an expert, or expert fees. Insurers must obtain FEMA approval to pay a SALAE 1 expense regardless of the dollar amount.

Only an insurer, or WYO vendor if authorized by the insurer (excludes adjusting firms and independent adjusters), can request outside professional services.

When making an assignment, insurers must verify the entity and that the individual from whom services are sought is qualified and licensed in good standing with the state where the insured property is located, before authorizing an inspection.

When making an assignment for a professional service:

- Specify the type of service needed including the covered property to be inspected. The assignment should be clear that non-covered property is not part of the assignment unless the assignment involves such determination. FEMA will not authorize expenses incurred to inspect or evaluate non-covered property, example: pools, pool decks, sidewalks, retaining walls that are not an integral part of the foundation, bulkheads, non-covered buildings, etc.

- Secure a pre-inspection expense cost estimate to confirm expenses are fair and responsible before authorizing the inspection. FEMA will not authorize payment for any expense that exceeds the original quoted fee unless the engineer can document pre-approval from the insurer or authorized vendor prior to incurring the expense.

- FEMA will not pay for multiple engineers to conduct an inspection unless pre-approval was received from the insurer with a detailed explanation that the inspection requires different expertise or disciplines to evaluate the damage, for example, a structural and electrical engineer.

- In addition, any co-signer of a report holding themselves out as a professional engineer (PE) must have a current license in the inspection state and include the engineer license number on the report.

- Engineer travel expenses must be fair and reasonable and conform with GSA travel rates. FEMA will not pay the following:

- o lodging within the contiguous United States;

- o food expenses; or

- o photos.

- Engineers' invoices must be itemized by time and expense (no lump sums), separately report inspection and travel time, and provide all applicable receipts for air travel, vehicle rental, hotel, tolls, parking, etc. Exceptions should be clearly explained and documented.

- Insurers may not request changes to final reports; however, insurers may request that experts prepare an addendum to the final report.

- Insurers must keep the entire expert report in the claim file and provide a copy of the final expert report and any addendums to the policyholder.

- Insurers must rely on the professional service to prepare requested reports in accordance with all applicable state laws regarding professional licensure and conduct. To be reimbursed for engineering expenses, documentation must validate that the engineer of record is qualified and licensed to work in the state of the property inspected. Insurers and their retained experts may not assert that they are exempt from state licensing laws because they are Federal employees, Federal contractors, or performing work for the Federal government unless FEMA expressly authorizes an exemption in writing.

B. Exclusive Reliance on Final Reports from Professional Services

When making claim decisions, insurers should only rely upon final reports that meet the proper disclosures and reporting standards for the report type involved. Insurers must use such reports in context with all other relevant information and data gathered throughout the claim investigation process when making a claim determination.

When a report involves a structural evaluation of the building, the professional service should disclose and report at least the following:

- Date of inspection
- Individual who performs the inspection
- Building description and foundation type – all components
- Site observations supported with annotated photographs, analytical discussion, and conclusion
- Cost-effective method to repair, when applicable
- Signature of the engineer of record with professional seal or state license number
- Name and curriculum vitae of all persons who assisted with the technical content of the report
- The engineer should not interpret SFIP terms and conditions or discuss coverage.

C. Retention and Disclosure of Final Expert Reports from Professional Services

For the purposes of 44 CFR 62.23(i)(10), FEMA considers a final report from professional service as a normal component of a claim file. Accordingly, whenever the insurer retains professional service to investigate the claim, the insurer must keep all reports in the claim file. When requested by policyholders, insurers must provide a complete copy of the requested report.

D. Avoiding Undue Influence on Analyses Performed by Outside Professional Services

Insurers and their representatives may not adopt any practice that may influence the opinions or recommendations of the professional service. Insurers may not request changes to reports. However, when the insurer or a representative has a question that requires a written response, they may request that the professional service prepare an addendum to the final report in response.

17   General Adjuster (GA) Re-inspection Request

👥 Claims Examiners

All re-inspection requests must come directly from the NFIP insurer or the Federal Insurance Directorate to NFIPFloodDisasterResponseMailbox@fema.dhs.gov.

The re-inspection program is designed to assist in maintaining quality claims processing within the NFIP. Re-inspections are performed in cooperation with the insurers. There are five types of re-inspections:

1. Special Assist;
2. Congressional;
3. FEMA Appeals;
4. FEMA Requests;
5. Random Claims Quality Check (RCQC).

For Special Assist re-inspections, the insurer claims management makes a request by email to the NFIP BSA at NFIPFloodDisasterResponseMailbox@fema.dhs.gov. The email subject line should include the policy number and the type of submission (ex. 1234567890 – Request for Re-inspection). The body of the email should contain the policy number, policyholder name, property address, date of loss, and a brief description of the issues. Attach a copy of the complete claim file or upload it to the SFTP site.

A GA will be assigned for a desk review or on-site re-inspection. The GA will contact the requestor to discuss the file and determine if an insurer will accompany the GA on the on-site re-inspection.

Congressional, FEMA Appeals, and FEMA Requests are all sent by FEMA's Federal Insurance Directorate.

RCQC is a practice by which the NFIP BSA chooses random claim files for review during disasters to determine if the adjusters are properly handling the claim.

18   Heating, Ventilation and Air Conditioning (HVAC) Equipment and Heating Machinery

18.1   HVAC Equipment

The SFIP will pay for damage to HVAC components, including air conditioning compressors in the open, connected to and servicing the building, when a component or the entire system suffers direct physical loss by or from flood. The SFIP defines direct physical loss by or from flood as, "loss or damage to insured property, directly caused by a flood. There must be evidence of physical changes to the property".[11] Elevated platforms that are attached to the building are covered.

Upgrades required due to change in cooling refrigerant or Seasonal Energy Efficiency Ratio:

When a new HVAC component replaces an existing component damaged by flood but is not compatible with the existing undamaged HVAC component, the system may not function properly or at all. The reason may be due to a different type of refrigerant, or a different Seasonal Energy Efficiency Ratio (SEER) rating designed for each unit. SEER is the standard used

---

[11] SFIP (II)(B)(12).

to measure the energy efficiency of building HVAC systems. As with refrigerants, federal regulations require periodic increases in SEER ratings. Both rules were established to help our nation consume energy more efficiently. Federal law requires the phase-out of older refrigerant types starting in 2010.

Although not covered by the SFIP, retrofit of the existing undamaged component could solve the issue of component incompatibility. The most common retrofit in an undamaged interior HVAC unit (air-handler) is to replace the evaporator coil (E-coil). With an undamaged exterior HVAC unit, a retrofit may be possible by replacing the compressor. Depending on the system and incompatibility issues, simpler modifications may be available by installing a pressure regulator or replacing the refrigerant with a different, but equally efficient, Environmental Protection Agency (EPA)-accepted variety.

In accordance with the SFIP, Section V.A.6-7, and because the SFIP only covers direct physical loss by or from flood to insured property, the NFIP insurer cannot pay for the cost to upgrade the HVAC system when the policyholder is forced to do so by law, regulation, or ordinance.

Additionally, the Pairs and Sets provision under the SFIP (Section VII.A. of the Dwelling and General Property Forms and Section VIII.A. of the RCBAP Form) does not provide coverage for the undamaged component as the provision states it will pay only the fair proportion of the total value of the pair or set that the lost, damaged, or destroyed article bears to the pair or set.

18.2   Heating Machinery

Heating machinery, in the insured building, connected to and servicing the insured building, is covered.

19   Identification of Building Equipment, Appliances, Electronics, and Mechanicals

The NFIP requires the adjuster to provide identifying information (manufacturer, model and serial number, and whenever possible, capacity, etc.) on major building equipment such as furnaces, central air conditioning units, and major appliances such as refrigerators, washers, dryers, televisions, etc.

The adjuster must provide available identifying information on all covered flood-damaged appliances, electronic, and mechanical devices to include the make, model number, and serial number, and include a photograph of any identifying tags or labeling. If this information is not accessible, or not available, the adjuster should document the items with a detailed description and explanation in the narrative report.

Air conditioning condensers and solar panels are covered even if set apart from the insured building. The SFIP does not cover other equipment, like electrical supply generators, air compressors, and substation transformers owned by the policyholder that may service the insured building unless the equipment is hard-wired and in an insured building as defined in the SFIP II.B.6 or in a building physically attached to the covered structure by means of a qualifying addition or extension per III.A.2. Generators stored in a building at the described location are personal property. Generators and other such equipment in a basement are not covered.

See Figure 44 for an example of a non-covered generator. It is not in a building as defined in the SFIP. See Figure 45 for an example of an attached utility shed. A generator is covered under the building when it is hard-wired to the building's electrical system, is installed within an area of the insured building, such as an attached utility shed or closet, or within an SFIP-covered porch or detached SFIP-eligible garage.

Figure 44 Non-Covered Generator

Photograph credit Generac

Figure 45. Attached Utility Shed

👥 Claims Examiners

The examiner should confirm the adjuster provided identifying information (manufacturer, model and serial number, and whenever possible, capacity, etc.) on major building equipment such as furnaces, central air conditioning units, and major appliances such as refrigerators, washers, dryers, televisions, etc. and follow-up to secure this information if not in the report.

20 Improvements and Betterments

The SFIP defines improvements as fixtures, alterations, installations, or additions comprising a part of the insured dwelling or the apartment in which the policyholder resides.

20.1 Tenants' Contents Only Policies

As explained in the SFIP Dwelling Form, Section III.B .4, if the policyholder is a tenant and has purchased Coverage B – Personal Property (contents coverage), the SFIP will cover such property, including the policyholder's cooking stove or range and refrigerator. The SFIP will also cover improvements made or acquired solely at the policyholder's expense in the dwelling or apartment in which the policyholder resides, but not for more than 10 percent of the limit of liability shown for personal property on the Declarations Page. Use of this insurance is at the policyholder's option but reduces the personal property limit.

The SFIP General Property Form, in Section III.B. 7–9, specifies coverage conditions for improvements and betterments for a tenant or condominium unit owner. Paragraph 7 makes clear that improvements acquired by or made at the expense of the tenant are covered, even if the tenant cannot legally remove them, such as a built-in walk-in freezer.

If a tenant has a contents policy in his or her own name, flood-damaged items that the tenant may claim as improvements and betterments under a covered loss will include all items purchased at the tenant's expense for which coverage would be provided under building coverage (Coverage A), and that have not been paid under Coverage A for the same loss event under a policy held in the building owner's name.

Insurers may refer to the lease agreement to determine which policy will respond.

20.2 Building Owner and Tenant Named on Same Policy with Coverage A

As stated in the General Rules section of the Flood Insurance Manual, the building owner must be named on a flood insurance policy with Coverage A. If the building coverage is purchased by a tenant due to a lease agreement, the tenant may be named as an additional policyholder on the policy. The NFIP does not designate any of the named policyholders as primary or secondary. The rule is intended to ensure that all parties with an insurable interest in the building are named on any claim settlement proceeds for building damage. Any claim payment would be made to all parties named as policyholders on the policy.

20.3 Duplicate Policies with Coverage A Not Allowed

Excluding residential condominium buildings, NFIP-insured buildings can have only one policy with building coverage (Coverage A). Section 100228 of the Biggert-Waters Flood Insurance Reform Act of 2012, codified at 42 U.S.C. § 4013(b), clarifies that the total aggregate liability for a non-residential building or non-condominium building designed for five or more families is $500,000 per structure. The law also reiterates that the maximum coverage available for a residential 1–4 family building or condominium unit is $250,000 per policy. The SFIP prohibits duplicate building coverage by the same policyholder. This means that the NFIP will only pay for building coverage under one policy, and the owner must be a named policyholder.

The NFIP also will not pay twice for the same covered loss (either Coverage A or Coverage B) when an RCBAP provides coverage for a condominium unit insured under the Dwelling Form.

21 Increased Cost of Compliance

The adjuster should provide the Increased Cost of Compliance (ICC) Brochure to the policyholder at the time of the inspection.

Claims Examiners

The examiner oversees or can directly handle ICC claims, which involves securing from the policyholder the necessary documentation to include:

- The community's substantial damage determination letter confirming a compliance requirement resulting from substantial damage. The community determination factors in all perils. For ICC, the SFIP requires the percentage of damage to be by or from flood, whether covered by the SFIP or not;

- When ICC is required for repetitive loss, the examiner confirms the community has a repetitive loss provision in its floodplain management ordinance, such as two losses during a 10-year period. The state or community must have a cumulative or repetitive loss provision already within its floodplain ordinance at the time of the flood. *See* Dwelling Form Section III.D.3;

- Bids to perform the work and confirmation that work is only for covered mitigation activities. The SFIP does not allow payment of the ICC claim until the approved mitigation activity is completed and the community has confirmed in writing that the activity resulted in a building that complies with their floodplain management ordinance. However, FEMA encourages advance payments when the policyholder signs a written agreement attesting the funds will be used only for eligible ICC mitigation work and agrees that any dollar amount not spent by a specific date will be returned to the insurer; and

- A new elevation certificate for provision to underwriting for re-rating the new policy.

The ICC Policyholder's Processing Checklist (See Appendix K) is a useful tool to send to the policyholder.

See Section 3 Increased Cost of Compliance of this manual for detailed guidance.

22 Inspection

The adjuster essentially has one opportunity to make a good first impression; that opportunity should not be wasted. FEMA expects the adjuster to be punctual for inspections and present oneself in a professional manner. Professional attire should be worn, for example: no ripped or torn jeans, t-shirts, offensive branding, etc. The adjuster should present their FCN card and any government-issued photo ID to the policyholder at the start of the inspection. When minors are present in the building that requires inspection, the adjuster should never enter unless there is an adult present, preferably the policyholder or policyholder's representative.

The adjuster's site visit to the insured property is the most important part of the claim handling process. Adjuster professionalism and empathy towards the policyholder for the loss to their property and potential financial ramifications, as well as meaningful communication, are key aspects to the inspection that help avoid issues. These three key aspects lay the groundwork for a prompt and successful claim resolution. The adjuster should spend time with the policyholder explaining the adjustment and claim processes and give a realistic timeline for completion of the estimate. This will help avoid future issues and help ensure a good working relationship. These conversations are the adjuster's investment in a successful claim result for the policyholder and for the adjuster.

The adjuster must provide the policyholder a copy of the Flood Insurance Claims Handbook and ICC Brochure and spend time reviewing the documents with the policyholder. The adjuster must discuss with the policyholder SFIP coverage and non-coverage issues, and how they apply to the loss, but cannot say whether the insurer will approve or deny the claim. The adjuster must confirm that the mortgagee is correct and identify all parties to the contract.

If the adjuster cannot inspect within a reasonable timeframe, the adjuster should promptly submit a status report explaining the cause(s) for the delay. The adjuster should also address inspection delays caused by the policyholder, or their representatives, including their failure to set a reasonable time and date to conduct the inspection and the reason for the delay. The adjuster should avoid visiting the insured risk without an appointment.

> **Claims Examiners**
>
> The examiner should send a Reservation of Rights (ROR) outlining requirements in case of loss when the policyholder, or their representative, either refuses an inspection or unreasonably delays the timeframe to conduct the inspection.

23 Letter of Map Amendment/Letter of Map Revision

23.1 Letter of Map Amendment Definition

A Letter of Map Amendment (LOMA) is an official amendment, by letter, to an effective NFIP map. A LOMA establishes a property's location in relation to the SFHA. LOMAs are usually issued because a property has been mapped as being in the floodplain, but the property is in fact on natural high ground above the base flood elevation.

The LOMA officially amends the effective NFIP map. The community maintains this public record. LOMAs are included on the community's master flood map and filed by panel number in an accessible location.

23.2 Letter of Map Revision Definition

A Letter of Map Revision (LOMR) is FEMA's modification to an effective Flood Insurance Rate Map (FIRM), or Flood Boundary and Floodway Map (FBFM), or both. LOMRs are generally based on the implementation of physical measures that affect the hydrologic or hydraulic characteristics of a flooding source and thus result in the modification of the existing regulatory floodway, the effective Base Flood Elevations (BFEs), or the SFHA. The LOMR officially revises the FIRM or FBFM, and sometimes the Flood Insurance Study (FIS) report, and when appropriate, includes a description of the modifications. The LOMR is generally accompanied by an annotated copy of the affected portions of the FIRM, FBFM, or FIS report.

All requests for changes to effective maps, other than those initiated by FEMA, must be made in writing by the Chief Executive Officer (CEO) of the community or an official designated by the CEO. The LOMR officially amends the effective NFIP map. The community maintains this public record. LOMRs are included on the community's master flood map and filed by panel number in an accessible location.

23.3   Obtaining a LOMA or LOMR

Obtaining a LOMA/R is the responsibility of the policyholder in conjunction with the designated community official.

The policyholder may download a LOMA/R application from the FEMA website. FEMA does not charge a fee to review a LOMA/R request, but requesters are responsible for providing the required mapping and survey information specific to their property. For FEMA to remove a structure from the SFHA through the LOMA process, Federal regulations require the lowest ground touching the structure, or Lowest Adjacent Grade (LAG) elevation, to be at or above the BFE.

The exception to this requirement is when the submitted property information shows that the structure is outside the SFHA. In this case, the property is referred to as "out as shown." If elevation information is required for the LOMA request, the requester should submit the elevation data requested on the MT-EZ Form.

23.4   How a LOMA or LOMR Applies to Claims

A LOMA or LOMR effectively removes a post-FIRM elevated building from the SFHA. If the policyholder obtains a LOMA or LOMR after the loss, its effective date is the date of the loss. This means that the coverage limitations to areas beneath the lowest elevated floor do not apply. A LOMA or LOMR may not be issued if the lowest adjacent grade of the property is below the BFE. If such a property has its lowest floor (enclosure floor) above the BFE, the property may comply with the NFIP Floodplain Management Regulations. The insurer should send claims involving such buildings to the NFIP BSA with a request for a waiver of the elevated building coverage limitation (See Waiver of Elevated Building Coverage Limitations, in this section of the manual, for instructions).

May 1, 2020

24   Lowest Elevated Floor Determination

Full coverage for post-FIRM elevated buildings in an SFHA begins at the lowest elevated floor. This is the lowest floor raised above ground, even if the pilings extend beyond it. For the purposes of coverage, false floors and raised floors that appear to be elevated do not qualify as the lowest elevated floor. See Figure 46 and Figure 47 as examples of non-elevated floors. A hanging floor would qualify as a lowest elevated floor for the purposes of full coverage – see Figure 48. Full coverage in a non-V zone starts at top of the floor. See the Flood Insurance Manual for definitions and additional information.

Figure 46. Sleeper System Installed Over a Concrete

Figure 47. False (Raised) Floor

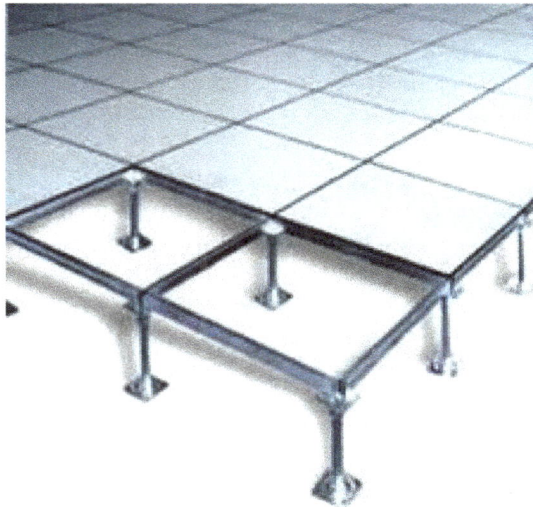

Figure 48. Hanging Floor

If an elevated floor is constructed over a crawlspace and the crawlspace is below the ground level on all sides, the building is not elevated and the building's lowest floor is the below ground level crawlspace floor, meeting the SFIP definition of a basement. If the building is rated elevated it will require correction.

An elevated building with an attached garage that has been converted to living space is considered a non-elevated building. The SFIP may require reformation. Please send a referral to the Underwriting Department.

Please refer to the Flood Insurance Manual.

25 Manufactured (Mobile) Home/Travel Trailer Worksheet

When concluding a covered loss on an SFIP-eligible mobile home or manufactured home, the adjuster's Final Report should include the NFIP mobile-home worksheet, the itemized building valuation, and building diagram. (MH Worksheet, FEMA Forms 086-0-17 and 086-0-18 at Appendix E)

The adjuster must determine the pre-loss valuation or book value of the home and complete an industry-accepted method of establishing pre-loss valuations of manufactured or mobile homes.

The valuation should be for the mobile home unit only and any extras that were installed at the factory. Any modifications, upgrades, and additions built or added on or in the unit after its purchase must be valued separately and explained in the adjuster's narrative report.

When establishing the value of the mobile home, consider the following:

- The cost to disconnect and reconnect existing utility connections;

- The cost to remove the damaged mobile home;

- Transportation costs; and

- The cost to set up the replacement mobile home on the existing foundation including tie-downs or anchors, etc.

The value would not include:

- The cost to comply with any code compliance except ICC if it qualifies;

- Upgrades; or

- The cost to relocate the mobile home on another location requiring a new foundation, extending or moving utility connections, etc.

Claims Examiners

The examiner should confirm that the adjuster appropriately completed a Manufactured (Mobile) Home/Travel Trailer Worksheet for every manufactured (mobile) home/travel trailer claim with a covered loss.

26 Non-Waiver Agreement

A non-waiver agreement allows the adjuster to investigate a loss where a potential coverage concern exists without waiving the rights of the program. A non-waiver agreement is necessary in these circumstances, even if there is evidence of a flood or flood damage to the insured property.

The adjuster secures a non-waiver signed by the policyholder for late reports or when the adjuster identifies a coverage issue. To the extent possible, the adjuster must include all known reasons for the non-waiver agreement. If the policyholder will not sign the non-waiver agreement, contact the insurer to send a Reservation of Rights letter. See Reservation of Rights in this section of the manual.

27 Notice of Loss

The first report or notice of loss from the policyholder is the first step in the claims process. The SFIP requires the policyholder to give prompt written notice of loss to the insurer. In addition to the normal information required on the notice of loss, every loss assignment to an adjusting firm should include a brief description of the loss, even if the loss is minor. Information about the loss, such as water depth, affected room areas, and unique circumstances such as accessibility, high valued property, and extent of the damage, is important as it helps to ensure assignment to an adjuster with the appropriate level of experience and will help to prioritize the loss.

When the policyholder delays the notice of loss, the adjuster should ask questions so he or she understands the circumstances. The concern here is, if an avoidable delay caused damage to undamaged property or increased damage from salvageable to non-salvageable property, the SFIP may not provide coverage and the adjuster will face challenges. A justified delay in such instances could be an order issued by local authorities or prolonged inundation which prevented the policyholder's prompt access to the insured property. There may be others, but it is important that the adjuster understand the delay and clearly report the explanation.

28   Overhead and Profit

Overhead and Profit (OHP) is added to an estimate when the complexity of the repairs requires coordination by a general contractor at a typical industry standard of 10 percent overhead, 10 percent profit. The adjuster should evaluate each claim and document support of their decision in the file.

General contractors' overhead expenses are the ongoing costs associated with running a business. Overhead expenses are typically categorized as indirect (general) or direct.

Indirect overhead costs are fees that a contractor pays on a regular basis that are not specific to a particular job, such as:

- Salaries and benefits for office personnel who may not work on the site, such as bookkeepers and administrative employees.

- Office rent, utilities, supplies, phone and internet lines, business insurance and, licenses, etc.

- Various ongoing expenses such as marketing, advertising, travel costs, legal fees, etc.

Direct overhead costs are typically those ongoing costs for a particular job, such as:

- Short-term office structures such as trailers, architect's stations, and leased office space,

- Project-specific salaries for foremen, schedulers, engineers, job superintendents, etc.,

- Job-specific equipment rentals (jackhammers, cranes, bulldozers, backhoes, etc.),

- Short-term water and sanitation facilities.

Contractors' profit allows a general contractor to earn their living.

When the policyholder performs the duties of a general contractor on some trades or repairs, the policyholder is entitled to a fair overhead allowance (not profit) for the time spent hiring, scheduling, and overseeing repair performance. This allowance is limited to 5 percent. The adjuster must fully justify a higher percentage.

NFIP typically omits general contractor OHP on adjuster-estimated allowances for:

- Cleanup

- Treatment against mold & mildew

- Building dry-out

- HVAC

- Kitchen appliances

- Carpet and padding

- Contractor receipts or quotes

These "Non-OHP trades" are mostly performed by the policyholder or outside services hired by the policyholder.

If the general contractor estimates or repairs include "Non-OHP trades," the adjuster should ensure justification, note the file, and apply OHP accordingly.

29 Payment and Paying the Undisputed Loss

The loss will be payable 60 days after the insurer receives the policyholder's proof of loss or within 90 days after the insurance adjuster files the adjuster's report signed and sworn to by the policyholder; and once the insurer reaches an agreement with the policyholder, there is an entry of a final judgment, or there is a filing of a valid appraisal award. (See 3 Appraisal for further guidance).

Claims Examiners

Important: If the insurer receives proof of loss that is not supported or agreed to, the insurer should pay the undisputed claim and issue a partial proof of loss rejection letter.

Remember, the lienholder is not required on payments under Coverage B – Personal Property unless there is a loan specific to the coverage. SBA loans can apply to personal property, Coverage C – Other Coverages, or Coverage D – Increased Cost of Compliance.

---

30 Perimeter Wall Sheathing

This topic addresses perimeter wall sheathing when flooded.

30.1 General Guidance on Perimeter Wall Sheathing

The SFIP provides coverage for perimeter wall sheathing that experiences a direct physical loss by or from flood. As with any loss claimed under the policy, a policyholder must prove the loss, and an NFIP insurer must, where appropriate:

- Invoke any options afforded to the insurer necessary to investigate a claim. See SFIP Section VII.K.

- Assert any applicable exclusion or limitation of coverage. *See* SFIP Sections, III, IV, and V.

- Retain a licensed engineer or other qualified professional to assist the insurer, as may be necessary.

Additionally, when a policyholder claims flood damage to perimeter wall sheathing, an NFIP insurer must verify:

1. The presence and classification of sheathing in an insured building at the time of a flood;

2. That floodwater came into contact and damaged such sheathing; and,

3. That no coverage exclusions or limitations, such as pre-existing damage or design defects, apply.

30.2 Determining Coverage of Damage to Perimeter Wall Sheathing

FEMA published Technical Bulletin 2- Flood Damage-Resistant Materials Requirements for Buildings Located in Special Flood Hazard Areas in Accordance with the New National Flood Insurance Program(TB2) to provide communities enforcing their local floodplain management requirements with guidance on which building materials FEMA considers flood damage-resistant. Using TB2, FEMA has developed the following guidance on the adjustment of claims for perimeter wall sheathing.

A.   Class 1 or 2 Sheathing

When Class 1 or 2 sheathing material is damaged directly by contact with floodwaters, the material is not salvageable. It is not necessary for a qualified professional, such as an engineer, to document the flooded sheathing material's condition. However, such professional services may be appropriate to investigate possible exclusions or to recommend methods of repair.

B.   Class 3 Sheathing

When Class 3 sheathing material is damaged directly by contact with floodwaters, it may not be salvageable. If questions arise over whether Class 3 sheathing material is salvageable, insurers may involve a qualified professional. Such professional services may also be appropriate to investigate possible exclusions or to recommend methods of repair. If the Class 3 material used for sheathing is documented as paper-faced gypsum, FEMA recommends the replacement of the affected portion if inundated and damaged directly by flood on the claimed date of loss, provided it was not previously flooded or damaged from another cause of loss or defect.

C.   Class 4 or 5 Sheathing

When Class 4 or 5 sheathing material is in direct contact with floodwaters, it is expected to be salvageable. If questions arise over whether Class 4 or 5 sheathing material is salvageable, insurers should involve a qualified professional. Such professional services may also be appropriate to investigate possible exclusions or to recommend methods of repair.

30.3 Determining Methods of Repair or Replacement of Damaged Sheathing

Once an NFIP insurer has determined that perimeter wall sheathing in an insured building experienced direct physical damage by or from flood and that no coverage limitations or exclusions apply, an NFIP insurer should handle the claim appropriately. The claim handling process should determine the type of sheathing material installed, the extent of damages incurred, and the appropriate scope to repair.

When perimeter wall sheathing experiences flood damage, an appropriate and reasonable repair can generally be made without demolishing the exterior surface of the building unless it is economically or physically impractical to do so. The adjuster must document the complete scope to repair the flood-damaged sheathing from the interior side. Insurers must adjust each loss on its own merits and base the appropriate repair method on the extent of damage and the construction type at the time of loss.

If the policyholder discovers additional damage after they complete repairs or improvements, the adjuster must base the additional estimate on the condition of the building immediately following the flood and prior to completion of the repairs or improvements. The adjuster should not make additional allowances to re-do elements of the repair, for example: if payment was made to repair and replace drywall, additional costs associated with replacing sheathing should not include repair and replace drywall.

The adjuster may need to consult with a local building official, qualified professional, or the policyholder's contractor to determine the most reasonable and cost-effective method of repair. Multiple methods of repair may exist, including alternative interior approaches or an exterior approach, so the adjuster should obtain at least one estimate for each approach to document and support claim payment.

Insurers may engage a qualified professional to address disagreements concerning the damage or method of repair.

30.4 Adjuster Considerations

In addition to the guidance provided above, NFIP insurers and adjusters should consider the following when investigating and adjusting claims for perimeter wall sheathing:

- The SFIP pays for the direct physical damage by or from flood. It does not cover the cost to match undamaged building components.

- The SFIP does not cover damage to sheathing or exterior siding, including masonry veneer, when installed in a wall that is below the lowest elevated floor of a post-FIRM elevated building located in a special flood hazard area or basement.

- Adjusters must take detailed photographs and document thorough observations to support their recommendations.

- Adjusters must identify and document any pre-existing damage to the perimeter wall sheathing from insect damage, rot, improper installation or construction defect, prior unrepaired flood damages, other evidence of deterioration from continuous exposure to moisture, or other non- covered causes.

31 Photographs

The adjuster should take as many photographs as necessary to portray the damage; to include photographs of undamaged property and damage from other causes. Photographs should document the flood damage and the condition and quality of building finishes and contents. The adjuster must label the photographs, provide the date, the room, and a description of what the photograph represents to include:

1. All sides, elevations, and foundation components of the building, to include any vents if applicable;

2. Interior and exterior water lines on the building;

3. All damaged rooms including any special architectural features;

4. Discrepancies pertaining to basements, elevated buildings, garages, additions, and extensions or other buildings requiring review for coverage determination;

5. Exterior and interior of cabinets and drawers;

6. Appliances and building equipment including make, model, serial number identification;

7. All undamaged rooms;

8. Representation of the damage to personal property; and

9. Photographs of the curbside debris including contents and building material set out at the curb.

10. Avoid taking or including photographs that can be considered inappropriate and have no bearing on documenting or supporting the claim.

32 Pollutants

The cost to test for and monitor pollutants is only covered if the ordinance or law was in effect at the date of loss. When a flood causes direct physical damage to covered building material containing asbestos, the removal and proper disposal of the covered building material is covered as part of the covered repair, including necessary abatement charges when incurred. The claim file should contain a copy of the mandated requirement for testing or monitoring, a paid invoice documenting the policyholder incurred the expense, other costs associated with increased disposal fees, and special handling process, including detailing, in the narrative.

The SFIP will not cover to test for, monitor, remove, or mitigate areas of the home not directly damaged by flood. For example, tile in the living room damaged by flood is found to contain asbestos, and asbestos was also found in insulation around plumbing lines not directly damaged by flood. Coverage is limited to the asbestos tile in the living room.

Under the Dwelling and RCBAP Forms, the cost to remove the flood-damaged building material containing asbestos is limited only by the building property coverage limit, less the deductible. The General Property Form contains a $10,000 limit for testing and monitoring of pollutants when required by ordinance or law and any damage caused by pollutants. Under this provision, excess damage greater than this limit may not be applied to the building deductible.

33 Porches

Porch design and construction has varied over time. It may be original to the building or an attached addition. A porch can be fully or partially enclosed, screened or open; it can be built on the ground or elevated.

A porch is covered if it shares a continuous roofline and continuous foundation type with the main dwelling.

If the porch is an addition or extension attached to and in contact with the dwelling by one of the five means of connection as fully described in Section III. Property Covered A.2., it can be covered.

The adjuster should use good judgment in determining coverage for a porch. Good judgment includes clear photographs of the complete construction of the porch's roof, walls, and foundation, and the reasonable explanation or documentation that justifies the coverage recommendation.

Adjusters should also keep in mind building materials that are used to construct a porch are exterior-rated, which may resist damage from flood inundation. The same is true with common porch furniture. The scope of loss should be reasonable, and the adjuster should consider if a repair and refinish is the extent of the loss. A scope that replaces porch building materials or porch contents should be documented on the claim file.

34 Prior Loss Request

The SFIP does not cover damage to insured property that occurred prior to the covered loss, including unrepaired damage from a prior flood. NFIP insurers must verify that damages from any prior loss have been repaired before the subject loss occurred and must exclude from the adjustment any unrepaired prior damages. This normally requires the NFIP insurer to obtain and review prior flood claim files prior to adjusting the loss.

May 1, 2020

For claims filed under the SFIP Dwelling form, an NFIP insurer may adjust a claim without obtaining a prior flood claim file if there is evidence of completed repairs following a prior flood loss. Examples of evidence include an inspection of the property that clearly shows repairs to or replacement of prior damage and a review of available documentation, such as paid contractor invoices and receipts.

FEMA relies on the flood adjuster and insurer personnel to evaluate and document in the claim file the evidence demonstrating prior repairs. If the adjuster cannot substantiate repairs based on their preliminary assessment, the adjuster should recommend obtaining and review of the prior loss file to the insurer. The adjuster should provide the insurer with adequate documentation and photographs of any unrepaired prior damage.

Claims Examiners

Examiners should identify prior losses as quickly as possible following a new report of a claim and provide the estimate and photographs to the adjuster to assist with confirming prior damage and repairs.

If the current insurer needs prior loss information on a claim handled by a previous insurer, the current insurer can make a request by email to the NFIP at NFIPClaimsMailbox@fema.dhs.gov. The email subject line should include the current policy number and the type of submission (ex.1234567890 – Request for Prior Loss Information). The body of the email should contain the current policy number, property address, and date of loss. It should also contain any information you have regarding the prior loss and your reason for the request.

Requestor should expect to receive an initial reply containing basic information, building amount paid and contents amount paid for each prior loss requested, within 48 hours of the request.

If a copy of the file is needed, the NFIP BSA will request the claim file from the previous insurer and relevant information will be forwarded to the requestor upon receipt; typically, within 72 hours.

35 Prompt Communications

NFIP flood adjusters must contact the policyholder within 24-48 hours of the claim assignment, or as soon as reasonably possible depending size and scope of the storm. This initial contact will preferably be by telephone; however, if contact by telephone is not possible, the adjuster will send the policyholder or designated agent an electronic message, postcard, or letter acknowledging the assignment and providing the adjuster's telephone number and any other means of contact.

FEMA expects the adjuster to return telephone or electronic messages within 24 hours after receipt of a message from a policyholder, agent, or company staff person. When unable to contact the policyholder, the adjuster should contact the carrier to seek guidance on how to proceed with the loss and document their efforts to make contact in the activity log.

FEMA expects adjusters to provide each policyholder timely status and to set appropriate expectations or to advise when issues arise.

 **Claims Examiners**

FEMA expects the examiner to:

- Return telephone or electronic messages within 24-48 hours after receipt of a message from a policyholder, agent, or adjuster;
- Reply to written communications within ten business days of receipt;
- If denying all or part of the claim, send partial or full denial letters within ten business days of claims closure; and
- Accept or reject the POL in whole or in part within seven to ten business days of receipt. Timely acceptance or rejection of the POL gives the policyholder time to file a request for additional payment if accepted, or an amended POL within the required time-frame if rejected.

Important: Retain electronic communications in the claim file.

FEMA may extend these time frames due to catastrophic events; the extension does not relieve the examiner of the responsibility of properly documenting the file.

36. Proof of Loss/Increased Cost of Compliance Waiver Request Process

 **Claims Examiners**

When the examiner receives the Final Report or POL after 60 days from the date of loss, or after the ending date of a FEMA-issued POL extension, the examiner must submit a POL Waiver request through PIVOT and receive approval on the waiver before issuing payment. The carrier does not have the authority to extend the timeframe for filing a POL per SFIP Section VII.D.

36.1 Navigating to the POL/ICC Waiver in PIVOT and Requesting Access

1. Access the PIVOT application: https://pivot.fema.gov
2. Click on the "Request Access" hyperlink
3. Complete the Access request form

36.2 Creating a New Waiver Request

1. Log into PIVOT and select the POL/ICC Waiver card, located under Claims Operations on the PIVOT homepage.
2. To create a new POL/ICC Waiver Request, click the "Create New Request" button at the upper left-hand corner of the POL Waiver homepage.

Quick Tip: Click the "POL ID" hyperlink to access existing POL/ICC Waiver Request Forms.

36.3 Submitting a Standard POL Waiver Form

After clicking the "Create New Request" button, a pop-up box will prompt you to select a form type. Please review the section above entitled Creating a New Waiver Request for additional details.

1. Select the Standard Waiver form type and click "OK" to access the Standard POL Waiver Form.
2. Tab down to complete each section of the waiver form.
3. Click the "Add Comment" button to include comments for FEMA to review.
4. Click the "Save" button to save the In Draft waiver form.
5. After completing the form, check the "Disclaimer" checkbox at the bottom of the form to

acknowledge acceptance.

6. After affirming the disclaimer, click the "Submit Waiver" button to generate the pop-up confirmation window.
7. Within the pop-up confirmation window, click the "OK" button to submit the waiver to FEMA as a New Request.
8. FEMA will review and approve or return the waiver request.

Quick Tip: Clicking the "Save and Exit" button will save the In Draft form and direct you back to the proof of loss Waiver homepage. The "Back" button will exit the page without saving the form. In addition, when you see in red at the top "POL Alert: This waiver is a possible duplicate" it means that a previous waiver was submitted on the claim. Additional payments must be submitted under the same waiver. You can locate the previous waiver by searching "All" by the insurers' policy number. Delete this submission and submit under the prior proof of loss waiver.

36.4 Submitting an ICC POL Waiver Form

After clicking the "Create New Request" button, a pop-up box will prompt you to select a form type. Please review the section above entitled Creating a New Waiver Request for additional details.

1. Select the ICC Waiver form type and click "OK" to access the ICC Waiver Form.
2. Tab down to complete each section of the waiver form.
3. Click the "Add Comment" button to include comments for FEMA to review.
4. Click the "Save" button to save the In Draft waiver form.
5. After completing the form, check both of the "Disclaimer" checkboxes at the bottom of the form to acknowledge acceptance.
6. After affirming the disclaimers, click the "Submit Waiver" button to generate the pop-up confirmation window.
7. Within the pop-up confirmation window, click the "OK" button to submit the waiver to FEMA as a New Request.
8. FEMA will review and approve or return the waiver request.

Quick Tip: Clicking the "Save as Draft" button will save the In Draft form and direct you back to the proof of loss Waiver homepage. The "Back" button will exit the page without saving the form. In addition, when you see in red at the top "POL Alert: This waiver is a possible duplicate" it means that a previous waiver was submitted on the claim. Additional payments must be submitted under the same waiver. You can locate the previous waiver by searching "All" by the insurers' policy number. Delete this submission and submit under the prior proof of loss waiver.

36.5 Accessing an Additional Payment POL Waiver Form

After clicking the "Create New Request" button, a pop-up box will prompt you to select a form type. Please review the previous section, Creating a New Waiver Request for additional details.

1. Select the Standard Waiver – Additional Payment or ICC Waiver – Additional Payment form type.
2. Use the Policy Number data field to search for the original Standard or ICC POL Waiver. Please note that all Additional Payment Waiver Forms must be associated with an existing approved POL Waiver Request.
3. Select the associated waiver and click "OK" to open a read-only version of the original Standard or ICC Waiver.
4. Locate section F. Additional Payment at the bottom of the waiver form.
5. Click on the "Add a new additional payment" button to access the Additional Payment Waiver Form.

👥 **Claims Examiners**

Quick Tip: You may also access the additional payment waiver by clicking the "POL ID" hyperlink of an existing approved waiver from the proof of loss Waiver homepage.

36.6 Submitting an Additional Payment POL Waiver Form

The "Add new additional payment" button will generate a pop-up box with the Additional Payment Waiver Form. Please review the previous section, Accessing an Additional Payment Waiver Form for additional details.

1. Complete the waiver form. Please note that all fields must be completed prior to submission.
2. Once the form is complete, check the "Disclaimer" checkbox at the bottom of the form to acknowledge acceptance.
3. After affirming the disclaimer, click the "Submit Waiver" button to generate the pop-up confirmation window.
4. Within the pop-up confirmation window, click the "OK" button to submit the waiver to FEMA as a New Request.
5. FEMA will review and approve or return the waiver request.

Quick Tip: Clicking the "Save as Draft" button will save the In Draft form and direct you back to the proof of loss Waiver homepage. The "Back" button will exit the page without saving the form.

36.7 Reviewing the Status of a Waiver Request

A. Organizing the POL Waiver Homepage by Adjudication Status

1. Locate the POL Waiver Status drop-down at the top of the POL Waiver homepage to filter waiver requests by adjudication status. Please note, the waiver status will always default to "All".
2. POL/ICC Waiver Requests can be sorted into the following categories:
3. **All:** Includes all waiver statuses.
4. **New Requests:** Includes initial wavier requests that have been submitted to FEMA, but that FEMA has not adjudicated.
5. **In Draft:** Includes saved, in-progress waiver requests that have not yet been submitted to FEMA.
6. **Action Needed:** Includes waiver requests that have been returned to the requester for editing, or that have been resubmitted to FEMA for adjudication.
7. **Approved Requests:** Includes waiver requests that have been accepted and approved by FEMA.
8. **Closed Requests:** Includes waiver requests that FEMA has returned to the requester but were not resubmitted within 10 calendar days. Please note that you can restore Closed Request waivers by clicking the "Restore" button located at the bottom of the closed waiver. The restored waiver will move to the Action Needed queue, with the insurer as the owner.

Quick Tip: Waivers may be withdrawn until they have been approved by FEMA, including New Request, In Draft, Action Needed, and Closed Request waivers. To withdraw a waiver, click the "Withdraw Waiver" button located at the bottom of the waiver forms or within the Additional Payment pop-up box.

B. Locating specific POL/ICC Waiver Requests to Review the Adjudication Status

The POL Waiver homepage can be sorted and filtered to locate specific waiver requests using policy information.

1. Locate the filter textboxes at the top of each column, and enter the specified policy information (i.e., POL ID or Policy Number) to locate a specific waiver request.
2. Click the column headers (i.e., Policyholder Name) to sort POL/ICC Waiver Requests by ascending and descending order.

Claims Examiners

3. After you locate a specific waiver, click the "POL ID" hyperlink to access and review the waiver request.

Quick Tip: You may check the status of an Additional Payment Waiver Request by clicking on the "POL ID" of the original or additional Payment request on the POL Waiver homepage.

36.8 Reviewing Returned Waiver Requests for Edits

Upon reviewing a POL/ICC Waiver Request, FEMA can approve or return the waiver. If the waiver is returned for edits, the requester may edit the waiver to address FEMA's comments.

1. Locate the POL Waiver Status drop-down on the POL Waiver homepage, and select Action Needed.
2. The Owner column denotes which party must take action in regard to a waiver request. If FEMA is listed as the owner, FEMA must review and adjudicate the resubmitted waiver. If the insurer or vendor is the owner, the insurer must review FEMA's comments, update the form as necessary, and resubmit the waiver request to FEMA.
3. To access and resubmit forms that require action, click on the "POL ID" hyperlink of the forms that lists the insurer or vendor as the owner.
4. Update the waiver form as requested by FEMA and add comments as necessary by clicking on the "Add Comment" button.

36.9 Editing and Resubmitting Returned Waiver Requests

Upon reviewing FEMA's comments on a returned POL/ICC Waiver Request, update the waiver form as necessary, and resubmit the waiver request to FEMA.

1. Update the data fields required by FEMA. If supporting documentation is requested, locate Section F. Document Upload, and click the "Attach File" button to locate supporting documentation files on your computer.
2. Once the appropriate file has been added, click the "Save" button to save the documentation to the waiver request.
3. Once the updates are complete, check the "Disclaimer" checkbox at the bottom of the form to acknowledge acceptance.
4. After affirming the disclaimer, click the "Submit Waiver" button to generate the pop-up confirmation window.
5. Within the pop-up confirmation window, click the "OK" button to resubmit the waiver to FEMA as an Action Needed request.
6. FEMA will review and approve or return the waiver request.

36.10 Exporting Waiver Request Data and Forms to Printable Format

The proof of loss Waiver homepage and the POL/ICC Waiver Request Forms can be exported to Microsoft® Excel, Comma Separated Values (CSV), and Adobe® Portable Document Format (PDF) documents.

1. Navigate to the proof of loss Waiver homepage and locate the "Excel" and "CSV" icons in the top right-hand corner of the page. Click on either icon to generate a printable version of the POL Waiver homepage.
2. To print a specific waiver request form, locate the specified waiver using the POL Waiver Status drop-down, the filter text boxes, and/or the column sort function. Please see Reviewing the Status of a Waiver Request, above, for additional information.
3. After identifying the specific waiver request, click on the "POL ID" to open the waiver form.
4. Within the form, locate the "PDF" icon at the top right-hand corner of the page. Click on the icon to generate a printable version of the waiver request form.

Claims Examiners

For additional technical support, you may contact fema-nfippivotsupport@fema.dhs.gov or fema-ucort@fema.dhs.gov.

37   Property Address Waiver

Claims Examiners

You may not endorse an SFIP to change the insured property location. This includes relocation from one unit to another unit within the same building and relocation of a mobile home or travel trailer to a new location. You may not submit an endorsement when it will result in a change to the actual building to be insured regardless of whether a loss has or has not occurred. You must submit a new application and a new premium. Any applicable waiting period for the SFIP to become effective will apply.

An endorsement may be submitted to correct an erroneous property address (example: one made through typographical error or an Emergency 911 property address change) when it does not result in a change of the building to be insured. You may make a correction in the case where there are no paid or pending claims, without a waiver from the Federal Insurance Administrator of the requirement to submit accurate information in Section I of the SFIP. You may correct the address in the following situations:

- The property address submitted on the Application was typed incorrectly, and the building description, coverage, and rating elements belong to the building at the address indicated on the correction endorsement; or
- The address used to describe the insured building indicated on the Application has changed with the United States Postal Service; or
- A postal address is being supplied for a descriptive or legal address originally provided on the Application.

In a situation where there is a pending claim, and the agent indicates that the address on the policy is not the correct address for the building intended to be insured, you may seek a waiver from the Federal Insurance Administrator of the requirement to submit accurate information in Section I of the SFIP in the following instances:

- The property address submitted on the Application was typed incorrectly, and the building description, coverage, and rating elements belong to the building at the address indicated on the correction endorsement, and the policyholder has no insurable interest in the building at the address incorrectly indicated on the application; or
- The address used to describe the insured building indicated on the Application has changed with the United States Postal Service. The agent must demonstrate that the building description, coverage, and rating elements belong to the building at the address indicated on the correction endorsement; or
- A postal address is being supplied for a descriptive or legal address originally provided on the Application. The agent must demonstrate that the building description, coverage, and rating elements belong to the building at the address indicated on the waiver request.

You may not pay a pending claim on a policy requiring an address change without FEMA approval.

When the request is not due to a typographical error or an Emergency 911 property address change, the waiver request must come from the insurer and be sent by email to the NFIP at NFIPUnderwritingMailbox@fema.dhs.gov. The email subject line should include the policy number and the type of submission (ex. 1234567890 – Property Address Waiver).

For a Property Address Waiver, the following documentation is required:

- The complete underwriting file; documentation that was used to issue the policy, for example: Flood Application, elevation certificate, photographs, etc.

👥 **Claims Examiners**

- A signed statement from a community official that the policyholder has no insurable interest in the property with the wrong address or that the property address does not exist.
- A signed statement from the agent as to why the wrong property address was written on the Application. This may indicate that the property address submitted on the Application was typed incorrectly, and the building description, coverage, and rating elements belong to the building at the address indicated on the correction endorsement.
- A copy of the current claim file and any previous claim files, if applicable.
- For corrections on multiple buildings, submit the following supporting documentation:
  - A sketch identifying each building.
  - A schedule listing the correct building addresses.
  - Photographs of each building showing the property address.

A Property Address Waiver is not required in the following instances:

- There is no open claim.
- There is a letter from the community indicating a change in the property address.
- The address change is due to an Emergency 911 property address change.

38 NFIP Coverage for Structures Where Controlled Substances are Manufactured or Distributed

The NFIP will not issue a policy to a person or entity that acknowledges the property to be insured is used in violation of 21 U.S.C. § 856, for example: a marijuana grower or dispensary; and the NFIP will void a policy and deny a claim where the NFIP discovers the property is likely in violation of 21 U.S.C. § 856 because it is used primarily and principally for the manufacture or distribution of a controlled substance.

The NFIP may not provide a flood insurance policy for structures identified by the property owner as utilized for the manufacture or distribution of a controlled substance. To do so would constitute a direct encouragement of illegal activity under federal law and be contrary to public policy.

The NFIP must void a flood insurance policy and deny coverage where the NFIP determines after a claim is filed that it is more likely than not that the primary or principal use of the insured structure has been the manufacture or distribution of a controlled substance.

In such a circumstance, providing insurance coverage would constitute a direct promotion, effectuation, or encouragement of a violation of the law and be contrary to public policy.

When there is a question of coverage, the adjuster must conduct a reasonable investigation to confirm the use of the property and report the information to the WYO or NFIP Direct to confirm coverage.

39 Record Request from Third Party Special Investigation Units for

Fraud Investigation

When a request is received from a third party's special investigations unit, such as from a wind insurer, disclosure of the WYO flood claim file for fraud is not authorized under the Privacy Act and NFIP's System of Records Notice (SORN).

The NFIP SORN's routine use exception to the Privacy Act allows disclosure to certain entities investigating fraud or potential fraud in connection with claims, subject to the approval of the DHS Inspector General. 79 Fed. Reg. 28747, 28751 (May 19, 2014), https://www.gpo.gov/fdsys/pkg/FR-2014-05-19/html/2014-11386.htm (allowing disclosure "[t]o property loss reporting bureaus, state insurance departments, and insurance companies to investigate fraud or potential fraud in connection with claims, subject to the approval of the DHS Office of the Inspector General").

The requesting party must make the request for disclosure direct to the DHS Inspector General at https://www.oig.dhs.gov/foia.

40 Release of Claim File Information to Policyholders

40.1 Integrity of Claim Files

NFIP insurers must ensure that claim files contain all documentation in their possession directly related to the adjustment, investigation, and payment of an individual claim.[12] Such documentation includes:

1. Declaration page or verifications of coverage applicable on the date of loss

2. Copies of claim payment checks

3. Correspondence to or from the insurer and policyholder regarding the claim at issue or underwriting issues relevant to the claim at issue

4. Communications between insurer, claims examiner, adjuster, and other insurer employees and contractors

5. Adjuster reports and supporting materials, including preliminary reports, final reports, estimates, log notes, and photographs

6. Materials submitted by the policyholder, including estimates or supporting documents including prior losses provided by the policyholder or policyholder representative

7. Proof(s) of loss and other requests for additional payment

8. Claim decision letters

---

[12] See 44 CFR 62.23(i)(10) (2018).

9. Denial letter(s)

10. Expert report(s) (example, engineering assessments)

Insurers should include electronic mail or other electronic communications in the file (either as print copies or in PDF or similar format).

NFIP insurers may only rely on documentation contained within a claim file when making a claim determination. NFIP insurers are not required to obtain drafts of the documents described above but must maintain and disclose them if acquired during the adjustment, investigation, or payment of a claim.

NFIP insurers must ensure that individual claim files do not contain materials unrelated to the claim. For instance, if an insurer receives communications pertaining to multiple policyholders, the insurer must remove the personally identifiable information of other policyholders who are not part of the claim file in question prior to including the communication in the claim file.

NFIP insurers may redact any privileged communications from a claim file prior to disclosure. Privileged communications are limited to privileges that the insurer anticipates will be asserted to preclude disclosure in court, such as the attorney-client privilege.

40.2 Disclosure of Claim Files

Policyholders may obtain a copy of their claim file by submitting a signed request to their NFIP insurer. At a minimum, the request must include the policyholder's full name, current address, and date and place of birth. The policyholder's signature must either be notarized or submitted with the following statement prescribed by 28 U.S.C. § 1746:

> I declare (or certify, verify, or state) under penalty of perjury that the foregoing is true and correct. Executed on (date).
>
> (Signature)

In addition, if a representative of a policyholder, such as an attorney or public adjuster, requests a copy of a claim file on behalf of their client, the representative also must provide a letter of representation that meets the requirements below.

40.3 Letters of Representation

NFIP insurers may not disclose a policyholder's information to a policyholder's representative or allow a representative to act on behalf of a policyholder without obtaining a letter of representation signed by all policyholders named on the policy. At minimum, a letter of representation must include the following:

1. Policyholder's full name.

2. Policyholder's current address.

3. Policyholder's date and place of birth.

4. Name of third-party representative.

5. Statement from policyholder authorizing authorized representative to act on their behalf and for the insurer to release records to the representative.

The policyholder's signature must either be notarized or submitted with the following statement prescribed by 28 U.S.C. 1746:

I declare (or certify, verify, or state) under penalty of perjury that the foregoing is true and correct. Executed on (date).

(Signature)

41 Remediation, Drying, and Emergency Service Contractors

Most flood losses with interior inundation require drying. When a loss is covered by the SFIP, there are four ways an adjuster can include the cost to structurally dry salvageable building materials on a claim:

1. By square foot method, which is similar to flood cleanup, when professional services or rental equipment are not involved. This allowance represents the estimated cost and time to structurally dry the building based on the owner's time and equipment, including the building's HVAC system. An increased allowance for treating against mold and mildew may be required on longer drying efforts. An average base unit price can be derived by adding these estimated allowances for an average loss, then dividing the sum by the square foot for an average size dwelling. This unit price may be adjusted based on the facts on the loss. It is also acceptable for the adjuster to simply list each allowance in the estimate without converting the allowance to a square foot unit price.

2. When professional drying or rental equipment is involved, but there is no properly completed "drying log," the number of dehumidifiers and air movers, and the number of days of drying is based on the following factors:

   a. The length of time floodwater remained inside the building.

   b. The reasonable period unsalvageable materials remained installed; and,

   c. The length of time after the removal of unsalvageable building items, building cleanup and sanitizing was performed, to the start of mechanical drying. The scope and costs must be reasonable and in line with water mitigation costs.

3. When professional drying services are performed and a properly completed drying log is provided along with the itemized invoice, the claim payment should consider the number and type of equipment for the duration of time validated by the drying log. The scope and costs must be reasonable and in line with water mitigation costs.

A drying log is a record of daily temperature and relative humidity readings of both indoor and outdoor air, plus moisture readings and the recorded location of affected and unaffected building materials, as well as the drying goal and dry standard for the affected materials. The properly completed drying log, an industry-standard, should also include a moisture map, the daily operating status of the building's HVAC system and all the instruments and equipment used by the technician.

4. The majority of the work performed to mitigate water damage can be addressed using line-item unit cost pricing that includes labor and profit. Lump-sum, unexplained charges, and charges based on time and expense should be investigated and documented to identify the charge and to ensure charges are not duplicated. Ancillary charges for travel, food, and lodging by the water mitigation company are not payable.

For more information, the claims professional may refer to the Structural Drying bulletin, Appendix F, in this manual or the Institute of Inspection Cleaning and Restoration Certification (IICRC). The IICRC is a certification and Standards Developing Organization (SDO), a non-profit organization for the inspection, cleaning, and restoration industries. In partnership with regional and international trade associates, the IICRC serves more than 25 countries with offices in the United States, Canada, United Kingdom, Australia, New Zealand, and Japan. The industry standard, *Standard and Reference Guide for Professional Water Damage Restoration*, is certified by the American National Standards Institute (ANSI). The document is officially known as ANSI-IICRC S-500 (2015).

42 Reporting

42.1 Timely Reporting

An adjuster should submit the NFIP Preliminary Report within 15 calendar days after receipt of the loss assignment. The NFIP Final Report is due 30 days later. An adjuster should conclude the claim within 45 days after the Preliminary Report. When the claim cannot be concluded within 45 days, an adjuster should file an interim report every 30 days until the claim is concluded or as directed by the claims examiner.

Claims Examiners

The examiner should confirm the following and maintain a proper diary to ensure compliance:

- NFIP Preliminary Report received within 15 days after receipt of the loss assignment.
- Signed NFIP Final Report received by 30 days after receipt of Preliminary Report or an interim report received every 30 days until the adjuster completes the adjustment.
- Signed proof of loss received from the policyholder within 60 days of the date of loss, or by the deadline of a FEMA issued proof of loss extension.

Important: The examiner must receive a signed Final Report or signed proof of loss by the 60th day or ending date of a FEMA issued proof of loss extension. If the examiner receives the signed document after the deadline, the examiner must submit a proof of loss waiver request to FEMA through UCORT and receive approval on the waiver request before issuing payment.

42.2 Preliminary Report

The adjuster's first report is the Preliminary Report Form. It is important to submit the Preliminary Report as soon as possible, preferably the same day as the inspection but no later than 15 calendar days after the assignment, along with perimeter photographs of the risk and photographs of the damage. The adjuster must complete all sections in the Preliminary Report as accurately and detailed as possible. When a unique circumstance develops with the assignment that delays the initial inspection, the adjuster should immediately submit a narrative documenting the insurer's claim file of the reason for the unavoidable delay. The report detailing the delay is to be submitted no later than the 15th day after the assignment. The form must be signed by the adjuster and include the active FCN.

All the data recorded in the Preliminary Report Form is important. The adjuster should complete the entire form and give special attention to:

A.   Reserve Amounts

The approximate value of the covered payable loss is important for financial reasons.

B.   Building Foundation Components

1. A building that has walls installed over top of a concrete slab is non-elevated, and has either slab-on-grade, raised slab-on-grade, or raised slab-on-stem wall foundation.

2. A building that has a floor installed above the ground level, supported by foundation walls, shear walls, posts, piers, pilings or columns, is an elevated building.

    –   If a concrete slab is installed within the foundation's perimeter, the slab is not considered structural to the foundation, unless it is six inches thick and reinforced with "re-bar" which is driven into the building's foundation.

    –   If an elevated floor is constructed over a crawlspace and the crawlspace is below the ground level on all sides, the building is not considered elevated, and the building's lowest floor is the below ground level crawlspace floor, meeting the SFIP definition of a basement.

C.   Measuring Waterlines

The adjuster must record the highest water line on the exterior and interior of the building, and the recorded interior waterline should not be higher than the exterior waterline. The adjuster should look for an exterior debris line on all buildings and provide measurements. It is advisable to have a photograph of the tape measure against the exterior and interior walls clearly showing the waterline measurement.

Plantings and shrubbery may retain debris so the adjuster should photograph and report that measurement. If the adjuster is not able to identify a debris line, address it in the narrative report.

1. Waterlines: Must be recorded in inches.

2. Exterior: Waterlines are always recorded using a positive number. Adjusters should measure the exterior water depth from the lowest point of the land immediately outside the building.

3. Basements: Measure the interior waterline from the floor above the basement down and record the value on the Preliminary Report with a negative sign in front of the recorded inches. This is necessary for FEMA actuarial purposes. If the water enters the main living area (the floor above the basement) – the measurement will be from that floor, up, and will show as a positive number. Please also note the height of the basement ceiling.

4. Elevated Buildings: Measure the interior water height in a crawlspace or enclosure from the lowest floor as defined in the Flood Insurance Manual. In non-V Zones, the reference point of the lowest floor is the top of the floor. In V-Zones, the reference point of the lowest floor is the lowest horizontal structural member. When the water depth is below the lowest floor, the number of inches should be represented by a negative number.

*To collect accurate data of areas damaged, it is necessary that every adjuster use either negative or positive numbers. A negative number reported indicates that flood water was found only in the basement. In the case of elevated buildings, the negative number indicates that floodwater did not enter above the floor used for rating.

Figure 49. Basement Interior Waterline

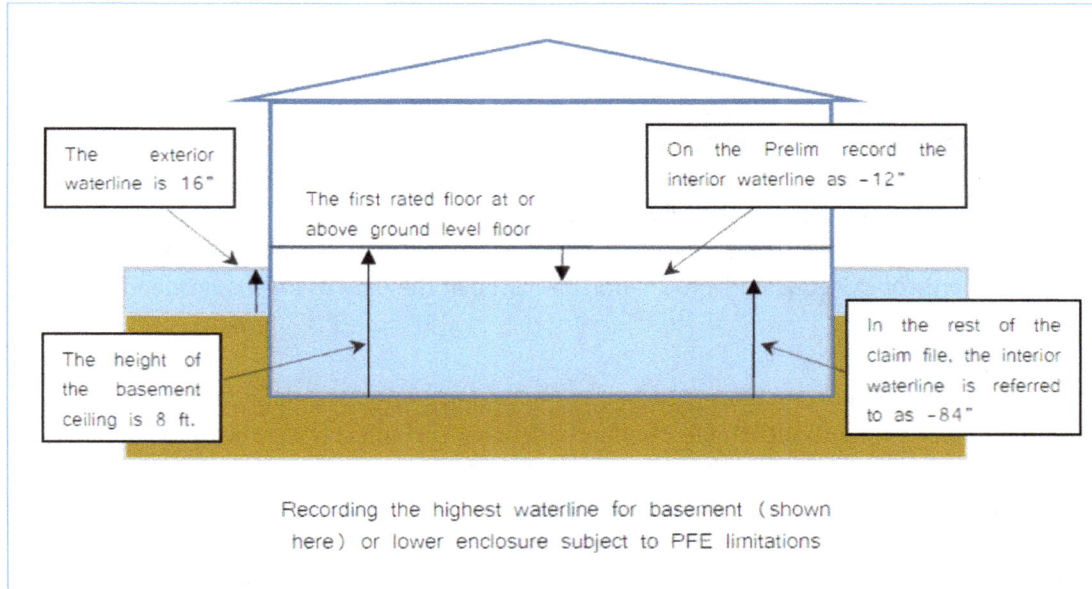

Diagram credit Anthony Thorne, FEMA

D.   Adjuster Memo to the Insurer

When a special issue arises from the loss inspection, the adjuster should include a narrative memo accompanying the Preliminary Report. This may involve a customer service issue with the policyholder or a representative, help support a large advance payment, request an expert, or submit an underwriting referral noting any potential policy rating issues.

Claims Examiners

The examiner ensures that the adjuster provides the NFIP Preliminary Report within 15 days after the adjusters' receipt of the assignment, along with perimeter photographs of the risk and photographs of the damage. The form must be signed by the adjuster and include the adjuster's FCN. Review the form for accuracy, underwriting or rating concerns, advance requests, and reserves. Communicate to the adjuster necessary changes, errors, or omissions. The examiner should refer any rating issues to their underwriting department.

The adjuster must recommend reserves on the Preliminary Report based on the initial inspection and provide updated reserves as the claim progresses. It is the adjuster's best approximation of the amount of damage to the covered building and personal property at the time of, and prior to, an estimate being prepared.

Claims Examiners

Flood systems set minimal reserves when a flood claim is open. The examiner must promptly update the claim reserves upon receipt of the Preliminary Report, any subsequent interim report(s) and Final Report. Company systems should have the ability to update reserves as payments are made.

42.3 Interim Report

The adjuster's interim report is required every 30 days after the Preliminary Report submission until the Final Report is complete, or anytime issues arise that the insurer should be aware of. It is important for the adjuster to inform the insurer why a claim remains open more than 45 days after the assignment. The interim report also gives the insurer assurance that the policyholder and their claim is receiving the proper care and attention. The report can be a brief memo notifying the insurer of the claim handling status, or it can be a copy of correspondence from the adjuster to the policyholder, which requests additional information or which serves as a reminder of previously requested information discussed at the date of the loss inspection.

42.4 Narrative Report

The NFIP Narrative Report serves as a summary of coverage, interests, claim activities, adjustment decisions, and settlement recommendations. The adjuster may need to provide multiple Narrative Reports when the circumstances are unusual, suspect, or especially complicated, and additional explanation is appropriate. Only include facts in reports. The narrative should outline relevant information based on facts that address who, what, where, when, and how. Conjecture, sarcasm, innuendo, or any other unprofessional language have no place in Narrative Reports. Adjusters should also provide specific details in the Narrative report when the adjuster's judgment is applied to any part of the loss adjustment.

Claims Examiners

The examiner should confirm that the Narrative Report properly summarizes the loss including coverage, points of interest, claim activities, adjustment decisions, and settlement recommendations and request an amended report if additional information is required to support the adjustment and payment recommendation.

42.5 NFIP Final Report

A policyholder who suffers flood damage to the insured property has only one claim arising from that event, regardless of the number of proofs of loss with documentation packages the policyholder may submit in support of that claim. The insurer's assignment of an adjuster to a loss plays a critical part in the claims experience for both the policyholder and the insurer. As the policyholder is tasked with certain responsibilities when a flood loss occurs[13,] the insurer assigns the adjuster to help the policyholder meet these responsibilities and to document the loss. The policyholder, with assistance from the adjuster, develops the agreed-to proof of loss during the Flood Claims Process.[14] The NFIP Final Report is required on all losses.

---

[13] See SFIP, Section VII. General Conditions, paragraph (J) "Requirements in Case of Loss"

[14] FEMA Fact Sheet, Flood Claims Process, https://www.fema.gov/media-library/assets/documents/114402

42.6 Proof of Loss

A proof of loss is a policyholder's signed and sworn statement of loss with documentation to support the dollar amount requested.[15] The proof of loss is not the claim and it is not just a form. FEMA encourages the policyholder, adjusters, and insurers to utilize the FEMA-generated proof of loss form when complying with the policy's requirement in case of a loss. However, completion and signing the form alone does not meet all SFIP requirements, and the policyholder must provide documentation to support the loss and dollar amount declared on the form.

The policyholder is required to submit a proof of loss within 60 days of the date of loss or within any extension granted by the Federal Insurance Administrator. The adjuster may assist the policyholder in completing the proof of loss; however, this assistance is only a courtesy. Policyholders must use their own judgment concerning the amount of the loss, and they must justify that amount. A fully completed NFIP proof of loss form, signed by the policyholder(s) with the required documentation is required on every claim on which the adjuster recommends payment.

A signed Increased Cost of Compliance (ICC) proof of loss is required on valid ICC Claims.

Proof of loss forms do not require a Notary. Electronic signatures are acceptable (see NFIP Insurers' Acceptance of Electronic Signatures in this manual).

FEMA expects the adjusters to communicate to policyholders that the proof of loss is not a waiver. Signing the proof of loss allows the policyholder to comply with the policy requirement to submit a proof of loss but does not prevent the policyholder from submitting an additional proof of loss, such as an amended proof of loss or replacement cost proof of loss form, for additional payment.

A payment arising from litigation is considered the settlement of a case and not a claim. Therefore, a proof of loss is not required for payments arising from litigation unless specifically directed by counsel.

Claims Examiners

The examiner reviews the Final Report and proof of loss to confirm accuracy and that the policyholder properly supported their claim for damage on the form.

When the proof of loss is not compliant in content or form, the examiner should reject the proof of loss and communicate the decision directly to the policyholder. However, when the examiner can support payment of a portion of the claim, issue a partial rejection of the proof of loss to allow payment of the undisputed claim. The examiner should provide written notification of the rejection to the policyholder explaining all issues and request the documentation required to resolve those issues.

---

[15] FEMA.gov, Proof of Loss, https://www.fema.gov/media-library/assets/documents/9343

43 Requests for Additional Payment

Claims Examiners

43.1 Handling of Requests for Additional Payment Prior to Repairs

A policyholder who has not completed repairs and is requesting additional payment is not required to prove how they spent funds previously paid on the same claim. If a policyholder has not completed the repair or replacement of items damaged by a covered loss, NFIP insurers may not deny requests for additional payment solely because the policyholder did not provide evidence that all amounts previously paid on the claim, plus the value of the deductible(s) and any applicable physical depreciation, were spent to repair or replace covered flood damage. NFIP insurers must evaluate such requests for additional payments using the same methods, procedures, and requirements used to evaluate the initial requests for payment.

While policyholders are responsible for substantiating their claims, NFIP insurers must make best efforts to assist policyholders and work collaboratively to reach agreement on the scope and cost to repair or replace covered damage, regardless of the documentation provided, and when necessary:

- Provide the policyholder with guidance on the documentation necessary to support the policyholder's request for payment.

- Assign an adjuster to review the claim and, when warranted, inspect the property.

- Confirm that the property for which payment is sought is covered by the SFIP. This review likely will assess whether the scope or price includes material improvements, repair re-design, costs incurred to comply with building codes, undamaged or non-covered property items, damage resulting from causes other than flood, pre-existing damage, duplicate allowances, or costs to repair that are outside of industry standards.

- Use the services of an expert when there are questions concerning whether the damage was caused by flood or the extent of the damage repairs.

43.2 Handling of Requests for Additional Payment When Repairs are Complete

Where repairs have been made before a request for additional payment is submitted, NFIP insurers must determine that funds previously provided were spent to make repairs and that the supplemental request does not duplicate the prior payment. Once payment is made to the policyholder, the NFIP has no control over the use of the funds. The policyholder may use the funds to repair the covered loss, repair losses that are not covered by the SFIP, or for any other use. Also, the deductible and any applicable depreciation are the responsibility of the policyholder and cannot be reimbursed as a part of any additional payment(s). Accordingly, if a policyholder does not have the funds to complete repairs, it does not necessarily mean there has been an underpayment.

To be eligible for additional NFIP payment, the policyholder must document that funds previously paid were used to repair or replace covered damage and must show with specificity that additional funds to repair covered damage are required. NFIP insurers should carefully review the evidence of actual loss, together with paid receipts, paid invoices, canceled checks, and other evidence of payment for repairs, to ensure that the policyholder is not seeking duplicate payments, payment for uncovered losses, or the values of applicable deprecation and the deductible(s) in a request for additional payment.

44 Reservation of Rights

Claims Examiners

The examiner may send a Reservation of Rights letter when the policyholder does not sign the non-waiver agreement, when there is a lack of cooperation on the part of the policyholder, or when it becomes necessary to compel some action on the part of the policyholder seeking compliance with policy conditions. Non-Waiver Agreements and Reservation of Rights letters must clearly state the issue in question. See Non-Waiver Agreement in this section of the manual.

45 Salvage

The adjuster should address the potential for a financial recovery in one of three ways:

1. Readjust the scope of damage from replacement (non-salvageable) to repair (salvageable) and reach an agreement with the policyholder on the cost to repair. This value should include any applicable cost to disassemble, clean, repair, refinish, reassemble, plus any handling by the repair provider.

2. Keep the scope of damage for the item as a replacement (ruined and non-salvageable) and reach an agreement with the policyholder on the "buy-back" value.

   a. The adjustment must specify the salvage and the buy-back value either within an appendix to the estimate, or within the estimate itself.

   b. The adjuster should keep in mind property damages settled under this option (2) ruined and non- salvageable, are no longer insurable or claimable on a future loss; hence the potential that option (1) (salvageable) is more suitable to the policyholder's interests.

3. When the policyholder is not amenable to either (1) or (2), the adjuster should promptly inform the insurer, who may instruct the adjuster to contact an outside third party such as a salvor. While uncommon for a loss on the Dwelling Form, residential salvage interest exists with hardwood furniture, HVAC units, and major household appliances, especially those with certain metals such as copper.

Financial recovery paid to the program by a third party salvor is contingent upon prompt coordination between the adjuster and the salvor. The insurer should retain a list of reputable salvors involved in past claims and make that list available to its adjusters. When applicable, the adjuster should discuss with the policyholder, the potential visit by a salvor soon after the adjuster's inspection. An inspection by the salvor only involves inventorying damaged items worth purchasing. The salvor may not take possession of any property before the loss is settled until it is agreed upon by the policyholder and the insurer. The salvor should promptly provide the salvage list and price to the adjuster for direction, and the adjuster should promptly discuss the matter with the policyholder and the examiner. The salvor is entitled to an inspection fee if the salvage offer is turned down by the insurer. See SALAE section in this manual for instructions to request approval to pay the salvor's fee. Otherwise, the salvors' fee is taken from the sale of the salvage. The salvor should issue payment for the overage to the insurer as a recovery. The insurer may allow the adjuster to make decisions involving salvage on its behalf.

The adjuster's narrative in the Final Report must address the "financial recovery" applicable to the loss. Oftentimes this portion of the narrative is omitted or is incomplete, which may lead to missed opportunities by the program. When financial recovery is not available, the narrative should explain why.

The adjuster's service charge is based on the gross loss at RCV before any salvage. The adjuster or the adjusting firm may not act as salvor on a loss, in whole or in part. This includes taking possession of the insured property for the inspection or purchase by a third party.

Claims Examiners

The examiner should confirm that the adjuster considered the salvage value of all replaced items. The insurer is entitled to a 10 percent salvage allowance only when there is an actual cash collection of salvage from the policyholder. The 10 percent allowance does not apply in any other situation.

The insurer's share of salvage recoveries (10 percent) must be deducted from the net recovery proceeds prior to remitting the remaining proceeds to the restricted bank account. The amounts of salvage recoveries reported to FEMA (via the recovery after final payment transaction) will be for the total recoveries, inclusive of the insurer's entitlement.

---

46 SFHAs and Non-SFHAs

46.1 Special Flood Hazard Areas (SFHAs)

High-Risk Zones

1. AE (replaces A1-A30)

2. A, AH, AO, A99, AR

3. VE (replaces V1-V30), V, VO

46.2 Non-Special Flood Hazard Areas (Non-SFHAs)

Low to Moderate Risk Zones

1. B, C, X

2. D (undetermined)

See the NFIP Flood Insurance Manual for descriptions of the stated zones.

47   Special Allocated Loss Adjustment Expense (SALAE) Processes

Claims Examiners

IMPORTANT: All SALAE expenses need FEMA authority to pay regardless of the dollar amount.

47.1 SALAE Type 1 – Engineering and Other Expert Fees

It is the insurer's responsibility to confirm that expert fees are reasonable for the work performed and to address questions prior to submitting the invoice to FEMA for authorization. Following are guidelines to aid examiners in evaluating SALAE Type 1 expenses:

- Reimbursement of SALAE Type 1 expenses need FEMA's approval of the exact amount of the incurred expenses.

- FEMA will not pre-approve expert assignments or fees; this is the responsibility of the insurer.

- Insurers must secure a pre-inspection fee quote from the expert prior to assignment. Engineers must seek authority from the insurer prior to incurring expenses that exceed the pre-inspection fee quote. FEMA will not authorize payment for any unapproved amount.

- FEMA will not accept lump-sum charges. All expenses on the invoice must be itemized by time and expense with hours rounded to the nearest whole and supported by receipts.

- To control expenses, engineering firms should assign the closest available engineer to the assignment location and use the most economical means to travel to the site. When this is unavoidable, the firm should provide an explanation and seek pre-authorization.

- Engineer travel expenses must be fair and reasonable and conform with GSA travel rates. Engineers are expected to apportion travel expenses between assignments. FEMA will not pay the following:

    o   lodging within the contiguous United States;

    o   food expenses;

    o   Travel time billed at the site study/inspection rate. Travel time must be reasonably discounted; or

    o   Mileage within 100 miles of loss location round trip.

- Experts must bill separately the administrative fee, site study/inspection, travel time (billed at no more than half the hourly rate for the site study), report preparation, peer review if applicable, travel expenses, mileage, etc. Experts must provide all applicable receipts for air travel, vehicle rental, hotel, tolls, parking, etc., and clearly explain any exceptions. Mileage can be charged for distances traveled exceeding 100 miles round trip and pro-rate between multiple assignments in the same area.

- The expert must thoroughly explain the need to use other subcontractors or vendors to complete the assigned task and itemize the charges. FEMA will not pay for multiple engineers or experts to conduct an inspection unless the expert receives pre-approval from the insurer with a detailed explanation or the inspection needs different expertise or disciplines to evaluate the damage, for example: a structural and electrical engineer.

- Experts should limit the number of individuals involved with producing the final work product to only those who are essential.

- The total billing involved with producing the final report should be reflective and representative of the complexity of the assignment.

Claims Examiners

- All expense submissions to FEMA require the specific recommendation for payment by the insurer's Principal Coordinator or their designee.

- **The following expenses are never reimbursable under SALAE Type 1:**

  o Engineering fees charged by an unlicensed engineer.

  o Engineer reports co-signed by an engineer who present themselves as a P.E. but are unlicensed in the state where the inspection took place.

  o Fees charged in excess of the pre-inspection fee quote unless there is evidence that the engineer secured pre-approval prior to incurring or charging the excess expense.

  o Undocumented expenses and expenses that exceed the GSA travel rates.

  o Photos.

  o Food expenses.

47.2 SALAE Type 1 (Expert Services) Reimbursement Requests

- A SALAE Type 1 is any expert expense incurred by the insurer as part of the claim investigation, including an Engineer, Surveyor, Architect, Salvor, Certified Public Account (CPA), or similar expert. FEMA reimburses insurers for use of such services.

- Insurers must request FEMA approval to pay all SALAE Type 1 expenses regardless of the dollar amount.

- SALAE Type 1 approval requests must include all supporting documents including the engineer report, any amended report(s), itemized invoices, and applicable receipts for travel, etc.

A. Navigating to the SALAE Module in PIVOT

- Accessing PIVOT and requesting access to PIVOT for a New User:

  o Access the PIVOT site: https://pivot.fema.gov

  o Click on the "Register" hyperlink

  o Complete the Registration form

  o Request access to Special Allocated Loss Adjustment Expenses (SALAE) module and include a reason for access to complete the registration

  o Following administrator approval via email, affirm the Rules of Behavior to access PIVOT

- Navigating to the SALAE homepage in PIVOT:

  o After logging in to PIVOT, select the "Special Allocated Loss Adjustment Expenses" navigational tile under "Claims Operations." This brings you to the SALAE homepage.

- SALAE Homepage Features:

  o The "create new request" button allows you to start a new SALAE Type 1 reimbursement request.

  o The Filter panel allows you to search and filter SALAE requests by policyholder name, policy number, insurer, engineering entity, owner, and status.

  o The "in-progress" tab displays SALAE requests that are in draft, in FEMA's queue for review, or ones that require additional information from the insurer prior to FEMA's determination.

  o The "complete" tab displays SALAE requests that are approved, rejected, or closed.

Claims Examiners

B. Submitting a New SALAE Request

- Step 1: Requestor Information Page
  - o The first step of the SALAE request submission process is to verify (or update if needed) the requestor information that is auto populated on the Requestor Information Page.
  - o After the requestor's information is verified, click "next" to continue to the SALAE Type Designation Page.

- Step 2: SALAE Type Designation Page
  - o Verify that "Type 1 (Expert Expense)" is chosen from the drop-down menu on the "SALAE Type Designation" page.
  - o After "Type 1 (Expert Expense)" is chosen, click "next" to continue to the Policy Information Page.

- Step 3: Policy Information Page
  - o Enter all the policy information on the Policy Information Page.
  - o After inputting the required information (denoted with "*"), click "next" to navigate to the Expert Service Information Page.

- Step 4: Expert Service Information Page
  - o Select the "type of expert" from the drop-down menu on the Expert Service Information Page.
  - o Click the "add new entity" button to add the expert services entity name(s) and address(es). Click "update" to save the entity details to the request. You can add up to three entities per request.
  - o Report the state Certificate of Authorization (COA)/Registration Number and expiration date. Some states do not license engineering firms; however, there may be a requirement for the firm to register with the Secretary of State.
  - o Enter the request details and justification for the expense.
  - o For engineering or surveyor services *only*, respond to additional questions.
  - o For engineering services *only*, click "add new engineer" to report the names and license information the engineer(s) conducting the inspection. Add a separate line entry to report the co-signer of the report, when listed as a P.E. Click "update" to save the engineer's information to the request.
  - o For engineering or surveyor services *only*, you must certify the request and electronically sign and date the certification.
  - o Click "next" to continue to the Documentation Upload Page.

- Step 5: Documentation Upload Page
  - o Upload all expert invoices and enter the invoice date and invoice number on the Documentation Upload Page. Click "select file" to browse for the appropriate file on your computer and then click "upload invoice" to save the file to the request.
  - o Upload all engineering reports and amended reports. Click "select file" to browse for the appropriate file on your computer and then click "upload report" to save the file to the request.
  - o Use the optional "Other" section on the Documentation Upload Page to upload other documentation. Click "select file" to browse for the appropriate file on your computer and then click "upload other" to save the file to the request.

👥 **Claims Examiners**

      o   Click "next" to continue to the Final Review Page.

- Step 6: Final Review Page
    - o   On the Final Review Page, you can review the information pertaining to the request that was previously entered.
    - o   If you need to update information prior to sending it to FEMA, use the "edit" link in the section headers to navigate back to the appropriate page.
    - o   After reviewing and verifying the information on the Final Review Page, you can choose to provide any additional comments or files they wish to attach to the SALAE request and submit to FEMA. You are required to click "add comment/file(s)" to save comments/files to the request.
    - o   Click "submit to FEMA" at the bottom of the Final Review Page to officially submit the request to FEMA for review. You will be redirected back to the SALAE homepage.
- Once FEMA provides a determination, insurer users will receive an email notification informing you of FEMA's review decision (approved, rejected, or additional information requested).

C. Providing Additional Information for a Specific SALAE Request

- To supply additional information on a request returned by FEMA:
    - a.   Filter requests by status: "Action Needed" on the SALAE homepage.
    - b.   Verify the policyholder's name, date of loss, and policy number to ensure you are entering the correct request.
    - c.   Click "open request" to enter the request and supply additional information.
- To review the request for more information:
    - d.   Scroll to the comment section on the Final Review Page and review the comment left by FEMA (comment also available in the email from UCORT).
    - e.   Respond to/carry-out FEMA's request prior to resubmitting the request.
        - i.   To edit information, go to the correct page and update the information and return to the Final Review Page for review and submission.
        - ii.   To supply more files, utilize the comment section on the Final Review page to upload documents and provide a description of the file. Click "add comment/file(s)" to save the file to the request.
    - f.   Click "return to FEMA" to re-submit the SALAE Type 1 request for review. Upon FEMA's review, you will receive an email notification, informing you that your request has been approved, rejected, or if more information is needed.

Important: If FEMA returns a request to the insurer, the requestor has 14 business days to provide the additional documentation or the request is automatically closed.

For technical support, contact fema-nfippivotsupport@fema.dhs.gov.

47.3 SALAE Type 2 (Adjustment Expenses) Reimbursement Requests

SALAE Type 2 is for extraordinary adjustment expenses that are not reimbursed by the applicable NFIP Adjuster Fee Schedule including efforts by the adjuster to establish the loss or coverage and necessary travel expenses. It is the insurer's responsibility to confirm that adjuster expenses over the applicable NFIP Adjuster Fee Schedule are reasonable for the work performed. Following are guidelines to aid examiners in evaluating SALAE Type 2 expenses:

- Reimbursement of SALAE Type 2 expenses need FEMA's approval of the exact amount of the incurred expense.
- FEMA will not pre-approve adjuster fees; this is the responsibility of the insurer.

👥 Claims Examiners

- Adjusting firms and adjusters must have pre-approval and agreement from the insurer before incurring or billing SALAE Type 2 expenses.

- All expenses must be fair and reasonable, billed at time and expense, and supported by receipts.

- The adjuster fee schedule fairly compensates adjusters for their time to adjust flood claims. This includes revising flood claims when necessary. There may be a time when allowing an adjuster to bill on time and expense makes sense due to the complexity of the claim. Time and expense must only be used when necessary and when clearly supported.

- When it is necessary for an adjuster to revise a claim, the adjuster fee schedule pays the adjuster the greater of:
  - the difference in the fee based on the revised claim
  - the CWOP fee.

  When an insurer authorizes an adjuster to bill on time and expense, the adjuster can only receive time and expense, not time and expense and the fee under the adjuster fee schedule. However, the insurer must offset the time and expense by the applicable fee under the adjuster fee schedule. Example SALAE Type 2 for time and expense:

  The initial adjuster fee was $800 based on the amount of loss per the published fee schedule. The adjuster submits an invoice for time and expense that total $937.50. The total expenses to date $1,737.50. Based on the revised claim, the adjuster would be owed the $395 CWOP fee. The examiner would deduct the $395 CWOP fee from the $937.50 time and expense and request a SALAE Type 2 for $542.50. The SALAE Type 2 entries would show as follows:

Expense Details					
Total expense amount previously approved:		Total adjusting expenses under this claim:	1737.5	Requested amount for approval:	542.5
Deduct applicable scheduled fee:	1195	Authorized SALAE 2 paid to date:	0	Fee schedule:	Adjuster Fee Schedule for DOL on or after 8/24/17

  The SALAE Type 2 request must include all fee bills to support the total adjusting expenses under the claim and confirm the original claim amount used to determine the initial fee and the revised claim used to determine the applicable adjuster fee based on the revised claim.

- Travel expenses must conform with GSA travel rates. Independent Adjusters are responsible to arrange for and incur lodging expenses within the 48 contiguous states. FEMA will only reimburse lodging expenses that exceed the average lodging expense normally incurred with the 48 contiguous states, not to exceed the GSA travel rates for lodging. FEMA will not reimburse the following:

- FEMA will not accept lump-sum charges and there is no longer a $500 rate for SALAE Type 2.

- The insurer must thoroughly explain in writing the reason it was necessary for the adjuster to incur the excess expense, details of the activity, what effect this activity or work had on the adjustment, any unusual circumstances, and why FEMA should approve the expense. All SALAE Type 2 approval requests must be accompanied by copies of the report (including any previous reports), all actual bills, and itemized time and expense sheets.

- If an adjuster conducts an inspection on a covered flood loss, with an active policy, and the policyholder withdraws the claim after an estimate is written, or fails to pursue the claim, the adjuster is paid the CWOP fee under Loss Adjusting Expense (LAE). In exceptional circumstances, the insurer can seek approval to pay the excess adjuster fee as a SALAE Type 2 when:

Claims Examiners

- o After the adjuster and the insurer makes several documented reasonable attempts, using all available contact sources (phone, mail, email, etc.), to secure the signed Proof of Loss so that the claim can be paid and the policyholder:
    - Provides written confirmation that they will not pursue the claim;
    - The policyholder withdraws the claim;
    - It becomes reasonably clear that the policyholder will not pursue the claim due to the policyholder's failure to respond to all attempts to secure a signed Proof of Loss. Documentation of all attempts to secure the signed Proof of Loss must be provided, and the insurer must send a letter to the policyholder advising that the claim is being closed without payment due to failure to pursue.

  - o FEMA will not give approval when the policyholder does not sign the Proof of Loss due to disagreement with the settlement or coverage dispute.

- The following expenses are never reimbursable under SALAE Type 2:
    - o CWOP adjuster fees for supplemental adjustments, regardless of the number of CWOP adjuster fees under any one claim
    - o Texas tax expenses are only payable as LAE per the published adjuster fee schedule and are never reimbursable under SALAE Type 2.
    - o To reimburse adjusting expenses on an invalid policy. An example: It is determined after the inspection and estimate that the insured property is in a COBRA requiring the policy to be rescinded.
    - o Undocumented expenses and expenses that exceed the GSA travel rates.

A. Navigating to the SALAE Module in Pivot

A. Accessing Pivot and requesting access to Pivot for a New User:
  - o Access the Pivot site: https://pivot.fema.gov "Special Allocated Loss Adjustment Expenses" navigational tile under "Claims Operations." This brings you to the SALAE homepage.

B. SALAE Homepage Features:
  - o The "Create new request" button allows you to start a new SALAE Type 2 reimbursement request.
  - o The Filter panel allows you to search and filter SALAE requests by policyholder name, policy number, insurer, engineering entity, owner, and status.
  - o The "In-progress" tab displays SALAE requests that are in draft, in FEMA's queue for review, or ones that require additional information from the insurer prior to FEMA's determination.
  - o The "Complete" tab displays SALAE requests that are approved, rejected, or closed.

B. Submitting a NEW SALAE Request

A. Step 1: Requestor Information
  - o Edit your personal and company information (as needed) and click "Next".

B. Step 2: SALAE Type Designation
  - o Select "Type 2 (Adjuster Expense)" from the drop-down menu.
  - o Click "Next" to continue with your submission.

C. Step 3: Policy Information
  - o Enter the policy information.
  - o Click "Next" to continue with your submission.

D. Step 4: Expense Details
  - o Complete the expense details.

Claims Examiners

- o Use the appropriate Fee Schedule to calculate the "Total Adjusting Expenses Paid to Date" and use the drop-down to indicate which Fee Schedule was used.
- o Click "Next" to continue with your submission.

E. Step 5: Documentation Upload
- o Enter invoice information.
- o Under Invoice, click "Select Files . . ." to browse for the appropriate invoice(s) and upload to the application.
- o Under "Other", click "Select Files . . ." to browse for other documentation related to the submission.
- o Click "Next" to continue with your submission.

F. Step 6: Review Your Submission
- o Review all information entered into the system.
- o Upon completion of data entry, click "Submit to FEMA."
- o Submission Complete

C. Notifying the Insurers

A. Once FEMA provides a determination, insurer users will receive an email notification informing you of FEMA's review decision (approved, rejected, or additional information requested).

D. Providing Additional Information for a SALAE Type 2 Request

A. To supply additional information on a request returned by FEMA:
- o Filter requests by status: "Action Needed" on the SALAE homepage.
- o Verify the policyholder's name, date of loss, and policy number to ensure you are entering the correct request.
- o Click "Open request" to enter the request and supply additional information.

B. To review the request for more information:
- o Scroll to the comment section on the Final Review Page and review the comment left by FEMA (comment also available in the email from UCORT).
- o Respond to/carry-out FEMA's request prior to resubmitting the request.
  - To edit information, go to the correct page and update the information and return to the Final Review Page for review and submission.
  - To supply more files, utilize the comment section on the Final Review page to upload documents and provide a description of the file. Click "Add comment/file(s)" to save the file to the request.
- o Click "Return to FEMA" to re-submit the SALAE Type 1 request for review. Upon FEMA's review, you will receive an email notification, informing you that your request has been approved, rejected, or if more information is needed.

Important: If FEMA returns a request to the insurer, the requestor has 14 business days to provide the additional documentation or the request is automatically closed.

For technical support, contact fema-nfippivotsupport@fema.dhs.gov.

47.4 SALAE Type 3 (Litigation Expenses) Reimbursement Requests

A. Reimbursement of SALAE Type 3

1. Approval for All Expenses

Type 3 SALAEs are reimbursed solely for litigation expenses. The regulations and the Arrangement do not authorize the reimbursement of other legal expenses, including pre-litigation matters or other legal advice. 44 C.F.R. § 62.23 and the Arrangement. Only actual litigation expenses related to a filed

Claims Examiners

lawsuit are reimbursable. Prior to the filing of a lawsuit, the matter is considered claims handling and ineligible for Type 3 SALAE reimbursement. This provision does not revise any of the expenses typically reimbursed throughout the claims handling process.

FEMA requires WYO Companies to seek FEMA approval for all litigation expenses incurred to defend a lawsuit within the scope of the Arrangement brought against an insurer for claims under a WYO Company-issued policy.

2. **Customary Standards**

    FEMA reimburses Type 3 SALAE Litigation expenses incurred by a WYO Company pursuant to the Arrangement subject to FEMA Office of Chief Counsel, FIMA Legal Division guidance and direction. The WYO Company is responsible for ensuring litigation expenses for which reimbursement is sought are consistent with its own customary standards, staff, and independent contractor resources, as it would in the ordinary and necessary conduct of its own business affairs, subject to the Act, the SFIP, the Arrangement, and other regulations prescribed by FEMA. 44 C.F.R. § 62.23(e). For example, if the customary standards of the WYO Company require a reduction of hourly rates or expenses or other limitations on payment for outside expenses, the WYO Company is required to do the same for any Type 3 SALAE-related expense.

    Under the Arrangement, FEMA is not responsible for payment to counsel representing WYO Companies. The WYO Company is responsible for paying its counsel without delay and for seeking reimbursement for eligible expenses under the Arrangement. WYO Companies must submit requests for reimbursement within 60 days of receipt of the invoice or bill from its outside counsel. If outside counsel will not submit an invoice or bill within the 60-day period, the WYO Company must notify FEMA of its existence and provide an explanation and estimation of when the outside counsel will submit the invoice or bill.
    Further, FEMA will deny any invoice or bill submitted after 180 days unless the WYO Company provides sufficient justification, or FEMA expressly and in writing waived the 180-day period authorizing an extension.

    Prior to seeking FEMA's approval for reimbursement, a WYO Company must review the invoice to verify the work was completed, accuracy of the billing, reasonableness of the expenses incurred, and that the reimbursement would be approved under the WYO Company's customary standards as submitted subject to the Arrangement, Act, Regulation and FEMA guidance. A certification signed by the WYO Company representative must be attached as a cover sheet or the expense will be denied. The certification must provide the following:

    I have reviewed and understand the FEMA guidelines that govern the Type 3 Special Allocated Loss Adjustment Expenses (SALAEs). I am responsible for reviewing and ensuring that Type 3 SALAE requests comply with the FEMA guidelines. I have reviewed the invoice for which reimbursement is sought, and to the best of my knowledge, information and belief, confirm that the invoice is reasonable, appropriate and complies with the applicable FEMA guidelines.

    Executed on (date).

    (Signature)

3. **Overhead Expenses are Not Reimbursable**

    Customary charges such as overhead, ordinary office supply costs, and local telephone costs are included in the hourly rate and are not reimbursable as Type 3 SALAE. The following expenses are considered overhead and generally are not reimbursable. FEMA will consider reimbursement on a case-by-case basis after pre-approval:

    A. Fees attributed to secretarial and administrative services;

    B. Organizing material for storage;

Claims Examiners

C. Unless an attorney is required, responding to inquiries concerning services, billing statements, cases files or audit letters;

D. Fees incurred for "learning time";

E. Scheduling and arranging meetings, depositions, examinations or other event scheduling;

F. Data entry, document scanning, document conversion to other electronic formats;

G. Arranging travel;

H. Time spent photocopying, collating, and faxing;

I. Bates stamping of documents;

J. Date stamping documents;

K. Management of personnel;

L. Annual or monthly fees for computerized legal research services such as LexisNexis, Westlaw, or Public Access to Court Electronic Records (PACER). Research time is reimbursable;

M. Rent for office space, equipment, or software;

N. Utilities including local and long-distance telephone service;

O. Charges for use of a teleconference line;

P. Meeting rooms in the assigned counsel's law offices for local depositions and conferences;

Q. Catering;

R. Facsimile charges of any kind;

S. Postage;

T. Meals or refreshments for anyone other than the attorney assigned to the case while attending meetings, depositions, or similar events;

U. Support staff salaries;

V. Technology costs such as depreciation on electronic devices, copiers, and other machinery;

W. The use of an outside vendor for copy services unless pre-approved by FEMA (In-house photocopy charges are limited to ten cents per page); and

X. Any other item associated with overhead or profit.

As noted above, FEMA recognizes there may be circumstances that warrant reimbursement of an expense listed above. Accordingly, FEMA may approve such expenses upon written request and appropriate justification by the WYO Company.

B. Limitations on Reimbursement for Discovery

Substantial legal fees and expenses are incurred as part of discovery. WYO Companies must monitor these costs. Depositions can provide critical information, but present one of the most significant litigation costs to the NFIP. FEMA will reimburse up to three depositions per case without preapproval. This does not apply to defending depositions. FEMA recognizes the need to ardently represent the Program. This provision is not intended to restrict or interfere with the outside counsel's ability to represent the WYO Company. The purpose of this provision is to provide better monitoring of discovery expenses. The WYO Company simply needs to provide a brief justification for the additional depositions to FEMA-NFIP-WYO-Litigation@fema.dhs.gov. The Write Your Own Oversight Team will promptly review and respond to all requests.

Video Teleconference for depositions and other proceedings is highly encouraged. Any questions should be referred to FEMA's Office of Chief Counsel.

Claims Examiners

C. **Navigating to the Litigation and Expense Module in Pivot**

   A. Accessing Pivot and requesting access to Pivot for a New User:
      - Access the Pivot site: https://pivot.fema.gov
      - Click on the "Register" hyperlink
      - Complete the Registration form
      - Request access to Litigation and Expense module and include a reason for access to complete the registration
      - Following administrator approval via email, affirm the Rules of Behavior to access Pivot

   B. Navigating to the Litigation and Expense module homepage in Pivot:
      - After logging in to Pivot, select the "Litigation and Expense" navigational tile under "Claims Operations." This brings you to the Litigation and Expense homepage.

For technical support, contact fema-nfippivotsupport@fema.dhs.gov.

47.5   SALAE Type 4 (Appraisal Expenses) Reimbursement Requests

SALAE Type 4 are expenses incurred under the SFIP Appraisal Clause.

- Reimbursement of SALAE Type 4 expenses need FEMA's approval of the exact amount of the incurred expenses.

- FEMA will not pre-approve appraisal fees; this is the responsibility of the insurer.

- FEMA will not accept lump-sum charges. All expenses must be fair and reasonable, billed at time and expense, and be supported by receipts.

- All SALAE Type 4 requests must be accompanied by copies of the report (including any previous reports), all actual bills, and any itemized time and expense sheets. The insurer must thoroughly explain in writing why FEMA should approve the expense.

- **The following expenses are never reimbursement under SALAE Type 4:**
  - FEMA will not approve expenses incurred by the insurer on an invalid Appraisal.

E. **Navigating to the SALAE Module in Pivot**

   A. Accessing Pivot and requesting access to Pivot for a New User:
      a. Access the Pivot site: https://pivot.fema.gov
      b. Click on the "Register" hyperlink
      c. Complete the Registration form
      d. Request access to Special Allocated Loss Adjustment Expenses (SALAE) module and include a reason for access to complete the registration
      e. Following administrator approval via email, affirm the Rules of Behavior to access Pivot

   B. Navigating to the SALAE homepage in Pivot:
      a. After logging in to Pivot, select the "Special Allocated Loss Adjustment Expenses" navigational tile under "Claims Operations." This brings you to the SALAE homepage.

   C. SALAE Homepage Features:
      a. The "create new request" button allows you to start a new SALAE Type 2 reimbursement request.

Claims Examiners

    b. The Filter panel allows you to search and filter SALAE requests by policyholder name, policy number, insurer, engineering entity, owner, and status.

    c. The "In-progress" tab displays SALAE requests that are in draft, in FEMA's queue for review, or ones that require additional information from the insurer prior to FEMA's determination.

    d. The "Complete" tab displays SALAE requests that are approved, rejected, or closed.

F. Submitting a NEW SALAE Request

A. Step 1: Requestor Information
- o Edit your personal and company information (as needed) and click "Next".

B. Step 2: SALAE Type Designation
- o Select "Type 4 (Appraisal Expense)" from the drop-down menu.
- o Click "Next" to continue with your submission.

C. Step 3: Policy Information
- o Enter the policy information.
- o Click "Next" to continue with your submission.

D. Step 4: Expense Details

    a. Complete the expense details.

    b. Fill in or use the "Auto Calculate" button to calculate the reimbursable amount.

    c. Click "Next" to continue with your submission.

E. Step 5: Documentation Upload
- o Enter invoice information.
- o Under Invoice, click "Select Files . . ." to browse for the appropriate invoice(s) and upload to the application.
- o Under "Other", click "Select Files . . ." to browse for other documentation related to the submission.
- o Click "Next" to continue with your submission.

F. Step 6: Review Your Submission
- o Review all information entered into the system.
- o Upon completion of data entry, click "Submit to FEMA."
- o Submission Complete

G. Notifying the Insurers

A. Once FEMA provides a determination, insurer users will receive an email notification informing you of FEMA's review decision (approved, rejected, or additional information requested).

H. Providing Additional Information for a Specific SALAE Request

A. To supply additional information on a request returned by FEMA:

    a. Filter requests by status: "Action Needed" on the SALAE homepage.

    b. Verify the policyholder's name, date of loss, and policy number to ensure you are entering the correct request.

    c. Click "open request" to enter the request and supply additional information.

B. To review the request for more information:

    a. Scroll to the comment section on the Final Review Page and review the comment left by FEMA (comment also available in the email from UCORT).

    b. Respond to/carry-out FEMA's request prior to resubmitting the request.

        i. To edit information, go to the correct page and update the information and return to the Final Review Page for review and submission.

        ii. To supply more files, utilize the comment section on the Final Review page to upload documents and provide a description of the file. Click "add comment/file(s)" to save the file to the request.

c. Click "return to FEMA" to re-submit the SALAE Type 1 request for review. Upon FEMA's review, you will receive an email notification, informing you that your request has been approved, rejected, or if more information is needed.

Important: If FEMA returns a request to the insurer, the requestor has 14 business days to provide the additional documentation or the request is automatically closed.

For technical support, contact fema-nfippivotsupport@fema.dhs.gov.

48   Statute of Limitations

48.1 Interplay Between the Extension of the Proof of Loss Deadline for NFIP Policyholders and the 1-Year Statute of Limitations in 42 U.S.C. § 4072 (VII.R. Suit Against Us)

NFIP Insurer

The SFIP is a Federal regulation promulgated by FEMA, which has three forms. The Dwelling form is found at 44 C.F.R. § 61, Appendix A(1), the General Property form is found in Appendix A(2), and the Residential Condominium Building Association Policy (RCBAP) form is found in Appendix A(3). In these regulations, FEMA established the 60-day proof of loss deadline. See Section VII(J) of the Dwelling and General Property forms and Section VIII(J) of the RCBAP form. The Associate Administrator of the Federal Insurance and Mitigation Administration has the authority to grant waivers of and extend the proof of loss deadline pursuant to 44 C.F.R. § 61.13(d). See also 44 C.F.R. § 61, Appendices A(1) and A(2), Section VII(D), and Appendix A(3), Section VIII(D).

Congress, in enacting the National Flood Insurance Act of 1968, as amended, (42 U.S.C. § 4001, et seq.) enacted a 1-year statute of limitations for an NFIP policyholder to bring a lawsuit after the complete or partial denial/disallowance of the policyholder's claim. See 42 U.S.C. §4072. This 1-year statute of limitations was incorporated into the SFIP by FEMA. See 44 C.F.R. § 61, Appendices A(1) and A(2), Section VII(R), and Appendix A(3), Section VIII(R).

Unlike the SFIP proof of loss deadline, which is a regulation created by FEMA, FEMA cannot extend the time limit for NFIP policyholders to bring a lawsuit. The applicable time limit to file a lawsuit was set by statute, not FEMA. Although FEMA has the administrative authority to extend the proof of loss deadline it established by regulation, FEMA lacks the authority to extend the time limit to file a lawsuit established by statute. This statute of limitations has never been extended.

It is important to understand that the proof of loss is not the claim. The claim is the assertion by the policyholder that they are entitled to be paid for a covered loss under their SFIP (i.e., the demand for money). An NFIP policyholder whose insured property is damaged by an event only has one claim arising from that event, regardless of the number of proofs of loss that the policyholder may submit in support of that claim. Even in the instance of an Increased Cost of Compliance (ICC) claim under Coverage D of the SFIP there is only one claim that arises from that substantial damage determination regardless of the number of proofs of loss submitted by the policyholder.

The SFIP sets forth the process that the policyholder must follow in supporting his or her claim in the General Conditions section of each form of the SFIP (which is Section VII for the Dwelling and General Property SFIP forms

NFIP Insurer

and Section VIII for the RCBAP SFIP form). For example, Section VII(J)(1) of the Dwelling SFIP form requires prompt written notice of the loss. Also, Section VII(J)(4) of the same form and its subparts set forth what information must be included for the proof of loss (which is the policyholder's statement of the amount of money demanded and submitted in support of their claim) and indicate that it must be sent within 60 days after the loss.

NFIP court rulings hold that if the policyholder does not comply with all the terms and conditions of the SFIP prior to filing a lawsuit (including the proof of loss requirements), then the necessary conditions for the policyholder to be able to bring a lawsuit have not been met. What this means is that, in the instance in which a denial letter has been issued such that the statutory 1-year to bring the lawsuit will run before a proof of loss extended deadline runs, the policyholder has to both file the lawsuit and have the required proof of loss requirements completed within 1 year of the date of the denial or partial denial of the claim. This situation will typically arise when the insurer determined that the policyholder did not suffer a "direct physical loss by or from flood" and there is no coverage under the SFIP. For example, if the insurer determined that floodwaters did not reach the insured building, a denial letter will be sent because there is no insured loss and no coverage under the SFIP.

In any event, FEMA requires NFIP insurers to continue to work with their policyholders. The NFIP can pay additional amounts if properly supported, even if the formal proof of loss deadline has passed. FEMA does this through the granting of the policyholder's request of an individual waiver of the proof of loss deadline through the insurer. The NFIP makes every possible effort to ensure that a proper claims payment and resolution of the claim are achieved in every instance.

The limited waiver and extension of the proof of loss deadline recognizes the difficulties policyholders may experience evaluating damage and supporting their flood insurance claim. The typical dispute arises after a policyholder received payment based on an adjuster's report and the insurer's approval and later believes there is additional uncompensated damage. However, as discussed above, there are instances when the claim may be denied for reasons that do not require an adjuster's report or proof of loss from the policyholder. Even in those claims where the insurer issued a denial letter early, the policyholder still has a full year from the date of that denial letter to collect all required documentation, file the proof of loss, and then file a lawsuit if believed necessary.

The extended time to file the proof of loss is an effective mechanism that allows policyholders to fully present their claims. For most claims, disputes will not arise until after the submission of the proof of loss and formal denial of the amount sought. While FEMA does all it can to assist NFIP policyholders, it does not have the authority to waive or extend the applicable statute of limitations.

49 Subrogation

Subrogation is the right of the insurer to claim damages caused by a third party and recover the claim payment by the insurer to the policyholder for the loss. Pursuant to 44 C.F.R. § 62.23(i)(8), FEMA has the right of first recovery in the event of any subrogation claim under the NFIP. The adjuster must consider subrogation on every flood claim, confirm the potential for subrogation, and address subrogation in the Narrative Report. This may require the use of an expert to confirm causation and verifying the potential at-fault party. Investigations should be timely to prevent the loss of key evidence that would allow a successful recovery. If the adjuster believes there may be potential for subrogation, the adjuster should complete FEMA Form 086-0-16 - Cause of Loss and Subrogation Report, to identify the potentially responsible third party and characterize how their actions may have caused or worsened flood damage.

WYO companies and the NFIP Direct cannot waive subrogation or otherwise complicate FEMA's right to pursue subrogation. SALAE Type 3 does not apply to proactive litigation such as subrogation. FEMA's Office of Chief Counsel (OCC) assumes primary responsibility for all subrogation recovery matters upon refusal by the WYO.

When reviewing a claim for subrogation, be sure to capture the who, what, where, when, and how of the third-party event that caused the flooding. Adjusters should ask policyholders about events like recent residential or commercial construction, changes to neighboring properties, drainage issues, city pumps, and recent road work projects.

👥 Claims Examiners

The insurer should evaluate subrogation recovery. Whether the insurer pursues recovery or not, the insurer should notify the NFIP BSA and submit the Cause of Loss and Subrogation Report and a copy of the claim and underwriting file.

Send subrogation-related documentation and information to the Office of Chief Counsel (OCC) at FIMA-OCC-Subrogation@fema.dhs.gov and cc a copy to the NFIP BSA via electronic mail at NFIPClaimsMailbox@fema.dhs.gov. Upon receipt of the information, the NFIP BSA will log the information. OCC will contact the insurer if additional information is required or necessary.

50 Underwriting Referral

It is important that the adjuster brings to the insurer's attention any issue involving a potentially improperly rated policy or ineligible building or contents promptly upon discovery. The sooner in the claims process the adjuster raises a potential problem, the sooner Underwriting (UW) can review the concern; minimizing delays to the loss settlement. A UW referral should cite the current rating of the policy, followed by the facts and supporting photographs. When the issue involves a potential basement or post-FIRM elevated building located within a special flood hazard area, but the adjuster is unsure about the facts, the referral should disclose this and recommend the insurer hire a qualified outside professional service.

👥 Claims Examiners

With an issue involving an elevation status of a floor level, an elevation certificate, or a written elevation study, a detailed "bird's-eye" drawing is typically necessary. A bird's-eye drawing plots all elevation points for each floor level, area or room, in addition to recording the elevation points along the building's exterior perimeter foundation, and high and low points at the described location. A report of this nature generally requires certification with a signature and seal from a professional land surveyor; however, some states also permit a signature and seal from a professional engineer. The insurer should ensure the professional it hires complies with all rules established by the state for land surveying.

The conversion of elevation "vertical datum" may also present a UW issue. A vertical datum is a base measurement point (or set of points) from which elevations are determined. Historically, the standard datum used by the federal government was the National Geodetic Vertical Datum of 1929 (NGVD 29). However, the North American Vertical Datum of 1988 (NAVD 88) is now the national standard. Elevation values based on different vertical datum cannot be used together directly since they are based on a different vertical reference point. When comparing the updated flood hazard data released by FEMA with elevation information on elevation certificates and other documents from different sources, the insurer must take care to ensure all elevations are in the same datum. If they are not the same, the insurer must apply a conversion factor so that the values are

👥 **Claims Examiners**

referenced to the same datum before they are used. Failure to do this can result in improper structure design (for example: building at the wrong elevation), which can have serious implications in terms of complying with community and state building requirements. Flood insurance rates can also be impacted, including eligibility for the Waiver of the Limitation or a Letter of Map Amendment or Revision.

The examiner must carefully review the adjusters' report for discrepancies in the declarations page, the preliminary report, or photographs, and immediately refer any discrepancies to the UW Department for review and provide the necessary supports, ex. photographs, surveyors report, etc.

How to address potential rating changes:

- When the rating change will result in greater coverage, the adjustment should proceed based on the current rating and revised once underwriting confirms the rating, reforms the policy, and collects the correct premium.

- When the rating change will potentially restrict coverage, have the adjuster secure a non-waiver agreement, or send a Reservation of Rights letter addressing the coverage issue. The adjustment continues and payment is issued based on the undisputed covered loss. The adjuster revises the estimate once UW confirms the rating, reforms the policy, and collects the additional premium.

The examiner should keep the policyholder informed through the process and communicate the change to the adjuster and the policyholder as necessary.

51 Waiver of Elevated Building Coverage Limitation

A Letter of Map Amendment (LOMA) or Letter of Map Revision (LOMR) removes the post-FIRM elevated building from the Special Flood Hazard Area (SFHA), and the elevated building limitations of the SFIP then do not apply to the area beneath the lowest elevated floor. The LOMA or LOMR obtained after the loss is effective as of the date of the loss.

If the lowest adjacent grade (LAG) of the property is below the Base Flood Elevation (BFE), this would prevent a LOMA or LOMR from being issued to the property owner, so that the property owner will not be able to obtain full coverage for the enclosure. (See Letter of Map Amendment/Letter of Map Revision in this section of the manual and the Flood Insurance Manual for additional information regarding LOMA and LOMR.)

However, there are buildings where the LAG is below the BFE, but the lowest floor elevation (LFE), the enclosure floor, is at or above the BFE. Such buildings comply with the NFIP Floodplain Management Regulations, in that the lowest floor of the building is elevated to or above the community's BFE. This means the enclosure does not have the higher risk of flooding that elevated building enclosures normally have. In such cases, a claim may qualify for a waiver of the elevated building coverage limitation.

The waiver applies to buildings located in SFHA zones beginning with the letter A where a BFE is available. Buildings located in SFHAs beginning with the letter V do not qualify for this waiver. The waiver is based on the current flood map and the use of a grandfathered flood map is not applicable. The flood zone on the current map must also be an AE flood zone. Consequently, the waiver is only applicable to the current loss, and a separate waiver request must be filed on any future claim to ensure the use of the current flood map, the proper flood zone, and BFE.

Claims Examiners

The examiner must send the waiver request by email to the NFIP BSA at NFIPUnderwritingMailbox@fema.dhs.gov. The email subject line should include the policy number and the type of submission (ex. 1234567890 – Waiver for Elevated Building Coverage Limitation).

Documentation to attach to the email must include:
- Complete Underwriting file.
- Documentation used to issue the policy.
- Current Flood Zone Determination.
- Elevation Certificate and datum conversions if applicable.
- Color photographs of all sides of the building and photographs showing machinery and equipment and location
- Copy of current claim file and any previous claim files if applicable.

The NFIP BSA will send an acknowledgement of receipt of the waiver request to the insurer. If additional information is required, the NFIP BSA will notify the insurer within 10 business days. Otherwise, the NFIP BSA will submit the packaged documents to the FEMA Underwriting Branch for review and determination. If all documentation is submitted timely and properly, the entire process should not take more than 15 business days.

---

52 Wildfires

52.1 Application of Post Wildfire Exception to 30-Day Waiting Period for New Policies

In general, new policies for flood insurance become effective following a 30-day waiting period.[16] However, the Biggert-Waters Flood Insurance Reform Act of 2012 provided an additional exception to this requirement related to flooding caused by post-wildfire conditions, referred to as the Post-Wildfire Exception.[17] Under the Post-Wildfire Exception, the standard 30-day waiting period does not apply to new policies if:

1. The covered property experiences damage caused by a flood that originated on Federal land;

2. Post-wildfire conditions on Federal lands caused or worsened the flooding; and,

3. The policyholder purchased the policy either:

   a. Before the fire containment date; or

   b. During the 60-calendar-day period following the fire containment date.

For the purposes of the Post-Wildfire Exception, the Federal Agency responsible for the land on which the post-wildfire conditions existed determines the fire containment date.

---

[16] See 42 U.S.C. 4013(c)(1); 44 CFR 61.11(c)

[17] See 42 U.S.C 4013(c)(2)(C) (added by the Biggert-Waters Flood Insurance Reform Act of 2012 § 100241)

Where a policyholder meets the requirements of the Post-Wildfire Exception, the insurer must make the policy effective at 12:01 a.m. (local time) on the date of the flood loss qualifying for the exception. Once the policy is made effective, the insurer must adjust and pay claims in accordance with the SFIP, including provisions governing a flood in progress and requiring that a flood occurs after the purchase of the policy.

52.2 Assistance with the Proper Application of Post Wildfire Exception

FEMA supports the application of the Post-Wildfire Exception by tracking containment dates for wildfires occurring on Federal lands and consulting when necessary with appropriate Federal agencies to determine whether post-wildfire conditions caused or exacerbated a flood. Insurers may request assistance with the proper application of the Post-Wildfire Exception by contacting FEMA- FIDClaimsMailbox@fema.dhs.gov.

53 Wind/Flood Loss

When adjusting wind/water losses, the adjuster should use established and proven investigative methods to document flood and wind damage to buildings and contents occurring during hurricane or storm events. "Wind/Water Investigative Tips" below can also be helpful.

The adjuster should record the process they use when approaching a wind and water claim. In addition to looking for signs of flood damage and a general condition of flood and documenting the exterior water line, the adjusters should note any exterior wind damage, such as missing shingles, turbines, or fascia damage. The adjuster should also photograph this damage and mention what was observed in the narrative report.

The SFIP only pays for direct physical loss by or from flood to the insured property. Once inside the building, the adjuster should always document the floodwater line. Damage below this line is typically flood damage (exceptions like wicking should be noted in the narrative report). Damage above the floodwater line is typically wind damage, such as water-stained ceilings or water damage at broken windows or exterior doors. This damage should also be photographed and mentioned in the narrative report.

53.1 Wind and Water Investigative Tips

1. Research local newspapers and check with the National Weather Service, or other agencies, to determine the specific data relative to the storm in the location of the claim. Specific information to look for includes wind speed data, storm surge data, flood height data, and other relevant information.

2. When damage is caused by a hurricane, tropical storm, nor'easter, or other event that may cause both wind and flood damage, determine and record the following (*check and record the timing and duration for each*):

Data Element	Measurement	Timing	Duration
Highest Wind Speed			
Barometric Pressure			
Amount of Rainfall			
Tidal Heights			
Storm Surge			
Wave Heights			

3. Record the distance and direction of the insured risk relative to the eye of the storm. Remember that the waves are higher to the right of the storm's path.

4. Research and record site conditions:

   – Original ground elevation

   – Distance from a body of water

   – After-storm ground elevation or other indications of scour

   – Amount and type of storm debris

5. Canvass the neighborhood for eyewitnesses and take their recorded or signed statements. Be certain to identify where each witness was at the time of the storm, document the wind speed versus wind gusts and flood levels each witness saw, and the time of day observed that each saw it. Record in the claim files only what each witness says verbatim—not hearsay or your own opinion.

6. Check for and photograph the debris line. Measure and record how many feet the debris line is from the shoreline and how many feet from the insured risk. Be sure to describe the topography in detail. Check for and photograph houses and objects adjacent to the insured risk. If the damage appears to be different from that of the insured risk, determine why and record the reason in the claim files. Usually, the damage is different for one of two reasons:

   – Different causes of damage (for example, a tornado can cut a relatively narrow path, leaving neighboring buildings relatively undamaged).

   – Different building construction and anchoring. Look for connectors or tie-down straps for elevated buildings and enclosures beneath elevated buildings. Check the pilings for evidence of scouring. Photograph the remaining pilings, showing patterns of the leaning pilings. Determine how deep the pilings were installed and measure the distance between pilings.

7. Determine and record in the claim file a complete description of the damaged or demolished building, including the type of construction; whether elevated (if elevated with an enclosure, be sure to indicate the type of enclosure – breakaway walls, open latticework, vents, etc.); number of floors (including basement); roof covering and pitch; windows, carports, etc.; and the building's relative position to the wind. It is also important to include a description of the foundation type (slab, piles, piers, etc.) and damage.

8. Photograph (close-up) the remains of connectors or tie-downs. Be sure to describe the size, type, method of installation, and the brand name.

9. Make a notation in the initial report where evidence suggests the insured risk was not built as securely as neighboring buildings. The flood insurer or adjuster may want to check the local building codes to determine if a building construction violation has occurred and document the claim files, both with copies of the code and the evidence of a violation. Document the age of the building and the effective dates of the building codes.

10. Check for and photograph any wind-caused openings in the building and missing roof shingles.

11. Check for and photograph all possible wind-related watermarks or stains visible on both the exterior and interior walls and ceilings of the building.

12. Check for and photograph all possible flood-related watermarks or stains visible on both the exterior and interior of the building.

13. Check for and photograph any watermarks visible on nearby trees or fence posts, or other buildings.

14. Other important considerations:

   – Causation must be determined in order to accurately adjust the loss.
   – The policyholder has a duty to provide the wind adjustment from the wind insurance carrier. Wind damage must be considered before any payment is made.
   – If stick building the covered structure, the non-covered wind damage has to be considered.
   – At no time will the SFIP pay more than the pre-loss value of the home, less claim payments from all other insurance.
   – The SFIP does not allow for constructive total losses.

Overall, flood claim adjusters should take special care when adjusting claims caused by both flood and other perils. In addition to thoroughly examining all flood damage, adjusters should also photograph and note evidence of damage caused by non-flood perils. General notations of damage caused by non-flood perils do not rise to the level of providing a professional opinion regarding causation, damages, or repair methods. Such notations can help resolve disagreements later in the claims process.

53.2   Handling guidance when wind carrier pays wind limits

The SFIP provides that flood insurance payments cannot exceed the value of the insured building before the loss. In addition to the provisions requiring proof of direct physical flood loss cited above, the SFIP expressly limits payment to the lesser of (a) the building limit of liability, (b) the replacement cost of covered property with materials of like kind and quality and for like use, or (c) the necessary amount actually spent to repair or replaced covered property.

A federal court has held that any flood payment is limited to the value of the structure before the storm minus prior insurance payments for damage to the same property[18].

The court stated that "coverages for both [wind and flood under separate insurance policies] does not entitle the plaintiff to double recovery in the event of a given loss.' Policyholders can recover under both a flood and non-flood policy when a flood and another covered peril combine to result in a total loss if they can segregate and prove the two types of damages. The policyholder should be given the opportunity to segregate which damages were caused by flood versus another non-flood policy to recover up to the entire pre-loss value of his home.

Setting expectations and conducting a prompt and detailed wind and water investigation is necessary to provide the best possible service to the policyholder. The adjuster must :

- Set proper expectations for the policyholder, explaining what is needed to confirm causation, direct physical damage by or from flood, and to set the amount of loss.

- Secure the services of a subject matter expert to document the cause of loss and damage by wind versus. flood.

- The adjuster may need a subject matter expert to determine the pre-loss value. A contractor's rebuild estimate that considers like-kind and quality construction is an acceptable method to prove the value.

- Determine the pre-loss value for the building immediately before the loss per VII. GENERAL CONDITIONS, V. LOSS SETTLEMENT 5. Amount of Insurance Required and attempt to reach an agreement with the policyholder. Once the value is established, the adjuster will deduct applicable depreciation, the wind payment, and flood deductible to determine the amount payable under the flood policy.

---

[18] See: Halmekangas v. State Farm Ins. Co., 2008.

54 Withdrawal Letters and Denial Letters

Claims Examiners

54.1 Withdrawal Letters

The examiner will issue a letter of withdrawal confirming the policyholder's voluntary withdrawal of the claim prior to or after inspection. A policyholder's withdrawal is not a denial and does not trigger the one-year limit to file suit or the 60-day timeframe to file an appeal; however, if an inspection occurred the letter should reflect the findings of the adjuster and address any applicable exclusions.

54.2 Partial Denial Letters and Full Denial Letters

Send letters to policyholders so that they are aware of the disposition of the claim and provide copies of estimates and inventories to support the claim payment and settlement.

Send a denial letter on all partial or full denial of claims. Denial letters must include all known reasons for the denial, citing the appropriate section of the SFIP supporting the denial, and include information regarding FEMA's formal appeals process (see Section 4 Appeals, in this manual).

Provide the policyholder a courtesy copy of experts' reports.

55 Oversight

55.1 Claims Oversight

FEMA maintains oversight of the NFIP claims processing performed by the insurers. This oversight is conducted primarily through claims and underwriting Operation Reviews and Random Claims Quality Checks (RCQC). The Operation Reviews are typically performed on closed claim files. An RCQC is conducted during disasters on open and closed claims. The RCQC review involves reviewing at least one claim from each adjuster to determine if the claim is on the right path and provide guidance as necessary. Additionally, insurers engage Certified Public Accounting (CPA) firms to perform biennial audits that include a claims audit section.

Adjusters and insurers should be mindful of the findings from the Operation Reviews, RCQC, and biennial audits.

The NFIP is a federal program and therefore subject to the scrutiny of the Department of Homeland Security (DHS) and other federal agencies, including the Government Accountability Office (GAO), the DHS Office of Inspector General (OIG), and the Office of Management and Budget (OMB). Adjusters and insurers should be aware and mindful of findings from the following audits: DHS Improper Payment Elimination and Recovery Information Act (IPERIA), DHS Financial Audit, and various GAO and OIG studies and reports.

Many of the findings can be avoided simply by adherence to good claims handling practices and knowing the terms and provisions of the SFIP. Helpful tips may be included in the findings. The following will identify findings and preferred methods when indicated:

A. Incorrect Estimate/Worksheet Calculation

1. Estimates are line-by-line, room-by-room using unit costs.

2. Depreciation to both building and contents are taken on a line-by-line basis.

3. Rooms should be described and identified, and the adjuster should verify that the estimate/worksheet and the building diagram match.

4. The adjuster should be careful to include only building items on the building estimate/worksheet; for instance, clothes washers and dryers are always contents and should not be included as building items.

5. Qualifications for Replacement Cost Loss Settlement should be clearly documented, including single-family residence, principal residence, insured to at least 80 percent of full replacement cost, or maximum available.

B. Insufficient Damage Documentation

1. Invoices may be needed to adequately support a commercial inventory or other complex claim items. A salvor or CPA may be required and must be approved by the insurer.

2. Photographs should adequately document the claimed damage – photographs of undamaged building elements and contents are also important as well as damage from causes other than flood.

C. Payment Processing Errors

The adjuster should make all payment recommendations clear. Other claim documents, including the estimate/worksheet, Final Report, and the proof of loss, should support the recommendations.

D. Covered Loss Exceeded the Value of Certain Items

1. Care is taken when items with Special Limits are claimed, not to exceed the amount of special limits in the aggregate.

2. Loss Avoidance Measures should be properly documented and supported with invoices or other documentation.

3. Property Removed to Safety claims should be properly documented and supported with invoices or other documentation.

E. Case Loss Reserving

The reserving system mandates that reports must be timely and reflect true reserves. The initial case loss reserve may be a system-generated amount based on criteria established by the insurer or it may be an individually set reserve based on the best knowledge of the loss at the time the reserve is established.

The insurer may also set a bulk catastrophe reserve. The NFIP Preliminary Report and each subsequent adjuster report should refine the case loss reserve amount as the insurer becomes aware of additional facts, inspections, and estimates. The goal is that this knowledge along with any reductions of partial or advance payments will result in a case loss reserve that closely reflects the value of all future payments and ultimately the value of the final payment.

55.2 Claims Operation Reviews Description of Findings

Claims payments arising out of policies issued by the insurer are issued from NFIP funds. FEMA performs claims operation reviews to confirm compliance with the rules of the program and the SFIP. The following are the description of findings that could result in a critical error finding.

Claims Examiners

A. No Signed Proof of Loss

The policyholder is required to send the insurer a complete, signed and sworn proof of loss (or for claim payments of $7,500 or less, the policyholder signs the adjuster's final report) within 60 days after the date of loss or within any extension granted by the Federal Insurance Administrator (Administrator). The proof(s) of loss must include documentation to support the amount requested initially and any requests for additional payment. Failure to have the required properly executed Proof(s) of Loss in the file is a critical error.

B. No Proof of Loss Waiver

When the policyholder submits a proof of loss after the 60-day SFIP time requirement or any extension granted by the Administrator, the insurer must request a waiver from the Administrator of the time required for the proof of loss. The insurer does not have the authority to extend the time required to file a proof of loss per the SFIP Section VII.D., "This policy cannot be changed nor can any of its provisions be waived without the express written consent of the Federal Insurance Administrator." Payments made without the required waiver are unauthorized. Such payments are critical errors.

C. Incorrect Close Without Payment (CWOP) Reason Code

The insurer must carefully review the adjusters' reports for claims that are to be closed without payment and close the claim file using the correct CWOP reason code in accordance with the National Flood Insurance Program Bureau and Statistical Agent (NFIP BSA), PIVOT (NFIP system of record). If the incorrect reason code results in an improper payment to the insurer, or to the adjuster, the payment is a critical error.

D. No Denial Letter or Improper Denial Letter/Withdrawal Letters

The insurer must carefully review the adjusters' reports for claims that are to be closed without payment. Denial letters are required on all denials of the entire claim or any portion of a claim and must include all reasons for denial known at the time of the letter citing the appropriate section of the SFIP supporting the denial. The denial letters must also include information regarding FEMA's formal appeals process. The insurer must also send letters to policyholders confirming their voluntary withdrawal of a claim. A policyholder's withdrawal is not a denial and does not trigger the one-year limit to file suit or the 60-day time frame to file an appeal; however, writing a policyholder that the review of the claim found no damage by or from flood is considered a denial. Due to the importance of the denial letters in the appeals process and the litigation process, failure to send a denial letter is a critical error.

E. Mortgage Issues

The SFIP, Section Q. Mortgage Clause states, "The word 'mortgagee' includes trustee. Any loss payable under Coverage A – Building Property will be paid to any mortgagee of whom we have actual notice as well as any other mortgagee or loss payee determined to exist at the time of loss, and you, as interests appear." The Mortgage

Clause is a contract within a contract. That is a contract between the mortgagee and the insurer within the contract between the policyholder and the insurer. Including the name of the mortgagee on each building claim payment is the surest method to keep this promise to the mortgagee. Building payments should include all known mortgagees. Failure to pay a known mortgagee when required is an error because of the potential exposure to not only the insurer, but also to the Federal Government If the failure to name the mortgagee results in expenditures of Federal funds, that failure is a critical error.

F. Underwriting Issues

The insurer must carefully review the adjusters' reports for any discrepancies from the Declaration page and refer any discrepancies to the insurer's UW Department for review. Non-money discrepancies may be non- critical errors; however, if the discrepancy would result in an endorsement involving a change in premium, it is a critical error.

G. Adjustment Issues

A claim file is deficient when the adjuster has not explained the facts satisfactorily enough to determine coverage, or when the coverage is misapplied. These issues may result in critical errors depending upon delay or monetary consequences.

H. Time Standards

The insurer must assign the notice of loss to an adjuster within 24 hours of the policyholder's reporting. The adjuster must contact or attempt to contact the policyholder within 48 hours of that assignment. The adjuster's preliminary reports are due to the insurer within 15 calendar days of assignment of the claim. In the absence of the preliminary report, the claims examiner should have requested the report from the adjuster and taken action if they recognize a trend with any particular adjuster and adjusting firm. Missing reporting deadlines may indicate too many claims to adjust. Time standard infractions that result in a significant delay in payment to policyholders are critical errors. All other unexplained time standard infractions are non-critical errors.

I. Special Allocated Loss Adjustment Expenses

All SALAE payments must be adequately documented with a valid reason for the payment and the proper SALAE type must be used. SALAE payments made without the required FEMA approval are improper payments. If the payment was ineligible, the error is considered a critical error.

J. Incorrect Payment Amount

Incorrect payment amount is the error for claim payments and adjuster fees that are improperly paid. The insurer must make immediate arrangements to address the incorrect payments. The insurer must make the correct payment to the policyholder or independent adjuster if underpaid or issue a reimbursement to the National Flood Insurance Program if overpaid. The use of an improper CWOP code can generate an incorrectly Allocated Loss Adjustment Expense (ALAE) payment. All incorrect payments are critical errors.

K. Deficient or Redundant Case Loss Reserves

The individual case loss reserves of the insurers do not effect the NFIP's balance sheet. The minimal test will compare the final case loss reserve(s) with the final payment(s). The insurer will need to revise its case reserve to reflect new information about an individual claim. However, it is not critical that reserves are decreased or increased in the same PIVOT (NFIP system of record) cycle that new information is learned. FEMA recognizes that there will be occasions where the insurer will want additional time to evaluate the new information before revising case reserves.

However, it is important that the claims examiner revise the reserves before the next payment. FEMA further recognizes that it is sound business practice for case reserves, collectively, to be somewhat redundant. Reserve redundancy of 10-15 percent is not discouraged.

Note: The above list is not exhaustive and may be changed with adequate notice.

56 Claim Overpayment Recovery

56.1 Claim Overpayment Recovery Process

Reimbursement to the NFIP of claim overpayments is not contingent upon recovery from the respective policyholder(s). Specifically, the insurer is responsible for the recovery of erroneous claim overpayments.

Upon receipt of written notification of flood claim overpayments, the respective insurer's flood insurance principal coordinator has thirty (30) days to respond to the notification from the NFIP using one of the two options below:

1. Submit the entire amount of the overpaid claim to the NFIP using one of two acceptable methods to avoid the creation of a federal debt collection item (see 55.2 below); or

2. Appeal this matter in writing to the NFIP and submit relevant, reliable, and verifiable supporting documentation. Additional time to gather supporting documentation for the purpose of the appeal must be requested in writing by the principal coordinator within 30 days of the date of the notification from the NFIP. A maximum of 60 days from the date of the notification may be granted by the NFIP for an appeal.

56.2 Methods of Claim Overpayment Reimbursement to the NFIP

A.   Method A:

1. Reduce the claim payment by the overpaid amount on the financial statement, Write Your Own Accounting Procedures Manual, Exhibit I, Line 115.

2. Reduce the claim payment by the overpaid amount on the PIVOT (NFIP system of record).

3. Issue a disbursement for the overpayment amount to the U.S. Treasury via ACH, internet, or wire transfer. Report the disbursement on the appropriate Exhibit VIII schedule.

4. Submit the supporting documents (policy number, date of loss, original loss payment, adjusted loss payment, original error code generated, and original error code date) to:

   > DHS-FEMA Debt Collection Office
   > Attn: NFIP/Debt Collection Officer
   > 400 C Street SW 6th Floor, SW
   > Washington, D.C. 20472-3010

B.   Method B:

1. Reduce the claim payment by the overpaid amount on the financial statement, Write Your Own Accounting Procedures Manual, Exhibit I, Line 115.

2. Reduce the claim payment by the overpaid amount on PIVOT (NFIP system of record)

   3. Payment can be issued in the amount of overpayment by wire transfer or manual check

made payable to NFIP. Record the payment check as a disbursement to the U.S. Treasury and report on the appropriate Exhibit VIII schedule.

4. Submit the manual check and supporting documents (policy number, date of loss, original loss payment, adjusted loss payment, original error code generated, and original error code date) to:

DHS-FEMA Debt Collection Office
Attn: NFIP/Debt Collection Officer
400 C Street, SW 6th Floor
Washington, D.C. 20472-3010

Section 3: Increased Cost of Compliance

1   Increased Cost of Compliance (ICC)

The NFIP encourages mitigation efforts and supports individual and local initiatives to mitigate future flood risks. ICC coverage currently provides eligible policyholders up to $30,000 towards the costs they incur to comply with minimum NFIP floodplain management regulation, state laws, or the local community ordinance. An NFIP policyholder now has up to six years from the date of loss to complete eligible compliance activities to a flood-damaged building in the ICC process described below. While there is only one NFIP flood claim, ICC (Coverage D) is a separate policy benefit, as is Building Property (Coverage A), Personal Property (Coverage B), and Other Coverages (Coverage C). A Coverage D payment is not subject to the Mortgage Clause as with a Coverage A payment. ICC is an additional amount of insurance above the Coverage A - Building limit of liability, but it cannot result in payment beyond the current Program maximums of $250,000 for dwelling, $500,000 for commercial, and $250,000 x the number of units under the RCBAP when combined Coverage A and Coverage D payments are made.[19]

The insurer only accepts ICC after the community has declared in writing that the insured building has been substantially damaged (see below) and the policyholder sends that substantial damage declaration letter, written by an official authorized to make the declaration to the NFIP insurer, on community letterhead. ICC pays benefits to eligible SFIP policyholders to comply with state, or local floodplain management law or ordinance affecting repair or reconstruction of a building damaged by flood.[20]

The following compliance activities are eligible for payment:

1. Floodproofing of the basement (for non-residential buildings only)
2. Relocation
3. Elevation
4. Demolition

or any combination of the above.[21]

In order to initiate, receive partial payment, and finalize an ICC claim, the policyholder property owner is required to provide the insurer with a copy of the substantial damage declaration letter they received from the community official confirming that the building is "substantially or repetitively damaged" and therefore requiring the property owner to comply with floodplain

---

[19] *See* SFIP (III)(D)(2). *See also* 42 U.S.C. § 4013(b); 44 C.F.R. § 61.6 (2018).
[20] *See* SFIP (III)(D)(3).
[21] *See* SFIP (III)(D)(1).

regulations ("substantially" and "repetitively" are both defined in the SFIP at Section III.D.3.(1) and (2)). If applicable, either substantial damage or repetitive damage must be adopted by the community in their floodplain management ordinance and enforced uniformly in the community. The policyholder's submission of a substantial damage declaration letter to the insurer demonstrates the policyholder's intent to file for ICC Coverage D benefits, and the insurer should begin the ICC benefit process.

Note: Some states, rather than the communities within the state, have land-use management authority. Floodplain management guidelines may be in state law and not in community ordinance. It is always good practice to include both in the claim file if there are questions.

For the purposes of ICC, flood damage must be to the percentage threshold adopted by law or ordinance although other damages may be involved, such as wind or fire. The percentage threshold is typically 50 percent but can be a lower threshold if adopted by law or ordinance.

Note that "substantial damage" and "substantial improvement" are often used interchangeably by a community official for all causes of loss. For the purposes of ICC Coverage D, substantial damage attributed only to flood is considered. All covered and non-covered damages sustained to the insured building by flood may be considered in the community's determination of substantial damage.

The policyholder or adjuster is required to obtain a copy of the local ordinance and confirm the community official's market value (not replacement cost value) for the insured building used to determine substantial damage. If the substantial damage letter signed by the authorized community official advises of the specific standard enforced against the building is included, this information can be used in lieu of obtaining the ordinance copy. The letter must also indicate the market value. It is important to note that FEMA never determines market value; it is solely determined by the community official.

Market value can be obtained from the following sources:

1. Independent appraisals by professional appraisers.

2. If the community prefers, a detailed estimate of the building's ACV as a substitute for market value.

3. Property appraisals used for tax assessment purposes can be used as a screening tool.

4. The value of the building taken from NFIP claims data can be used as a screening tool.

5. Qualified estimates based on the sound professional judgement made by the staff of the local building department or local or state tax assessor's office.

6. A copy of the detailed signed contract from the policyholder's contractor confirming a start and completion date of the mitigation work to be performed. The contract must show the contractor's and policyholder's (property owner's) signatures.

A community is a governmental body with the statutory authority to enact and enforce zoning, building codes, subdivision, and other land use control measures. The authority of each unit of government varies by State. Eligible communities can include:

1. Cities

2. Villages

3. Towns

4. Townships

5. Counties

6. Parishes

7. States

8. Native American tribes and Alaskan villages

1.1 ICC Requirements for Advance or Partial Payment:

The policyholder may request an advance or partial payment from their insurer to help cover the cost of the eligible compliance measure(s) subject to the insurer's approval once supporting documentation and a signed ICC proof of loss for the partial payment amount have been submitted. Previous FEMA guidance dated April 24, 2013, under Bulletin w-13024 (Appendix H) stipulates the requirements and guidelines for issuing an ICC advance:

Section III of the SFIPs, "Coverage D," authorizes ICC Coverage[22]. Section III.D ICC benefits are available to eligible properties for floodproofing, relocating, elevating, or demolishing a structure following a flood (or any combination of these activities). The SFIP allows for up to $30,000 in ICC benefits to be paid towards these activities, subject to the statutory limitation that the combined total amount paid for building damages under Coverage A of the SFIP and ICC benefits paid under Coverage D of the SFIP cannot exceed the statutory limit on coverage for any structure (currently $250,000 for residential structures)[23]. Under the terms of the Policy, ICC benefits are not payable until after the eligible work is completed[24].

The National Flood Insurance Program encourages mitigation efforts and supports individual and local initiatives to mitigate future risks, and allowing advance payments will further that goal.[25] Accordingly, to facilitate implementation of ICC and to effect mitigation measures to reduce the risk of future loss, FIMA Associate Administrator issued a conditional waiver of the provision in the SFIP Coverage D, subpart (5)(e),[26] that requires completion of ICC work before payment, and

---

[22] See 44 C.F.R. Pt. 61, App. A(1)-(3).

[23] *See* 42 U.S.C. § 4013.

[24] *See* 44 C.F.R. pt. 61, App. (A)(1)-(3)(III)(D)(5)(e).

[25] *See* 61 Fed. Reg. 49720 (1996).

[26] 44 C.F.R. pt. 61, App. (A)(1)-(3)(III)(D)(5)(e).

authorizes partial advance payments up to 50 percent of the available ICC limits or $15,000. Specifically, the NFIP insurers may advance up to one-half of the available ICC funds under an SFIP to an eligible policyholder, conditioned upon:

1. The policyholder signing a written agreement that the funds will be used only for eligible ICC work, and

2. The policyholder signing a written agreement that if all or part of the advanced funds are not used within the permitted time limits for completing the eligible work (or any extensions that may be granted of that time), the policyholder agrees that those amounts not spent on such eligible work will be refunded.

If a policyholder fails to complete the ICC eligible work within the authorized time, the policyholder must return the ICC funds provided. Failure to do so will subject the policyholder to any available administrative, civil, or criminal remedies. Those remedies include, but are not limited to, a determination that an SFIP is void pursuant to its General Conditions, Sections (VII)(B) and (G)(3) or (VIII)(B) and (G)(3)[27], a Federal debt collection action[28], and legal actions under State or Federal laws.

If the policyholder does not agree to the above conditions, the terms of the SFIP will apply (i.e., no amount of ICC benefits will be paid until after completion of eligible work).

All other terms and conditions of the SFIP for ICC claims, including the ICC proof of loss requirements, are not affected by the conditional waiver.

The conditional waiver applies to all ICC claims made on or after February 11, 2013.

If an insurer issues payment in accordance with the terms and conditions set forth here and properly documents ICC advance partial payments, FEMA will apply these standards in all reviews or audits of files, including any reviews under the Arrangement or the Improper Payment Information Act of 2002.[29] However, if payment is incorrectly made to a policyholder, if a claim is not properly documented, if the insurer omits an additional named policyholder or mortgagee from being listed as an additional payee, or if the insurer otherwise does not act consistent with the obligations set forth in the Arrangement or applicable law, the insurer will be responsible for the erroneous payment.

1.2   Required ICC Claim File Documents and Requirements

Once the work is complete, the policyholder must provide the flood adjuster or insurer with all final ICC documents, such as a post-FIRM elevation certificate or a floodproofing certificate, including any other supporting documentation confirming completion of the work.

---

[27] 44 C.F.R. pt. 61, App. (A)(1)-(2)(VII)(B), (G)(3), App. A(3)(VIII)(B), (G)(3).
[28] *See* 44 C.F.R. §11.1-11.2.
[29] Pub. L. No. 107-300, 33 U.S.C. § 3321 (amended by Pub. L. No. 111-204 (2010)).

May 1, 2020

The local community official must also inspect the compliant building or demolished area and provide the property owner with a certificate of occupancy, or a letter confirming compliance with floodplain management regulations has been met.

Once all required ICC documents are received, including confirming all other eligibility criteria, an insurer sends the policyholder an ICC proof of loss form for final payment that must be signed, dated, and returned to the insurer for processing.

The insurer issues the final ICC payment once all required steps have been completed relating to the eligible compliance measures and the building complies with minimum NFIP floodplain management regulations and the community ordinance. This process requires that the policyholder work closely with their local officials to ensure that the ICC work is completed timely. This also requires that the policyholder work closely with the flood adjuster and claims examiner to ensure timely submission of all required ICC documents. Please note that there can be no duplication of allowances considered in the underlying flood claim and ICC Coverage D nor does ICC provide coverage for deterioration or rot conditions of the building, additional costs associated with structural modifications, upgrades, or any additional increase in square footage.

Table 13. Required ICC Claim File Documents

Document	Details
Copy of the community's floodplain management ordinance.	• Once FEMA provides a community with the flood hazard information upon which floodplain management regulations are based, the community is required to adopt a floodplain management ordinance that meets or exceeds the minimum NFIP requirements. • The overriding purpose of the floodplain management regulations is to ensure that participating communities take into account flood hazards, to the extent that they are known, in all official actions relating to land use management.
Permit copy for floodplain development associated with the compliance measure.	• Must be valid and must not be expired. • A permit is required before construction or development begins within any Special Flood Hazard Area (SFHA). Permits are required to ensure that proposed development projects meet the requirements of the NFIP and the community's floodplain management ordinance. • A community must also review all proposed developments to ensure that all necessary permits have been received from those governmental agencies from which approval is required by Federal or State law.
Photographs	• Detailing the compliance measures' progress from start to completion.

Document	Details
Elevation Certificate (EC), for elevation projects.	• This can be pre- or post-construction. • The elevation certificate (EC) is an administrative tool of the NFIP, which is to be used to provide elevation information necessary to ensure compliance with community floodplain management ordinances, to determine the proper insurance premium rate, or support a request for a Letter of Map Amendment (LOMA) or a Letter of Map Revision (LOMR) based on fill. – *Letter of Map Amendment.* An amendment to the current effective FEMA map, which establishes that a property is not located in an SFHA. A LOMA is issued only by FEMA.[30] – *Letter of Map Revision.* An official amendment to the current effective FEMA map. A LOMR is issued by FEMA and changes flood zones, delineations, and elevations.[31]

1.3 What to Know Concerning Elevation, Demolition, Relocation, and Floodproofing of a Flood-Damaged Building:

A. Elevation

The ICC claim file should include:

1. Documentation on what elevation the building will permanently be raised to, including the required Base Flood Elevation (BFE), adopted ABFE (Advisory Base Flood Elevation), Best Available Data including any freeboard requirement.

2. Costs to set up equipment, elevate, and temporarily support the building.

3. Permit for floodplain development.

4. Cost to build the new compliant foundation.

5. Temporary support (cribbing).

6. Confirmation of the total number of vents and costs, if applicable to the elevation project.

7. Drawings of the projected building perimeter footprint, including dimensions of any attached garage and ground-level utility room, if applicable.

8. Confirmation of the first-floor living space square footage in comparison to the original flood-damaged building as the ICC payment will be limited to the costs to mitigate the building as it was at the time of loss because there is no coverage for any additional costs associated with structural modification, upgrades, or any additional square footage increase.

9. Pre-mitigation elevation certificate, if needed.

---

[30] *See* 44 C.F.R. pt. 70; *see also* https://www.fema.gov/letter-map-amendment-loma.

[31] *See* 44 C.F.R. pt. 65; *see also* https://www.fema.gov/letter-map-revision.

10. Post-mitigation elevation certificate.

11. Costs associated with disconnecting required utilities (electricity, water, sewer, or gas).

12. Costs associated with reconnecting required utilities (electricity, water, sewer, or gas; extensions and modifications).

13. Costs associated with reconstruction of egress (steps and railing plus allowances of 16 square feet of landing) front and rear or under the building.

14. Cost of the installation of a platform for an air conditioning unit.

15. Cost to separate an attached garage, if applicable.

16. Architectural and engineering fees associated with a design for elevating an eligible insured building.

17. Before and after photographs of the structure and site.

Table 14. Covered vs. Non-Covered Elevation Expenses

Covered Elevation Expenses	Non-Covered Elevation Expenses
• Architectural and engineering fees associated with a design for elevating an eligible insured building. • Cost of permits. • Pre-mitigation elevation certificate, if required. • Disconnecting required utilities (electricity, water, sewer or gas). • Clearing of plant-life and excavation around the insured building for the setup and installation of lifting equipment and supports. Cost to separate an attached garage. • Elevation of the insured building to minimum required height (BFE or freeboard). • Temporary support (cribbing). • Removal and disposal of pre-mitigation insured building foundation components, when applicable (see Demolition). • Construction of the compliant foundation. Required minimum flood venting. • Re-connection of required utilities (extension or modification). • Re-construction of egress (steps & railings plus 16 SF landing), front and rear of the structure, or under the structure. • Installation of platform for air-conditioning equipment. • Post-mitigation elevation certificate.	• Elevation of any structure other than the insured building. • Elevation of the insured building already at the minimum required height. • Elevation of the insured building above the minimum required height. • Elevating the insured building outside of a Special Flood Hazard Area, except when required according to an existing local community flood management ordinance. • Code upgrades unrelated to State or local floodplain management law or ordinance. Added improvements, remodeling, or additions. • Disconnection, elevation, and re-attachment of decks or walkways. • Re-attachment of garages or grade level utility closets. • Repair, removal, reinstallation or replacement of exterior siding or masonry veneer. • Re-grading and re-seeding of lawns or the replacement of plant-life. • Other surfaces (sidewalks, driveways, patios, etc.) or structures (fences, containment or retaining walls, etc.) outside the perimeter exterior walls of the insured building. • Expenses not included in the covered elevation expenses above. • Allowances for items already considered under Coverage A – Building Property. • Any payable amount over the NFIP's maximum for Coverage A – Building Property, on any single loss.

B. Demolition

The ICC claim file should include:

1. Cost to demolish the insured building or foundation (plus associated cartage and dump fees).

2. Cost to demolish other covered items other than the insured building, if applicable.

3. Cost to grade and stabilize the building site or fill for basements.

4. Cost of clearing the existing building site of any remaining materials of the insured building, such as the foundation.

5. Cost to disconnect and cap required utilities (electricity, water, sewer or gas).

6. Cost to grade and stabilize the site in accordance with state or local regulations.

7. Before and after photographs of the structure and site.

The property may be redeveloped after demolition is complete, subject to all applicable Federal, state, and local community laws and regulations.

Table 15. Covered vs. Non-Covered Demolition Expenses

Covered Demolition Expenses	Non-Covered Demolition Expenses
<ul><li>Cost of permits.</li><li>Demolition of an eligible insured building.</li><li>Disconnect and cap required utilities (electricity, water, sewer and or gas) in accordance with State and local regulations.</li><li>Cartage of debris (demolished insured building) and dumpsite fees.</li><li>Clearing the existing building site of any remaining materials of the insured building, such as the foundation.</li><li>Grade and stabilize the building site in accordance with State or local regulations (fill for basement foundation voids).</li></ul>	<ul><li>Demolition of an insured building already in compliance with State or local floodplain management law or ordinance.</li><li>Demolition of other surfaces (sidewalks, driveways, patios, etc.) or structures (detached garages and carports, sheds, playsets, fences, containment or retaining walls, etc.) outside the perimeter exterior walls of the insured building.</li><li>Re-grading and re-seeding of lawns or the replacement of plant-life.</li><li>Expenses not included in the covered demolition expenses above.</li><li>Allowances already paid in a claim under Coverage A – Building Property.</li><li>Any payable amount over the NFIP's maximum for Coverage A – Building Property, on any single loss.</li></ul>

C. Relocation

The ICC claim file should include:

1. Confirmation of the moving route preparation.

2. Costs for the building, transport, mileage, and cost.

3. Costs associated with installation and anchoring of the building to the new foundation.

4. Costs to disconnect electricity, water, sewer and gas and reconnection charges for electricity, water, sewer, and gas.

5. Architectural and engineering fees associated with a design for relocating an eligible insured building.

6. Permit for floodplain development.

7. Costs associated with clearing of plant life and excavation around the insured building to allow setup, installation of lifting and transportation of equipment and supports.

8. Costs associated with preparation, elevation, and transport of the insured building to the new site.

9. Cost to clear the existing building site of any remaining material of the insured building, such as the foundation.

10. Cost to construct the compliant foundation of the new site.

11. Cost to install and anchor the insured building to the foundation at the new site.

12. Cost to connect required utilities at the new site, electricity, water, sewer, or gas.

13. Before and after photographs of the structure and site.

Table 16. Covered vs. Non-Covered Relocation Expenses

Covered Relocation Expenses	Non-Covered Relocation Expenses
• Architectural and engineering fees associated with a design for relocating an eligible insured building. • Cost of permits. • Clearing of plant-life and excavation around the insured building to allow the setup, installation of lifting and transportation equipment and supports. • Preparation of the moving route. Disconnect and cap required utilities in accordance with state and local regulations. Preparation, elevation, and the transport of the insured building to the new site. • Clearing the existing building site of any remaining materials of the insured building, such as the foundation (see Demolition). • Construction of the compliant foundation at the new site (see Elevation). • Installation and anchoring of the insured building to the foundation at the new site. Connecting required utilities at the new site (electricity, water, sewer, and or gas).	• Relocation of any structure other than the insured building. • Elevating the insured building at the new site located in a non-SFHA. • Expenses not included in the covered relocation expenses above. • Allowances already paid in a claim under Coverage A – Building Property. • Any payable amount over the NFIP's maximum for Coverage A – Building Property, on any single loss.

D. Floodproofing

The ICC claim file should include:

1. Completed Floodproofing Certificate.

2. Photographs of shields, gates, barriers, or components designed to provide floodproofing protection to the building.

3. Written certification from a licensed professional engineer that all portions of the building below the BFE are made watertight or substantially impermeable to the passage of water and must perform in accordance with Title 44 Code of Federal Regulations (44 CFR § 60.3(c)(3)).

See the Flood Insurance Manual for information regarding floodproofing.

Eligible structures for floodproofing:

1. Non-residential buildings in A zones (floodproofing is not allowable in any V zones). The specifications for floodproofing ensure that the building is watertight, its floodproofed walls will not collapse, and the floor at the base of the floodproofed walls will resist flotation during flooding conditions.

2. Residential dwellings with basements, located in zones A1-30, AE, AR, AR Dual, AO, AH, and A with BFE that are within communities specifically approved and authorized for residential floodproofing by FEMA. For residential buildings, the building must be watertight without human intervention.

Table 17. Covered vs. Non-Covered Floodproofing Expenses

Covered Floodproofing Expenses	Non-Covered Floodproofing Expenses
<ul><li>Architectural and engineering fees associated with a design for floodproofing an eligible insured building.</li><li>Cost of permits.</li><li>Floodproofing certification completed by a design professional for non-residential buildings.</li><li>Installation of watertight shields for doors and windows.</li><li>Reinforcement of walls to withstand floodwater pressures and impact forces generated by floating debris.</li><li>Membranes and other sealants to reduce seepage of floodwater through walls and wall penetrations.</li><li>Installation of drainage collection systems and sump pumps to control interior water levels, collect seepage, and reduce hydrostatic pressures on the slab and walls.</li><li>Installation of check valves to prevent backup of floodwater or sewage through utilities.</li><li>Anchoring the building to resist flotation, collapse, and lateral movement.</li></ul>	<ul><li>Floodproofing of any structure other than the insured building.</li><li>Code upgrades unrelated to state or local floodplain management ordinance.</li><li>Expenses not included in the covered floodproofing expenses above.</li><li>Allowances already paid in a claim under Coverage A – Building Property.</li><li>Any payable amount over the NFIP's maximum for Coverage A – Building Property, on any single loss.</li><li>Measures such as floodwalls independent from the building, berms, and levees around buildings are not allowable floodproofing measures under the NFIP.</li></ul>

1.4 Assignment of Coverage D, ICC Benefits

FEMA authorizes policyholders the ability to assign their ICC claim payments when eligible to be included in a FEMA-sponsored flood mitigation grant involving eligible ICC compliance activities. The policyholder's agreement to transfer this interest is accomplished by submitting the Assignment of Coverage D – Increased Cost of Compliance Coverage Form (Appendix I) to the local authorities, state, or community administering the grant. Once the policyholder assigns the ICC claim, the local authorities, state, or community will be responsible for completing the eligible mitigation activity. Upon receipt of the completed Assignment of Coverage D Form, the insurer should process the ICC claim in the customary manner up to the policy limit of $30,000, when available.

Therefore, adjusters and insurers are required to verify and include the required ICC documentation based on the selected mitigation activity as they normally would.

A. Steps for the Assignment of Coverage D – Increased Cost of Compliance Coverage:

1. Policyholder consents to the assignment of the ICC claim payment.

2. The community official will provide the policyholder with an Assignment of Coverage
    D Form (Appendix I).

3. The policyholder signs the form and provides the signed form to the community official.

4. The community official sends a copy of the completed form, along with the community's
    signed declaration of substantial damage to the NFIP Bureau & Statistical Agent at
    NFIPClaimsMailbox@fema.dhs.gov, or PO Box 310, Lanham, MD 20703-0310.

5. NFIP BSA maintains a database of the ICC information submitted by the community. The
    NFIP BSA then sends the documents to the appropriate insurer, with instructions. The
    insurer will then assign an adjuster.

6. The assigned adjuster contacts the policyholder to advise s/he has the claim and
    contacts the local community official to coordinate and help complete the claim.

7. The adjuster receives/reviews the contract for demolition, elevation, relocation or
    floodproofing to determine the cost.

8. The adjuster has the community official sign the proof of loss once the claim value
    has been determined.

9. The adjuster sends the final report, along with the proof of loss to the insurer for payment.

10. The insurer issues the check to the community and advises the NFIP BSA of the
    amount of the claim payment.

NOTE: The policyholder cannot assign an ICC claim when the owner transfers the title of the
property to a new property owner. The SFIP allows the policyholder to assign the policy in
writing when policyholder transfers title, but not a flood or ICC claim.

1.5 Grants

ICC benefits can be used as the non-Federal cost share that is the policyholder's responsibility for
SFIP policyholders participating in a FEMA mitigation grant.

FEMA offers three Hazard Mitigation Assistance (HMA) grant programs to assist the states, U.S.
territories, federally recognized tribal governments, and local communities in implementing cost-
effective, long-term hazard mitigation measures including elevation. All three have different
periods of funding availability and eligibility considerations.

1. **Hazard Mitigation Grant Program (HMGP)** provides grants to states and local
    governments to implement long-term hazard mitigation measures after a major
    disaster declaration to protect public or private property through various mitigation
    measures. When a Federal disaster declaration is made, new opportunities for

mitigation funding may be available.[32]

2. **Pre-Disaster Mitigation (PDM)** Program provides funds to states and local communities annually, so they may continue to achieve a higher level of risk management capability through the implementation of hazard mitigation planning and mitigation projects prior to a disaster event. This is a competitive grant program that addresses many different types of natural hazards.[33]

3. **Flood Mitigation Assistance (FMA)** Program is competitive and focuses solely on flood mitigation. The FMA program provides funds on an annual basis to states, territories, federally recognized tribes, and local communities for projects that reduce or eliminate the long-term risk of flood damage to buildings insured under the National Flood Insurance Program.[34]

Individuals may not apply directly to the State for assistance from any of these programs; however, local governments may sponsor an application on their behalf. FEMA awards mitigation grant funds to the state, which disburses those funds to its communities. States have the primary responsibility for prioritizing, selecting, and administering state and local hazard mitigation projects.

1.6   Cost Share

Cost-share, also known as the "non-federal share" or "non-federal match", is the portion of the costs of a FEMA mitigation grant that is the policyholder's responsibility not borne by the federal government. The authorizing statute for each HMA program establishes the minimum cost share. The total cost to implement approved mitigation activities is generally funded by a combination of federal and non-federal sources. Both the federal share and the non-federal cost share must be for eligible costs used in direct support of activities that FEMA has approved in the grant award. Contributions of cash, third-party in-kind services, materials, or any combination thereof, may be accepted as part of the non-federal cost share.

To meet cost-sharing requirements, the non-federal contributions must be reasonable, allowable, allocable, and necessary under the grant program and must comply with all federal requirements and regulations.

The terms of the SFIP, Coverage D, control what a policyholder is paid under the policy. The terms of the grant and any non-federal cost-share are separate and distinct from the terms of the SFIP. The recipient (state, territory, or federally recognized tribe) and FEMA's regional HMA program offices will make and verify a determination that an assignment of the ICC claim has not resulted in a duplication of benefits for purposes of the grant.

---

[32] 42 U.S.C. § 5170c.

[33] 42 U.S.C. § 5133.

[34] 42 U.S.C. § 4101(c).

May 1, 2020

1.7 Some ICC Issues

A. Sale of the Structure

The sale of a building from one individual to another is a contract between those individuals and should not involve the NFIP. The NFIP contract is with the policyholder who owned and insured the building on the date of loss, and it will or has met those obligations. If the purchaser must repair the building to meet the community's floodplain management ordinance, the cost of that obligation should be reflected in the purchase price.

B. Converting or Retrofitting a Building

ICC covers second story conversions, which are accomplished by abandoning the lower enclosed area making it non-habitable as long as the enclosed area is raised above ground level by foundation walls, shear walls, posts, piers, pilings, or columns. A new second story is constructed usually when the depth of the base flood is more than four or five feet. The roof and roof framing are removed, and a new second story is built on top of the lower level. Considerations such as cost, final appearance, the strength of the existing foundation, and the need to address other natural hazards should also be considered. The building must meet the requirements of floodplain management and the community ordinance. The building after reconstruction must also meet the SFIP definition of an elevated building.[35] The policyholder is required to submit a certification statement from a registered design professional to certify under seal that the structural design, plans, specifications, and method of construction are in accordance with accepted standards of practice in addition to meeting or exceeding the minimum floodplain management requirements of the NFIP and building codes.

C. Filling a Subgrade Basement

Coverage is available under Coverage D ICC to fill in a basement and then elevate the existing home to meet the SFIP definition of an elevation building if this activity is required by the community enforcing their floodplain management ordinance as it relates to elevation.

D. Mitigation Measures

Mitigation measures completed prior to the issuance of the substantial damage declaration will not be considered. Substantial damage determinations for the purposes of ICC claims cannot be issued after repairs have been started or mitigation completed, as it is no longer possible to verify that the building was out of compliance and the cost of repairs attributed directly to flood.

---

[35] *Section II.B.14.14 Elevated Building. A building that has no basement and that has its lowest elevated floor raised above ground level by foundation walls, shear walls, posts, piers, pilings, or columns.*

E.   Elevating on Fill

Elevation on Fill is allowed in A and AE zones to comply with NFIP minimum standards; however, some communities prohibit the use of fill in their ordinances. The insurer should review the community ordinance to verify the use of fill.

Note: Allowing a claim for fill dirt only is not true mitigation with no structure in place. ICC is concerned with completed mitigation to the insured building and or a replacement structure.

F.   Itemized Contractor Estimates

Lump-sum estimates are not acceptable for ICC purposes. The ICC adjuster is required to write their own estimate to ensure the integrity of the pricing provided by the contractor is correct. The examiner must also review the ICC estimate for validity which includes identifying non-covered allowances related to ICC.

G.   Asbestos Abatement

The SFIP excludes the cost associated with enforcement of any ordinance or law that requires any policyholder or others to test for, monitor, clean up, remove, contain, treat, detoxify, or neutralized, or in any way respond to or assess the effects of pollutants.[36]

H.   Opening in Foundation Walls and Wall Enclosures

Non-engineered openings are used to meet the NFIP's prescriptive requirement of one-square-inch of net open area for every square foot of enclosed area. As an alternative, engineered openings that have characteristics that differ from non-engineered openings may be used provided they are designed and certified by a registered design professional as meeting certain performance characteristics. FEMA Technical Bulletin 1, Openings in Foundation Walls and Walls of Enclosures Below Elevated Buildings in Special Flood Hazard Areas, August 2008 may be helpful.

1.8   ICC U-CORT Waiver Process

A FEMA waiver is required when the timeframe to complete an eligible mitigation activity has expired. Once the eligible and approved mitigation activity is complete, the NFIP insurer on behalf of the policyholder will request that waiver using FEMA's U-CORT. The insurer may submit a request directly to FEMA through FEMA's U-CORT requesting authorization to pay benefits to the policyholder. The insurer must confirm that the rights of the Program have not been prejudiced by the late submission and provide the Administrator with a valid reason for the delay when the request is submitted. The policyholder and insurer must work together to ensure that the ICC claim meets all eligibility and documentation requirements. FEMA reviews and approves each request on a case-by-case basis. *The ICC work must be completed before the waiver is*

---

[36] SFIP (III)(D)(5)(b).

submitted to FEMA for consideration of payment. A waiver should not be submitted to FEMA for pre-approval.

See Section 2 of this manual for details on the ICC waiver process.

This ICC process is not exhaustive, and additional supporting documents may be required as deemed necessary by the insurer. Not all buildings qualify for an ICC payment. ICC also does not provide coverage for any duplication of an item included in the SFIP Coverage A-Building Property payment made or for any amount over the Program's statutory limit for the type of building insured.

This page was intentionally left blank.

Section 4: NFIP Claims Appeals

1   NFIP Claims Appeals

NFIP policyholders file claims with their insurers after experiencing a flood. In general, most claims will settle without dispute. However, a policyholder may disagree with their insurer in some cases, and when their insurer denies all or part of their claim, they may appeal the insurer's final claim decision to FEMA.

FEMA reviews policyholder appeals concerning final claim determinations because FEMA oversees the NFIP but recommends the policyholder work with their adjuster, the adjuster's supervisor, and the insurers prior to filing an appeal. The insurers and their representatives are in the best position to quickly address a specific claim problem. The NFIP policyholder has the right to appeal any denial directly to FEMA when they cannot reach an agreement on the determination of a claim along with any denial of all or a portion of their claim.

1.1   Eligibility

A policyholder may appeal a full or partial denial of a claim by the insurer and must appeal within 60 days of the date of the insurer's written denial letter. The policyholder appeals to FEMA by email at FEMA-NFIP-Appeals@fema.dhs.gov or by postal or express mail at FEMA, 400 C Street SW, 6th Floor Washington, DC 20472-3010.[37] FEMA calculates the 60-day time frame as follows: FEMA begins counting the day after the date on the denial letter and counts every Saturday, Sunday, and legal holiday. If the 60th day is a Saturday, Sunday, or legal holiday; FEMA extends the period to the next day that is not a Saturday, Sunday, or legal holiday. FEMA considers an email electronic time stamp, U.S. Mail postmark, or express carrier acceptance date as the time of submission to FEMA.

Federal regulation prohibits policyholders who have filed suit against their insurer or entered into appraisal to determine the amount of their loss from appealing their denial to FEMA.[38] With an appraisal, an impartial third party determines the value of the covered scope of damage, when the insurer and policyholder disagree on that dollar amount.[39]

1.2   Filing an Appeal

In addition to the name of the policyholder(s) and the property address, appeal letters must include:[40]

1. The flood insurer's denial letter;

---

[37] See 44 C.F.R. § 62.20(e)(1) (2018)
[38] See 44 C.F.R. § 62.20(c)(1); (d) (2018)
[39] See SFIP, Section VII or Section VIII. General Conditions, paragraph (P) "Appraisal"
[40] See 44 C.F.R. § 62.20(e) (2018) for requirements

2. The flood insurance policy number (from the policy's declarations page);

3. Contact information;

4. Letter of Representation: If the author of the letter is a representative of the policyholder (for example: a relative, a public adjuster, an attorney, or a translator), he or she should indicate the relationship and provide documents verifying and authorizing the relationship. A letter of representation allowing access to personal information under the Privacy Act, 5 U.S.C. § 552a must include:

   – The policyholder's full name, current address, date and place of birth, the name(s) of the representative(s), and the policyholder's signature;

   – The following statement from the policyholder: "I expressly grant permission to FEMA to release my records to this third-party representative.";

   – The policyholder must have this document notarized **or** include the following statement:

   "I declare under penalty of perjury that the foregoing is true and correct. Executed on <DATE>. <SIGNATURE>."[41];

5. The details of the policyholder's concern; and

6. Documentation that illustrates, explains, and supports the policyholder's position.

FEMA reviews the incoming appeal package and then requests the claim file from the insurer to verify the information the insurer relied upon is current and accurate. To best address the issue(s) raised in an appeal, FEMA encourages policyholders to provide as much detail and documentation as needed to support their position in the initial appeal.

Policyholders should provide all information relevant to their particular issue(s).[42] Policyholders can access a sample list of documentation in the NFIP Flood Insurance Claims Handbook. This list serves as an example, and policyholders need not submit all the documentation listed; only the documentation that applies.

FEMA may require additional information depending on the circumstances of the disagreement. The policyholder is allowed an additional 14 calendar days to supplement the appeal file, using the same process and information described above.[43]

---

[41] See 28 U.S.C. § 1746.

[42] See 44 C.F.R. § 62.20(e)(4) (2018)

[43] See 44 C.F.R. § 62.20(f)(2) (2018)

1.3   What to Expect

FEMA will review the claim file to determine if the insurer properly evaluated and paid the claim based on the terms and conditions of the SFIP.

The policyholder may raise new questions or provide documentation in the appeal that they did not present to the insurer before the insurer denied the claim. FEMA may recommend submitting any additional documentation that the policyholder may have directly to the insurer to support their claim(s) for additional payment or to preserve the policyholder's appeal rights.

FEMA begins its process by acknowledging receipt of the appeal in writing to the policyholder and requesting the claim file from the insurer. During the appeal process, if the insurer is able to resolve the appeal issue(s) in favor of the policyholder under the terms and conditions of the SFIP, FEMA encourages them to do so.

At the conclusion of the appeal, FEMA will provide its decision in writing with specific information concerning the resolution of the appeal.[44]

FEMA's response will address each issue raised on appeal in one of two ways:

1.   FEMA will inform both the policyholder and the insurer of its determination and recommend the most appropriate action(s) to the insurer when FEMA agrees with the policyholder.

2.   FEMA will explain its decision in plain language with references to the SFIP and other relevant publications when FEMA disagrees with the policyholder. FEMA may also suggest actions the policyholder can take to achieve a different outcome.

1.4   Insurer Responsibility

Policyholders must have a formal letter of denial, in whole or in part of the policyholder's claim, from their insurer to appeal a decision to FEMA.[45] For the policyholder to comply with FEMA's requirements for the appeals process, the insurer must provide a properly written denial letter to policyholders when they deny a claim, in whole or in part. The insurer must include the following elements in all denial letters:

1.   **The date of the denial letter.** The date of the initial denial letter begins the one-year period from which the policyholder may file suit; the denial letter date also triggers the 60-day period to file an appeal with FEMA under Title 44, Code of Federal Regulations, Section 62.20.

2.   **The name(s) of the policyholder(s), the mailing address, and the loss location.** While straightforward, these elements are especially important when policyholders involve

---

[44] See 44 C.F.R. § 62.20(f) (2018)
[45] See 44 C.F.R. § 62.20(b) (2018)

legal representatives, public adjusters, or other representatives when submitting a claim for payment (i.e., the proof of loss).

3. **The date of loss.** Necessary when policyholders file claims for the same properties across multiple events.

4. The date(s) the policyholder submitted a request for payment (example: advance payment, proof of loss) or failed to comply with a material term of the SFIP (example: failed to submit a timely proof of loss). Sequentially, a denial letter should be issued only after the policyholder submits a signed and sworn proof of loss, signs the final adjuster's report, or fails to comply with a material term of the SFIP.

5. **The item(s) denied with the corresponding dollar amount denied, whenever applicable.** Denial letters should avoid general terms such as "various items" or "finished items in a basement," and instead list the items not covered by the SFIP.

6. **A plain-language explanation for the non-payment or non-coverage.** Rather than quote the SFIP at length, the denial letter should explain why the SFIP does not provide coverage.

   - **Example:** "The Standard Flood Insurance Policy does not cover shrubs. We, therefore, must deny the part of your claim seeking payment for shrubs. This limitation appears in the SFIP in Section IV, Paragraph 6."

   - **Note:** "The above-referenced claim has been closed without payment. IV. Property Not Covered 6. Land, land values, lawns, trees, shrubs, plants, growing crops, or animals[.]"

7. Citations to the relevant sections of the SFIP and a web link to the SFIP. This should complement the plain-language explanation, not replace it.

Insurers should continue to acknowledge coverage restrictions in their communications with policyholders. Nothing in this section is intended to broaden coverage or change standard claims- handling procedures.

With every denial, the insurer must also include an attachment that explains the rights of the policyholder after a whole or partial denial. FEMA is providing the Policyholder Rights document (Appendix G). WYO Companies may modify this document to the extent that they want to include any brand identity or contact information elements. FEMA intends for this attachment to replace the previous standard paragraphs in the denial letters themselves concerning appeals and litigation. The Policyholder Rights document provides policyholders with the option to submit flood insurance appeals by email.

When the reasons given in the denial letter do not agree with the facts of the claim, or if the SFIP citation referenced does not fully support the denial decision, the letter may be faulty and result in a premature or ineligible appeal. In such a case, FEMA will forward the policyholder's letter to the insurer requesting that they deal directly with the policyholder to resolve the matter by making a final determination and send an adequate denial letter. Insurers should continue to acknowledge coverage restrictions in their communications with policyholders.

Finally, FEMA currently receives appeals prior to the policyholder receiving a denial letter. FEMA reminds the insurers that the SFIP does not authorize adjusters to approve or disapprove claims, or to tell the policyholder whether the insurer will approve the claim.[46] The adjusters may answer general flood insurance coverage questions in the effort to provide good customer service to policyholders but should also inform policyholders that the insurer provides the final claim decision. FEMA asks that the insurers have their adjusters inform policyholders that they cannot file an appeal until they receive a denial letter. The proper sequence for claims-handling and dispute resolution is explained in the FEMA Fact Sheet, "Flood Claims Process" available on fema.gov.

---

[46] See SFIP, Section (VII)(J)(8)

This page was intentionally left blank.

Appendix

Appendix	Document
Appendix A – Adjuster Fee Schedule	Appendix A Adjuster Fee Schedule_eff0824
Appendix B – ICC Fee Schedule	Appendix B ICC Fee Schedule_eff 090120
Appendix C – FEMA Policy Guidance for Closed Basin Lakes	Appendix C FEMA Policy Guidance for Closed Basin Lakes
Appendix E – NFIP Claims Forms	Appendix E NFIP Forms.docx
Appendix F – Bulletin w-13025a Structural Drying	Appendix F Bulletin w-13025a Structural Drying
Appendix G – Policyholder Rights	Appendix G Policyholder Rights
Appendix H – Bulletin w-13024 Increased Cost of Compliance Amendments	Appendix H w-13024 Increased Cost of Compliance Amendments
Appendix I – Assignment of Coverage D	Appendix I Assignment of Coverage D
Appendix J – BVLA Methods and FAQs	Appendix L BVLA Method and FAQs.doc

Appendix	Document
Appendix K – ICC Policyholders Processing Checklist	 Appendix K ICC Policyholders Processing

Appendices are made available online at https://www.fema.gov/media-library/assets/documents/169171.

Acronyms and Abbreviations

Acronym	Acronym Definition
ACO	Adjuster Claims Office
ACV	Actual Cash Value
ADA	Americans with Disabilities Act of 1990
ALE	Additional Living Expenses
ANFI®	Associate in National Flood Insurance®
ANSI	American National Standards Institute
APDA	Adjuster Preliminary Damage Assessment
ASC	Areas of Special Consideration
BFE	Base Flood Elevation
BVLA	Building Valuation Loss Assessment
CBIA	Coastal Barrier Improvement Act
CBRA	Coastal Barrier Resources Act
CBRS	Coastal Barrier Resources System
CFR	Code of Federal Regulations
CPA	Certified Public Accountant
CSA	Controlled Substances Act
CWOP	Closed Without Payment
DHS	Department of Homeland Security
DRC	Disaster Recovery Center
E&O	Errors and Omissions
EC	Elevation Certificate
EMI	Emergency Management Institute
FBFM	Flood Boundary and Floodway Map
FCN	Flood Control Number
FEMA	Federal Emergency Management Agency
FICO	Flood Insurance Claims Office
FIMA	Federal Insurance and Mitigation Administration
FIRM	Flood Insurance Rate Map
FIS	Flood Insurance Study
FMA	Flood Mitigation Assistance

Acronym	Acronym Definition
FRO	Flood Response Office
GA	General Adjuster
GAO	Government Accountability Office
GFIP	Group Flood Insurance Program
GP Form	General Property Form
HFIAA	Homeowner Flood Insurance Affordability Act of 2014
HMA	Hazard Mitigation Assistance
HMGP	Hazard Mitigation Grant Program
HVAC	Heating, Ventilation, and Air Conditioning
ICC	Increased Cost of Compliance
IFICO	Integrated Flood Insurance Claims Office
IHP	Individuals and Households Program
IICRC	Institute of Inspection Cleaning and Restoration Certification
Insurer	NFIP Direct and WYO Companies
IPERIA	Improper Payment Elimination and Recovery Information Act
JFO	Joint Field Office
LAG	Lowest Adjacent Grade
LOMA	Letter of Map Amendment
LOMR	Letter of Map Revision
NFIP	National Flood Insurance Program
NFIP BSA	National Flood Insurance Program Bureau and Statistical Agent
NFIP Direct	National Flood Insurance Program Direct Servicing Agent
NWS	National Weather Service
OHP	Overhead and Profit
OIG	(DHS) Office of the Inspector General
OPA	Otherwise Protected Areas
POL	Proof of Loss
RCBAP	Residential Condominium Building Association Policy
RCQC	Random Claims Quality Check
RCV	Replacement Cost Value
RL	Repetitive Loss
SALAE	Special Allocated Loss Adjustment Expense
SAP	Single Adjuster Program

Acronym	Acronym Definition
SF	Square foot/feet
SFHA	Special Flood Hazard Area
SFIP	Standard Flood Insurance Policy
SRL	Severe Repetitive Loss
U.S.C.	United States Code
UAV	Unmanned Aerial Vehicle
UCORT	Underwriting and Claims Operation Review Tool
UW	Underwriting
WYO Company	Write Your Own Company

Questions or suggestions regarding content or formatting errors in the NFIP Claims Manual, or suggestions for improvement should be directed to FEMA-FIMA-ClaimsManual@fema.dhs.gov.

All claims coverage questions should be directed to the insurer. The insurer may consult with FEMA at FEMA-FIDClaimsMailbox@fema.dhs.gov.

U.S. Small Business Administration
Table of Size Standards
matched to the 2017 NAICS
SBA size standards date August 19, 2019